Organizations Evolving

Second Edition

Howard E. Aldrich and Martin Ruef

SAGE Publications

London • Thousand Oaks • New Delhi

First published 1999
Second edition published 2006

SAGE Publications Ltd
1 Oliver's Yard
55 City Road
London EC1Y 1SP

SAGE Publications Inc.
2455 Teller Road
Thousand Oaks, California 91320

SAGE Publications India Pvt Ltd
B-42, Panchsheel Enclave
Post Box 4109
New Delhi 110 017

British Library Cataloguing in Publication data

A catalogue record for this book is available
from the British Library

ISBN-10 0-4129-1046-3   ISBN-13 978-1-4129-1046-0
ISBN-10 0-4129-1047-1   ISBN-13 978-1-4129-1047-7 (pbk)

Library of Congress Control Number: 2005930969

Typeset by C&M Digitals (P) Ltd., Chennai, India
Printed and bound in Great Britain by TJ International Ltd, Padstow, Cornwall
Printed on paper from sustainable resources

Contents

List of Tables and Figures

Figures

Preface to the Second Edition

The first edition of this book had one author; now, there are two of us. When Sage asked Howard to consider updating the first edition of this book, he realized that so much had happened in the intervening five years that he could no longer tackle this task alone. Fortunately, he needed to look no further than around the corner of his office to find another scholar who had deep interest in evolutionary theory and organizational analysis. Martin joined the faculty at the University of North Carolina, Chapel Hill, in 1999, the year the first edition was published. He had just completed his Ph.D. in sociology at Stanford University, an institution that some see as the crucible for many of the perspectives we discuss in this book. Working with Dick Scott gave him a deep appreciation of the institutional approach, while doing a post-doctoral fellowship in the Stanford Graduate School of Business fostered his interest in ecological analysis. Collaboration on the book was complicated by Martin's move back to Stanford's Graduate School of Business in 2002 and his subsequent move to Princeton University. Being back on the East Coast, in the same time zone, and in a Department of Sociology seemed to speed things up a bit. Whatever the cause, we have found that this has been a remarkably agreeable and productive project.

Why a second edition? First, young organizational researchers continue to produce robust empirical generalizations that strengthen the case for an evolutionary approach. We felt enough new material had accumulated that we could justify discarding some of the material in the first edition and replacing it with work published in the last five years. Second, sympathy for the evolutionary approach has grown, as evidenced in dynamic research designs that have generated insights into change processes. Reviews of the book's first edition were remarkably positive, and many reviewers commented on the ability of an evolutionary understanding to bring unity to the growing field of organization studies. The book was well received in both the sociology and management research communities, as it won the Max Weber award for Best Book from the American Sociological Association's Section on Organizations, Occupations and Work in 2000, and the George R. Terry Award from the Academy of Management for the best management book published in 1999. Third, we have seen signs of an emerging synthesis of the ecological and institutional perspectives, as well as a decidedly historical turn in many empirical projects. As we argue in the book, period and place are now central features of any sophisticated organizational analysis.

What is new in this edition? First, in addition to providing citations to the most recent work in the field, we have added new sections on organizational forms, community evolution, and methods for studying organizations at multiple levels.

We added a short methodological appendix that reviews research methods in terms of units of analysis, mode of data collection, and observation plan. Second, we found that the book is used as a text in many upper division undergraduate classes as well as graduate seminars, and so we have added review questions and exercises at the end of each chapter. Third, in many chapters, we have added a lengthy research case, illustrating the chapter's concepts. The rich descriptions add life to the concepts and principles and show how they can be applied to real historical examples.

As in the first edition, the book contains about 1,000 references. Their publication dates reveal something about our own intellectual predilections, as well as the "evolution" of the evolutionary approach to organizational analysis. In many respects, the 1970s and 1980s were watershed years for the development of organizational theory, in general, and the evolutionary approach, in particular. Articles, chapters, and monographs from these decades represent roughly 30 percent of our references. The 1990s were a period of fervent empirical refinement of many organizational perspectives and this is paralleled in our References, which devotes nearly half of its listings to this decade. The years since the publication of the first edition have involved further empirical refinement of many organizational perspectives, as well as increased attention to processes that are central to an evolutionary perspective, such as entrepreneurship and organizational emergence. We cannot aspire to a complete survey of the recent literature because it would involve nearly every article from specialized journals such *Administrative Science Quarterly* and every third or fourth from general-purpose journals, such as the *American Journal of Sociology* and *American Sociological Review*. Even a selective approach to this recent literature yields over 150 references to publications from 2000 through 2005, as reflected in our References section.

Acknowledgments

Our task was made immeasurably easier because of the friends and colleagues who helped us with advice. Many of the same people who were involved with the first edition helped, in numerous ways, with the second edition. Because we already thanked them in the preface to the first edition, which follows this preface, here we will single out only those people who truly served double duty for us. Two people who read the first edition from cover to cover did the same for this edition: Ted Baker and Linda Renzulli. Steve Lippmann celebrated the completion of his dissertation at the University of North Carolina by also reading the entire book draft. Perhaps having Howard and Martin on his dissertation committee added urgency to his task! Valery Yakubovich also read the entire draft and provided comments. Phil Kim's work with Howard and Martin on entrepreneurial teams contributed insights to Chapter 4, and Linda Putnam and Joel Iverson read Chapters 5 and 6 and provided extensive comments as well as new references for us. Geoffrey Hodgson and Thorbjørn Knudsen have kept us apprised of the latest developments in evolutionary economics. Klye Longest updated all the domestic and international statistics, proofed the references, and suggested new interpretations of data and concepts.

In the preface to the first edition, Howard noted that he had not been cooped up, hermit-like, as he was writing. His good fortune continued as he worked on this edition. In addition to visiting many of the same institutes and universities as before – AILUN in Sardinia, the Aarhus School of Business, and the University of British Columbia in beautiful Vancouver, among others – his Scandinavian connection strengthened when the Swedish Foundation for Small Business Research (FSF) gave him an 'entrepreneurship researcher of the year' award in 2000, allowing him to return repeatedly to Denmark, Norway, and Sweden over the past five years. When he became chairman of the sociology department in 2003, his travel slowed a bit, but his colleagues have always been understanding about receiving emails from places with alien keyboards that add strange symbols to his messages. In the first edition, Howard commented on the contributions his family had made. Now that he has been made a grandfather, three times over, he hopes that Gavriel Tzvi, Jackson, and Yaakov will carry on the family's love of travel. (All three already have their own passports and two have their own frequent flyer cards.)

Martin has benefited from the collective knowledge of colleagues and students at the University of North Carolina, Stanford, and Princeton University. His approach to organization studies has benefited in particular from the example set by Dick Scott, a generous mentor and one of the most prolific scholars in the field. A number of ideas in this second edition were 'trial' tested on Martin's students in both advanced undergraduate and graduate courses and we thank them for their honest and constructive feedback. Finally, Martin would like to thank his family for their support during the writing of this book (and beyond). In 2003, he returned to North Carolina to marry Jennifer, a social worker and true-blue Tarheel. As work on this book was nearing completion in 2005, Jennifer gave birth to their first child, Edison. He has yet to learn about formal organizations, but already has a great deal to teach about life.

Preface to the First Edition

In 1979, in the preface to my book, *Organizations and Environments*, I wrote:

> In trying to write a book on organizational sociology for both students and colleagues, I decided there was no point in either reviewing all of the 'perspectives' advanced by theorists in the past two decades, or in re-creating the seemingly endless debates over measurement and method that have plagued the field. Rather, I have attempted to present a perspective that integrates concepts and research findings from all social science disciplines studying organizations, while retaining the gains made by historically and politically sensitive investigators in the United States and abroad. With a slight shift of emphasis from an original investigator's intentions, I found that a great deal of the literature in economic history, industrial economics, the social-psychology of organizations, organizational sociology, and political sociology could be integrated into an encompassing framework.

Twenty years later, in 1999, my intentions remain the same: I seek an overarching framework that organizes an inquiry into the issues surrounding organizational *change*. As I will explain in Chapters 1 and 2, I use an evolutionary approach because it is a generic framework for understanding social change. The approach is applicable at multiple levels of analysis and directs our attention to the processes of variation, selection, retention, and struggle that jointly produce patterned change in evolving systems. I first use the evolutionary approach to explain how new organizations are constructed, and in later chapters I explore the historical context in which populations and communities emerge.

How to use this book

This book was written to be read in chapter order. Concepts are defined when they first appear and arguments in subsequent chapters build on those that have come before. However, I have provided an extensive index for people who wish to skip around. I have tried to make it easy for users to see other applications of a concept, and so I have listed most of the relevant pages on which the concept appears. The index also indicates where to find international examples, as I have noted the pages on which examples from nations other than the United States are mentioned.

Given the substantial changes in the field over the past two decades, there is very little overlap with the literature reviewed in my 1979 book. Of the roughly 1,000 references, a little more than 50 percent are from the 1990s and about one-third are from the 1980s. The *Administrative Science Quarterly* is the most cited reference, with about 7 percent of the citations. Together the two Academy of Management journals received about 6 percent of the citations, and the three major American sociology journals account for another 10 percent. The remaining 77 percent of the references are selected from a wide range of journals and books, representing a variety of disciplines and approaches.

I maintain a Web page for the book on my Web site at http://www.unc. edu/~healdric/. The page shows examples of course syllabi that use the book and also provides space for comments and discussion. Please visit the site.

Intellectual origins

In the past, I have used a number of different terms to describe my perspective, but I now prefer the label 'evolutionary.' I admit to a certain inconsistency over the last several decades in labeling the research stream to which I was contributing. In the early 1970s, I argued that an 'organization-environment' perspective would correct a common problem with traditional approaches which were 'using single organizations instead of populations of organizations as the frame of reference' (Aldrich, 1971: 280). I argued that organizational properties had been 'investigated without regard to their contributions to fitness in varying or diverse organizational environments' (Aldrich, 1971: 281–282). Then, in 1975, building on Pfeffer's (1972) several papers on 'organizational interdependence,' and Yuchtman and Seashore's (1967) 'system resource approach,' I used the terms 'resource dependence' and 'resource dependence perspective' (Aldrich, 1976a, 1976b; Mindlin and Aldrich, 1975: 382). However, in retrospect, I probably should have built more explicitly on my earlier observations regarding the need to study populations.

Then, given the opportunity to collaborate with Pfeffer on a review article concerning 'environments of organizations,' I chose the term 'natural selection model' to contrast my way of thinking with Pfeffer's, which we labeled the 'resource dependence model' (Aldrich and Pfeffer, 1976). Many of the themes I developed with Pfeffer in that review article were elaborated upon in my 1979 book, where I referred to the approach as 'population ecology' interchangeably with 'natural selection model.' Bill McKelvey convinced me that the term 'population ecology' was too narrow for what we were doing, and so in 1983 we chose the phrase 'population perspective' (McKelvey and Aldrich, 1983).

Now, I am convinced that it is best to use the terms 'evolutionary perspective,' 'evolutionary approach,' or 'evolutionary theory,' because evolutionary thinking in the social sciences has matured and shed some of its earlier unwarranted connotations. For further discussion of this issue, see my discussion of the excess baggage carried by the term 'evolution' (Aldrich, 1979: 51–54). Baum and Singh (1994a), for example, managed to recruit a large group of scholars to a conference expressly focused on using evolutionary theory to study organizations, a feat unimaginable back in the 1970s. Subsequently, Baum and McKelvey (1999) had no difficulty finding scholars willing to contribute to a conference explicitly focusing on evolutionary issues. I hope my book encourages others to begin thinking in evolutionary terms.

Acknowledgments

I enjoyed writing this book, although it took years longer than I expected. When Sue Jones and I had a celebratory signing dinner in Las Vegas in 1992, she thought

I would be delivering a manuscript to Sage Publications in a few years. When she turned over the editorship to Rosemary Nixon in 1996, we realized that 'book years' rather than 'book months' had become the metric of choice. Sue provided wonderful encouragement in the early years, and Rosemary never wavered in supporting the project, no matter how many self-imposed deadlines I missed.

Along the way, many friends and colleagues became implicated in my efforts, and to prevent them from disclaiming any responsibility for the results, I've decided to give them due credit. First, many of the book's ideas were initially developed in collaborative writing with my doctoral students and other colleagues. Udo Staber initially worked with me at Cornell University on a study of trade associations and subsequently on studies of social networks. Jane Salk joined that effort while a doctoral student at North Carolina, along with Jack Beggs. Ellen Auster also worked with me at Cornell and went on to conduct research on interorganizational strategies. At the University of North Carolina, Amanda Brickman Elam, Pat Ray Reese, Linda Renzulli, and Cathy Zimmer were involved in research on entrepreneurship and social networks, with Paola Dubini collaborating on an Italian replication of that work. Arent Greve and Bengt Johanisson carried out the Scandinavian part of that research. Ted Baker opened my eyes to strategic human resource issues involved in entrepreneurial activities and has been an invaluable co-author on numerous projects. Also at the University of North Carolina, Courtney Sheldon Hunt sparked my curiosity about the possibility of empirical research on electronic commerce, and Amy Kenworthy showed me that Don Campbell still had much to teach me. Jane Weiss's influence lives on to the extent that an historical and comparative flavor informs my writing. Her vibrant presence is sorely missed.

Bill McKelvey and I, as fellow admirers of Donald Campbell's contributions, made a pilgrimage to visit Don in Syracuse. We subsequently wrote a series of papers together. Marlene Fiol rekindled my passion for the social psychology of organizations, reminding me of the lessons Dan Katz and others at Michigan had taught me but which I had suppressed. Mary Ann Von Glinow stirred my interest in human resource issues confronting new firms, and Gabriele Wiedenmayer co-authored several papers with me on the ecological analysis of organizational foundings. Peter Marsden not only recruited me to Chapel Hill but also joined me in several efforts to review the state of the art in organizational sociology. Nancy Langton and Jennifer Cliff gave me a Canadian perspective on human resource management in small and medium sized enterprises. In Japan, Toshihiro Sasaki worked with me on a study of research and development consortia, Tomoaki Sakano and I studied entrepreneurial networks, and Tamiki Kishida tried to persuade me of contingency theory's value.

Second, many people read at least part of the book and made written comments on it. At the top of the list are five truly self-sacrificing souls who read the entire book at least twice, not only providing critical comments but also proposing new text that substantially improved my arguments: Ted Baker, Heather Haveman, Anne Miner, Linda Renzulli, and Pat Thornton. Their advice and encouragement reaffirmed for me the value of strong ties and the joy of supportive colleagues. Others read specific chapters or passages and provided incredibly helpful criticism: Kristina Ahlen, Linda Argote, Joel Baum, Nicole Biggart, Bill Gartner, Mary Ann Glynn, Lisa Keister, Jonathan Levie, Benyamin Lichtenstein, Leann Mischel, Mark Mizruchi, Jim

Moody, Donnie Parker, Jeremy Reynolds, Paul Reynolds, Huggy Rao, Soodi Sharifi, Toby Stuart, Mark Suchman, Jim Wade, and Theresa Welbourne.

Third, undergraduate and graduate students in my organizational sociology and entrepreneurship courses at the University of North Carolina patiently endured multiple drafts of the book and provided constructive feedback. There are too many of them to list, but their contributions live on in the concrete examples and valuable references they contributed. Fourth, my colleagues in Chapel Hill provided a supportive environment in which to discuss not only organizational theory but also my other great passion, the teaching of sociology. In particular, I want to thank Arne Kalleberg, Rachel Rosenfeld, Glen Elder, Lisa Keister, Sherryl Kleinman, and Judith Blau. My office staff did a superb job in putting the book together. Deborah Tilley began the effort, Erica Dawson and Leslie Whitley kept it going, and Jennifer Carpenter masterfully put the final pieces together.

Over the past decade, while this book was taking shape, I did *not* sit cooped up in a dark garret or seaside cabin, as so many other authors seem to claim. Instead, I enjoyed the hospitality of many institutes and universities around the world. Several times, I spent the late spring and early summer months teaching at SDA-Bocconi, in Milan, and at Keio Business School, in Yokohama. Because of the generosity of the University of British Columbia's College of Commerce and Administration, my wife and I spent several summers in Vancouver. I have enjoyed yearly visits to Vienna, teaching in Josef Mugler's Institute for Small and Medium Enterprises at the University of Economics, and also to Sardinia, teaching in Giulio Bolacchi's AILUN program. Mike Useem introduced me to Professor Bolacchi, and Woody Powell and Paul Hirsch have joined me in sustaining an American sociological spirit in AILUN. My 'Scandinavian connection' has proved particularly fruitful, with frequent seminars in Uppsala, Stockholm, Linköping, Jönkoping, Bergen, and a current part-time visiting appointment at the Norwegian School of Business in Oslo. In particular, I thank Maja Arnestad, Magnus Aronsson, Gunn Birkelund, Per Davidsson, Arent Greve, Sølvi Lillejord, Leif Melin, Torger Reve, and Olav Spilling. Many other overseas colleagues have welcomed me for short visits that have broadened my outlook and showed me alternative 'ways of seeing.'

Traditionally, authors conclude their acknowledgments with a painful reference to the sacrifices of their families and an apology for lost time. Those who know my family, however, would not find that claim credible. Our two sons matured magnificently during the 1990s, in part due to study as Morehead Scholars at the University of North Carolina. Steven gave up a career in physics for several years in investment banking and then returned to college for his MBA at Stanford. After graduation, he married Allison and founded an Internet commerce firm. Daniel pursued his interest in Japan with study overseas and an MA in Asian Studies at Berkeley. After marrying Yael and spending a year in Israel, he entered a Ph.D. program in Political Science at Harvard. My wife's inclination for adventure, noted in my 1979 book, continued. Penny spent time swimming with Dolphins in Mexico, teaching on a Navajo reservation in Arizona, snorkeling with the Manatee in Florida, following Orcas off the coast of Vancouver Island, and reading stacks of books in the off-season. Even though my involvement in many of my family's pursuits probably doubled the time it took to finish this book, I could not have asked for a better and more selective environment.

1

Introduction and Themes

Why are organizations important? They are the fundamental building blocks of modern societies and the basic vehicles through which collective action occurs. Their products constitute the infrastructure of societies, shaping the context for organizations of succeeding generations. Through organizations, people pursue activities too broad in scope to be accomplished by individuals or families acting on their own. Accordingly, organizations mediate the influence of individuals on the larger society. For example, most news headlines in the mass media concern the actions of organizations, such as the International Monetary Fund, the World Cup Organizing Committee, or the Microsoft Corporation. Wherever an organization succeeds in attracting enough people and resources, centers of potential social action are created. They mold the social landscape, as individuals affiliate with or abandon them (Ahrne, 1994). We need to know more about how organizations emerge and grow.

Opportunities for the creation of special-purpose organizations increased with urbanization and with economic, political, and social differentiation. The resources required to construct organizations grew more abundant with the development of a money economy and the spread of literacy (Stinchcombe, 1965). The spread of legal institutions protecting property transactions and economic participation created a stable context within which entrepreneurs could look forward to appropriating the gains from organizational foundings (Collins, 1997). Consequently, organizations, rather than individuals or families, became the units of stratification in modern societies. Families now gain or lose wealth through their organizational affiliations, not their historic lineage.

Organizations are shaped by the contexts in which they are established. Thus, contemporary organizations reflect the impact of their historical origins in societies characterized by growing affluence and competition over the control and distribution of wealth (Roy, 1997). Innovations in organizational structures, made possible by the growth of supportive legal, financial, and logistical infrastructures in 19th-century industrial societies, spurred the development of huge organizational projects. In the United States, for example, large national railroads emerged as people struggled to find methods of overcoming the problems of coordinating the passage of shipments across hundreds of miles of rugged terrain (Chandler, 1977). In the 20th century, the production of mass-market consumption goods, such as automobiles and televisions, was made possible by the rise of large vertically integrated manufacturing firms (Lawrence and Dyer, 1983).

Similarly, in the public sector, welfare-state social policies are now implemented through large government agencies that can process thousands of cases on an impersonal and universalistic basis (Orloff and Skocpol, 1984). When the United States found itself behind in the 'race into space' in the early 1960s, President Kennedy committed the nation to putting a man on the moon within the decade, and he created an enormous organization – the National Aeronautics and Space Administration – to accomplish the task. In many industries, employment agencies and brokers affect the allocation of well-paying jobs and structure the careers of workers in the industry. For example, elite talent agencies in Hollywood have had a significant effect on the employment rates and earnings of television and movie writers (Bielby and Bielby, 1999).

Major tasks in many domains are addressed not by single organizations, but by sets of interdependent organizations. *Policy domains* consisting of government bodies, corporations, political groups, and non-profit associations, collectively influence governmental policy formation and agenda setting (Laumann and Knoke, 1987). The National Cooperative Research Act of 1984 allowed businesses that normally compete with each other to establish consortia for conducting research on processes or products that benefit an entire industry (Aldrich and Sasaki, 1995). Interorganizational arrangements between hospitals, doctors, and university laboratories have been created by the National Cancer Institute to coordinate cancer research and treatment, and interorganizational arrangements have replaced asylums for the delivery of mental health services at the community and societal levels (Scott and Black, 1986).

The concentration of power in organizations contributes not only to the attainment of large-scale goals, but also to some troublesome actions (Coleman, 1974; Vaughan, 1999). Some of the negative consequences of organized action arise as by-products in the normal course of business, whereas others are the result of callous disregard of the public interest. During the 'Love Canal' episode in Buffalo, New York, hazardous waste contamination was the result of the careless disposal of unwanted hazardous materials by chemical manufacturers (Levine, 1982). Price-fixing scandals in the heavy electrical equipment industry (Baker and Faulkner, 1993), insurance fraud in the health care industry (Vaughan, 1983), and accounting scandals at Enron and WorldCom provide further examples of the capacity of organizations to do harm as well as good. Complex technical systems managed by organizations, such as airline transportation or nuclear power plants, periodically have 'normal accidents' with catastrophic consequences (Perrow, 1999).

Organizations disband at a high rate in modern societies. By *disband*, we mean that an organization ceases to exist as an operating entity, for whatever reason. Not all marginal, non-competitive, or troubled organizations disband quickly. Many marginal organizations linger on, declining or deteriorating over a period of years or even decades (Meyer and Zucker, 1989). For organizations that permanently shut down, dramatic events such as organizational bankruptcy may stigmatize owners and managers (Sutton and Callahan, 1987). Owners and managers are not the only people affected by organizational disbandings, as losing one's job at a declining or downsizing organization can also be a traumatic experience for workers (Cappelli et al., 1997). Because many workers' identities and sense of self-worth are bound up in their jobs, business closures can severely shake their self-confidence. Conversely, other workers – particularly those in skilled high-technology fields – have come to accept more contingent relationships with their employers (Barley and Kunda, 2004).

As organizational participants and publics, we seem to have an ambivalent feeling about the organizations in our lives (Smelser, 1998). First, we might consider organizations as our servants, making possible an infinitely more varied and full life than would otherwise be possible. Optimistically, history shows organizations serving *our* needs. Second, we might view the growth of an organizational society as a record of people enslaved and dominated by organizations, subject to arbitrary and impersonal dictates, and nearly powerless to fight back (Perrow, 1991; Roy, 1997; Weber, 1963: 203–204). Some have even argued that, in postmodern society, the issue is no longer relevant – individuals have ceased to exist (Baudrillard, 1983). These contradictory images motivate much of the literature on organizations in the scholarly and popular press. Writers assert that the tension between individuals and organizations can be a liberating, alienating, or destructive force. Whatever the answer, organizations constitute the dominant feature of the modern social landscape.

Our goals for this book

We had three goals in mind in writing this book. First, we wanted to write about the challenges of studying *organizations*, not just organizational theory. Organizations are fascinating social units, of many shapes and sizes, but most of them are overlooked by the field of organization studies. Driven by data convenience and substantive biases, contemporary books and journals tend to focus heavily on publicly traded firms, numbering around 7,000 businesses in the United States. The millions of organizations that are neither listed on any stock exchange nor staffed by graduates of business schools appear less frequently in our research, except in sub-fields like entrepreneurship. Of course, we do not mean that this book is a handbook of organizational statistics, devoid of theoretical interpretation. We do seek, however, to ground the book in research designs that capture organizations in all their diversity, rather than to write as if the Fortune 500 were the only creatures in the organizational zoo. We focus primarily on businesses, but other kinds of organizations are also covered.

Second, we wanted to write about the *emergence* of organizations, not just their existence. Organizational scholars have done an excellent job in explaining how things work in organizations that have been around for a while, but not how they came to be that way. In contrast, we are interested in the genesis of organizations, organizational populations, and communities. Even really large organizations started small, usually, but the absolute miracle of their creation does not seem to interest most organization theorists. It should. Without understanding why and how new social units emerge, we miss the connection between the ongoing creative ferment in human societies and the particular realizations of it in organizations. Thus, we give more attention to the early days of organizations, populations, and communities than do most other organization studies' books and articles.

Third, we wanted to write about the *evolutionary processes* through which new organizations, populations, and communities emerge, using an approach that cuts across academic disciplines. We have been disappointed that most research on organizations focuses on structure and stability rather than emergence and change. By ignoring the question of origins, researchers have also avoided the question of why things persist. In contrast, the evolutionary approach treats origins and persistence as inseparable issues. In doing so, evolutionary models encompass many levels and units of analysis and thus typically take an inter-disciplinary perspective on change processes.

The eclectic nature of organization studies draws scholars from economics, history, political science, psychology, sociology, and elsewhere. Disciplinary boundaries have never meant much in organization theory, and members of particular theory groups publish in topical as well as discipline-based journals. We use an evolutionary approach, as we explain in Chapters 2 and 3, because it is a generic framework that can address various theoretical paradigms. Applicable at multiple levels, it directs our attention to the processes of variation, selection, retention, and struggle that jointly produce patterned change in evolving systems. In the early chapters of this book, we use it to portray how new organizations emerge as people mobilize resources in pursuit of opportunities. We focus on time measured in weeks and months. In later chapters, we focus on time measured in years and decades, as we examine the historical context in which organizations, populations, and communities evolve. We show how an evolutionary approach helps us connect history and social structure.

In keeping with our theme of depicting the full variety of organizations in industrial societies, we present some information on the organizational landscape. We show the similarity in organizational size distributions across societies, as well as the enormous disparity between the tails of the distributions. Finally in this chapter, we describe our plan for the book, indicating the topics we will cover in each chapter and the logic underlying their order.

Organizations: an overview

After we explain the three dimensions of our definition of formal organizations, we examine the shape of the organizational landscape in the United States and Western Europe.

Definition of organization: the three dimensions

What are organizations? A simple definition is that organizations are goal-directed, boundary-maintaining, and socially constructed systems of human activity (Aldrich, 1979). This definition focuses attention on the social processes involved in the genesis and persistence of organizations. Some definitions add other criteria, such as a deliberate design, the existence of status structures, planned durability, orientation to an environment, and substitutability of personnel (Meadows, 1967; Scott, 2003). However, we believe these features follow from the three key processes marking off organizations from other types of social units, such as families and friendship circles. Organizational analysis of other types of social units is certainly possible, but we focus on goal-directed organizations.

Goal direction
Goal-directed behaviors and the deliberate design of activity systems are features marking organizations off from other collectivities, such as families and small groups. Organizations are purposive systems in which members behave as if their organizations have goals, although individual participants might personally feel indifferent toward

those goals or even alienated from them. In some cases, organizational goals are codified explicitly in the form of charters, mission statements, and strategy documents (Saloner et al., 2001). More often, however, goals are implicit, complicating the distinction between members' and organizational goals, as well as the definitional division between organizations and other collectivities.

Concerted collective action toward an apparent common purpose also distinguishes organizations from social units such as friendship circles, audiences, and mass publics. Such social units typically do not have a focused agenda and are easily deflected into aimless or purely sociable activities. By contrast, comparisons of actual outcomes to desired targets have a substantial effect on whether organizations will continue a line of action or change it (Simon, 1955). Because many organizational forms are now institutionalized in modern societies, people readily turn to them or construct them when a task exceeds their own personal abilities and resources (Meyer and Rowan, 1977; Zucker, 1988). For example, people raising funds for social or political causes almost always set up a voluntary association, complete with a charter, officers, a bank account, and regular meetings (Knoke, 1990).

Goal setting by owners or leaders must take into account potentially conflicting preferences of other organizations and individuals supplying their resources. For example, participants must be enticed or coerced into contributing to the organization's activities: businesses pay people to work for them, and many non-profit organizations offer more intangible benefits, such as sociable occasions. Because organizations need resources from their environments, they are subject to diverse uncertainties, and may be vulnerable to exploitation or external control if they depend on outsiders (Pfeffer and Salancik, 1978). Contemporary research often focuses on how these external dependencies are managed by organizations, thus highlighting the second dimension of our definition: the boundary between organizations and their environments.

Boundary maintenance

Organizations share their feature of socially constructed boundaries with other types of collectivities. In contrast to those collectivities, however, organizations tend to establish an authoritative process to enforce membership distinctions. For example, large businesses have human resource management departments that select some people and exclude others, creating a strict distinction between 'employees,' who are entitled to organizational benefits, and 'non-employees,' who are not. Voluntary associations have membership committees that perform similar functions. Distinctive symbols of membership may include unique modes of dress and special vocabularies. In leisure parks, such as Disney World, employees' personal identities disappear under their costumes and they become 'cast members' and 'performers' (Van Maanen and Kunda, 1989). The establishment of an organization implies a distinction between members and non-members, thus setting organizations off from their environments (Weber, 1978).

From an organization's perspective, survival as an entity depends on its ability to control its boundaries. Using the criterion of boundary-maintenance, friendship circles or casual associations would not be considered organizations, whereas most social clubs and fraternal associations would be. Circles or casual groupings of people are relatively easy to enter and exit, possessing a fleeting existence, at best. Boundary-maintaining processes become visible on occasions when they are severely tested. For example, they became visible when ethnic minorities in the United States first sought admission to exclusive social fraternities, country clubs, and elite law firms (Smigel, 1964).

In some theories of organizations, boundary maintenance includes stripping away or attempting to control those aspects of personal identity and external commitments that would interfere with rational decision making (Weber, 1978; Simon, 1997). Emotional attachments cloud judgment and may lead people into 'irrational' decisions. Organizations are thus structured in ways to suppress or at least compensate for the excess baggage that people bring with them. Such theories build on assumptions about human behavior that feminist theorists, among others, reject. Mumby and Putnam (1992: 471–474) argued that *bounded rationality* isolates and suppresses 'the emotional/physical self from the process of organizing.' They argued for an alternative model of *bounded emotionality*, in which 'nurturance, caring, community, supportiveness, and interrelatedness are fused with individual responsibility to shape organizational experiences.' Their critique highlighted the difference between models of organizations generated by management theorists, concerned with organizational effectiveness, and more encompassing models, concerned with understanding how and why organizations have evolved. For our purposes, the concepts of bounded rationality and bounded emotionality both emphasize the embeddedness of organizations in their environments.

Activity systems

Organizations have activity systems for accomplishing work, which can include processing raw materials, information, or people. Activity systems consist of bounded and interdependent role behaviors – sets of routines and bundles of activities (Nelson and Winter, 1982). The interdependencies are often contingent upon the techniques used (Thompson, 1967). We use the term *routines* as a generic term, following Levitt and March (1988: 320): 'the forms, rules, procedures, conventions, strategies, and technologies around which organizations are constructed and through which they operate.' Although routines have traditionally been viewed as sources of organizational inertia and inflexibility, more recent accounts stress their evolutionary and dynamic properties (Feldman and Pentland, 2003).

Many routines are inter-personal, but many others require that humans interact with non-humans (e.g. machines and other artifacts), and the study of such interactions has spawned an extensive literature on technology and innovation (Bechky, 2003; Zuboff, 1988). Indeed, Latour (1993) argued that sociologists have been unable to really understand organizations because such complex units are more than just the sum of their human members. He asserted that theories must take account of people in organizations interacting with non-people, such as products and technologies. Under their own power, machines often act without discernible human intervention, and the results of their actions can pose constraints for the machines' nominal owners.

The division of labor between activities in organizations leads to role differentiation and specialization of functions. In smaller organizations, *role differentiation* – people fulfilling different roles in the organization – may simply involve a difference between a leader or manager and other members. Larger organizations are typically highly differentiated. During the 1960s and into the 1970s, researchers investigated the relation between organizational size and role differentiation (Blau, 1970; Child, 1973). They found that organizational growth produced problems of coordination and control, resulting in attempts to simplify structures and create new subunits and divisions (see Cullen et al., 1986, for a review).

Within organizations, goal direction and boundary maintenance manifest themselves as issues of coordination and control, as authorities construct arrangements for allocating resources or integrating the flow of work. These internal structures affect the perceived meaning and satisfaction of individual participants by, among other things, differentially allocating power and affecting the characteristics of jobs. *Control structures* – arrangements that shape the way participants are directed, evaluated, and rewarded – are constrained by participants' multiple external social roles. Some complement, but others conflict with organizational roles. Over the past few decades, organizational sociology has gradually expanded its scope to include more of the external uncertainties associated with organizational life.

With few exceptions, organizations are not self-sufficient. They must depend on interchanges with their environments for their sustenance. Environments include technical elements – information and other resources – directly tied to the accomplishment of work, as well as cultural or institutional elements – rules, understandings, and meanings about organizations – that are shared in the wider society (Meyer and Scott, 1983). Early attempts to theorize about relations between organizations and environments attempted to sharply demarcate the two and sought taxonomies of environments (Emery and Trist, 1965). Following the insights of institutional and social network theorists, we now recognize that environmental influences penetrate organizations in many different ways.

The organizational landscape

In keeping with a central theme of the book, we should know the contours of the organizational landscape before theorizing about it. Discussions of organizations in books and journals often nourish an aura of unreality among scholars, conveying an image of organizations as monolithic behemoths with massive power. On the contrary, the vast majority of organizations are small and short-lived, coming and going on a much shorter timescale than the humans who create and run them (Kaufman, 1985). A comprehensive understanding of organizational evolution must recognize this reality. We can start by recognizing the limitations of information commonly used in our research.

Historically, the broad field of organizational studies has examined many types of organizations. Researchers have studied government agencies (Blau, 1955; Selznick, 1949), churches and non-profit organizations (Gusfield, 1963), educational institutions (Clark, 1970; Stinchcombe, 1964), and various forms of for-profit organizations. However, much contemporary research shows a bias toward large, publicly held organizations, and this bias affects the kinds of organization theory we build (Clegg and Hardy, 1996). A similar problem of selection bias affects research on other events which are the outcomes of historical processes, such as comparative studies of political systems (Geddes, 1990).

Corporations constitute a minority of all businesses, and publicly traded firms are a minority of all corporations. In the United States, publicly traded firms on the three national and several local stock exchanges comprise around 7,000 businesses, amounting to less than two-tenths of one percent of all organizations using a corporate form. Many organization researchers, especially those interested in financial performance measures, rely on this small set of publicly traded firms because data are readily available in reports filed with the Securities and Exchange Commission, the Federal Trade Commission, and other organizations. However, when only the oldest and largest firms constitute our samples, many historical details are lost. We miss the process by which organizations aged, evolved through periods when competitors were eliminated, and developed the distinctive differences that made them hardier than their peers.

Industrial societies contain a substantial number of organizations, but most are quite small. Over 5.7 million businesses with at least one employee were active in the United States in 2001 (Small Business Administration Website FAQ, 2004), and there are thousands of governmental, non-profit, membership, and voluntary associations. For example, in 2004 there were 15,000 American Legion posts, 1,000 local League of Women Voters groups, 7,710 Rotary clubs, 2,100 local Elks lodges, and 2,200 adult branches of the NAACP. In 1991, almost 70 percent of all Americans reported belonging to at least one association (Schofer and Fourcade-Gourinchas, 2001). Over 3 million belonged to the American Legion and over 1 million to an Elks lodge. Figures for voluntary association membership are similar in other nations (Curtis et al., 1992).

How can we learn more about the actual organizational landscape? Detailed information on businesses in the United States and other countries has been rather sporadic in the past, but it has improved as governments have sought more detailed information on which to base economic policy decisions. In the United States, the Small Business Administration (SBA) has assumed most of the responsibility for collecting and publishing data on businesses, using information from other government agencies as well as the private sector. Because the various agencies involved have used somewhat different definitions and cover slightly different target populations, comparability across data sources and years is highly problematic. In the Appendix, we briefly review the relative merits of research designs that have been used to collect information on formal organizations.

Given the wealth of organizational statistics that are available, we now highlight three descriptive features in particular, presenting cross-national data when possible. First, the size distribution of businesses and non-profit organizations is highly skewed, with a small number of very large organizations. Second, although the number of large organizations is small, they tend to achieve a dominant share of resources (e.g. revenues and assets). Third, even though most people work for large organizations, smaller organizations have a relatively large share of all employees.

Although the data we present below are contemporary, readers should recognize that the properties we identify have been stable features of the organizational landscape for some time. For instance, the skewed distribution of business organizations was already a well-known empirical fact in the 1950s (Simon and Bonini, 1958) and commentators recognized the importance of small organizations as employers long before recent booms in entrepreneurial activity (Granovetter, 1985). From an evolutionary perspective, then, an important theoretical question is how these properties persist in the aggregate, alongside tremendous variation in the composition of the organizational landscape over time. As discussions in the theoretical literature and in later chapters make clear, these properties arise because of basic evolutionary processes, such as organizational founding, growth, and dissolution (Simon and Bonini, 1958; Carroll and Hannan, 2000).

Most organizations are small

The size distribution of business firms tends to be log-normally distributed, as does the size distribution of voluntary associations (see Sutton, 1997, for a review). At one tail of the distribution, there are a very large number of small organizations. At the

Table 1.1   Size of firms by industry: United States, 2000

	Percent of firms* in size class			Percent of employees working in firms with 100 or more employees
	Size class 1–19	Size class 1–99	Size class 100+	
All	89.1	98.2	1.8	64.2
Agriculture, Forestry, Fishing, and Mining	89.8	97.5	2.5	57.1
Construction	91.1	98.9	1.1	30.0
Manufacturing	72.3	93.2	6.8	76.3
Transportation, Communications, Public Utilities	86.6	96.9	3.1	77.5
Wholesale Trade	85.2	96.8	3.2	53.0
Retail Trade	90.1	98.4	1.6	65.0
Finance, Insurance, Real Estate	92.6	98.1	1.9	70.1
Professional Services	93.3	98.8	1.2	49.5
Administrative Services	87.5	96.3	3.7	77.4
Educational Services	74.7	93.6	6.4	72.8
Health Care and Social Services	87.7	96.8	3.2	70.5
Accommodation and Food Services	79.9	97.6	2.4	54.1
Other Services	89.2	96.6	3.4	55.7

*Only firms with employees are included in the percentages
Source: Small Business Administration (2002), Table A.7

other tail, a small number of very large organizations exist. In 2000, the SBA estimated that 89.1 percent of the approximately 5.7 million firms with employees in the United States employed fewer than 20 workers, as shown in Table 1.1. Over 98 percent of all firms employed fewer than 100 employees. Nearly 99 percent of EU-based firms employed fewer than 50 employees, and over 92 percent employed fewer than 10 workers, although this proportion varied by country, as shown in Table 1.2. In 2002, over 99 percent of Japanese establishments employed fewer than 100 employees (Japan Statistics Bureau, 2001: Table I-4–1).

Large firms are economically dominant

Second, measured by assets, large firms dominate the corporate world. In 2000, most of the approximately 5 million corporations in the United States had less than $100,000 in assets, and they accounted for less than 0.2 percent of all corporate assets (Internal Revenue Service, 2003). By contrast, the top 0.002 percent of corporations with a quarter of a billion dollars or more in assets held about 90 percent of all corporate assets. In 2000, about 90 percent of all active corporations held assets of less than 1 million dollars, and this large group of approximately 4.5 million firms accounted for just over 1 percent of all corporate assets. The largest 9 percent of all corporations therefore controlled over 98 percent of all corporate assets.

Table 1.2 European Union: employment share by member state and employment size, 2003, selected nations

Nation	Percentage employment share of firms with:				
	0–9 employees	10–49 employees	50–249 employees	250+ employees	Total percent
Denmark	36	20	17	27	100
France	37	16	14	33	100
Germany	34	18	13	35	100
Greece	57	17	13	13	100
Italy	57	17	10	16	100
Spain	50	20	12	18	100
United Kingdom	32	15	12	41	100
*All EU Nations**					
Employment Share	39.4	17.4	13.0	30.3	100
Percent of Firms	92.3	6.5	1.0	0.2	100

*'All EU Nations' includes, in addition to those shown, Austria, Belgium, Finland, Iceland, Ireland, Luxembourg, Norway, The Netherlands, Portugal, and a non-EU nation, Switzerland. Excludes agriculture, hunting, forestry, fishing, and some 'non-market services.'
Source: ENSR. Observatory of European SMEs (2003), Table 1.2.

Detailed information reveals that concentration varies over time within particular corporate sectors. For example, among the 7,887 commercial banks in the United States in 2002, the 184 largest banks with 3 billion dollars or more in assets controlled about 80 percent of all assets (U.S. Department of Commerce, 2003). By contrast, credit unions are mostly state and local membership-based institutions holding fewer assets than banks. In 2002, only 9 of the 9,688 credit unions held more than 3 billion dollars in assets, representing only about 10 percent of all credit union assets. The merger and acquisition movements of the past several decades led to further consolidation in some industries, but the overall concentration of corporate assets has apparently not increased very much (Stearns and Allan, 1996).

Small organizations are significant employers

Third, measured by employment share, large firms still have a very large share of total employment. Nonetheless, small firms play an important role in labor markets. In the United States in 2000, about 36 percent of all employees worked in firms that employed fewer than 100 people. In the agricultural, forestry, and fishing sector, and in construction, substantially less than half of employees worked in firms with more than 100 workers (Small Business Administration, 2002: Table A.7). In three industries, more than 70 percent of the workforce worked in large organizations: (1) manufacturing, (2) transportation, communication, and public utilities, (3) finance, insurance, and real estate. In the EU, firms with 50 or more workers employed about 43 percent of the private sector labor force in 2003, but variation across countries was substantial, as shown in Table 1.2.

In Germany and the United Kingdom, large firms employed around half the labor force, whereas Greece and Italy had very large small-firm sectors, with firms over 50 employing just over 26 percent in both countries (ENSR, 2003: Table 1.2).

Taken individually, small organizations may appear to have a relatively minor effect on their environments. However, analyses at the population or industry level often show that small individual effects can cumulate into sizable collective effects. For example, Barnett and his colleagues studied telephone companies in Southeast Iowa, active between 1900 and 1917, and telephone companies operating in Pennsylvania between 1877 and 1933 (Barnett and Amburgey, 1990; Barnett and Carroll, 1987). They found that small firms – taken individually – consistently had the smallest effects on other firms. However, taken at the population level, small firms in both studies consistently had the strongest effects because of their greater numbers. More important, from an evolutionary perspective, large organizations have their roots in small ones. They do not burst onto the scene fully formed, but rather emerge from among cohorts of peers, many of whom do not survive the startup process and most of whom do not grow to textbook-salient size.

Plan of the book

We use an evolutionary approach to explain the genesis of organizations, population, and communities in modern industrial societies. While offering a framework for understanding, we also wish to keep images of organizational reality in the foreground. Accordingly, we draw on many case histories and offer extended examples of recent research. We emphasize that the processes of emergence are grounded in local and historical contexts, but also that certain generic regularities are apparent.

The book is organized into five sections. The first introduces the evolutionary approach and puts it in the context of other approaches. The second section contains three chapters that use an organizational level of analysis and focus on the role of individuals and groups in the creation and maintenance of organizations. In the third section of the book, we examine organizational transformation and make the transition to a population level of analysis by exploring the historical context of organizations and social change. The fourth section includes two chapters at the population level of analysis, with the first focusing on the emergence of new populations and the second on the reproduction of established populations. In the fifth section, we move to a community level of analysis, drawing upon the earlier chapters to explore how entrepreneurship and relations between populations affect the dynamics of community emergence. Each chapter concludes with a series of study questions and exercises that highlight relevant theoretical debates and suggest empirical areas requiring further research.

Plan for the chapters

In the first section of the book, Chapters 2 and 3 set the stage for what follows by describing the evolutionary approach and how it relates to other perspectives. In Chapter 2, we examine three issues. First, we define and explain the four generic processes that drive evolution and generate the critical events occurring in the life histories of organizational entities: variation, selection, retention, and struggle. Second, we illustrate the promise and challenges of an evolutionary approach, via a detailed historical case study of Wedgwood Pottery. Third, we review some of the central issues affecting research design in an evolutionary approach, including selection biases that may impair our ability to identify evolutionary processes, the problem of defining organizational novelty, and the various levels of analysis that may be addressed. We emphasize that the evolutionary approach is applicable across multiple levels, thus setting the stage for a review of approaches that focus on different units of analysis.

In Chapter 3, we argue that a diversity of approaches to organizational studies is not only tolerable but also necessary, given the subject matter. Because the evolutionary approach is an overarching perspective, we believe that it is flexible enough to serve as a metatheory within which other approaches are acknowledged and appreciated. Evolutionary models do not specify the engines driving variation, selection, and retention, and thus they depend upon ideas from other approaches for their power. We review six approaches: institutional theory, the interpretive approach, organizational learning theory, population ecology, resource dependence, and transaction cost economics. We consider how each approach deals with variation, selection, and retention. Using an evolutionary lens, we also discuss a few of the key issues and debates surrounding each approach, as well as the contributions each makes to understanding organizational evolution.

In the second section of the book, Chapters 4, 5, and 6 take up the question of the conditions under which organizations emerge and coalesce as social units. Organizations display a bewildering variety of forms because they have been created in response to a wide range of problems and have emerged under widely varying environmental conditions. In Chapter 4, we explore the process by which new organizations are founded. People who initiate activities that might culminate in a viable organization are called *nascent entrepreneurs*. In applying an evolutionary perspective, we focus on two aspects of the process by which nascent entrepreneurs move toward creating a fledgling organization: their pursuit of organizational knowledge, and their mobilization of resources around an activity system. Most organizations start small, with little in the way of capital requirements, and thus social support and knowledge gained through social networks figure heavily in their ability to keep the activity going. We highlight the network context of startup activity through a research illustration of a study that has sampled nascent entrepreneurial teams across the United States and analyzed their demographic and network composition.

Chapter 5 continues the theme of emergence by asking how founders and other participants solve two related problems. First, they must discover how to maintain organizational boundaries, and second, they must learn how to reproduce their organizational knowledge. These discoveries must endure from day to day, and over generations of members. Boundary maintenance is problematic because members play ambivalent roles in organizations: as users of what organizations offer because of their control over resources, and as supporters of what organizations must do to reproduce themselves. We pursue these themes by focusing on the processes by which new organizations recruit applicants and construct reward and control systems. We draw extensively on social psychological research in this chapter to explain how the boundaries of groups and organizations become real, taken-for-granted reference points.

In Chapter 6, we examine how *organizational forms* emerge out of the routines and identities that develop around organizational tasks, driven by local exigencies as well as authoritative directives. We argue that founders spend much of their time hiring employees and centrally allocating some roles. At the same time, other roles are emerging through the creation of idiosyncratic jobs. Under these conditions, an organization's coherence as an entity is problematic because founders' activities are constrained by the relations members establish with one another. Through their interaction, members must learn and share organizational knowledge, and use it on a daily basis. We present a perspective on organizational forms that is grounded in interaction between members and their cognitive schemata. We review an ethnographic study of software support hotlines to illustrate the usefulness of a routine-based approach to understanding organizational forms. The image of organizations as boundary-maintaining systems also raises the issue of the extent to which organizations maintain a homogeneous identity. Using Martin's (2002) analysis of organizational culture, we argue that multiple strands of meaning run through most organizations, especially after they have become bounded entities.

In the third section of the book, we examine the issue of transformation within organizations and within cohorts of organizations experiencing large-scale social change. The issue of how frequently and under what conditions organizations change has provoked some of the most spirited debates in organizational studies. For example, strategic choice theorists have argued for managerial autonomy and adaptability, whereas ecological and institutional theorists have tended to stress organizational inertia and dependence. If organizations are relatively inert after they are created, then new organizations are the primary source of variety in populations. Organizational founding processes would be responsible for the modification of populations over time. If, however, organizations change significantly and frequently over their life course, then existing organizations are the major source of diversity in populations.

Of course, we know that organizations sometimes change. The key questions are how often do they change, to what extent, and under what conditions? Moreover, even if organizations do change, they may not change fast enough to keep up with their environments. Some organizations adapt readily to every environmental challenge, whereas others succumb to the first traumatic event they face. In Chapter 7, we offer a definition of transformation as a major change occurring along three possible dimensions: changes in goals, boundaries, and activities. Major changes involve a break with routines and a shift to new kinds of competencies that challenge existing organizational knowledge. The evolutionary framework calls our attention to several dimensions of the transformation process, including the extent of member involvement in them. We also consider the conditions under which transformation disrupts organizations and thus potentially threatens organizational coherence and survival.

Some organizational transformations occur not only within populations but also across entire communities of populations, on a sweeping historical and geographical scale. Others are mundane, repetitive events that are individually insignificant but that have substantial cumulative effects. Most transformations lie somewhere in between. All are time-dependent historical processes. In Chapter 8, we argue that we must embed our explanations in an historical context to study population-level transformations, and we present a framework for classifying and interpreting historical transformation processes. We borrow from population demographers a conception of history as comprising age, period, and cohort effects. Using a research illustration about elite recruitment in the Chinese Communist Party over nearly half a century, we underscore how history can be a key feature of an evolutionary explanation.

In the fourth section of the book, we focus on a population level of analysis, examining the dynamics of new population emergence and the persistence of established populations. In Chapter 9, we examine the social processes surrounding the emergence of new populations, from pioneering ventures through early stages of growth, until a new form proliferates and the population becomes established. Organizational forms reflect the knowledge and resources available to nascent entrepreneurs during a specific historical period. Resource availability is historically contingent, based upon conditions during a particular historical epoch, and thus certain kinds of organizations cannot be founded until the relevant competencies and routines are available or until entrepreneurs develop them. Competencies and routines used in organizing are culturally embedded and historically specific, and thus populations founded in different eras embody different organizational forms (Stinchcombe, 1965). In constructing new populations, nascent entrepreneurs either develop new competencies and routines, or else combine old ones in novel and innovative ways.

Chapter 10 is based on the observation that populations of organizations in modern societies are constantly undergoing processes of expansion, contraction, and change. If all newly founded organizations persisted forever, then the study of organizational evolution would be confined to issues of founding, adaptation, and inertia. However, we know that organizations disband at a fairly high rate, and a sizable literature has developed on organizational mortality (Baum, 1996; Carroll and Hannan, 2000; Ruef, 2002b). Organizations can cease to exist as separate entities in two ways: by completely dissolving – the process by which the vast majority of organizations disband – or by becoming part of a different entity through merger or acquisition. Less than 1 percent of the incorporated firm population in any given year disappears because of mergers (Small Business Administration, 1998), but about 10 percent of the businesses in the United States cease to exist as separate entities each year (Small Business Administration, 2004). Similar rates have been found in other Western capitalist economies, such as the United Kingdom (Ganguly, 1982). We examine the impact of external events on the viability of different forms of organizations, using a research illustration that emphasizes competition between chain stores and independent retailers.

In the final section of the book, we move to the community level of analysis. An organizational community is a set of populations linked by ties of commensalism and symbiosis. The evolution of communities depends on the simultaneous processes of variation, selection, retention, and struggle at the population level, aggregated across the various populations constituting an organizational community. The dynamics of community legitimation also affect the course of organizational evolution. Thus, the same evolutionary model used to explain organizational foundings and the emergence of new populations can also be applied to community development.

Mutual interdependence (between different units) and competition and cooperation (between similar units) sort populations into niches. Dominant populations drive others into subordinate positions and ancillary roles. In Chapter 11, we build on Hawley's (1950) conception of the community level of analysis, focusing on relations between populations. We offer a typology of eight forms of population interdependence, ranging from full competition to full mutualism or symbiosis. Dominance and power relations also play a role in community structure, especially when entrepreneurs struggle to carve out new niches and gain legitimacy for their organizations and populations. We examine two aspects of this process: (1) entrepreneurs' roles in building new populations from discontinuities in technology, norms and values, and laws and regulations, and (2) collective action by interest groups and associations that builds community level legitimacy, especially directed toward the state.

Study Questions

1. Employing the definition of formal organizations as goal-directed, boundary-maintaining activity systems, identify some problematic cases in the 'gray area' between organizations and other social groups. Examples might include youth gangs, social movements, and professional conferences, among others. Develop a taxonomy that accounts for deviations from the definition of organizations.
2. Some methodological individualists argue that the study of organizations is reducible to the study of individual participants and stakeholders. How would you defend the idea of an organizational science, in light of these arguments? Why is it important to study organizations apart from individual actors?
3. In our review of descriptive organizational statistics, we noted that past research has often been developed based on biased views of the organizational landscape (e.g. the misconception that large firms are numerically prevalent). What are some other 'myths' about organizations that you think are commonly held among academics or the general public? What research designs could you employ in an effort to falsify those misconceptions and why?

Exercises

1. Find and evaluate a source of information on businesses or non-profits in another nation. You may use the Internet, but should also consult with your reference librarian for help in locating reliable and up-to-date figures.
2. Map the organizational population of your community. Prepare a distribution of firms by employment size.
3. Interview a local politician or public administrator about changes in the local business population.
4. Write your own 'organizational autobiography' in terms of the organizations that have shaped your life.

2

The Evolutionary Approach

In this chapter, we take up three issues. First, we define and explain the four generic processes that drive evolution and generate the critical events occurring in the life histories of organizational entities. The processes subsume other processes, such as mutation, recombination, random drift, learning, institutionalization, convergence, reorientation, entrepreneurship, cooperation, and competition. Second, we consider the utility of the evolutionary approach through an historical case study, examining the emergence of bureaucracy at Wedgwood Pottery in late 18th-century Britain. Finally, we review three key issues of research design that an evolutionary approach must consider, noting points of disagreement among theorists. These include selection biases that may affect a research design, the problem of defining novelty in routines, organizations, and organizational forms, and the choice of the units of analysis involved in an evolutionary process. Some theorists favor focusing on *activities and structures* on which evolution operates, such as routines, competencies, and jobs, whereas others favor *bounded entities* that carry activities and structures, such as groups, organizations, populations, and communities.

Evolutionary processes

Evolution results from the operation of four generic processes: variation, selection, retention, and the struggle over scarce resources (Campbell, 1969). They are listed in Table 2.1, along with definitions and examples. Evolutionary theory is not a set of deductively linked law-like statements (Sober, 1984). Instead, it is 'a concatenated system of loose, but apparently true and heuristic propositions ... it poses interesting questions, provides clues to their solution and, perhaps most crucially, generates testable hypotheses' (Langton, 1984: 352). The four generic processes comprising evolutionary theory are necessary and sufficient to account for evolutionary change. If processes generating variation and retention are present in a system, and that system is subject to selection processes, evolution will occur. Most importantly, as Dennett (1995), Hull (2001), and others have noted, these mechanisms need not be restricted to the biological level. The principles we draw upon are generic ones, applicable to social as well as biological systems.

Table 2.1   Evolutionary processes

Evolutionary process	Definition	Example
Variation	Change from current routines and competencies; change in organizational forms • *Intentional*: occurs when people actively attempt to generate alternatives and seek solutions to problems • *Blind*: occurs independently of conscious planning	• Within organizations: problemistic search • Between organizations: founding of new organization by outsiders to an industry • Mistakes, misunderstandings, surprises, and idle curiosity
Selection	Differential elimination of certain types of variations • *External selection*: Forces external to an organization that affect its routines and competencies • *Internal selection*: Forces internal to an organization that affect its routines and competencies	• Market forces, competitive pressures, and conformity to institutionalized norms • Pressures toward stability and homogeneity, and the persistence of past selection criteria that are no longer relevant in a new environment
Retention	Selected variations are preserved, duplicated, or otherwise reproduced	• Within organizations: specialization and standardization of roles that limit discretion • Between organizations: institutionalization of practices in cultural beliefs and values
Struggle	Contest to obtain scarce resources because their supply is limited	• Struggle over capital or legitimacy

Beginning with Spencer (1898), scholars have been interested in social applications of evolutionary analysis. Darwin's variation-selection-retention model has attracted more and more adherents, as evolutionary theory has shed the taints of early misunderstandings, such as that 'evolution' implies 'progress.' However, the term 'evolution' still provokes negative emotional reactions from some social scientists. Many of them have been reluctant to consider the evolutionary approach because of misunderstandings caused by authors who confuse old-fashioned social Darwinist ideas with modern evolutionary ideas. For example, Giddens' (1985) portrayal of evolutionary principles was incomplete and slanted because he relied on authors with outmoded ideas, as Hodgson (1993: 41–42) pointed out. As evolutionary applications become more common, we expect such misunderstandings to diminish in frequency and intensity.

Over the past few decades, Boyd and Richerson (1985), Dawkins (1986), Dennett (1995), and Hull (2001) have provided lucid explanations of evolutionary thinking, and Nelson (1994) has applied evolutionary ideas to economic change. Many researchers have used evolutionary principles in their investigations. For example, McPherson invoked an explicitly Darwinian evolutionary model in a series of projects investigating the growth and decline of voluntary associations (McPherson, 1990; McPherson and Ranger-Moore, 1991; McPherson et al., 1992). Lomi and Larsen (1998) used computational models to analyze the dynamics of localized competition in organizational populations. Such empirical projects demonstrate the gains that follow from exploiting the natural affinity between evolutionary principles of explanation and a substantive focus on organizational- and population-level change.

Variation

Variation is a useful analytic starting point for understanding evolution. Any departure from routine or tradition is a variation, and variations may be intentional or blind. *Intentional variations* occur when people or organizations actively attempt to generate alternatives and seek solutions to problems. They result from conscious responses to difficult situations, planning sessions, advice from outside consultants, and so forth. *Blind variations*, by contrast, occur independently of conscious planning. They result not from intentional responses to adaptation pressures but rather from accidents, chance, luck, conflict, malfeasance, and so forth (Brunsson, 1985; March, 1981). Variations are the raw materials from which selection processes cull those that are most suitable, given the selection criteria. The higher the frequency of variations, whatever their source, the greater the opportunities for change.

Sociological theorists often pose the relative importance of intentional variations as the problem of *agency*: how much scope do people have for independence and creativity in the face of social structural constraints on their understanding and behavior (Emirbayer and Mische, 1998)? Agency is an important problem, but we need to separate the question of whether actors are free to take autonomous action from the question of whether their actions – from whatever intentions – are consequential. By 'consequential' we mean that the world actually changes because of an actor's behavior. Of course, some actors enjoy greater access to wealth, power, and prestige than others, and their actions thus have a greater likelihood of succeeding than those of less privileged actors. The evolutionary approach separates the issue of the conditions under which variations are produced from the issue of the conditions under which they are selected and retained.

Evolutionary theory posits that a great deal of sociocultural variation is blind with respect to individuals' or organizations' needs. People's needs may well explain their reasons for generating variations as they engage in search behavior, trying to solve problems, but 'need' does not explain the solution. Blind variations can be as effective as deliberate ones. Selection of variations follows from their consequences, not from the intentions of those who generated the variations (Langton, 1979).

Variation within organizations

Sources of *intentional variation* within organizations include: (1) formal programs of experimentation and imitation; (2) direct and indirect incentives offered to employees; and (3) encouragement of unfocused variation or 'playfulness' (Miner, 1994). Organizations often attempt to induce exploratory variation by institutionalizing experimentation in projects, programs, divisions, and other officially sanctioned activities (Burgelman, 1983). For example, the six computer industry firms examined by Brown and Eisenhardt (1997) relied on a variety of low-cost probes into the future, including experimental products and strategic alliances. Sitkin (1992: 239) argued that innovative organizations should design systems for promoting intelligent failure as a method of constructive experimentation: 'Failure can induce experimentation that, in turn, leads to increased variation in organizational response repertoires.' Variation may also be introduced as individuals and groups improvise in dealing with unforeseen circumstances, working under pressures not permitting lengthy contemplation of alternatives (Moorman and Miner, 1998).

Incentives for variation from standard routines include making *innovation* part of employees' job descriptions, financially compensating workers whose ideas are selected for further evaluation, and creating competitions between work groups with recognition as a symbolic reward. Planned transfer of people across units diffuses knowledge about new practices throughout an organization. Miner (1994) argued that some organizations tolerate occasional unfocused variations as the cost of keeping creative but slightly eccentric employees. Managers sometimes also encourage unfocused variations because they recognize that induced variations are often not radical enough to break through to new ground. Such policies are important because they help generate and sustain organizational heterogeneity that would otherwise disappear because of pressures to conform.

Variations are also sometimes deliberately suppressed within organizations. Dominant groups and coalitions may constrain opportunities for variation to prevent challenges to their power and privilege (Pfeffer and Salancik, 1978). Powerful groups may create unobtrusive structures and promote interpretive principles that shape people's perceptions of what is necessary and possible (Burns and Dietz, 1992; Perrow, 1986). For example, in her study of the Dow and DuPont Chemical companies, Draper (1991) documented how company doctors defined occupationally induced hazards as a problem of unique, individual susceptibility and withheld information from workers. Had they defined the problems as due to workplace arrangements and practices, knowledgeable workers might have switched jobs or taken collective action to demand better protection from the hazards. Instead, workers sought outside medical attention or simply lived with their disabilities.

Sources of *blind variation* in organizations include: (1) the everyday variation generated by members fulfilling their roles as organizational participants, involving trial and error learning, luck, imitation, mistakes, passion, misunderstandings, idle curiosity; and (2) member reactions to unexpected environmental 'jolts' (Meyer, 1982) such as membership turnover, labor strikes, financial crises, legal scandals, and the like. Variations may occur in an organization's jobs, as workers forget standard routines, invent new ones, hear gossip about better practices, drop or unplug things, pursue creative insights, and become discouraged or bored. Variations can also occur in work groups, especially those involving demographic changes (Lawrence, 1997). Variations crop up as new members are included, old ones are fired or laid off, tasks are transferred, and members come to like each other more.

At the department and upper management levels within organizations, variations include a mix of deliberate and blind actions. New managers try to look good by reorganizing things, and research and development labs create products for which markets must be found. They also include marketing departments selling products that organizations have not yet found a way to build, and newly minted MBAs discovering that everything in their organization needs to be re-invented. Blind variations may also be interjected when other organizations are imitated. When managers of California savings and loan institutions were searching for models to follow in their diversification efforts in the 1980s, they ignored similar organizations and imitated successful organizations larger than themselves (Haveman, 1993c). By trying to copy from dissimilar organizations, rather than their peers, they increased the likelihood of unintentionally introducing discordant elements into their structures.

What is the relative mix of purposeful and blind variations? Corning (1974) argued that most variations within organizations are purposeful. Indeed, we have many accounts of managers behaving in very sensible and deliberate ways (Mintzberg, 1974). Managers, almost by definition, believe that most of what they do is *not* blind; they assume that they can use their skills, when faced with uncertainty and risk, to improve their situations (March and Shapira, 1987). In contrast to the many hopeful views of purposeful variation, other theorists have not been so sanguine. Kaufman (1985: 54) listed the challenges facing managers in uncertain environments, including reconciling differences of opinion, coping with irrationality in decision processes, and struggling with imperfect attempts to implement decisions. His conclusion was that 'a successful response to an environmental challenge can be a very fortuitous thing.' Campbell (1982, 1994) held the belief – shared by Weick (1979) – that most variations are blind. Nelson and Winter (1982: 11) argued for a mixed position: 'it is neither difficult nor implausible to develop models of firm behavior that interweave 'blind' and 'deliberate' processes. Indeed, both elements are involved in human problem solving itself and are difficult to disentangle.'

Organization- and population-level variation

A crucial feature of an evolutionary framework is that it must consider not only variations *within* existing organizations but also variations introduced by *new* organizations or *new* organizational populations. Variations are potentially introduced into populations and communities whenever new organizations are founded. Intentions play a pivotal role in the goal-directed activities involved in organizational foundings, as we point out in Chapter 4. Most founders apparently intend to reproduce the characteristics of organizations perceived as successful. They thus avoid departures from the norm in their population. Nonetheless, mistakes in copying are frequent, haphazardly introducing blind variation into new organizations. Although failures and errors can be fruitful because they stimulate further variation (Sitkin, 1992), many prove fatal.

Some foundings are deliberately undertaken as departures from established organizational forms. If successful, such radical innovations transform the conditions of existence for other organizations by destroying the competencies on which they are based (Tushman and Anderson, 1986). Examples include the development of new product classes, such as automobiles replacing horse-drawn wagons (Lawrence and Dyer, 1983), or close substitutes for existing products, such as diesel for steam locomotives (Marx, 1976). In Chapter 9, we examine the conditions facilitating foundings that are so radical that they generate entirely new organizational populations.

Naturally, variations at the population level may also be discouraged by organizations with a vested interest in existing arrangements. In their history of the radio broadcasting industry, Leblebici et al. (1991: 358) found that outsiders to the system introduced most new practices. Innovations were initiated by 'shady traders, small independent stations, renegade record producers, weaker networks, or enterprising advertising agencies. The powerful parties who had vested interests in the institutionalized conventions used their resources to maintain the status quo or introduced practices that confirmed established conventions.' Many of the variations pioneered by outsiders were eventually adopted by dominant organizations, and others triggered legislative and regulatory responses that reshaped the industry.

Selection

Forces that differentially select or selectively eliminate certain types of variations generate a second essential evolutionary process: *selection*. Some variations help organizations acquire resources or legitimacy and are thus selected. Selection criteria are set through the operation of market forces, competitive pressures, the logic of internal organizational structuring, conformity to institutionalized norms, and other forces. If selection criteria favor administrative rationality and formalized control structures within an industry, then adaptive organizations will switch to the new practices. Bureaucratically structured organizations will survive at the expense of non-bureaucratic organizations. For example, during World War II, several forces accelerated the trend toward bureaucratic personnel practices. In a wide range of industries, three factors favored bureaucratization: (1) governmental intervention in labor markets, (2) growing union pressures, and (3) the increasing influence of professional personnel specialists (Baron et al., 1986; Baron et al., 1988).

Selection within organizations

Within organizations and work groups, internal diffusion, imitation, promotion, and incentive systems may be selective in ways that enhance fitness, decrease it, or are simply irrelevant. Scholars of strategic choice argue that managers can often introduce positive internal selectors, first by establishing the strategic direction of an organization and then by favoring elements of organizational design that are consistent with the logic, scope, goals, and competitive advantage of that strategy (Saloner et al., 2001). Others offer less omniscient portraits of organizational leaders, noting that positive selection is often introduced in a mode of 'firefighting' (i.e. reacting to current problems) rather than strategic planning (Mintzberg, 1974).

Management and business strategy writers usually focus on selection systems that improve fitness, whereas an evolutionary approach alerts us to the possibility that many selection systems are irrelevant or not tightly connected to environmental fitness. These systems preserve organizational diversity that is not tied to current environmental conditions. Organizations that are somewhat protected from their environments may even move *away* from external relevance, as in so-called 'ossified' or 'permanently failing' organizations (Meyer and Zucker, 1989). Three types of internal selectors contribute to the loose coupling of internal selection and environmental fitness: (1) pressures toward stability and homogeneity (Campbell, 1969); (2) the persistence of past selection criteria that are no longer relevant in a new environment (Campbell, 1994); and (3) the willingness of some organizational founders and leaders to accept a low performance threshold (Gimeno et al., 1997).

First, pressures in work groups and organizations often encourage internal stability and cohesion. Frequent interaction between members leads to positive reinforcement of interpersonal behavior that is rewarding for the people involved, and to the elimination of incompatible behavior (Kanter, 1977). Such shifts in choices or attitudes within a group have been explained from a number of social psychological perspectives, including social comparison, self-categorization, and network influence theories (Friedkin, 1999). Interdepartmental and other intra-organizational activities are similarly influenced towards maintaining consistency, independently of external environmental pressures.

Second, internal selection criteria may continue as vicarious representatives of past external criteria. Procedures that were once selected because they fit the context may be irrelevant or even maladaptive to the current situation. As an organization repeats the practices, members become proficient at reproducing them day after day and thus are more likely to continue using them. The self-reinforcing process contributes to organizational stability, but can also lead to *competency traps* that inhibit the discovery of potentially adaptive alternatives (Levitt and March, 1988). Members may simply continue doing what they know best, rather than searching for more effective options.

Third, investments in human capital specific to a particular organization, psychic income from association with the organization, and the costs of switching to another activity make some founders and leaders less sensitive to low organizational performance than others. Founders and leaders may become attached to an organization for what it represents, rather than for what it accomplishes. They may also perceive that their skills are more valuable inside the organization than elsewhere. For example, Gimeno et al. (1997) followed 1,547 firms over three waves of data collection from 1985 to 1987. They examined the determinants of firm performance and decisions to discontinue the firm, and found that owners differed in the threshold of performance they were willing to accept. Owners who were more intrinsically motivated and had a family history of business ownership were 'more likely to accept a lower level of economic performance to remain in business' (Gimeno et al., 1997: 771). They also found that older owners had a lower threshold of performance than younger ones and were willing to remain in business despite low returns.

Organization- and population-level selection

Organizations exhibiting maladaptive variations in technology, managerial incompetence, non-conforming norms, or other problematic acts are likely to draw fewer resources from their environments and therefore are more likely to decline in performance. For example, in 2000–2001 over 679,000 business establishments were discontinued in the United States (Small Business Administration, 2004). Over time, populations are more apt to be characterized by the attributes of surviving organizations than by the attributes of those that disbanded. However, the speed of this change will depend on the founding rates of organizations with other attributes, as well as on individual differences in sensitivity to selection pressures, as we noted above.

Strong selection pressures explain the high degree of similarity in the psychological profiles and business operating practices of men and women owners, and ethnic minority and non-minority owners, within small business sectors. Competition from similar businesses leads to similar opening hours, credit practices, and staffing patterns, particularly use of family labor. For example, regardless of their ethnicity, business owners in English inner cities in the early 1980s tended to employ their children, to compensate for their inability to hire regular employees (Zimmer and Aldrich, 1987).

At the population level, consistent selection criteria may drive organizations toward a standard set of routines. Under the requirements of Title IX of the Education

Amendments of 1972 enacted by the U.S. Congress, colleges and universities in the United States have moved toward equalizing the amount of money that they spend on men's and women's sports. In addition to governmental pressures, colleges and universities were under growing pressure in the 1990s from the National Collegiate Athletic Association (NCAA), the private non-profit organization regulating college sports. The NCAA laid down procedures regulating student recruitment, the number of coaches allowed in a sport, practice schedules, and so forth. Thus, in an example of population-level selection forces, the athletic programs of major universities began converging on a similar set of practices, without regard to a particular college or university's local history.

Variations that culminate in *collective action* within a population can blunt or enhance the impact of selection pressures. For example, individual firms in an industry's early days may succeed in forming an employer's association to deal with workers' wage demands. The employer's association can standardize costs across the industry (Staber and Aldrich, 1983). As long as the employer's association monitors and enforces any agreements reached, wages in the ensuing period are a constant for all organizations in the population. Consequently, wage differences across firms will not be a source of selection pressures.

Collective action can create *cooperative alliances* between populations of producers, suppliers, and distributors that transform a formerly competitive community into a set of mutually interdependent populations. In the Prato textile-producing region of Italy, pressures toward shorter product cycles led to the vertical disintegration of hundreds of firms and resulted in a flourishing population of thousands of new firms. New ventures were launched by foremen and mechanics, and the focus of production shifted from large integrated firms to constellations of many smaller firms, led by a primary firm (Lorenzoni and Ornati, 1988). Collective action persists in such cases only if institutionalized, and the barriers to it are formidable (Moe, 1980; Olson, 1965; but see DeNardo, 1985).

Retention

A third evolutionary process involves the operation of a *retention* mechanism for the maintenance of positively selected variations. Retention occurs when variations are preserved, duplicated, or otherwise reproduced so that the selected activities are repeated on future occasions or the selected structures appear again in future generations. Retention processes allow groups and organizations to capture value from existing routines that have proved – or been perceived as – beneficial (Miner, 1994: 85). When environments change slowly, replication of selected variations is the key to continuity in organizational existence. Without the constraints on variation provided by retention mechanisms, gains from selected variations would rapidly dissipate.

Retention within organizations

Stability in the structure and activities of individual organizations is a central focus of traditional organizational analysis, and management textbooks are filled with techniques for the perpetuation of a specific organizational form. Smircich (1983: 341), following Meadows (1967), argued that organization theory is 'dominated by the concern for the problem of social order.' Documents and files are the material embodiment of past practices and are handy references for persons seeking appropriate procedures to follow. For example, accounting and information management systems create categories that channel and document certain activities, directing members' attention toward them and away from undocumented activities (Walsh and Ungson, 1991). Organizational memory also inheres in physical resources such as buildings and machines (Latour, 1993).

Retention within organizations is greatly facilitated by humans' inherent abilities to acquire habits. As Hodgson (2004a) pointed out, an ability to learn valuable behaviors so thoroughly that they become automatic gives humans a great advantage in routine situations. Habits can be contrasted with instincts, which are wired into humans. Instincts represent fundamental drives that shape the environment in which habits are learned, but cannot themselves become the basis for a full-fledged repertoire of responses. Were humans totally dependent on instincts, they would be helpless in complex and rapidly changing situations they had not encountered before. Habits, such as standard ways of solving problems constituting threats to survival, help people economize on information processing and interpretation. Habits allow people to draw on habitual dispositions, thus reducing their cognitive loads so they can attend to the unique aspects of new situations.

Specialization and standardization of roles limit members' discretion and buffer organizations against unauthorized variation from official policies. However, loose coupling within organizations creates opportunities for deviance that are sometimes hard to root out. Members may over-generalize from official tolerance for some kinds of deviance and infer that other sorts will also be tolerated. Centralization of authority and formalization of duties also limit role discretion, channeling members' activities in ways that make them more accountable to higher authorities. Selected routines, structures, and procedures thus help preserve existing organizational forms, if organizations continue to fit the relevant selection criteria.

Organization- and population-level retention

At the population level, retention preserves the technological and managerial competence that all organizations use, collectively, to exploit the resources of their environments. For example, the survival of a particular type of personal computer firm is not terribly consequential to the survival of its population. The entire population's survival depends on the total pool of technological and managerial competencies held by all personal computer firms. Thus, when the Osborne Computer Company, a pioneering firm, went bankrupt in the early 1980s, its employees and customers simply switched to other firms in the population. Variations possessed by particular firms contribute to the total pool but do not determine its collective fate. Of course, a single firm might *develop* an innovation that enhances a population's survival chances, but that would depend on the diffusion of the innovation throughout a large sector of the population.

Retained variations are passed, with more or less additional variation, from surviving organizations to those that follow, and from old to new founders, employees, and managers. Replication occurs via people observing one another, through training and education, learning appropriate rules of behavior, and interacting with machines and documents. Linkages between organizations facilitate the *diffusion* of variations, whereas isolated organizations contribute little or nothing to future generations. The movement of people between organizations facilitates knowledge diffusion (Phillips, 2002), as do alliances, consortia, and other strong ties (Strang and Soule, 1998). For example, Burns and Wholey (1993) found that cooperative interorganizational relations between hospitals increased the likelihood of their adopting a matrix organizational structure when others in their region did so.

Diffusion of variations across organizations may be limited, however, because of factors that inhibit interorganizational learning. Diffusion of many innovations may be blocked by impermeable organizational boundaries. Organizations often cling to traditional ways or display a reluctance to trust outside information. Decisions on *which* variations to copy are clouded by ambiguity in outcomes observed from a distance (Abrahamson, 1991). Tacit knowledge embedded in an organization's routines may mislead outsiders into imitating the wrong variations. Finally, unforeseen circumstances such as hostility, mistakes, incompetence, and an unwillingness to learn also impede diffusion. Accordingly, not all variations are diffused to new organizations, introducing a large element of uncertainty into the process.

Knowledge of previously successful forms is institutionalized in the socialization apparatus of societies – schools, families, churches, public agencies – and in cultural beliefs and values defended by dominant organizations and institutions. With industrialization, there has been a trend toward the externalization and rationalization of culture. Oral traditions are now less important than the material artifacts of societies, such as written records, machines, and general capital improvements. Technological change, especially in the form of information transmission and retrieval systems, has vastly simplified the task of preserving administrative knowledge (Zuboff, 1988; Cortada, 1993).

Social stability and its effects on retention are seen most clearly in the role the state plays in the creation and maintenance of organizations. As the major constraint on organizational formation and persistence, the state's role appears in many guises: political stability and ideological legitimation, educational systems, improvements in transportation and communication networks, national economic planning, and other state investments. These forces affect the terms on which resources are made available to organizations. For example, state-supported school systems not only help maintain continuity in knowledge between generations by producing educated students, but also certify graduates as amenable to the disciplined regimen sought by potential employers (Collins, 1979). Institutions such as calculable law, an independent judiciary, and state-insured banks raise the probability that organizational forms, if successful, will persist and that unimaginative entrepreneurs will be able to copy them (Stinchcombe, 1965; Collins, 1997).

Struggle

Underlying selection pressures and the search for effective variations lies the scarcity of resources within organizations, between organizations, and between populations. Struggle occurs within organizations, as members pursue individual incentives as well as organizational goals. As we discuss in Chapter 6, some theories view an organization as a unified whole with a personality and goals of its own. Others focus on organizations as collections of individuals. Individualistic approaches view 'the emergence of organizations, their structure of roles, division of labor, and distribution of power, as well as their maintenance, change, and dissolution … as outcomes of the complex exchanges between individuals pursuing a diversity of goals' (Georgiou, 1973: 308). Barnard (1938) took this position in his influential portrait of organizations as incentive distributing devices. In these views, a scarcity of the things people value creates a need for organizational control systems and mechanisms for distributing incentives.

Organizations pursue many scarce resources, including time. Peoples' free time is limited in industrialized societies, and organizations want their share of it. Employing organizations, voluntary associations, work groups, and other entities often want the full commitment of members, but they cannot obtain it because members would then accomplish nothing else in their lives. Employers come closer to realizing this ideal than voluntary associations. *Greedy institutions* (Coser, 1974) want more, and must fight members' families and friends for them. In the United States, some organizations cope by expanding their hours and operating seven days a week. Voluntary associations routinely do this, but many businesses do, as well. All-night supermarkets, gas stations, restaurants, and convenience stores have 'colonized the night' (Melbin, 1987) as a way of expanding their domains without adding to fixed investments.

Most attempts to found new organizations fail and many organizations disband within a few years, as we note in Chapter 4. In a world of limited resources, only some organizations can obtain the land, labor, capital, and other things they need to survive. In Chapter 7, we point out that most organizations do not grow and that most very large organizations are a result of mergers and acquisitions, not internal growth. Even long-lived organizations remain vulnerable to environmental change, as shown by turnover on lists such as the Fortune 500.

Struggle also occurs between populations. When a particular type of organization proliferates, a struggle over resources and opportunities occurs, fueling the selection process between that population and other populations. Sometimes organizational populations expand rapidly because opportunities are diverse and resources abundant. As populations evolve, however, or resources become scarce, competition over resources increases mortality rates and lowers founding rates. Cooperative schemes that protect populations may arise, buffering some against resource scarcity. For example, ties to important community and state institutions may serve as a transformational shield by providing extra resources and legitimacy to some populations (Miner et al., 1990). However, complex cross-unit cooperative arrangements, such as coalitions, cartels, and many forms of interorganizational alliances, are highly vulnerable to short-term deviations. Members of such arrangements are under heavy pressure to make their own unique adaptations to local conditions.

Summary

Using these four principles, evolutionary theory explains how particular forms of organizations come to exist in specific kinds of environments. Variation, selection, retention, and struggle occur simultaneously rather than sequentially. Analytically, the processes may be separated into discrete phases, but in practice they are linked in continuous feedback loops and cycles. Variation generates the raw materials for selection, by environmental or internal criteria; retention processes preserve the selected variation. But retention processes also restrict the kinds of variations that may occur, and competitive struggles as well as cooperative alliances may change the shape of selection criteria. The process is not necessarily historically efficient, as March (1994) pointed out. Using a computer simulation with plausible parameter settings, Carroll and Harrison (1994: 720) showed that 'path-dependent processes can often generate outcomes other than those implied by historical efficiency.' Thus, the organizations and populations we observe at a given moment are not the 'most fit' in any absolute sense. Rather, their forms reflect the historical path laid down by a meandering drift of accumulated and selectively retained variations.

Research Illustration 2.1   The Evolution of Bureaucracy

John Langton's (1984) analysis of Wedgwood Pottery provides a useful illustration of an evolutionary perspective using a case study methodology. Wedgwood is a British organization that was founded in the 18th century on the basis of Josiah Wedgwood's (1730–1795) extensive experimentation with ceramics, glazes, and colors. The firm still exists today, perhaps best-known for Wedgwood's innovative development of Queen's Ware, a cream-colored china, and Jasper Ware. Using an evolutionary perspective and detailed historical data, Langton sought to explain the emergence of bureaucracy at the pottery factory between its founding in 1759 and Wedgwood's death, as well as the subsequent bureaucratization of the British pottery industry.

The case study built on Weber (1978), who argued that authority systems would tend to evolve from charismatic and traditional forms to legal-rational forms, but did not provide a theoretically-motivated explanation for how this evolution occurs. Langton suggested that a variation-selection-retention (VSR) framework can readily provide this explanation. Josiah Wedgwood began with a number of *intended variations* at his factory, including the modification of work routines that would allow the mass production of superior but affordable pottery. He committed himself to an early version of scientific management, seeking to 'make such machines of the men as cannot err' (McKendrick, 1961: 34). *Blind variations* at the potbank deviated from Wedgwood's intentions, including such typical craftsman practices as drinking on the job, working flexible hours, taking Mondays off, and disregarding inefficiency or waste.

A variety of selection pressures, both those internal to the pottery factory and those affecting the pottery industry as a whole, favored the new work ethic advanced by Wedgwood. With respect to *internal selection*, Wedgwood replaced rules of thumb by rationalized administrative practices borrowed from his friend in London, Matthew Boulton. He also changed the way workers were hired and trained, and implemented a wide array of positive and negative sanctions within his factory. In many respects, however, *external selection* pressures – which favored the survival of the pottery factory itself – were even more significant. On the demand side, a rising standard of living throughout the 18th century changed British consumption patterns. The growth of coffee and tea drinking created an increased demand for earthenware, and traditional pottery manufacturers were unable to keep up. Improvements in transportation and communication, such as canals and paved roads, made long-distance movement of goods safer and cheaper. The labor force was also changing, as the Enclosure Movement forced many peasants off the land, thus making them available for wage labor. John Wesley, a Methodist preacher and a powerful public speaker, convinced workers to give up their traditional ways and turn more of their energies to work and the prospects of salvation. Wedgwood took advantage of these changes by creating a pottery factory that departed substantially from the organizational practices of traditional firms in the industry.

Wedgwood's innovations would have been short-lived if they had not become institutionalized at the pottery factory. The process of *retention* occurred through the creation of several permanent features of bureaucracy. As opposed to the artisan standard of autonomous craftsmanship, clear job descriptions and rules were introduced. The simple guild-like organization of the traditional potbank involved a two-tiered master–worker relationship that relied strongly on nepotism. By 1775, it was replaced by a more complex hierarchical career structure, with advancement based on job performance. Whereas production at the traditional potbank was unreliable, the Wedgwood factory came to be regulated by documented routines and systems for book-keeping.

In keeping with an evolutionary point of view, Langton's argument suggests that the outcome at the pottery factory ultimately depended on the interaction between Wedgwood's actions and the context of the times. Wedgwood's pottery factory was selected because it produced superior products more cheaply than his competitors, given the resources available in that era. The success of Wedgwood's innovations eventually led to a new commercial pottery industry that displaced the older, cottage-based population.

While provocative, the argument also highlights some difficulties in Langton's research design. Like any case study, the examination of Wedgwood Pottery raises the question of *generalizability*: elements of the VSR framework here reflect the idiosyncratic context of an 18th century pottery factory. How can these be generalized to help account for the emergence of bureaucracy in other contexts? Langton (1984: 346–349) himself anticipated these concerns, implying that the inclusion of criteria drawn from other theories can help flesh out an evolutionary account. For example, mainstream economists may argue that Wedgwood's bureaucracy faced favorable selection because it minimized transaction costs (Williamson, 1994), while Marxists will suggest that it maximized control of the work process and allowed the exploitation of workers. In Chapter 3, we consider in greater detail how other organizational paradigms can be mapped to an evolutionary framework along these lines.

Research design in evolutionary analysis

Like any principled social scientific analysis, an evolutionary perspective requires that organizational theorists think carefully about three research design questions. These questions are not narrowly methodological but rather raise basic theoretical questions. First, what is the most appropriate *unit of analysis*: routines and competencies; work groups, divisions, and organizations; or populations and communities? Second, given the importance of emergence as an outcome in evolutionary analysis (see Chapter 1), how can we best define when routines, organizations, or organizational forms are *novel* in character? Third, given evolutionary theory's emphasis on an accurate portrayal of selection mechanisms, how can we ensure that our research designs do not impose *selection biases* themselves, thus obscuring basic evolutionary processes?

Units of analysis

Three possible units of analysis have been proposed: (1) routines and competencies within organizations; (2) organizations as a whole; and (3) entire organizational populations or communities. In one version of the first view, organizational learning theorists have also suggested focusing on *bundles* of routines and competencies, rather than taking them one at a time. In contrast, proponents of the second view tend to treat an entire organization as a single interconnected bundle. Some theorists have also proposed populations and communities as units of analysis. In the eclectic spirit of Hodgson and Knudsen (2004), who advocated multiple levels of analysis, we review the options without offering a strong recommendation for any specific perspective.

Routines and competencies as units of analysis

Three interpretations of the term 'routine' have been proposed: routines as behavioral regularities, cognitive regularities, and propensities (Becker, 2004). First, many analysts use the term to indicate recurrent patterns of interaction between members, emphasizing the collective and observable nature of routines (Nelson and Winter, 1982). Second, others treat routines as cognitive regularities, such as rules and standard operating procedures that members follow when they work and interact (March and Simon, 1958). Third, in a departure from the first two uses, Hodgson and Knudsen (2004) depicted routines as propensities that can trigger behavioral and cognitive regularities, thus emphasizing their probabilistic nature. This conception of routines as stored capabilities, rather than directly observable regularities, greatly complicates research. Nevertheless, it allows us to avoid an essentialist notion of routines as either 'all or nothing' patterns sustaining organizational activities. Although we favor the 'propensities' interpretation, most of the research we cite in this book follows one of the other two interpretations. It would be premature to settle on one interpretation, given the diversity of opinions and the growing number of contributions to this issue, e.g. Feldman and Pentland (2003).

Theorists examining evolution inside organizations have focused on the differential survival of strategic initiatives (Burgelman and Mittman, 1994), job roles (Miner, 1991), and administrative rules (March et al., 2000). They view organizations as composed of a mix of routines and competencies that can vary somewhat independently of one another and are thus available for selective retention. From this perspective, evolutionary processes affect the course of change – at whatever level – by their selective effects on the entities embodying routines and competencies. Organizations, then, are the temporary repositories of competencies and routines that are held by their members and embedded in their technologies, material artifacts, and other structures. The distribution of these competencies and routines in a population depends on the selective survival and growth of organizations that contain different combinations of them. Analysis should therefore focus on conditions favoring the selection of routines and competencies, with organizational survival a secondary consideration.

Using this view of organizations and populations, McKelvey (1982) proposed an ambitious scheme for classifying organizational forms. He defined organizational species as 'polythetic groups of competence-sharing populations isolated from each other because their dominant competencies are not easily learned or transmitted' (McKelvey, 1982: 192). A polythetic group is one where: (1) each member possesses many properties, p, of a set of properties, P, (2) each p in P is possessed by many members, and (3) no p in P, is possessed by all members (McKelvey and Aldrich, 1983: 109).

McKelvey proposed his definition as a way of avoiding the grouping idea underlying traditional conceptions of organizational form, in which all the members of a population possess the same set of properties and the classification scheme focuses on the average in a population. Contemporary accounts of organizational forms tend to be more flexible, although formal definitions continue to rely on a minimal common identity that is shared across organizations and is enforced by an external audience (Pólos et al., 2002).

Routines and competencies may be *bundled* into complementary sets and even tightly coupled at the organizational level. If so, then these bundles drive the fates of the organizations that carry them, rather than routines and competencies taken in isolation (Levinthal, 1991). The effect of individual features of a system may depend upon the presence of other features, a condition called *epistasis* (Miner and Mezias, 1996: 93). To the degree that certain routines and competencies complement one another, selection will depend on whether entire sets are present in an organization.

Organizations as units of analysis

A second line of inquiry, pursued primarily by population ecologists but also by other theorists, treats organized entities as units of analysis, rather than the routines and competencies within the entities. To be a unit of selection, an entity must have the characteristics of a bounded system and have boundary-maintaining processes organized around the persistence of the unit and the perpetuation of its activities. Work groups, departments, divisions, organizations, and populations have this character, although in varying degrees.

Population ecologists, in particular, have focused on organizations as the units selected via an evolutionary process. They posit that changes in populations occur through the selective elimination of certain organizations and the survival of others. Even within this perspective, the choice of units of analysis can vary widely, ranging from establishments – physical sites occupied by an organization – to conglomerates – involving legally separate, but highly interdependent, organizations (Carroll and Hannan, 2000). Most analysts have avoided the extremes in this respect, emphasizing organizations as legally- and socially-defined entities, rather than physical locations or conglomerate groups.

Evolutionary ideas have also been applied to the emergence and decline of entire populations (Aldrich and Fiol, 1994; Renzulli, 2005; Ruef, 2000, 2004). Hannan and Carroll (1995: 29) argued that some forces affecting the organizational world can only be seen at the population level, and they defined organizational populations as 'specific time-and-space instances of organizational forms.' Thus, a population is identified not only by a generic label, such as 'public bureaucracy,' but also by the historical period and society in which it exists. Consequently, an ecological researcher would identify a subject of inquiry as 'the set of public bureaucracies in Japan between 1946 and 1993.' We examine the conditions promoting the emergence of new populations in Chapter 9.

Baum and Singh (1994a) advocated adding organizational communities to the list of bounded entities that can be selected, but other theorists have disagreed (Campbell, 1994). Do communities, for example, have sufficient coherence as entities to be selected as communities? Communities certainly stand toward the top of the evolutionary hierarchy, encompassing multiple populations. Under conditions of tight sociopolitical coupling, we can imagine selection occurring at the community level. However, as this is an under-researched area in organizational evolution, we will leave the issue open for now and return to it in Chapter 11.

Defining novelty

An evolutionary perspective takes the emergence of organizational phenomena as a key object of explanation, including the genesis of new routines and competencies, of organizational forms that depart from existing modes of organizing, and even of new social institutions. In many respects, these variations constitute the raw material that is subject to subsequent processes of selective retention or elimination. Schumpeter (1934) identified entrepreneurship broadly with 'the carrying out of new combinations' of such organizing activities. But how do we know when the activities of an individual or group are novel by historical or contemporary standards?

The research literature has tended to apply three standards in judging the novelty of an evolutionary variation, including: (1) an *egocentric* standard that takes into account the intentions of organizational participants themselves; (2) an *altercentric* standard that considers the opinions of selected peers or experts; and (3) a *holistic* standard, which relies on systematic sampling of organizational activities or structures. The egocentric criterion is most appropriately applied when a variation involves an intended departure from existing practices. Ruef (2002a) used this criterion in operationalizing attempts at innovation within a sample of business entrepreneurs. Elaborating on Schumpeter's (1934) categories of innovation, he included activities such as the attempted introduction of a new product or service; the development of a new method of production, distribution, or marketing; the development of new supplier linkages; attempted entry into an unexploited market niche; and the attempted reorganization of an organizational population. Implicitly, historical research often invokes an egocentric standard of innovation, relying on autobiographies, letters, diaries, or public statements produced by entrepreneurs. In his review of the historical literature on Josiah Wedgwood, McKendrick (1961: 30–31) noted that many of the early accounts of Wedgwood's methods drew from the English entrepreneur's personal letters.

An obvious methodological problem that arises with the egocentric standard of novelty is that organizational participants may over- or understate the novelty of their activities, depending on whether their social environment entails pressure toward deviance or conformity. Moreover, egocentric definitions are generally inadequate in judging blind variations, even when applied retrospectively. *Altercentric* definitions seek to counter these shortcomings by relying on the informed opinions of outside experts – e.g. industry specialists, stock market analysts, academics – who are not directly responsible for a purported variation. The most commonly used indicators in this respect are patents or trademarks, which have the advantage of being publicly available forms of external validation that correlate highly with other measures of novelty (Ahuja, 2000). Several drawbacks should also be noted, including the limited ability of entrepreneurs to patent or trademark most organizational variations, the differing propensity and ability among entrepreneurs to seek legal protection for their ideas, and the differing salience of legal protection across historical and national contexts. Both egocentric and altercentric definitions of novelty risk conflating the appearance of a variation with the selective retention of that variation, insofar as the attention of entrepreneurs and experts tends to be directed at successful creative action.

A third, holistic, approach to defining novelty relies on systematic sampling schemes to identify creative action. For example, Scott and colleagues (2000) sought to delineate the appearance of new institutional frameworks in the American health care field, tracking the sector's evolution from its early domination by physician interests to its more recent orientation toward the market. A simple altercentric definition of institutional change relied on the opinions of academic experts and a periodization produced by major legislative events. An holistic definition, on the other hand, tracked all significant regulatory events in the field, as well as a host of quantitative indicators, over half a century. Even though both definitions were in agreement on the periodization of major, discontinuous, institutional change, the holistic definition revealed a great deal of incremental transformation that would have been missed otherwise. Naturally, it is far easier to apply such systematic sampling in a retrospective, historical analysis than in a prospective research design. As Damanpour (1988) has noted, prospective designs that impose an investigator's definition of novelty are likely to miss significant aspects of organizational innovation.

Selection bias

One of the most difficult principles of the evolutionary approach for social scientists to accept is the indeterminacy of outcomes, which must be explained after the fact (Dennett, 1995). An evolutionary perspective treats the future as very much an open question. Rather than directly constructing populations, communities, or societies, people construct solutions to very specific problems. The accumulation of solutions might eventually result in organizations, then populations, then communities, but the process may conceivably require tens of thousands of trials and errors, occurring within historically conditioned constraints. Many accounts of organizational change ignore this sense of indeterminacy.

A methodological consequence of the emphasis on indeterminacy is that research designs examining evolutionary processes must be careful not to select cases based only on successful outcomes. The routines, organizations, and organizational forms that we observe today are outcomes of a long-running evolutionary process. If we only sample the organizational phenomena that have survived, we end up ignoring the numerous failures. Moreover, when our research designs impose such *success biases*, they obscure the selection mechanisms of interest to evolutionary theorists.

Success bias is a special case of a more general problem in research design, called *selection bias*. Sample selection bias occurs when the full range of values on an outcome variable cannot be observed (Berk, 1983). For instance, suppose that we seek to understand the determinants of growth among business firms, but we only have a sample of Fortune 500 companies. If organizational growth is dependent on existing organizational size (see Sutton, 1997), then this sampling criterion effectively constrains the range of outcomes that we obtain, jeopardizing the causal inferences made from our study.

Whereas this type of selection bias pertains to a constraint imposed on *quantitative* variations in outcomes, evolutionary theorists must also be attentive to selection bias that ignores *qualitative* variation. Following our discussion of novelty, let us assume that we seek to explain the emergence of the worldwide automobile industry. Clearly, this will require that we collect data on the industry, as well as the various social movements that legitimated it (e.g. Hannan et al., 1995; Rao, 1994). It is equally important, however, that we develop a *counterfactual* analysis that addresses the alternative modes of transportation that struggled against the automobile, but were subsequently marginalized as substitutes (Klein and Olson, 1996).

Conclusions

Following Ritzer (2006), the evolutionary approach may be described as a *metatheory*, an overarching framework that permits comparison and integration of other social scientific theories. Evolutionary theory applies to many levels of analysis: groups, organizations, populations, and communities. Variation, selection, retention, and struggle are processes occurring within all social units and across levels. Evolutionary theory does not provide a set of law-like statements governing these processes. Instead, the perspective takes what it needs from other approaches that we review in the next chapter, as befits its eclectic nature. Whether promiscuous borrowing will corrupt its products is not yet clear, but theoretical eclecticism has not seemed to harm other long-lived perspectives, such as 'contingency theory' (see Hodgson, 1993, for a related defense of evolutionary economics).

Major issues are still under debate, including the question of what is being selected in evolutionary processes (e.g. routines versus organizations), how novel evolutionary variations can be defined, and what research designs are most appropriate in capturing the indeterminacy of outcomes that is a key feature of evolutionary analysis. Rather than offering more definitive views on these issues at this stage, we will deepen our understanding of the relevant substantive phenomena in the following chapters and review a range of research designs that address our methodological concerns in distinctive ways.

Study Questions

1. To what extent can an evolutionary approach treat 'external' selection processes as being truly exogenous? Langton pointed out that Wedgwood helped petition Parliament for the development of a transportation infrastructure that would help his factory get products to market. List and explain two principles we can use to take account of the agents that construct a social environment.
2. As managers engage in intentional variation of routines and simultaneously contribute to internal selection criteria, the line between 'variation' and 'selection' can become ambiguous. What distinctions would you propose to help guide evolutionary analysis?
3. Perrow (1985) criticized Langton's study for ignoring the social costs of bureaucracy, such as the coercion and exploitation of workers. Can an evolutionary perspective be applied to understand – and even resolve – social problems, given the indeterminacy of outcomes in this approach?
4. Develop your own critique of Langton's case study, emphasizing the three issues of research design raised in the chapter – i.e. unit of analysis, definition of novelty, and selection biases.

Exercises

1. Pick an organization in which you participate, e.g. as an employee, volunteer, or student. Identify some of the evolutionary mechanisms that allow the organization's practices to persist from week to week.
2. Using each of the three interpretations of 'routines,' identify some routines in the organization you chose for #1 and design a research project to document them.

3

How the Evolutionary Approach Relates to Other Approaches

Paradigm proliferation in organization studies has given us a wealth of perspectives from which to view organizations and organizational change. Despite apparent confusion among conflicting theoretical claims, distinct points of clarity stand out in this academic briar patch. As Reed (1996: 33) noted, 'Organization studies is constituted through shared lines of debate and dialogue which establish intellectual constraints and opportunities within which new contributions are assessed.' Collective judgments, codified in rules and norms, emerge from negotiation and debate, resulting in new vocabularies and grammars for organizational analysis. The resulting perspectives are a product of their times, and many are swept away by subsequent historical currents (Aldrich, 1988). Some remain, however, and gain so many adherents that they qualify as schools of thought or theory groups.

Within organization studies over the past several decades, a handful of rather distinct approaches has emerged through fluctuating periods of relentless competition and tolerant cooperation. The evolutionary approach holds out the promise of using these views to achieve an integrated understanding – although perhaps not an integrated theory – of organizations. Such eclecticism delights some but disturbs others. For example, Pfeffer (1993: 620) argued that 'without working through a set of processes or rules to resolve theoretical disputes and debates, the field of organization studies will remain ripe for either a hostile takeover from within or from outside. In either case, much of what is distinctive, and much of the pluralism that is so valued, will be irretrievably lost.'

We believe that a diversity of approaches is not only tolerable but also necessary, given our subject matter. We also believe that the evolutionary approach serves as an overarching framework – or metatheory – within which the value of other approaches can be recognized and appreciated. The evolutionary approach constitutes a set of concatenated principles and uses multiple approaches to explain particular kinds of changes. Evolutionary models are not causal, because they do not specify the engines driving variation, selection, and retention. Instead, the models are algorithmic, specifying that *if* certain conditions are met, *then* a particular outcome will occur (Dennett, 1995: 48–60). In explaining any particular evolutionary *if–then* path, a theorist may be obliged to draw upon ideas from several approaches. To give readers a sense of how the model of variation, selection, retention, and struggle uses other approaches to explain organizational change, we review six of them: organizational ecology, institutional theory, the interpretive approach, organizational learning theory, resource dependence, and transaction cost economics (TCE).

We consider how the chosen perspectives deal with issues of variation, selection, and retention. We also offer a review of critical issues under debate within each approach, as well an assessment of their contributions to an evolutionary understanding. A summary of the six perspectives' relation to evolutionary theory is given in Table 3.1. We present the six approaches in alphabetical order, as their precise historical ordering and current standing are subject to dispute.

The ecological approach

The ecological approach explains organizational outcomes in terms of the demographic composition – size and distribution – of organizational populations and the resource environments they are located within. It emphasizes foundings and disbandings as sources of population level change, and downplays transformations. Ecological approaches to organizational analysis focus on relations between organizations and thus complement more micro-analytic approaches, which focus primarily on social relations within organizations. Ecologists assume that organizational populations can be identified that have *unit character*, responding in similar ways to environmental forces (Hawley, 1950). Populations are dependent upon distinct combinations of resources – called *niches* – supporting them. Because they compete for resources within the same environment, organizations in a population are in a state of competitive interdependence. Competition pushes organizations toward adopting similar forms, resulting in greater homogeneity or specialization of forms within different niches. Organizations, in a sense, find niches to protect themselves against competition. Organizations often make common cause with one another as they compete with other organizations and populations, thus creating a mutualistic state of cooperative relations. Competitive and cooperative interdependencies jointly affect organizational survival and prosperity, resulting in a distribution of organizational forms adapted to a particular environmental configuration (Carroll and Hannan, 2000; Hannan and Freeman, 1989).

Variation, selection, and retention

Organizational ecology has mainly looked for variation between organizations, via differences across organizations produced during their foundings. Ecologists assume that the most important processes to study are population demographics, or what Carroll and Hannan (2000) called *vital events*: patterns of foundings, transformations, and disbandings. These events constitute the dependent variables in most ecological analyses. Ecologists appreciate, even celebrate, the high level of volatility generated by these events. Sources of intra-organizational variation have been relatively neglected, in part because the preferred research design is the single population

Table 3.1   Six perspectives on organizations: relation to evolutionary theory

Perspective	Variation	Selection	Retention
Ecological	• Variation introduced via new organizations	• Selection results from fit between organizations and environment	• Retention through external pressures and internal inertia
Institutional	• Variations introduced from external origins, such as imitation	• Selection via conformity	• Retention through transmission of shared understandings
Interpretive	• Variation introduced as people negotiate meaning through interaction	• Selection via emergent understandings and compromise	• Retention is problematic; depends on learning and sharing
Organizational learning	• Variation via problemistic search or information discontinuities	• Selection results from fit to target aspiration level or existing organizational knowledge	• Retention in programs, routines, and culture
Resource dependence	• Variation introduced as managers try to avoid dependence	• Selection via asymmetric power relations	• Retention a temporary result of coalitions and bargaining
Transaction cost economics	• Variation introduced via intendedly rational action	• Selection involves actions to minimize transaction costs	• Retention via transaction-specific investments

census, covering long spans of time and observing all vital events, but yielding fewer details about particular organizations (Carroll and Hannan, 2000: Chapter 5).

Selection, within population ecology models, results from the degree of fit between organizations and their environments. For example, small and highly efficient organizations will do better than small and inefficient organizations in impoverished environments with widely scattered resources. Selection criteria are embedded in an organization's surroundings, although selection itself is a joint product of organizational and environmental characteristics. Populations emerge as a result of processes that segregate one set of organizations from another, such as incompatible technologies, market demands, or institutional actions such as governmental regulation (Hannan and Freeman, 1986). Populations are also subject to blending processes that blur the boundaries between them, such as the rise of shared technologies, common markets, and institutional actions such as deregulation. In their simpler models, population ecologists argue that organizations are relatively powerless against the combined weight of their competitors and other external forces.

With regard to retention processes, population ecology explanations explicitly presume a model of organizations as structurally inert – changing at rates slower than their environments, although they usually do not specify the precise form of internal replication processes. Structural inertia hinges on the daily success of reproduction processes. Hannan and Freeman (1984) argued that structurally inert organizations are produced by the combination of external selection of organizations displaying reliable and account-able structures *and* the power of internal institutionalization. Externally, organizations become embedded in networks of obligations and commitments as they age, pressuring their leaders to continue with past practices. Internally, members develop a homogeneous outlook, come together around vested interests organized to protect traditional practices, and adopt hiring and promotion policies that lock existing structures in place.

Issues under debate

Ecologists have focused their analyses on the founding and disbanding of organiza-tions in populations. Even though most studies have been at the population level of analysis, organizations have been the actual unit of selection studied. Astley (1985) noted that ecologists have generally neglected the community level, preferring to focus on intra-population dynamics rather than on the origins of new populations. Only recently have studies examined the rise and fall of entire populations (Aldrich and Fiol, 1994; Ruef, 2000, 2004). Studies of community-level processes are also increas-ing (e.g. Barnett and Woywode, 2004), and we will discuss them in Chapter 11.

In earlier analyses, assumptions concerning structural inertia deflected ecologists' attention away from transformation, but signs of change are apparent. Many orga-nizational ecologists have begun to relax the assumption that adaptation is a rare phenomenon, and have examined the 'relative roles of adaptation and selection in evolutionary change … [and] the relationship between transformation and selection processes' (Amburgey and Rao, 1996: 1278). Levinthal (1991) argued that selection and transformation are neither competing nor complementary processes, but rather are fundamentally related. Without stable structures, selected because they are best suited to their contexts, organizations would have no platform on which to create transformed structures. Ecological models now explicitly include transformation processes, as evidenced in work by Barnett and Carroll (1995) and Dobrev and col-leagues (2002). Because ecologists ordinarily study entire populations, rather than only the fastest-growing or largest organizations in them, they are particularly well placed to study the conditions under which transformation occurs. With longitudi-nal data on organizations that did not change, as well as those that did, ecologists can identify the preconditions of transformation. Ecological analyses of foundings have also begun to examine the social processes involved in organizational startups (Ruef, 2005).

Ecological research has been primarily concerned with aggregates of organizations, and thus it has downplayed the role of individual actors and their interpretations. Also, because their data sets encompass such a broad historical sweep, ecologists typically have obtained only limited information on the internal structural features of the organi-zations in a population. However, a recent strand of organizational ecology recognizes that the internal demographic composition of organizations – their membership or lead-ership profile – may also prove fateful for organizational life chances. In the *genealogi-cal* approach to internal demography, the process of interest involves the transfer of resources and routines from old to new organizations. Phillips (2002) emphasized the movement of high-ranking employees who stop being members of one organization (a 'parent') to become founders of another (its 'progeny'). Among Silicon Valley law firms, he found that greater transfers between parents and progeny decreased the life chances of the parent organizations but increased the life chances of their progeny in the 50-year period after World War II.

Ecologists assume that essential differences between types of organizations can be captured with the concept of *organizational form*. Debate has occurred over whether forms need to be defined *a priori*, rather than invoked pragmatically in the context of each empirical study (McKelvey and Aldrich, 1983). In theory, analysts recognize the existence of an organizational form when external audiences enforce a common identity through sanctions (Pólos, et al., 2002). In practice, organizational forms tend to be defined on the basis of common labels applied to organizations in industry censuses, trade directories, newspapers, phone books, and other archival sources.

Contributions

One of ecology's major contributions has been to the business policy and strategy literature, where it has focused attention on *organizations* as a unit of analysis, rather than *decisions*. It has made organizational survival and failure a salient outcome in studies of organizational performance. Analysts interested in strategic outcomes have also blended ecological with institutional and learning models in a sign of fruitful theoretical eclecticism. For example, in two special issues of the *Strategic Management Journal* in 1994 and 1997 devoted to competition, four of the 14 empirical papers were explicitly ecological and focused on organizational survival as an indicator of successful strategies. Barnett et al. (1994) examined the relative competitive advantages of single-unit versus multi-unit retail banks in Illinois, and Rao (1994) found that victories in certification contests enhanced firms' reputations and improved their life chances. In an analysis that combined ecology with institutional economics, Silverman et al. (1997) showed that trucking firms improved their life chances when they followed policies aimed at minimizing transaction costs. Ingram and Baum (1997) combined ecological and learning models in their examination of hotel chain failures in the United States. Even business strategy theorists not using ecological models often feel compelled to make at least a passing reference to population ecology explanations.

Population ecology has exhibited the greatest theoretical and methodological consensus among all the sub-fields in organization studies (Pfeffer, 1993). The academic social structure maintaining the population ecology theory group has created a body of cumulative research and theorizing that builds tightly upon work that preceded it. By choosing a limited number of problems, using a small set of agreed-upon concepts, and maintaining rigorous standards in research design and statistical analysis, population ecology has enjoyed a level of visibility and influence far out of proportion to the relatively small number of researchers who actually practice its craft. One sign of its growing theoretical and empirical base is the increasing use of computer simulations that model and test ecological principles (Carroll and Harrison, 1994; Bruderer and Singh, 1996; Lomi and Larsen, 1998; Barron, 2001). Simulations require investigators to make their assumptions explicit and to choose model parameters that are empirically plausible; ecologists now have the findings and the tools to make such simulations possible.

The institutional approach

The institutional approach focuses on the objectified and taken-for-granted nature of organizations and organizational environments, as perceived by participants. It emphasizes the value-laden character of institutions and the way in which organizational actions are legitimated when cloaked in an institutionally acceptable rhetoric. In reviewing developments in institutional theory in sociology, political science, and economics, Scott (2001: xx) argued that the ascendance of institutional theory was simply 'a continuation and extension of the intellectual revolution begun during the mid-1960s that introduced open systems conceptions into the study of organizations.' Actually, Parsons' two (1956) essays in the inaugural volume of the *Administrative Science Quarterly* were the first explicit statements on organizational environments as institutional-cultural phenomena. He argued that institutional patterns within organizations must be compatible with those of other organizations and social units within society, and he explored the institutionalized rules governing organizational behavior. Parsons also identified supra-organizational societal norms as the context within which authority and interorganizational contracts are carried out.

As with other wide-ranging theoretical perspectives, institutional theory has many faces (DiMaggio and Powell, 1991; Tolbert and Zucker, 1996). *Institutionalization* itself has several meanings, depending on which institutional theorist one reads, although the meanings are certainly complementary. Selznick (1957) originally developed the theme of institutionalization as a process of instilling values, and his students and intellectual heirs subsequently pursued that line of inquiry (Clark, 1956; Perrow, 1986; Stinchcombe, 1964; Zald, 1970). Institutional theorists often claim Berger and Luckmann (1966) as intellectual forefathers, although Berger and Luckmann did not identify what they were doing as 'institutional theory.' They elaborated the theme of institutionalization as a process of creating reality, and depicted actors as creating an external reality that was subsequently objectified, taken as real, and internalized by others.

Using the language of Berger and Luckmann, Zucker (1987) pointed to the exterior, objective, and non-personal character of something that has been institutionalized. It takes on rule-like, social fact quality, and when embedded in a formal structure, its existence is not tied to a particular actor or situation (Meyer and Rowan, 1977). Tolbert and Zucker (1996) described the processes involved in the growth of deeply shared meanings among social actors as *habitualization* and *objectification*. Habitualization is the rise of patterned problem-solving behaviors, and objectification is the elaboration of shared social meanings attached to these behaviors. Some institutional analysts have treated institutions as distinct societal systems, in keeping with a long tradition in sociology that explores the characteristics of the family, religion, the economy, government, and education.

Variation, selection, and retention

Institutional theorists have treated variation primarily as external in origin, generated as organizations are forced to respond to, adapt to, or imitate the ebb and flow of normative and regulatory currents in their environments. Some analysts have treated variation as arising from organizations responding to events at higher levels of analysis, such as changes in populations and communities (Zucker, 1987). When *environments* are treated as institutions, analysts have typically adopted a reproductive theme, focusing on how system- or sector-wide social facts are copied on the organizational level, with governmental units or professional associations seen as the usual source of such facts (e.g. Ruef and Scott, 1998). As a consequence of adopting externally-generated facts in pursuit of legitimacy, the technical core of an organization is de-coupled from direct evaluation on the grounds of efficiency. Meyer and Rowan (1977) argued that schools, R&D units, and government agencies maintain a facade of standardized, legitimated, formal structures while actually allowing variation in internal practices because of practical considerations. Schools can thus claim that they are effective because they meet state-mandated guidelines for their curricula, while ignoring actual data on student achievement.

When *organizations* have been treated as institutions, analysts have typically adopted a generative theme, examining the creation of new cultural elements by organizations, with small groups and managers often acquiring new facts by imitating other organizations (Zucker, 1987). Internal organizational processes and the example set by similar organizations thus generate new cultural elements. However, as in population ecology, such theories have paid limited attention to entrepreneurship and the creation of new organizations. As shown in Scott's (2001) comprehensive review of the field, the term *entrepreneurship* seldom appears in connection with institutional theory, with a few notable exceptions. Based on his study of Silicon Valley semiconductor startups, Suchman et al. (2001) proposed an *institutional ecology* of entrepreneurship to understand how institutional intermediaries, such as consultants and lawyers, influence the flow of resources and cognitive templates into new organizations. DiMaggio (1988) discussed the role of *institutional entrepreneurs*, focusing on people who mobilize resources *within* organizations to change them.

Selection forces in institutional theories arise from the constraining role played by cultural elements, such as symbols, norms, and rules. Selection processes in institutional theory tend to involve conformity to external norms, constituted and sustained by political actors in organizational fields (Meyer, 1994). Rather than conform, organizations sometimes pursue alternative strategies, including compromise, avoidance, defiance, and manipulation of institutional norms (Oliver, 1991). Norms cohere within *organizational fields*, sets of interacting groups, organizations, and agencies oriented around a common substantive interest, such as medical care, educational policy, or support for the arts (DiMaggio and Powell, 1983). Analysts define fields based on their research interests. Depending upon an analyst's purpose, a field could include suppliers, labor unions, consumer groups, regulatory agencies, trade associations, and other organizations.

Struggles within organizational fields occur over non-material as well as material resources, and the most intense struggles develop over who will have the power to shape rules and norms (Fligstein and Freeland, 1995). Organizations change their structures to conform to an institutionalized pattern supported by powerful legitimating forces outside their boundaries (DiMaggio and Powell, 1983). Delegitimating forces also affect organizations, as pointed out by Oliver (1992) and Davis et al. (1994). When an organizational form falls out of favor and loses legitimacy, as corporate conglomerates did in the 1980s, actors in that societal sector cease adopting that form and move on to others.

Scott (1987), following Meyer and Rowan (1977), argued that in modern societies, symbolic systems have become formally rationalized, with government and the professions playing a key role. The professionalization of school administration, for example, has made school superintendents very sensitive to what similar organizations are doing. School reforms have tended to spread quickly from district to district as they have become institutionalized. Similarly, differentiated departments in universities persist because codified typifications about universities have become institutionalized in the American academic system (Scott, 2001: 79–80). One outcome of successful imitation is enhanced organizational stability, and perhaps also a higher level of efficiency. Success comes from imitating others, not from an organization's own technical achievements.

A common theme running through all faces of institutional theory is environmental influence over organizations. Scott (1987) identified seven different forms of institutional explanation, differing by which types of institutional elements were examined and which causal mechanisms were posited. Most of the verbs used to describe organization–environment relations carry the connotation that environments dominate or overpower organizations, and in this respect, institutional theory resembles population ecology. Organizational structures may be *imposed* by a higher authority, such as via the coercive power of government (Guthrie and Roth, 1999), or *authorized* by a higher authority when a subordinate unit voluntarily seeks its approval (Ruef and Scott, 1998). Structures may be *induced* when a higher authority offers incentives or generates ambiguity for organizations (Zorn, 2004), or *acquired* when organizations deliberately choose a structural model, such as via imitative or normative isomorphism (DiMaggio and Powell, 1983). They might also be *imprinted* when new organizations take on the attributes of their surroundings (Boeker, 1988), *incorporated* when organizations adapt to the degree of differentiation in their environments (Selznick, 1957), or *by-passed* when participants pay more attention to normative pressures than technical requirements (Meyer and Rowan, 1977).

Retention mechanisms are typically subordinated to selection processes in institutional theory. Like ecologists, institutional theorists tend to treat the persistence of organizational entities as relatively non-problematic. They argue that people experience much of the social world as a taken-for-granted constraint and thus not available as raw material for conscious choice. People do something not because it is the normatively 'correct' thing to do or the rationally 'best' thing to do, but because it is the *only* thing to do. Institutional theories highlight the forces that create and maintain organizations as coherent, integral units, focusing on large, long-lived organizations. Forces such as socialization and charismatic leadership promote the transmission of shared meaning, increasing the likelihood of the successful daily reproduction of an organization.

Institutional theory might benefit from paying more attention to the psychological literature on habits (Hodgson, 2004a; Wood et al., 2002). When Berger and Luckmann (1966), Tolbert and Zucker (1996) and others write of habituation, sedimentation, and other such processes, they are referring to the ways in which some action has come to have an automatic character. In the language of psychology, the behavior has become controlled by a stimulus, rather than by goals. Once controlled by a stimulus – such as situational cues provided by other people, signs and artifacts, and so forth – people no longer have to reflect on their actions.

Issues under debate

Commenting on Scott's early portrayal of institutional explanations, Heydebrand (1989: 333) argued that 'while the scope of institutionalism has been widened, its internal coherence and precision has been weakened by incorporating various strands of traditional sociology.' Because of its broad scope, institutional theory has seemed to bridge the action versus structure debate that divides much of organization theory. However, Hirsch and Lounsbury (1997) contended that this sense of inclusiveness is misplaced, because the 'new' institutional theory has departed substantially from the 'old' institutional tradition. Whereas the old institutionalism included classic studies of organizational conflict and transformation, such as Selznick (1949) and Clark (1956), Hirsch and Lounsbury (1997: 408) argue that the new version neglects 'endogenous change, process, volition, organizations as units, informal relations, conflict, attitudes, and unanticipated consequences.' Echoing an argument made earlier by DiMaggio (1988), they were particularly critical of what they saw as the 'new' institutionalism's relative neglect of interest-based and local action, and their replacement by explanations claiming the embeddedness of actions within larger, constraining structures. Czarniawska (1997: 192) voiced a similar concern: 'On the one hand, the *construction* of institutions implies and demands a proactive vision of human actors, busying themselves with plotting, performing, accounting for what they do, and thus producing reality as they know it. On the other hand, the notion of institutions suggests *accretion*, a passive process not under anyone's control, just happening.'

Hirsch and Lounsbury's prescription for institutional theory's alleged failings involved three lines of research. First, they called for historical studies that would examine the micro-level actions generating organizational changes. Second, they wanted more studies of how institutions become sites of struggle, and sometimes even unravel. Ironically, DiMaggio (1991) has carried out such a study, examining the role of professional interest groups in American museums in the early part of the 20th century. Third, they suggested focusing on how and why the strength of institutions varies, perhaps using a social network perspective. Institutional theorists would not disagree with such a call, as many of them have also advocated the analysis of organizations in network terms, e.g. DiMaggio (2001) and Powell (1990). Although several programmatic statements have included admonitions to produce more process-oriented research, actual studies to date have mostly taken the existence of institutions for granted and have examined their adoption and diffusion, rather than their creation.

Hirsch and Lounsbury's (1997) critique of institutional theory as neglecting power and conflict has been echoed by others. Although DiMaggio and Powell's (1983) typology mentioned three types of isomorphism, subsequent work has mostly used the concept of mimetic isomorphism. Mizruchi and Fein (1999) found that of the 160 articles in six major journals that cited DiMaggio and Powell between 1984 and 1995, 115 merely mentioned the article, with no additional discussion. Of the remaining 45, only 26 attempted to operationalize one of the types, and the majority focused only on mimesis. After analyzing the characteristics of authors who had used DiMaggio and Powell's ideas, Mizruchi and Fein (1999: 677) concluded that mimetic isomorphism has dominated research applications because it is 'consistent with the dominantly held view among leading North American organizational researchers that emphasizes cognitive decision-making processes at the expense of interorganizational power and coercion.'

Contributions

The broad reach of the institutional perspective is its major strength, making it potentially relevant to all levels of analysis and all spans of time, from micro-level interactions to large-scale change in nation-states. As Jacobs (2005) noted, core works in institutional theory – such as DiMaggio and Powell's (1983) influential article – are among the most cited in organization studies and sociology journals. Scott (2001: xx) himself observed that the concept of institution 'has continued to take on new and diverse meanings over time, much like barnacles on a ship's hull, without shedding the old.' Consider its message: reality is socially constructed; taken-for-granted rules and norms govern social life; symbol systems in modern societies have become increasingly rationalized; and so forth. This broad sweep has blurred the boundaries between the institutional perspective and other perspectives, opening up possibilities for very fruitful collaboration. For example, the concepts of 'population' and 'population growth' in population ecology have been heavily influenced by institutional theory. In asking 'where do organizational forms come from?' Hannan and Freeman (1986) modified their earlier concept of population, based in biological ecology (Hannan and Freeman, 1977) in favor of a concept based on principles of social construction derived, in part, from institutional theory. Similarly, Hannan and Freeman's (1989) model of population growth took account not only of new populations' needs for material resource mobilization, but also of their dependence on institutional processes that legitimate them.

Institutional theorists have shown a willingness to work at many levels of analysis, from organizations to world systems, and have also taken on major issues that other, more narrowly focused perspectives have avoided. For example, Suchman et al. (2001) investigated law firms' contributions to the growth of high technology firms in Silicon Valley, and Thornton (2004) examined changes in publishing firms in the college marketplace over three decades. Edelman (1990) studied the influence of new labor legislation on the expansion of due process rights for American workers, and Dobbin (1994) analyzed the political changes that affected the development of national transportation systems in three nations. Despite pressures from applied fields to focus on narrow issues such as efficiency and intra-organizational problems, institutional theory has succeeded in expanding organization studies' scope and vision. Practitioners of institutional theory have kept alive the issues that stand at the heart of sociologists' interests, such as concerns for social inequality and long-term historical changes in social norms and values.

The interpretive approach

The interpretive approach focuses on the meaning social actions have for participants at the micro level of analysis. It emphasizes the socially constructed nature of organizational reality and the processes by which participants negotiate the meanings of their actions, rather than taking them as given. Unlike institutional theorists, interpretive theorists posit a world in which actors build meaning with locally assembled materials through their interaction with socially autonomous others. The various interpretive views have in common their focus on an actor's perspective on life in organizations, and they stress that organizational members must take into account the constraints of their social and physical environments (Fine, 1984).

Interpretive theorists are not interested in actors as individuals but rather as members of social categories. We define interpretive scholarship quite broadly, and thus would include Blau's (1955) classic study *Dynamics of Bureaucracy*, based on non-participant observation in several bureaucracies. We would also include more recent monographs, such as Biggart (1988), who used a Weberian social action approach to study women's participation in direct-selling organizations, and Hochschild (1983), who used a symbolic interactionist perspective to study firms' exploitation of their women employees' emotions in dealing with customers. A more traditional example of interpretive scholarship is Duneier (1999), who engaged in participant observation to understand the social organization and experiences of street vendors in New York City. Several versions of the interpretive perspective were also displayed in a special issue of the *Administrative Science Quarterly* on organizational culture (Smircich, 1983).

Interpretive researchers disagree over whether to focus on symbols and cognition or on actual behaviors. Some persons who call themselves cultural researchers study values or cognitive interpretations, focusing on the stories, myths, ceremonies, and rituals they collect through ethnographic research or surveys within organizations (Stewart, 1998). For example, Ingersoll and Adams (1992) argued that people interpret organizational actions using *meaning maps* that are heavily shaped by the books and stories they read as children. They found that children's stories in the United States portrayed people as happiest when they embraced their organizational roles. Stories also depicted people as accepted and satisfied when they found their own special slot. Other interpretive researchers focus more on observed behavior and job histories, rather than on stories (Barley and Kunda, 2004). Some cultural researchers argue very strongly against a purely cognitive approach and take a more materialist approach, maintaining that considerations such as power and privilege heavily affect culture, as well as an observer's ability to understand it. For example, Kunda's (1992) ethnographic portrait of cultural norms in an East Coast high-technology firm depicted senior management as deceitful and manipulative, whereas employees were depicted as victimized and exploited.

Variation, selection, and retention

In the interpretive view, variation in organizational structures emerges through social interactions in which people negotiate, compromise, accept others' definitions of what they are to do, and then act on them. Variations are generated within organizations, as people cope with problems involving the reproduction of their organizations from one day to the next. By making agreements to do things, people write scripts in which they then become social actors. They delegate themselves to play social roles, and then are constrained to fulfill the roles (Latour, 1993). In most interpretive accounts, the scripts are never all-encompassing because people possess the capacity to learn as they go, attending to their contexts, and they thus preserve the provisional nature of much social interaction. However, some interpretive-based models treat organizations as simply the site in which contending societal forces collide and members work out their differences. Clegg (1989) expressed such a view, and Burrell (1988), in his appreciative remarks on Foucault, also came close to this position.

Selection within interpretive models results from negotiation, compromise, and emergent understandings, as members interact in replicating or modifying the routines and competencies of their organizations (Strauss, 1978). For example, social order within medical schools results from students' negotiation between distinct medical values, including perspectives that emphasize clinical experience, medical responsibility, and academic success (Becker et al., 1961). Interest group models implicitly assume that selection criteria reflect an emergent structure of ideological and cultural dominance. The resulting dominant view sets individual preferences and suppresses incompatible interpretations. The interpretive view fits with other theories that focus on selection processes generated by actors' contributions to sustaining ongoing social interaction. Other theories include views of organizations as marketplaces of incentives (Dow, 1988; Georgiou, 1973), as arenas of class conflict (Clegg, 1989), and as sense-making entities (Weick, 1995).

Retention mechanisms are a very salient issue for interpretive theorists, because they implicitly view organizations as less coherent and stable than do ecological or institutional theorists. They tend to treat organizations as associations of self-interested parties, sustained by the rewards they derive from their association with other members or with the organization itself (Swanson, 1971). This view leads to the expectation that organizations are constantly at risk of dissolution. The reproduction of organizational structure depends on participants continually negotiating a shared understanding of what they are doing (Garfinkel, 1967). Selected variations that represent successful solutions to problems must be shared, in some way, to be retained. In all cases, learning from one's predecessors sustains the reproduction process.

Many, but not all, interpretive theorists emphasize the different, conflicting views that coexist in organizations, with such differing views potentially undermining an organization's coherence as a stable entity. Some versions are similar to institutional theory in positing socialization processes as leading to normative consensus. In others, replication is accomplished only via an uneasy truce between contending parties with divergent understandings of what should be done. Meyerson's (1991a) account of hospital social work examined the tension between two very different models of treatment: a medical model and a psychosocial model. She described how social workers learned to live with the ambiguity resulting from the models' simultaneous existence. Some workers responded to the tension by becoming cynical, whereas others denied the ambiguity altogether.

Issues under debate

Because it sees social reality as built from the bottom up, the interpretive perspective allows room for the play of chance, creativity, and accidents. When well done, interpretive accounts remind us that at the micro-level, the future remains open (within limits), and strategy, ambition, accidents, luck, and other forces drive changes in social life. For example, in his account of the Tenerife air disaster, Weick (1991) showed how cumulative ambiguities and misunderstandings in communication across organizations resulted in the death of hundreds of people. However, interpretive accounts are also vulnerable to a researcher's attempts to 'explain everything,' tying up loose ends and constructing too tidy an explanation. Martin (2002), for example, noted that investigators studying organizational culture from an *integration perspective* usually constructed explanations portraying organizations as unified, harmonious, and homogeneous. By contrast, investigators using a *differentiation perspective* have been more attentive to ambiguities, inconsistencies, and the existence of organizational subcultures.

At one extreme, theorists within the interpretive approach tend to assume that interactions and negotiations take place between actors with fixed preferences. In contrast, Weick's (1979) learning model, in which people discover or modify their preferences as they interact, presents a more subtle view of selection forces within organizations. Organizations, whether unified or differentiated in their cultures, can persuade individuals to accept a new interpretation of their behaviors. At the other extreme, critical theorists have claimed that people may be manipulated into a view of the world more compatible with the organization's interests, as opposed to their own (Perrow, 1986).

Some theorists argue that organizational actors essentially create the context to which they react, thus creating a closed explanatory loop (Weick, 1979). Not every theorist goes this far, but the concept of *enactment* – that actions precede interpretation and interpretations create a context for action – places heavy demands on anyone conducting research on why people and organizations behave as they do. Given what we know about cognitive heuristics and attribution bias, how much can we trust participants' self-reports about their actions? Intensive field-based studies and ethnographies are an alternative to self-reports, but such studies are time consuming and expensive. Nonetheless, they are invaluable for spelling out the conditions under which variations result in enactment, and the extent to which enactment is intentional or blind.

Contributions

One of the great strengths of the interpretive approach is that many of its practitioners rely heavily on direct observation and field work, rather than surveys and organizational records, thus avoiding the *trained incapacity* of most sociologists (Reiss, 1992). Survey researchers, according to Reiss, force respondents to speak to us 'in our own words,' rather than their own. Ethnographers with a cultural focus often spend lengthy periods in the field, observing participants' behaviors. For example, Barley (1990) spent one year observing changes in role relationships resulting from the introduction of a potentially innovative technology in two radiology departments. These reports from the field give us a closer look at processes within organizations, although they are still filtered through a lens wielded by the researcher, and thus subject to charges that authors are 'performing an act of ventriloquism' (Czarniawska, 1997: 198). Deconstructionists have disabused us of romantic notions that ethnographers offer unvarnished 'voices from the field'. Well-done ethnographies make readers aware of the author's voice and what it represents.

Ethnography is extremely time-consuming and emotionally draining. Many field workers only accomplish a single substantial ethnography before going on to write shorter essays and commentaries, e.g. Willis (1977) and Stewart (1989). Nonetheless, their work has illuminated the emotional foundations of action within organizations. Golden-Biddle and Locke (1997) wrote an historical account of the development of Glaser and Strauss's 'grounded theory' approach to fieldwork and also provided guidelines for analyzing data collected using that approach. Kleinman and Copp (1992) wrote passionately of the emotions raised by fieldwork, as researchers struggle with difficult issues. Fieldworkers must grapple with defining their roles vis-á-vis their subjects, coming to terms with negative feelings about the people whom they study, coping with time pressures when analyzing an intractable body of field notes, and trying to construct a valid account. Kleinman and Copp argued that fieldworkers enact a variety of social identities in the field, only one of which is 'professional researcher'. Their account reveals, in passing, one reason why true field-based ethnographies are so rare in organization studies, as well as why they are so valuable.

The organizational learning approach

The organizational learning approach focuses on how individuals, groups, and organizations notice and interpret information and use it to alter their fit with their environments. Some changes may improve their fit, whereas others may worsen it, and organizational learning has no inherent link to success. Two strands of theory and research on organizational learning have developed over the past five decades: the adaptive learning perspective and the knowledge development perspective (Glynn et al., 1994). The adaptive learning perspective, pioneered by Cyert and March (1963), treats organizations as goal-oriented activity systems that learn from experience by repeating apparently successful behaviors and discarding unsuccessful ones. Within the adaptive learning framework, theorists distinguish between incremental or single-loop learning and radical or double-loop learning (Argyris and Schön, 1978). At the extreme, trial and error models of learning that emphasize simple repetition of 'what works' can be seen as evolutionary processes with undirected variation and a constrained set of selection processes. Since its original formulation, March (1981), his students (Levinthal, 1991; Levitt and March, 1988; Denrell and March, 2001), and others, have modified the approach to take into account a variety of constraints on organizations' capacities to learn from experience. For example, in his simulation model contrasting exploration and exploitation as conflicting strategies, March (1991) used assumptions that implicitly ruled out radical learning under the most plausible scenarios. Subsequent contributors have also moved the perspective away from a purely behavioral approach and toward a more cognitive approach. For example, Greve (2003) drew on many concepts and principles from social psychology in developing his performance feedback model of organizational learning.

The second strand of the learning approach, the knowledge development perspective, treats organizations as sets of interdependent members with shared patterns of cognition and belief (Weick, 1979, 1995). Learning occurs as patterns of cognitive associations and causal beliefs are communicated and institutionalized. Sense-making and enactment are critical activities in the learning process, and researchers have studied the development of knowledge structures and causal maps within organizations, as well as their diffusion between organizations (Argote, 1993). The knowledge development perspective emphasizes that learning is not limited to simple trial and error or direct experience. Instead, learning can be inferential and vicarious, and organizations can generate new knowledge through experimentation and creativity. Although the learning approach shares much in common with the interpretive approach, it differs by explicitly taking a developmental view of organizational activities. Institutional theories have drawn heavily from the learning approach, with some researchers contributing to both (DiMaggio, 1997). The knowledge development perspective conceptually and empirically fits with work on technological evolution and organizational knowledge creation and deployment (Tushman and Anderson, 1986).

Variation, selection, and retention

From the adaptive learning perspective, variations are generated when performance fails to meet targeted aspiration levels, triggering problem-driven search routines.

Called *problemistic* search by Cyert and March (1963), variations from standard operating procedures follow well-understood heuristics and involve localized investigations that cease when satisfactory solutions are found. Following trial and error logic, a failure of standard procedures could result in their replacement by new ones, thus generating further variation. Such models raise the question of whether organizations will recognize a 'failure,' simply ignore it, or redefine their objectives (Milliken and Lant, 1991; Sitkin, 1992; Staw et al., 1981). From the knowledge development perspective, variation increases under conditions of cognitive confusion and misunderstanding, such as when knowledge acquired across group or organizational boundaries must be integrated into existing causal maps and beliefs. Changes in interpersonal and interorganizational networks may bring new information or interpretations into a unit, triggering a round of sense making (Gulati and Gargiulo, 1999). In a more subtle fashion, the creation of new and idiosyncratic jobs may create openings for the importation of new meaning systems into an organization (Miner, 1992).

Selection among variations in the adaptive learning perspective occurs when managers compare the results of their actions to pre-set aspiration levels. In keeping with the tenets of problemistic search, managers should keep those variations that helped them reach targets and try other variations to replace those that failed. In short, successful actions tend to be repeated (March, 1981). Unsuccessful actions should provoke further search. However, learning models also allow aspiration levels to shift with experience, with targets tending to adapt to actual performance levels over time. Selection in the knowledge development perspective results from the compatibility of new information and beliefs with current knowledge. Prior organizational learning creates knowledge structures and sets of conceptual categories that filter subsequent information and thus influence further learning. Cohen and Levinthal (1990) borrowed the term *absorptive capacity* from industrial economics to refer to the level of stored knowledge and experience that make organizations better able to learn from further experience.

Retention mechanisms are critical for learning theorists, because without a way to store and retrieve new routines or knowledge, organizations gain nothing from experience. From an adaptive learning perspective, the results of problemistic search are stored in routines and *performance programs* that can be reused when needed (March and Simon, 1958; Nelson and Winter, 1982). Learning is then embodied in sets of interlocked role behaviors, supported by job descriptions, socialization, training programs, written rules, and other externalized manifestations of what has been learned (March et al., 2000). From the perspective of knowledge development, retention occurs when the culture of an organization is altered: its belief system, causal maps, and other aspects of the knowledge structure. The new system of shared cognition and beliefs directs members' attention to those features of the environment made salient by new conceptual categories. Based on the two perspectives in organizational learning, theorists argue that learned information is retained in organizational memory in two ways (Cohen and Bacdayan, 1994): as declarative memory, involving facts, propositions, and events, and as procedural memory, involving skilled actions, competencies, and routines.

Cognition can plausibly play a role in any of the three processes of variation, selection, and retention within organizations. Therefore, the line between microevolutionary and organizational learning models is somewhat fuzzy. When models treat variation as directed by actors' intentions, or posit selection and retention processes that involve cognitive and inferential processes, learning models become more distinct from evolutionary approaches (Miner and Mezias, 1996). Nonetheless, committed evolutionary theorists would argue that the cognitive and inferential processes people use are themselves the products of a long-term cultural evolutionary process, thus situating learning models within a larger evolutionary framework (Dennett, 1995: 370–400).

Issues under debate

The community of theorists and researchers using the organizational learning approach has been extremely productive over the past several decades, but a number of of its members have been critical of its lack of integration (Huber, 1991). Organizational learning theorists have often been content with merely pointing out the flaws in rational actor assumptions (Cohen and Sproull, 1991). Because it offers a clear alternative to the more rationalistic models in industrial economics and the more aggregate models of population ecology, the organizational learning approach has attracted the attention of institutional theorists. Like the institutional approach, the organizational learning approach encompasses a diversity of research streams. Relying on the participants' own self-critical remarks, we have identified a few issues that are receiving a great deal of attention from learning theorists.

First, Glynn et al. (1994) noted the difficult methodological problems posed by the complexity of learning models and attempted to apply them across levels of analysis. With regard to complexity, learning models tend to include constructs representing how participants view their environments, as well as constructs representing environments. From experimental work by social psychologists on cognitive heuristics, self-perception, and attribution, we know that participants are often not very good reporters on their own perceptions and beliefs (Kahneman et al., 1982). In addition, because learning theories are explicitly about change over time, researchers must create dynamic designs to follow their subjects over time. Behavioral theorists, working from the adaptive learning perspective, often confront these issues by conducting computer simulations or creating simulated organizations in laboratory experiments. In addition, these researchers sometimes go beyond individual cognition by seeking measures of learning and memory at the organizational or higher levels of analysis. By contrast, cognitive researchers working from the knowledge development perspective have adapted by doing applied case studies, while also doing laboratory experiments. The result has been a gulf between these two groups and a paucity of dynamic field-based studies of actual learning organizations.

Second, a related methodological issue concerns the process by which observers attribute changes in organizations' actions to learning. 'Not all organizational learning is manifested in observable actions … and not all changes in an organization's actions reflect learning' (Glynn et al., 1994: 63). Some changes are simply random variations. Other actions are the result of *imitation*. Some theorists would treat imitation as simply 'action' unless participants have learned the underlying rationale for what they copied, arguing that only *intentional learning* should count as real learning. Other theorists argue that imitation of apparently effective action represents a form of vicarious trial and error learning at the level of an entire organization.

Third, scholars in several traditions have argued that organizational memory and action should be distinguished from the mere aggregation of individual level cognition

(Walsh, 1995). For example, Hutchins (1991) described how a group of people collectively discovered a new process for navigation after the breakdown of equipment aboard a ship. The participants were not individually aware of the actual new process they had enacted. Separating 'action' from 'learning' under such conditions is a daunting task. It requires investigators to probe the very core of an organization's knowledge system and to delineate carefully their constructs and levels of analysis.

Similarly, Weick and Westley (1996) raised the issue of whether the literature on organizational learning is really about an organizational level phenomenon, or simply about individuals learning within organizations. They argued that some theorists have ignored the issue by simply treating organizational learning as learning by individuals within an organizational context. In that respect, organizations are no different from laboratories, small groups, or any other context in which individuals might learn. Other theorists have argued that organizations learn the same way that individuals do, and thus we can readily transfer our theories of individual learning to organizations. Weick and Westley (1996: 456) suggested that we treat organizations as cultures – as repositories of knowledge and as self-designing systems – and focus on the process by which organizing unfolds to create 'learning moments.' Their suggested program closely resembles the approach we have labeled as 'interpretive,' but situates it thoroughly within an organizational context.

Contributions

The organizational learning approach is particularly well-suited for explaining organizational evolution, and indeed some of its adherents adopt evolutionary language in their work, e.g. Miner (1991). Organizational learning, whether from the adaptive learning or knowledge development perspective, is firmly anchored in the behavioral sciences. From this harbor, it ties organization studies to the disciplines of psychology and social psychology. It also is on the frontier of the growing field of cognitive science, one that cuts across the biological and behavioral sciences (DiMaggio, 1997). Such cross-disciplinary cooperative work increases the likelihood of creative theoretical insights, which, following learning theory, we would expect to come from scholars working on the edge of established fields.

The concept of distributed learning and learning embedded in systems of interaction is a new development with great promise (Weick and Roberts, 1993). 'With its emphasis on the construction of information through organizational interactions, a system interaction approach to organizational learning offers a shift in perspective, from an emphasis on the content of learning to the emergent process of learning' (Glynn et al., 1994: 75). Organizational learning thus becomes something accomplished with others, rather than alone, and theorists must attend to the structure of role relationships and interpersonal networks that sustain shared knowledge. This view could link the organizational learning approach to anthropological theories of culture and sociological theories of social networks and collective action.

The resource dependence approach

The resource dependence approach focuses on strategic actions undertaken by organizations to manage interdependencies with other organizations in their environment. It emphasizes some of the same constraints on action as the transaction cost economics (TCE) approach, but takes a more explicitly political approach to managerial motives, focusing on the trade-off between autonomy and survival. Interorganizational relations are the basic unit of analysis, although it has also been applied to other types of relations between subunits. Applications range from micro to macro, across units of analysis from individual managers, to organizational subunits, to firms, to alliances and joint ventures, to interorganizational networks (Burt, 1983; Casciaro and Piskorski, 2005; Mizruchi and Galaskiewicz, 1993; Zajac and Westphal, 1996).

The perspective was born in the early 1960s, when Levine and White (1961) and Litwak and Hylton (1962) argued that the behaviors of organizations in the social services sector could be explained by examining interorganizational exchanges. Government regulation and support were critical to such organizations, and they also operated in situations of resource scarcity, depending upon other agencies and organizations for much of what they needed. At about the same time, Emerson (1962) was developing a theory of power based on dependence relations, which Blau (1964: 118) subsequently reformulated to derive 'power imbalances from the conditions of exchange.' In the field of organization studies, Thompson (1967), Zald (1970), and other sociologically oriented theorists extended and applied many of the premises of resource dependence to interorganizational relations. For example, Thompson (1967) argued that organizations coped with uncertainty by regulating their boundaries and managing internal interdependencies.

Aldrich and Pfeffer (1976) sketched out the differences between resource dependence and evolutionary approaches, but Pfeffer and Salancik (1978) offered the first extensive presentation of the argument. They added concepts from political sociology, industrial economics, and social psychology to create a compelling account of managers struggling to control their organization in the face of external threats. Even though they titled their book *The External Control of Organizations*, they actually offered many strategies by which managers could blunt the impact of external threats and win more autonomy for themselves.

Variation, selection, and retention

With respect to variation, Pfeffer and Salancik (1978) formulated a fundamental premise in their book that remains at the heart of the perspective: beyond the normal interdependencies grounded in the interorganizational division of labor, some interdependencies are sought (or avoided) because of the power and control possibilities inherent in them. Variations are driven by managers' and administrators' efforts at avoiding becoming dependent on others, while making others dependent on them. Attempts to avoid dependencies may take the form of minor tactical adjustments to internal structure, such as reducing the impact of uncertain supply schedules by increasing stockpiles, or major strategic changes, such as mergers to restrain interorganizational competition. Pfeffer and Salancik (1978) depicted decision-makers attempting to gain power so that they can manage their environments, as well as their organizations. They conceptualized environments as being composed of multiple interest groups, and posited that managers must find ways of neutralizing hostile groups or aligning themselves with those groups that will protect their organizations.

Selection forces are inherent in asymmetric power relations. Power, in this scheme, is based on Emerson's (1962, 1972) concept that one's power resides implicitly in another's dependency. The parties in a power relationship are tied to each other by the dependence of one on the other, or perhaps by mutual dependence. The dependence of an actor **A** on another actor **B** is 'directly proportional to **A**'s *motivational investment* in goals mediated by **B**, and inversely proportional to the *availability* of those goals to **A** outside of the **A–B** relation' (Emerson, 1962: 32). The dependence of **A** on **B** provides the basis for **B**'s power over **A**, as **B** is in control of, or otherwise has influence over, goods and services that **A** desires. To the extent that **A** cannot do without the resources and is unable to obtain them elsewhere, **A** is dependent on **B**.

Thus, the power to control or influence others resides in control over the resources they value (see Aldrich, 1979: 268–273). Organization differentiation and specialization of function are likely to lead to interorganizational dependencies whenever organizations manage to acquire monopoly control over important resources, and are able to defend their positions. Going beyond TCE's idea of exchange, the resource dependence perspective asserts that one consequence of competition and cooperation over scarce resources is the development of dependencies of some organizations on others. Burt's (1983) network analysis of the American economy and firm profitability was one of the few attempts to test the idea of the impact of dependence on a large scale. He showed that industrial sectors that depended on other, better-organized sectors paid a price in reduced profitability. Given the aggregate nature of his data, however, he could not examine whether a firm's survival was directly affected by resource dependence.

Retention of viable structures is potentially problematic from a resource dependence perspective, given its emphasis on an organization as 'a coalition of groups and interests, each attempting to obtain something from the collectivity by interacting with others, and each with its own preferences and objectives' (Pfeffer and Salancik, 1978: 36). In this quasi-market environment, participants gain and lose power through processes of bargaining, negotiation, and compromise, and thus organizations are constantly at risk of dissolution. Following Barnard's (1938) lead, Pfeffer and Salancik argued that control and influence in organizations depends upon the importance of managers' and subunits' contributions to the organization's survival and success. Organizational units that provide their organizations with the most critical resources become the most powerful (Crozier, 1964). However, Astley and Zajac's (1990) research on 163 subunits in 20 large corporations in the Pacific Northwest of the United States did not support this resource dependence hypothesis. Instead of subunit power being generated by the balance of exchange dependencies between the units, power arose from workflow interdependencies embedded in a firm's division of labor. If retention processes are embedded in an organization's task structure, rather than pure exchange dependencies, then organizational reproduction is less problematic.

Issues under debate

Like institutional theory, resource dependence has blossomed into a wide-ranging perspective that is often invoked by analysts who admire the theory's scope and clarity. However, some unresolved issues remain. Some critics argue that even though resource dependence theory has been widely used, key elements of the theory have not been empirically tested. Pfeffer (2003: xvi) himself acknowledged that 'there is a limited amount of empirical work explicitly extending and testing resource dependence theory and its central tenets,' while Casciaro and Piskorski (2005) lamented the largely metaphorical role of the theory in organizational discourse. Two issues in particular deserve more attention: how resource dependence ought to be defined, and whether dependence or ordinary market-driven forces generate various forms of interorganizational relations.

One definitional issue concerns whether dependence is an objective or perceived state of affairs. Pfeffer and Salancik (1978) used objective measures of environmental conditions, such as four-firm concentration ratios and the number of alternative sources of a resource, in their models of constraints on organizational transformation. An interorganizational relationship may objectively be one of dependence of a subordinate on a dominant organization, but this may only be a *potential* problem for the dependent organization (Aldrich, 1979: 272–273). The effects of dependence may only be felt when a dominant organization makes demands upon a subordinate organization. Thus, the effects of dependence may be invisible unless the subordinate organization perceives its situation of potential dependence. As Fligstein and Freeland (1995: 31) noted, 'In murky social worlds, perceiving interdependencies is not always a straightforward task. Moreover, even if this occurs, actors must be able to impose their interpretation of the strategic contingency on others.'

Another definitional issue concerns the theoretical dimensions that underlie the concept of resource dependence. Casciaro and Piskorski (2005) argued that two dimensions in Emerson's (1962) framework have commonly been conflated in past empirical studies: (1) *power imbalance*, reflecting the power differential between two organizations; and (2) *mutual dependence*, reflecting bilateral dependencies within a dyad. Each underlying dimension has distinct implications for organizational efforts to manage resource dependence. Analyzing mergers and acquisition (M&A) activity among U.S. public companies between 1985 and 2000, Casciaro and Piskorski found that mutual dependence between firms promoted M&A events. By contrast, power imbalance served as a deterrent, because neither power-advantaged nor power-disadvantaged organizations had an incentive to enter such relationships.

With regard to alternative interpretations of resource dependence research, Donaldson (1995: 161) questioned explanations based on power and political processes. He argued that much of the evidence offered by resource dependence theorists in support of their position could be re-interpreted as being the result of market forces. A condition of asymmetric dependence in the marketplace might simply reflect specific supply and demand conditions, with no residual compliance obligations remaining after completion of the market-based transaction. From this point of view, an organization would suffer only a temporary disadvantage in most dependent relations, as the dominant organization extracts its price when the transaction is completed but gains no long-term advantage. Similarly, Zajac (1988), after examining interlocks across boards of directors, observed that researchers investigating interorganizational relations should be cautious in inferring that they truly represent an organizational strategy for dealing with dependence. Instead, the observed relations may simply be a consequence of unrelated actions. Research on interlocks has also generally ignored their historical and spatial context, focusing on their consequences rather than their causes (Mizruchi, 1996; Kono et al., 1998).

Contributions

The resource dependence perspective has influenced research on a variety of organizational issues centered on interorganizational relations, as Galaskiewicz (1985) noted in his review of studies of resource procurement and allocation, political advocacy, and organizational legitimation. Mizruchi (1992: 64–66) observed that research on interlocking directorates has often used resource dependence explanations, although the cross-sectional nature of most studies has somewhat undercut their value. Scott (2003: 118–119) credited the resource dependence perspective with discerning and describing strategies used by organizations to change and adapt to their environments. For example, Burt's (1982, 1992) structural theory of action and power is grounded in a resource dependence view of relationships. Fligstein and Freeland (1995) argued that scholars influenced by the resource dependence perspective have generated important criticisms of the rational adaptation approach to organizational change. Unlike the ecological and institutional views of organizations, resource dependence theorists take a very active view of organizations' relations to their environments. Active subjects are usually apparent in their work, and thus resource dependence principles are potentially a bridge across the action versus structure divide in organization studies (Reed, 1988).

Resource dependence resembles the interpretive perspective in treating organizations as marketplaces of incentives and arenas of conflict between contending interests. In some versions, it also resembles institutional theory in its stress on the powerful constraining influence of socially constructed truths on organizational actions. Fligstein (1990, 1996) built his political-cultural approach to organizational analysis by drawing on resource dependence and institutional theory principles. He emphasized the political processes inherent in interorganizational relations and the stabilizing influence of widely held and legitimated cultural understandings. However, the extremely diverse use theorists have made of resource dependence raises the question of the coherence of its intellectual core. Unlike ecological theory, which has accumulated a set of empirical generalizations by vigorously pursuing a narrow set of issues, resource dependence seems permanently fixed upon Emerson's initial insight – that power and dependence are intimately related. As such, it has the status of an auxiliary theory that is invoked in the context of specific research questions, but not one that itself benefits from any theory group's sustained research program.

The transaction cost economizing approach

The transaction cost economizing approach, or TCE, focuses on how managers decide to solve the dilemma of choosing between markets and hierarchies in organizing economic activity. TCE treats transactions as its basic unit of analysis and focuses on the specific selection pressures driving organizational change in competitive environments (Williamson, 1994). Organizational arrangements governing any particular exchange depend on the cost effectiveness of those arrangements, compared with alternatives (Hesterly et al., 1990). Given 'human nature as we know it' (Williamson, 1981), the ultimate explanation for the structuring of transactions is the constraining effect of external conditions on social actors.

Owners and managers of organizations face, at the extreme, two choices about how to structure their activities. Should they purchase the goods or services they need on the open market, or should they bring the production of such necessities inside their organization? They can obtain what they need by engaging in transactions with other independent actors in the market, or they can internalize the production of the needed resource, thus subjecting it to their own hierarchical control. TCE theorists recognize that organizations actually comprise a mix of market- and hierarchy-based activities. They recognize intermediate forms in between markets and hierarchies, such as professional societies and hierarchical contracts (Bradach and Eccles, 1989; Powell, 1990). Hodgson (2002), however, rejected the notion of intermediate forms, arguing that if organizations are truly bounded entities, then organizations and markets represent a simple dichotomy, not a continuum.

Variation, selection, and retention

In dealing with variation in organizations, TCE posits actors who have rational intentions but who also face constraints on their capabilities. TCE emphasizes the serious limits to human information-processing and monitoring capabilities, and takes a rather jaundiced view of human nature. Two assumptions derived from the Carnegie school tradition of March and Simon (1958) dominate TCE thinking about social behavior: actors operate within the constraints of *bounded rationality*, and much of human behavior is driven by *opportunism*. Most actors are intendedly rational, but they are denied textbook rationality because of human limitations. They are precluded from making optimal choices by cognitive deficiencies and peculiarities, limits on information availability, and constraints on information processing. Information search costs, in particular, lead most actors to choose satisfactory, rather than optimal, alternatives. Actors must also contend with the tendency of other actors to behave opportunistically, pursuing their own self-interest at the expense of others.

Williamson's treatment of opportunism differs from Simon's (1985: 303), as Simon treated lack of trustworthiness in humans as a result of 'frailties of motive and reason', whereas Williamson's explanation is much less benign. He noted that opportunism 'can take blatant, subtle, and natural forms' (Williamson, 1994: 81), with Machiavelli's advice to the Prince constituting one end of the spectrum and bureaucrats' tendencies to feather their own nests at the other end. In the middle is strategic opportunism, which is only effective if carried out subtly. 'Self-interest seeking with guile' is Williamson's clever description of the normal state of human affairs. In short, actors tend to lie, cheat, and steal to further their own ends. They withhold information or distort it, conceal preferences, and practice a variety of other deceptions.

Given a resource-scarce environment, actors will be under pressure to find ways to economize on transactions' costs. TCE models make selection a matter of matching organizational actions to organizational goals. 'Goals' are typically defined as the efficient use of resources in the competitive context of a market. Selection processes posited by TCE turn on the consequences of human shortcomings. Given bounded rationality and opportunism, transactions with other actors are almost always problematic and potentially quite costly. Williamson (1981) hypothesized that three dimensions to transactions are particularly important to the type of relationship established: the frequency of the transaction, uncertainty surrounding the transaction, and the level of *transaction-specific investments*. The more frequently an actor enters into transactions with specific other actors, the greater the pressure to find economical ways for handling the relationship. One-time spot transactions are not worth bothering about, and indeed would not be legitimately described in terms of the language of relationships.

Bounded rationality and opportunism produce uncertainty in transactions, thus requiring actors to expend more resources than they might prefer, given their gains. Uncertainty need not result from strategic opportunism by others, but may simply result from honest disagreements between 'honest, ethical people who disagree about what event transpired and what adjustment would have been agreed to initially had the event been anticipated' (Alchian and Woodward, 1988: 66). Hodgson (2004b) made a similar point, arguing that misinterpretation, misunderstanding, and disagreement are significant sources of contract non-compliance. In the language of evolutionary theory, transaction structures that reduce uncertainty by preventing misunderstanding and disagreements will have a selective advantage over those that do not, if the structures cost less than simply tolerating the uncertainty. Managers ignoring selection pressures would waste resources on inefficient structures and thus put their firms in peril, as Silverman et al. (1997) found in their research on the longevity of trucking firms.

Retention, in TCE models, is anchored in the transaction-specific investments made by the parties to a relation, in black-letter contracts, and in the mutual monitoring and enforcement that accompanies repeated transactions. *Transaction-specific investments* refer to the resources actors invest in a relationship to keep it going. For many one-time, market-based transactions, maintenance of the relationship is not a relevant issue. If, however, one of the parties to a transaction has an interest in ensuring that it persists, then that party must invest some resources in maintaining the relationship itself. Otherwise, purely self-seeking behavior will destroy rather than sustain the relationship (Swanson, 1971).

Institutional and interpretive theories treat transaction-specific investments as induced or motivated by purposive or solidary incentives (Clark and Wilson, 1961), whereas TCE theorists stress materialistic or self-serving motives. As Loasby (1995: 475) pointed out, TCE theorists 'follow the standard American practice in construing self-interest as narrowly focused selfishness,' and mostly neglect other motivations and incentives, such as trust. However, surveys of the American public suggest that TCE theorists may have accurately captured the real level of trust people are willing to place in others they do not know. Bellah et al. (1996: 510) noted that 'the proportion of Americans who say that most people can be trusted fell by more than a third between 1960, when 58 percent chose that alternative, and 1993, when only 37 percent did.'

Williamson acknowledged that 'farsighted contracting,' which he recommended to deal with critical contingencies, should not be taken to extremes. Noting that economists make the assumption that 'economic actors have the ability to look ahead, discern problems and prospects, and factor these back into the organizational/ contractual design' (Williamson, 1994: 88), he argued for 'plausible farsightedness,' rather than hyper-rationality. Moreover, because actors are contracting for an incompletely known future, their *ex ante* agreements must allow room for *ex post* realignments, when new situations are encountered (Nickerson and Silverman, 2003). The reasoning of contemporary TCE theorists sounds very much like evolutionary thinking, differing primarily in the greater confidence they place in 'farsightedness.'

Issues under debate

Granovetter (1985) strongly criticized TCE, arguing that it reflected two contradictory assumptions about human behavior. He argued that TCE draws on an *under-socialized* conception of humans because individuals are presumed to behave atomistically, as isolated actors. Under-socialized people act without regard to the social damage they do, or the impressions they leave with others. However, TCE also draws on an *over-socialized* conception when it assumes that individuals will voluntarily refrain from completely ruthless behavior. Do actors only follow the rules in playing competitive games if they have thoroughly internalized the norms of 'civilized' behavior? Nilakant and Rao (1994) agreed with Granovetter that agency theory and the other new institutional economics models probably overstate the role of individually oriented economic incentives in organizations and understate the importance of social exchange: reciprocity, cooperation, and trust.

Williamson (1994: 97), responding to criticisms that TCE neglects trust, noted that 'trust' has many functional substitutes, as credible commitments can be reached through the use of bonds, hostages, disclosure rules, agreements on how disputes will be resolved, and so forth. 'Albeit vitally important to economic organization, such substitutes should not be confused with (real) trust.' Although this concession opened the door to a possible compromise with Granovetter's approach, Williamson went on to argue that 'calculated risk' and 'calculated trust' occupy distinct places in social and economic life. 'Calculated trust' – of the real kind – is found in people's personal lives, and 'calculative risk' is found in their commercial lives. In contrast, Jones et al. (1997: 922) detected a point of common ground between Granovetter and Williamson, because both emphasize that frequency and reciprocity of contacts create conditions for informal control – building on trust – within relations.

The development of TCE as an empirical field within organization studies has been hampered by several problems. Theorists have had difficulty in operationalizing the concept of transaction costs *a priori*, and they have also been reluctant to conduct dynamic analyses of organizations actually adapting to their environments (Shelanski and Klein, 1995). TCE research has also been troubled by a fundamental ambiguity about whether organizations are really units of analysis (Hirsch et al., 1990). Most research has been descriptive, rather than hypothesis testing, using cross-sectional designs, and has focused on very large publicly held corporations (Hesterly et al., 1990). David and Han (2004) conducted a meta-analysis of 63 journal articles that tested TCE hypotheses, selected after a systematic search of articles abstracted in ABI/Inform and EconLit. They found surprisingly little agreement among researchers on how to operationalize TCE's constructs and propositions, and how to test them. They also found low levels of empirical support for TCE's core argument, with many results not supportive of TCE.

Transaction cost models have the potential of generating falsifiable hypotheses, to the extent that transactions' costs can be spelled out *a priori*. However, the lack of a strong research tradition, and disagreement on how to measure key constructs, inhibit TCE from accumulating a stock of reliable and valid empirical generalizations. Moreover, with its reliance on cross-sectional observations and its eagerness to attribute existing structures to the constraining effects of markets, it mostly ignores evolutionary issues. Hesterly et al. (1990) pointed out that much of TCE theorizing is implicitly functionalist. Functional thinking can be helpful in leading us to consider the benefits of a current structure, which can then direct our search for historical explanations (Dennett, 1995: 124–145). However, functionalist explanations fall short to the extent that they infer the origins of a structure by only examining its consequences, rather than the processes that brought it about.

Contributions

TCE has played a constructive role in pushing ahead the frontiers of organization theory. Williamson has worked unceasingly on creating a formalized, deductive scheme from which propositions may be derived. Beginning with plausible assumptions about human behavior, Williamson and his followers have crafted a strong challenge to non-economic theories. He has pushed theorists from other perspectives to consider alternative explanations for the organizational forms they observe, asking them to examine the costs and benefits of various arrangements. In his concern with 'the main case' – a theory's claimed domain of applicability – he has challenged others to 'sort the wheat from the chaff' and develop the 'refutable implications' of their arguments (Williamson, 1994: 86).

As economic thinking and rational choice models have continued to attract organization theorists' attentions, TCE has achieved a solid foothold in organization studies (Perrow, 1986: 219–257). David and Han (2004: 37) found that references to TCE in the Social Science Citation Index had grown faster than references to institutional theory, population ecology, and resource dependence. Even investigators whose studies were not conducted within a TCE framework sometimes feel compelled to mention it, anyway (Pennings et al., 1994). Among some economic historians, TCE has been recognized as offering 'the most promising framework for approaching the general rise of the modern business corporation' (Schmitz, 1993: 84), such as the emergence of vertical integration in the U.S. auto industry (Langlois and Robertson, 1989). Other historians have been less sanguine (Coleman, 1987). Regardless of problems in its research program, TCE has shown continued vitality as a well-developed, clearly articulated theory of comparative economic organization, with adherents ready and willing to answer attacks from their critics.

Summary: the six perspectives

Evolutionary theory is not a closed, logical deductive system, but instead comprises an overarching metatheory with a set of concatenated principles. Applied across multiple levels of analysis, it is open to multiple approaches for explaining particular kinds of changes. Over the past several decades, at least six viable perspectives on organizations have emerged that provide a rich set of ideas and principles on which evolutionary explanations can draw. In this chapter, we have reviewed the collective judgments, as represented in books and articles, that have emerged from negotiation and debate among the practitioners of these six approaches. In the rest of this book, we will draw upon these ideas in constructing evolutionary explanations.

Ecological analysis reminds us of the volatility of organizational populations, focusing on foundings and disbandings over a population's life cycle. By taking a long-term view, ecology makes salient the significance of historical events for population and community development. Because the scholars pursuing ecological research focus on building empirical generalizations through replication of key findings, they have laid much of the groundwork for evolutionary analysis. Institutional theorists emphasize the socially constructed nature of organizations and populations. Institutionalization as a process of instilling socially constructed entities with value occurs at all levels of analysis, and thus institutional theory allows theorists to link events at multiple levels. Institutional theory has also served as a counterweight to arguments from strategic management and TCE theorists about 'choice' by reminding us that inherited traditions, custom, and habits drive many organizational and managerial behaviors.

Interpretive approaches treat people as active agents influencing their own fate, as does much of the work in the organizational learning approach. People often disappear in other perspectives. By contrast, many interpretive theorists construct their explanations by doing direct observation of organizational life in the field. By focusing on the social-psychological processes involved in creating and sustaining meaning, the interpretive approach allows room for the play of chance and creativity in organizations. Transaction cost economics makes assumptions about human behavior that trouble many sociologists, and it has challenged proponents of other views to make their assumptions and propositions explicit. TCE provides evolutionary analysis with a framework in which to examine the costs and benefits of alternative organizational arrangements that might be selected via evolutionary forces.

Several approaches give a prominent place to human agency, but the resource dependence perspective is the most vigorous advocate of aggressive intervention. It emphasizes the strategies used by organizations to change or even control their environments, while recognizing the severe limits on such action. Like the institutional and organizational learning approaches, resource dependence models allow theorists to link multiple levels of analysis by tying the interests of organizational coalitions to organizational strategies, which in turn reflect judgments about an organization's position in its environment. Resource dependence is the most overtly political model of the six, but institutional theorists have also tackled many issues involving power and dominance. The organizational learning approach contains, in many respects, a parallel set of concepts and principles to those of the evolutionary approach. Although not made explicit in every article or book, the variation-selection-retention model is the foundation for analyses of learning in any context, whether by individuals, groups, or organizations. Because much of the work in organizational learning theory is grounded in social psychological and cognitive theories of human behavior, it allows researchers to formulate clear propositions about the conditions under which people act as agents of their own fate.

Conclusions

Each of the six approaches offers something of value to an evolutionary perspective on organizations. In practice, an evolutionary analysis borrows selectively from them, as befits its eclectic nature. Evolutionary theory remains open to the unexpected and the improbable, thus sharing something in common with interpretive and organizational learning approaches. As in the institutional approach, its explanations cut across levels of analysis and encompass both the short and the long run in organizational life cycles. Evolution is a locally adaptive process whose course is not predetermined and thus has something in common with ecological and TCE approaches that also stress local selection processes. Finally, the evolutionary approach emphasizes that few people know exactly what they are doing, or why. Consistent with resource dependence theory, organizations are therefore vulnerable to the influence of aggressive agents who know what they want, and are willing to work hard to get it.

In return for this eclectic borrowing, the evolutionary perspective adds value to each of the approaches. It suggests how approaches that highlight very different features within organizations might be integrated with one another. It also suggests how relatively specific processes – such as entrepreneurship, opportunism, coalition-building, and conformity – can be analyzed using a general framework of variation, selection, and retention mechanisms. The evolutionary perspective thus offers hope for an holistic understanding of organizations and improved accumulation of knowledge across diverse substantive areas.

Study Questions

1. We use the evolutionary approach as a metatheoretical framework to integrate the various perspectives on organizations. Are there some perspectives that fit more comfortably within an evolutionary frame than others? What features of the six perspectives reviewed in the chapter influence how well they can be conceptualized in evolutionary terms?
2. Recall the three research design issues raised in Chapter 2: choice of unit of analysis, definition of novelty, and selection biases. To what extent do you think these will affect empirical work conducted under the rubric of each of the six theoretical perspectives?
3. Consider your own views on the issue of theoretical pluralism in organizational studies. Is this a sign of intellectual vitality in the field? Or a major impediment to theoretical accumulation and integration?

Exercise

1. Choose a recent journal article on some aspect of organizational change and identify if the authors used one of the six perspectives we discussed in this chapter. If yes, to what extent does the article exhibit the strengths and weaknesses we noted? If no, did the authors use another perspective or create an eclectic perspective of their own? Why?

4

Entrepreneurs and the Emergence of New Organizations

The classic approach to organizational emergence, as represented by the entrepreneurship literature, focused on the traits and dispositions of the founders themselves, rather than the social landscape (Aldrich and Wiedenmayer, 1993). Knowledge and actions were not tied to a particular context, nor did researchers pay much attention to the process itself. At the other extreme, the sociological alternative to the traits approach was to focus on the societal level, taking account of culture and history, but at a very abstract level (Stinchcombe, 1965). Only in the past few decades have investigators begun to analyze the process connecting individuals, new organizations, and social context, filling the gaps in our knowledge about emergence.

From an evolutionary perspective, our focus on entrepreneurship reflects four themes in recent theory and research. First, Stinchcombe (1965) argued that people construct organizations that are culturally embedded and historically specific, reflecting societal conditions at a particular historical conjuncture. If entrepreneurs do not deviate from accepted organizational forms, they ensure the reproduction of existing organizational populations and thus reproduce the current social order. Consequently, in societies characterized by tendencies toward social inequality in the distribution of income, wealth, political power, and other valued resources, we might expect to see such inequality reproduced via the founding of new economic organizations (Tilly, 1998).

Second, entrepreneurship challenges the existing social order to the extent that it lays the foundation for the creation of new populations. Organizational ecologists have mainly focused on dynamics within existing populations, noting that most founding attempts reproduce existing organizational forms and comprise incremental rather than novel additions to the organizational landscape (Carroll and Hannan, 2000). By contrast, evolutionary theorists have focused on the generation of new populations, analyzing the conditions under which new forms of organizations carve out niches for themselves (Aldrich and Fiol, 1994). Whether a new organization simply copies an existing form or strikes off into novel territory depends upon the extent to which its founding members possesses diverse outlooks and skills, as well as on the socio-political context in which it is created.

Third, a high level of startup activity continuously introduces *potential* variation into the organizational populations of most industrial societies. Each year in the United States, between six and eight percent of the adult working population takes action to start a new venture (Gartner et al., 2004: Appendix A). By their early fifties, more than 40 percent of American men will have experienced a spell of self-employment (Müller and Arum, 2004). Studies in several Western European nations have discovered very similar rates. High startup rates reflect, in part, the limited resource requirements for initial founding efforts. Most organizations begin with little capital. Few begin with any paid employees.

Fourth, fierce selection pressures batter most founding attempts. Based on survey and ethnographic accounts, the founding process appears complex, chaotic, and compressed in time. Only about half the group of potential founders succeed in creating an initial operating entity, and fewer than one in ten new ventures grow (Duncan and Handler, 1994; Reynolds and White, 1997). Accordingly, much of the potential variation represented by diverse foundings disappears under the weight of selection forces. Observing that a higher proportion of new organizations fail than old ones, Stinchcombe (1965) coined the term 'the liability of newness.' He argued that new organizations, especially those with new forms, face constraints on viability because people must learn new roles, create new routines, and scramble for resources under severe time pressures. Subsequent research has shown that a liability of smallness (Aldrich and Auster, 1986) explains much of the tendency for new organizations to fail (Baum and Amburgey, 2002).

In this chapter, we focus on the process by which founders construct new organizations. Most research has examined business foundings, rather than non-profit or public sector organizations, but we consider a broad set of organizations whenever possible. Social networks frame the context of nascent entrepreneurs' actions, with some structural locations faring better than others. We describe three types of network ties and their consequences for entrepreneurial action, and we split the startup process into two sub-questions. Under what conditions do founders obtain and use knowledge, and under what conditions do they obtain capital and other resources?

Nascent entrepreneurs require several types of knowledge, and we examine their sources, including work experience, advice from experts, and copying from existing organizational forms. Knowledge structures in use involve various entrepreneurial heuristics, such as optimism and overconfidence. We examine the extent to which skill at framing issues and using stories to convey a vision of an emerging venture contributes to the founding process. In the final section, we show that most nascent entrepreneurs begin with few resources, getting most of what they need from informal sources.

Disputes over the definition of entrepreneurship

'Entrepreneur' and 'entrepreneurship' constitute somewhat contested terms, especially outside of the community of scholars who regularly publish in entrepreneurship journals (Gartner, 1988). Debates over the meaning of the terms were a regular feature of conference presentations and journal articles in the 1970s, as the field struggled for academic legitimacy. Some of the debates reflected the field's attempt to distinguish the field of 'entrepreneurship' from the field of 'small business studies,' which had been the traditional home of people studying business startups. The debate also reflected disciplinary disputes over units and levels of analysis, methods, and theoretical perspectives (Gartner, 2001). Articles offering conceptual schemes, taxonomies,

Table 4.1   Four competing interpretations of the term 'entrepreneurship'

Interpretation	Problems posed
High growth and high capitalization	Selection bias: growth is an outcome; high capitalization does not guarantee growth
Innovation and innovativeness	Selection bias: difficult to classify acts as innovative *a priori*
Opportunity recognition	Endows entrepreneurs with special cognitive powers
Creation of new organizations	Difficult to determine when new social entities emerge

and typologies defining 'entrepreneur' appeared regularly after the Babson College entrepreneurship conferences began in the 1980s.

Four competing perspectives highlight the themes in this continuing debate, as shown in Table 4.1. First, some scholars argue that high capitalization and high growth businesses are the proper focus of entrepreneurship studies. They distinguish such businesses from so-called 'lifestyle' or traditional businesses, which are purportedly founded by people contented with low growth and low returns to their enterprises (Carland et al., 1984). Second, based on their reading of Schumpeter, others argue that entrepreneurship should focus on innovative activity and the process by which innovations lead to new products and new markets. For example, business strategy authors often use the term 'entrepreneurial' in referring to managers and executives who take innovative action in established firms, associating it with 'corporate venturing,' 'intrapreneurship,' and similar neologisms (Kanter, 1989).

Third, following Kirzner (1997), some scholars argue that 'opportunity recognition' constitutes the heart of entrepreneurship and entrepreneurial activities (Shane and Venkataraman, 2000). From this perspective, the critical issue is not initial capitalization but rather the ability of some individuals to detect potentially valuable opportunities overlooked by others. Stevenson and Gumpert (1985), for example, defined entrepreneurship as the pursuit of opportunities without regard to resources currently controlled. This view accords with the outlook of investors and business strategy theorists, who often talk of the importance of future considerations, such as prospective market size, in funding ventures.

Fourth, some entrepreneurship researchers counsel focusing on what it is that entrepreneurs are trying to do, which is to found a new organization. For example, in his review of the literature on the alleged traits of entrepreneurs, Gartner (1988) argued that entrepreneurship should be studied by focusing on the behaviors and activities of people trying to create businesses, rather than on their psychological states and personality characteristics. From this perspective, entrepreneurs are people who create new social entities. This view fits the conventional use of the term 'entrepreneur,' referring to those who found an organization, regardless of its size.

Problems with several of these perspectives became apparent as entrepreneurial studies evolved from mostly policy-oriented writing and case studies toward a more empirically oriented research field. First, confining studies of entrepreneurship and entrepreneurial ventures to high growth companies introduces a strong selection bias into research. Growth is an *outcome* of an uncertain process, and research has shown that it is difficult to predict which firms will grow. For example, PC Connection began with $8,000 in a small town in rural New Hampshire in 1982, and despite its humble beginnings, grew to sales of about $300 million by 1995 (Chura, 1995). Regardless of their intentions, many innovative and opportunity seeking entrepreneurs create short-lived ventures. Even highly capitalized firms run into problems they cannot overcome, as the Internet dot-com bust in 2000 demonstrated. Understanding which activities lead to successful startup and growth, in varying environments, requires that researchers cast as wide a net as possible, beginning with even very modest and unlikely startup efforts.

Second, using degree of innovativeness as a criterion for picking entrepreneurs and entrepreneurial ventures to study also introduces selection bias into research, as we discussed in Chapter 3. Innovation is typically a classification of activities as new to a particular set of users and a particular environment, and is thus relative to existing conditions (Rogers, 1995). *A priori*, it is difficult to classify which acts are innovative and which are not, until they have been introduced and others' reactions gauged.

Third, opportunity recognition scholars work with the implicit assumption that the domain of potential opportunities studied includes those that could lead to business startups (Fiet, 2002). The perspective seems to endow some entrepreneurs with extraordinary cognitive powers. For example, Shane and Venkataraman (2000: 220) argued that, 'although recognition of entrepreneurial opportunities is a subjective process, the opportunities themselves are objective phenomena that are not known to all parties at all times.' Researchers must then discover what distinguishes those who recognize opportunities from those who do not. More generally, a major problem for organization theorists has been the pervasive belief that explanations for entrepreneurial achievements must be sought in cognitive traits, such as 'achievement motivation' and 'self-confidence.' Unfortunately, for theorists pursuing this avenue of investigation, such traits are widely shared and do not differentiate between entrepreneurs and other people. Moreover, some traits traditionally associated with entrepreneurial activity – such as financial risk-tolerance – are *more* common in the general population than among nascent entrepreneurs (Xu and Ruef, 2004).

Fourth, treating entrepreneurship as the creation of new organizations requires that investigators identify when new social entities begin. As goal-directed, boundary-maintaining, activity systems, organizations become new social entities that have a taken for granted presence in a society. Katz and Gartner (1988) noted that the boundary between pre-organization and organization is ambiguous, and suggested four criteria for identifying when an organization comes into existence: (1) intentionality, perhaps as reflected in stated goals; (2) mobilization of necessary resources; (3) coalescence of boundaries, such as through formal registration and naming of the entity; and (4) the exchange of resources with outsiders.

Given the problems posed by the first three perspectives shown in Table 4.1, we suggest reframing the issue of emergence by focusing on two questions suggested by the fourth perspective. First, through what process do founders construct new organizations? Organizations, as we have defined them, are goal-directed boundary-maintaining activity systems, and organizational founders must attend to all three components of this definition in constructing an organization. Our scheme for analyzing organizational emergence builds on the pioneering work of Katz and Gartner (1988), whose achievement was to drive home the point that organizational emergence is not a linear, step-by-step process. Instead, emergence involves uneven development along several lines, any one of which might be stopped well short of an organization's successful founding. Because the process of boundary construction critically shapes organizational emergence, we devote the next chapter to it.

Second, what selection processes affect whether new organizations reproduce or depart from existing organizational forms, routines, and competencies? This question raises a perplexing methodological issue for anyone using current research findings. Organizations need founders. But organizations cannot recruit them, because organizations don't exist until founders construct them. Thus, we typically identify founders only *after* we have already identified their organizations. If we only study entrepreneurs after their organizations have attracted enough public notice to be included in standard sampling frames, we overlook a critical phase in the founding process (Kalleberg et al., 1990). At that point, selection processes have winnowed out many interesting variations (Katz and Gartner, 1988). We also miss the process by which new organizations with innovative routines and competencies set in motion the genesis of new populations, a topic we consider in Chapter 9.

Nascent entrepreneurs and innovation

Through what process do organizations emerge? Behind this rather innocent framing of the question lies a host of thorny issues, beginning with the question of what language theorists should use for describing the process. We use the terms 'founding' and 'constructing' rather than 'birth,' because 'birth' implies a smooth process that occurs in uniform stages from conception to development. We emphasize the *contingent*, and sometimes disorderly, aspects of organizational emergence.

Nascent entrepreneurs

The concept of *nascent entrepreneur* captures the flavor of a contingent founding process. A nascent entrepreneur is defined as someone who initiates serious activities that are intended to culminate in a viable organization. Reynolds (2000) developed procedures for defining and studying nascent entrepreneurship, carrying through on the entrepreneurship field's budding interest in the entrepreneurial process rather than just outcomes (Gartner, 1988). Although Reynolds defined nascent entrepreneurs strictly for a business context, the principles of networking, resource mobilization, and entrepreneurial enactment apply to non-business startups as well. In evolutionary terms, nascent entrepreneurs are a major source of organizational variations, beginning with their intentions and continuing through their actions toward a realized founding.

The stages of nascent entrepreneurship are shown in Figure 4.1, involving three transitions and four periods. Transition I is triggered when someone begins thinking about trying to start a new business – alone or with others. Ever since Weber's (1963) early work on the Protestant work ethic, the social context driving this transition has been a central topic in economic sociology. Recent efforts have studied a diverse set of factors leading to entry into nascent entrepreneurship, including life history, human capital, financial capital, interpersonal networks, and organizational context (Carroll and Mosakowski, 1987; Davis et al., forthcoming; Müller and Arum, 2004). In the process, common presuppositions concerning the drivers of entrepreneurship have been challenged. For example, one counter-intuitive finding concerns the characteristics of previous employers of potential entrepreneurs. While transitions into entrepreneurship generally decrease when individuals are employed in large, stable bureaucracies, these

ADULT POPULATION →	(I)→	NASCENT ENTREPRENEUR→	(II)→	FLEDGLING NEW FIRM→	(III)→	ESTABLISHED NEW FIRM
∇		∇		∇		∇
(Conception)		(Gestation)		(Infancy)		(Adolescence)

Activities involved in gestation that were reported in Panel Study of Entrepreneurial Dynamics (PSED), 1998–2000, which collected a representative sample of nascent entrepreneurs in the U.S.

Activity	Percent that completed activity by first follow-up interview	Average months until completion
Bought or leased facilities/equipment	79	24
Received money from sales	75	25
Opened bank account	60	23
Established credit with supplier	58	24
Completed product or service	57	(N/A)
Devoted full time to business	51	27
Achieved positive monthly cash flow	45	38
Filed federal income tax return	43	18
Hired employees to work for wages	33	33
Listed number in phone book	33	31
Paid social security taxes	29	26
Paid state unemployment taxes	18	26
Listed with Dun & Bradstreet	9	34

N = 374

Figure 4.1   Organizational emergence: from conception to adolescence

Source: Adapted from Reynolds (2000) and Carter et al. (2004).

organizational contexts actually *increase* the transition rate among the *founders* of those ventures (Dobrev and Barnett, 2005). The underlying reason may be that organizational growth dilutes the personal connection that founders have to their startups and spurs a search for new entrepreneurial opportunities.

Following Transition I, an emergent organization is in a gestation phase, in which nascent entrepreneurs engage in startup activities to further their objectives. For example, nascent entrepreneurs may lease facilities or equipment, or hire employees for pay. Although a single startup activity might seem like a low threshold for this phase, most people who say they are 'now trying to start a new business' report engaging in several behaviors. In the Panel Study of Entrepreneurial Dynamics (PSED), over half of the nascent entrepreneurs reported that they were devoting their full time to the business in a 24-month follow-up after initially being surveyed (Carter et al., 2004). In the same follow-up, the majority of nascent entrepreneurs said they had completed a product or service for sale or delivery, established credit with a supplier, opened a bank account, received money from the sale of goods or services, and purchased or leased equipment or facilities.

Three characteristics of these activities illustrate the complexity of the founding process. First, many different combinations of activities have been uncovered and the activities do not form a scale of any kind. Of 14 possible startup activities investigated by Carter et al. (1996), 60 of the 91 inter-correlations between the activities were below 0.2. Second, the activities occur in many different orders before a fledgling business is established. Nascent entrepreneurs follow no fixed sequence of activities, although the timing of activities may be predictable once structural, strategic, and environmental contingencies are taken into account (Ruef, 2005). Third, the follow-up wave of the PSED indicates that, on the average, about 29 months elapsed between the time someone began to organize a business initially and the time that they *perceived* the startup had become an operating enterprise (Carter et al., 2004). However, the variance was considerable – some nascent entrepreneurs even considered their business to be operational before they had completed any other startup activities.

How many nascent entrepreneurs actually make the transition labeled II – constructing a fledgling firm? In the past, small numbers of cases and sample attrition have hampered research on this transition. Reynolds and White (1997) estimated that about half of the nascent entrepreneurs made the transition, with the average founder taking a little less than a year to achieve fledgling status. Using the larger PSED sample, Carter et al. (2004) found that roughly equal numbers of entrepreneurs reported an operating business (31 percent) or active startup efforts (30 percent) in a two-year follow-up. The rest either gave up entirely (19 percent) or considered the startup effort to be underway but currently inactive (20 percent). Based on these estimates, up to a million or so startups in the United States achieve infancy each year. Additional theory and empirical analysis are required to guide the investigation of the third transition to an 'established' new firm in nascent entrepreneur studies.

Outcomes of the founding process are highly uncertain. In many cases, nascent entrepreneurs' initial ideas are not realized, because their intentions are misguided or they cannot mobilize needed resources. At any given time, then, we observe only a surviving fraction of a much larger pool of startups begun but abandoned by nascent entrepreneurs (Katz and Gartner, 1988). Failure to appreciate the level of turnover and turbulence in populations has blinded social scientists to the organizational fermentation simmering just below the surface in modern societies. Most new organizations are quite small and short-lived, but, without the survivors of this process, organization studies would have little subject matter.

Reproducers and innovators

The overwhelming majority of nascent entrepreneurs start small *reproducer* rather than *innovator* organizations. On a continuum between the two poles of reproducer and innovator, *reproducer organizations* are defined as those organizations started in an established population whose routines and competencies vary only minimally, if at all, from those of existing organizations. They bring little or no incremental knowledge to the populations they enter, organizing their activities in the same way as their predecessors. *Innovative organizations,* by contrast, are those organizations started by entrepreneurs whose routines and competencies vary significantly from those of existing organizations (Ruef, 2002a). Many such organizations will not survive, as their departures from existing routines and competencies are unworkable or fall outside current selection criteria. For example, many attempts to combine resources in new ways are fatal and others are perceived as illegitimate.

Some innovative foundings use routines and competencies that vary in ways favored by selection criteria. The new organizational knowledge they carry may thus transform an existing population or create a new one. From a population point of view, they have created *competence-enhancing* or *competence-destroying* innovations (Anderson and Tushman, 1990). Competence-enhancing innovations involve substantial improvements that build on existing routines and competencies within a product/service class and can be adopted by existing organizations (Abernathy and Clark, 1985).

For example, most typewriter manufacturers switched relatively smoothly from producing mechanical typewriters to producing electric ones.

Most innovations are competence-enhancing rather than competence-destroying (Schmookler, 1962; Tushman and Anderson, 1986) and can thus be adopted by existing organizations. Startups are at a disadvantage because existing organizations can easily blend competence-enhancing innovations into their operations. In contrast, competence-destroying innovations require new knowledge, routines, and competencies in the development and production of a product/service. They fundamentally alter the set of relevant competencies required of an organization. Accordingly, they put existing organizations at a disadvantage. We review this distinction at greater length in Chapters 8 and 9.

The continuum from reproducer to innovator is defined by outcomes, not intentions (Aldrich and Kenworthy, 1999). Some entrepreneurs deliberately intend to depart from existing knowledge, whereas others give it no thought. Irrespective of intentions, individuals face a tension between deviating from existing competencies and conforming to them. Cultural pressures toward obedience often intimidate individuals with deviant ideas. Entrepreneurs whose business plans lie outside current expectations for their industry may find no one who understands or accepts what they propose to do (Hargadon and Douglas, 2001). Moreover, nascent entrepreneurs depend heavily on their social networks for knowledge concerning opportunities, the range of feasible variations, and perceived selection criteria. Negative feedback from their network ties may inhibit entrepreneurial departures from the norm, directing action down narrow channels. Given the centrality of social networks in influencing conformity, information diversity, and trust, we turn now to an examination of the network context of entrepreneurship.

The social network context

Social networks play a significant role in many facets of organizational emergence. Indeed, the larger network structure in which entrepreneurs are embedded constitutes a significant portion of their opportunity structure (Aldrich and Whetten, 1981). Nascent entrepreneurs' *personal networks* – the set of persons to whom they are directly linked – affect their access to social, emotional, and material support. All nascent entrepreneurs draw upon their existing social networks and construct new ones in the process of obtaining knowledge and resources for their organizations. For example, Baker et al. (2003: 265) noted that the founders they studied 'relied on their pre-existing networks as the primary means of access to the welter of resources needed during and after founding.' Regardless of their personal networking abilities, nascent entrepreneurs who occupy impoverished social locations may find themselves cut off from emerging opportunities and critical resources.

Network analysts distinguish between two complementary dimensions of someone's social relations: their diversity or heterogeneity, and their affective or emotional strength. The usefulness of any relation is context dependent. In the context of entrepreneurial networks, people need access to information and other resources. Thus, multiple diverse contacts are important, regardless of their strength. We first explain why diversity in social relations may convey advantages to entrepreneurs, and then consider the contribution of relational strength to entrepreneurial action.

The importance of diversity

Diversity in network ties is crucial for nascent entrepreneurs, as diversity increases access to a wider circle of information about potential markets, new business locations, innovations, sources of capital, and potential investors. By *diversity* we mean ties to persons of differing social locations and characteristics, along a variety of dimensions: gender, age, occupation, industry, ethnicity, and so forth. Diversity depends on the range of sectors through which a nascent entrepreneur moves. Ties can be *bridges* between sectors where a nascent entrepreneur currently has no direct ties (Granovetter, 1973). Diversity also depends on the number of structural holes in a nascent entrepreneur's network. *Structural holes* exist when persons to whom entrepreneurs are linked are not themselves connected to one another (Burt, 1992). For example, a nascent entrepreneur may have direct ties to a banker and an accountant, neither of whom knows the other.

A network made up of homogeneous ties may be of limited value to a nascent entrepreneur. In homogeneous networks, information known to one person is rapidly diffused to others and interpreted in similar ways (Granovetter, 1973). Two forces promote homogeneity in personal networks. First, people tend to associate with others who have similar social characteristics (Marsden, 1987; McPherson and Smith-Lovin, 1987; McPherson et al., 2001), a process commonly termed *homophily*. Second, people tend toward emotional and personal *balance* across their social relations (Cartwright and Harary, 1956; Davis, 1963). For example, a nascent entrepreneur's strong friendship with someone increases the likelihood of that person becoming friendly with other persons strongly linked to the entrepreneur. Thus, if a nascent entrepreneur has a lawyer as a close friend, and that lawyer has a bank loan officer as a close friend, then the entrepreneur is also likely to become friendly with the loan officer.

As ties to the same kinds of people accumulate, the marginal value of each successive tie drops. Ties to more than one person with similar characteristics or in similar social locations are *redundant* and thus of questionable value in providing new information (Burt, 1992). An entrepreneur gains little new information from talking to more than one person, if all of them are in nearly identical social locations or share many characteristics in common. For this reason, Burt (1992) argued, when it comes to the flow of information, the strength of ties is less important than whether they are non-redundant with other ties. We turn now to the contribution of strong and weak ties to entrepreneurial action.

The importance of tie strength

The types of relationships that make up a person's total set of relations can be classified according to the strength of the relationship: strong, weak, and indeterminate or fluctuating (dealing with complete strangers). A network's level of diversity depends, in part, upon the mix of strong and weak ties (Ruef, 2002a). Models of entrepreneurship and business life cycles emphasize the context-dependent nature of the three types of relations. For nascent entrepreneurs, strong and weak ties may be more important than contacts with strangers for the mobilization of resources in the early stages of business development. Later, when a newly founded organization has achieved some stability, arm's-length transactions and contacts with strangers assume more importance.

The most reliable relationships in a personal network are *strong ties*, which are usually of long duration. People rely on strong ties for advice, assistance, and support in all areas of their lives, such as asking for help in dealing with an ethical dilemma at work, or asking someone to watch their children on short notice. They are long-term, two-way relationships, not governed by short-term calculations of self-interest. Many contain an implicit principle of reciprocal obligations. Consequently, strong ties are typically more reliable than other ties and involve a strong degree of trust and emotional closeness (Granovetter, 1993; Marsden and Campbell, 1984). Individuals tend to make heavy investments in this type of relationship, requiring fairly frequent contact with the other person.

Because of the effort involved in creating and sustaining a strong tie, most people have in the order of 5 to 20 strong ties in their personal networks (Fischer, 1982). Researchers have found that the exact number of strong ties reported is very sensitive to how people are asked to think about their relations. In research on entrepreneurial networks, investigators typically find that most business owners report 3 to 10 strong ties, e.g. Aldrich et al. (1989). Results from studies inside organizations have produced similar figures (James, 2000). Attempting to manage large numbers of ties may produce role strain. Nonetheless, gains from extensive ties with others may outweigh the costs (Aldrich, 1979: 259–263; Marks, 1977). A business owner's strong tie network usually consists of a majority of close business associates, a few friends, and one or two family members (Aldrich et al., 1996).

Strong ties provide a sheltered sector within which entrepreneurs can avoid the opportunism and uncertainty otherwise possible in market-mediated transactions (Williamson, 1994). In social situations where people expect to deal with each other over an extended period, strong ties yield three benefits: trust, predictability, and voice. *Trust* tells founders whom they can count on in difficult situations, and it substantially enhances predictability in relations. *Predictability* refers to how the other party will behave if situations change. And, finally, using *voice* in a relation means the persons involved will make their complaints known and negotiate over them, rather than silently sneaking away (Hirschman, 1972). Long-term relationships enhance these benefits, increasing the likelihood of further interaction. Increased frequency of contact, in turn, carries many benefits. Through frequent contacts, strong bonds develop, tacit knowledge is transferred, and each party develops more informal control over the other (Jones et al., 1997: 922).

Surprisingly, perhaps, strong ties with family members do not often translate into financial support from them. Nationally representative data, as well as community studies, show that – with the possible exception of spouses – only founders from a handful of ethnic minority groups can count on much financial support from family members (Aldrich et al., 1996; Bates, 1997; Renzulli, 1998). Family members, as strong ties, provide emotional support for nascent entrepreneurs, but often they are not in a position to supply capital. Indeed, too great a reliance on family members may put nascent entrepreneurs at a disadvantage (Renzulli, 1998). A panel study in the Research Triangle Area of North Carolina found that the greater the proportion of kin members in a nascent entrepreneur's business discussion network, the lower the odds of that person actually starting a business (Renzulli et al., 2000). However, institutional and organizational context may also affect the salience of family ties. In China, kinship networks have been linked to both the founding and growth of private enterprises. However, in this same environment, the development of collective enterprises does not appear to be facilitated by strong ties (Peng, 2004).

Strong ties often form the core of a founding team. In a representative U.S. sample of startups studied by Ruef et al. (2003), respondents were asked, 'How many people will legally own this new business?' The average team of owner-founders in the sample included 1.7 persons. Apparently about half of startups are solo efforts, about a third are based on people related by marriage or kinship, and the rest are teams of unrelated individuals (Ruef et al., 2003). In the retail and services sectors, where most businesses are small, about half of all married owners in the United States and England report that their spouse participates in the running of the business (Aldrich et al., 1983).

Whereas strong ties are based on trust, *weak ties* are superficial or casual and normally involve little emotional investment. Weak-tie relationships are typically of shorter duration and involve lower frequency of contact. They are also less reliable and more uncertain than strong ties and often fade into dormancy, although they can be revived when assistance is required. They can be thought of as arm's-length relations, involving persons whose handshake we seek but whose full support we cannot count on.

Individuals have many more weak ties than strong ties. Examples of weak ties include relationships with customers or clients who are known on a first-name basis but with whom interactions are still 'businesslike.' In contrast to strong ties, weak ties are more likely to be characterized by opportunism, uncertainty, and exit, as depicted in the transaction cost economics perspective (Williamson, 1994). *Opportunism* is potentially present in typical market-like transactions that are driven by self-interest and involve little or no room for trust. *Uncertainty* in a tie stems from difficulty in predicting a partner's actions. *Exit* is often the route taken by people faced with opportunism and uncertainty. Going elsewhere to complete a transaction involving a weak tie is easier than struggling in negotiations for a better deal (Hirschman, 1972). However, conditions of high transaction-specific investments inhibit exit.

A third type of network relationship can better be described as *contacts*, rather than ties. These types of network relations are created for pragmatic purposes with strangers or individuals with whom nascent entrepreneurs have no prior relations. Contacts with strangers are typically fleeting in duration and require little or no emotional involvement. An example of a contact with a stranger would be buying a piece of equipment from a person who advertised in a trade publication. TCE theorists would describe such events as 'spot market' transactions.

The association between diversity and tie strength

In contrast to strong ties, people are less concerned with balance in their large circle of weak ties. The persons with whom we have weak ties, such as casual acquaintances, are less likely to know each other than are those with whom we have strong ties, such as close friends. Heterogeneity is both more likely and more tolerated among our weak ties. Contacts with casual acquaintances that are different from the nascent entrepreneur can be links to diverse others, each of whom has a close circle of persons unknown to the entrepreneur.

If these strangers have information or resources of value, then nascent entrepreneurs can gain access to them indirectly through the diversity of their weak ties. They could also accomplish the same goal by diversifying their strong ties, but that requires very intense and often unsettling maneuvering (Burt, 1992). We would thus expect successful nascent entrepreneurs to emerge from positions that are connected to diverse information sources, as well as from positions benefiting from a reliable set of strong ties. Indeed, Ruef (2002a) found that network diversity – a mix of strong ties, weak ties, and contacts – tended to promote innovation in a sample of entrepreneurs who had graduated from a U.S. business school.

Social networks and gender

The historical under-representation of women in ownership is clearly linked to their exclusion from men's business discussion networks (Carter, 1994). If women do not occupy key posts in banks, investment firms, and other financially significant positions, then the odds of men encountering them in daily business relations are reduced (Rytina and Morgan, 1982). In the PSED sample, women were only about 60 percent as likely as men to be nascent entrepreneurs (Ruef et al., 2003). Founding rates for women-owned businesses in Western Europe are also substantially lower than the rates for men-owned businesses (ENSR, 2004). In 2001, about 22 percent of entrepreneurs in Europe were women, varying from a low of about 14 percent in Greece to about 30 percent in France. Observing low rates of business formation by women in Israel, Lerner et al. (1997: 320) attributed the low rates of business ownership to women's restricted access to government and business contacts, limiting their abilities to 'obtain information and resources necessary for business creation and growth.'

Men's inclusion of mostly other men in their networks reflects the societal distribution of power and ownership positions, as well as the tendency of men to choose others like themselves (Kanter, 1977). For example, research in the 1980s and 1990s in the United States, Canada, Italy, Northern Ireland, Japan, Sweden, and Norway found that men business owners seldom had women in their strong tie circles (Aldrich et al., 1989; Aldrich and Sakano, 1998), with spouses constituting one notable exception (Ruef et al., 2003). Such gender homogeneity within men's strong tie circles creates a substantial barrier to the free flow of information to women.

Historically, women's *labor force participation rate* – the percentage of women over 16 who are employed or looking for work – began to increase in the United States in the late 1940s, and in 2002 stood at 63.4 percent, compared to 76.4 percent for men (U.S. Department of Labor, 2003). In the past, a lower participation rate, combined with occupational sex segregation, kept women out of many high-paying jobs (Rosenfeld, 1992). As employment opportunities improved for women over the past several decades, women have founded businesses at a much higher rate than in earlier generations, raising the likelihood that men's business discussion networks will change. Businesses that were majority-owned by women grew from less than 5 percent in 1970 to over 26 percent by 1997 (U.S. Department of Commerce, 2001). If firms owned equally by men and women are included, the figure jumped to about 44 percent in 1997.

Indeed, the growth of many voluntary associations for women dedicated to business networking has already substantially raised the visibility of women owners in the business community (Moore and Buttner, 1997). Three examples are the National Association of Women Business Owners (NAWBO), the National Women's Business Council, and the Committee of 200. Founding members of the Committee of 200 in 1982 included Katherine Graham of the Washington Post, Sherry Lansing of 20th Century Fox, Patricia Cloherty of Patricof & Co. Ventures, Christie Hefner of Playboy Enterprises, and Muriel Siebert of Muriel Siebert & Co. It now includes the owners and top officers of the largest women-owned firms in the United States.

Social networks and ethnicity

Rates of entrepreneurship vary substantially across ethnic groups because members of particular demographic groups have occupied very different structural positions, including their social network context (Aldrich and Waldinger, 1990; Portes and Sensenbrenner, 1993). A group's representation among entrepreneurs has been highly dependent upon the era in which they emigrated to a host society and on the reception they received. For example, during certain periods in American history, immigrant status was a spur to business formation. Some socially marginal ethnic or religious groups, such as Japanese or Jewish immigrants, have been a much greater proportion of the entrepreneurial population than of the general population during these selected periods in the late 19th and early 20th centuries. These groups immigrated during eras when economic opportunities were expanding, but found their paths blocked in nearly all directions except for small business ownership.

Ethnic solidarity and networking capacity have facilitated business ownership for many immigrant groups (Light, 2005). Groups have benefited from a strong internal market for finding business opportunities and raising capital (Wilson and Portes, 1980). For example, in Zimmer and Aldrich's (1987) study of businesses in three English cities, only about half of the owners relied upon formal channels for information about the site they eventually chose for their business. With regard to capital, Asians drew on family and friends to a much greater extent than whites in raising funds for their business. With multiple sources of capital available, Asians appeared less isolated in their social networks than whites.

Given trends in globalization, immigrant social networks now often develop transnationally, as well as locally. *Transnational entrepreneurs* are individuals who often travel abroad for their enterprises and believe that the success of those enterprises depends on regular ties with foreign countries. In their Comparative Immigrant Entrepreneurship Project (CIEP), Portes and colleagues (2002) sampled entrepreneurs who migrated to the United States from Colombia, the Dominican Republic, and El Salvador. They found that the entrepreneurs' social networks contained a large number of non-local ties, with the ratio of non-local to local ties averaging 0.77 to 1. However, they also noted that only small proportions of the three groups were actively involved in transnational activities.

In contrast to many immigrant groups, African-Americans in the United States have faced more systematic barriers to business ownership, including severe residential segregation (Butler, 1991; Feagin and Imani, 1994). (African-Americans are not themselves a traditional immigrant group, given the conditions under which they were brought to the United States. But the great northward migration of African-Americans, starting around the end of World War I, created conditions at their destinations that resembled those of European and Asian groups.) Even after some African-American owners established a foothold in some economic niches, many thriving business communities were disrupted and ultimately broken up by foreign immigration. Many others succumbed to the economic dislocations of the Depression Era (Drake and Cayton, 1945). Since then, African-American owners have made some gains, but their self-employment levels are still below those for many groups that have immigrated to the United States since the 1960s, e.g. Koreans and Cubans (Light and Gold, 2000).

Research Illustration 4.1 The Structure of Founding Teams

Our analysis of structural variation in founding teams within a nationally representative sample highlights several features of the networking context affecting entrepreneurs (Ruef et al., 2003). We used the first wave of the Panel Study of Entrepreneurial Dynamics (PSED) to collect demographic and social network information on the founding teams of 816 business startups in the United States. The sampling methodology emphasized *nascent* entrepreneurs, identifying individuals who 'are now trying to start a business' and excluding operational ventures – specifically, those with more than 90 days of positive cash flow.

From an evolutionary perspective, our principal interest was in mechanisms that would promote or inhibit variation in founding team structure. We proposed five distinctive mechanisms, including: (1) *homophily*, the tendency of entrepreneurs to group based on similar ascriptive characteristics (e.g. gender, ethnicity, national origin); (2) *functionality*, the tendency to group based on diverse achieved characteristics (e.g. business skills); (3) *status expectations*, the tendency of high-status entrepreneurs to attract more colleagues than low-status entrepreneurs; (4) *network constraint*, the limitation of group diversity due to pre-existing network ties; and (5) *ecological constraint*, the limitation of group diversity due to the segregation of entrepreneurs by geography or industry. Our empirical findings suggested that founding team structure in the United States is driven to a large extent by homophily and constraints imposed by strong ties. Controlling for the heterogeneity introduced by spouses, we found that all-male or all-female teams occur at a rate that is roughly four times that expected by chance. Moreover, the rate of ethnic homophily is almost ten times that of gender homophily, and can even be greater among minority groups. Perhaps the only significant source of diversity on the founding teams is the tendency of entrepreneurs to work with spouses or live-in partners, which decreases gender homogeneity substantially.

Methodologically, our study illustrates two key features involved in evolutionary analyses of emergent organizations. First, as noted in Chapter 2, analysts must be careful *not* to select organizations based only on successful outcomes. Given the existing social network literature, there may be good reason to doubt the efficacy of teams developed largely on the basis of demographic homogeneity and strong ties. But without a sampling strategy that targets nascent entrepreneurs, we would have little prospective evidence to adjudicate the efficacy of different structural arrangements which may appear during organizational gestation.

Second, the study calls attention to the importance of *counterfactuals* in evolutionary analysis. Due to the influence of sample size, homophily, and strong tie constraints, some types of founding teams may be absent from a given sample. For instance, our sample does not include any larger founding teams (five or more members) that are mixed-gender, feature a female majority, and exclude spouses or partners. Nevertheless, it is critical that one acknowledge that such founding teams are clearly possible, even when they are not observed empirically. Failure to do so can lead to underestimation of the mechanisms (e.g. homophily) that produce founding teams in the first place.

Given its emphasis on variation, our study could be criticized for not yet producing a full evolutionary account of founding team structure. To complete the explanation, one would need to address the selection mechanisms that affect the founding teams. For instance, are some team structures more prone to interpersonal conflict and, thus, dissolution? Does the structure of the teams predict whether the nascent entrepreneurs will eventually create an operational organization?

One would also need to address processes of retention. What types of teams are most likely to experience founder turnover? How does this affect the knowledge and routines used to create a new venture? These issues of personnel retention have been examined for the top management teams of established organizations (e.g. Boone et al., 2004), but remain to be addressed systematically among founding teams.

Summary

Social networks affect organizational emergence by structuring the context in which nascent entrepreneurs must act. Disadvantaged network circumstances limit entrepreneurial possibilities for many people. Nascent entrepreneurs who occupy advantageous social locations have access to emerging opportunities and critical resources, whereas those in impoverished locations must rely much more on their personal networking abilities. Regardless of their structural positions, the use of brokers and other networking strategies enables some founders to increase their access to resources and opportunities. Initial access only allows nascent entrepreneurs to begin the founding process, however. They must obtain knowledge and find ways to turn it into organizational routines and competencies. In the next section, we examine the types and origins of entrepreneurial knowledge, as well as its use.

Knowledge: types, origins, and uses

Organizations are the dominant, taken-for-granted tools of collective action in our world. Given the extent to which knowledge of organizations as a social form is deeply embedded in the cultures of industrial societies, we cannot give a brief answer to the question, 'Why was an organization formed?' The 'why' question implicitly takes us to an historically situated analysis of why people turn so readily to organizations, rather than using other problem-solving strategies. That question is beyond the scope of our book. Satisfying answers are available in the works of social historians and others on the transformation of Western societies since the 17th century (Polanyi, 1944; Wallerstein, 1974). We believe that 'why' questions in particular cases can almost always be re-phrased as 'how' questions without loss of theoretical power. Effective collective action often *means* organization, whereas *no* organization generally means isolated and inconsequential action. In situations requiring large-scale efforts, people do not face the 'choice' of organization versus non-organization, but rather the question of '*How* can we build an organization in this instance?'

Therefore, we take for granted the existence of fundamental rules of organizing in all modern societies. In most Western industrial societies, rules of organizing are part of the behavioral repertoire of socialized adults who understand and use them as guides through most social situations. Indeed, 'models of organization are part of the cultural tool kit of any society and serve expressive or communicative as well as instrumental functions' (Clemens, 1993: 771). Clemens (1993) noted that women's groups between 1890 and 1920 introduced models of organization from the voluntary association sector into the political arena. These social movements rested on cultural assumptions about the efficacy of voluntary organization in American society. Potential entrepreneurs simply take such culturally defined building blocks of rules for granted, thus channeling most new ventures in the direction of reproducing existing organizational forms (Carroll, 1993). The rules and their origins are certainly worthy of analysis, but that task deserves more attention than we can give it in this book.

In the next section, after defining some key terms referring to the types of knowledge used by nascent entrepreneurs, we point out the special conditions under which entrepreneurial knowledge is developed. We define organizational knowledge as the routines and competencies that are specific to an organizational activity system and embedded in its internal selection processes. Schemata, or organized knowledge structures, rest atop procedural and declarative knowledge and such knowledge can be obtained through several channels. Copying is a particularly attractive option, because it is cheap, but it can also be dangerous.

Types of knowledge

Nascent entrepreneurs develop organized knowledge structures through experience, and they use those structures as templates to give information form and meaning (Walsh, 1995: 281). For example, Lowstedt (1993) found that founders' cognitive structures and how they thought about organizing affected the eventual structure of their emergent organizations. Fiske and Taylor (1991: 149) called organized knowledge structures *schemata*, which they defined as 'cognitive structures that represent organized knowledge about a given concept or type of stimulus.' Schemata encompass both the structure and the content of knowledge. They are grounded in early socialization experiences and thus depend upon fundamental cultural rules, but they also change throughout people's lives as they learn from experience. When schemata are treated as the basis for making decisions, cognitive theorists speak of a top-down view of information processing. However, cognitive theorists also recognize that knowledge structures develop with experience and use, thus building learning and social interaction into their theories (Harris, 1994; Walsh, 1995). We discuss schemata extensively in Chapter 6 (for definitions of schemata, see Table 6.2).

Forms of memory
Much of the knowledge needed for constructing new organizations exists as stored information and experience in the *memory* of nascent entrepreneurs and those working with them to create an organization (Huber, 1991; Moorman and Miner, 1998). Two kinds of memory are relevant to organization building: procedural and declarative (Cohen and Bacdayan, 1994), as shown in Table 4.2. *Procedural memory* refers to the things people know because they have a stored stock of routines and skills they apply to familiar situations. For example, setting up and operating an electronic checkout machine is a routine procedure for managers who have done it many times before. Such knowledge comes not only from experience, but also can be learned from others, although at some cost. Procedural memory tends to be use-specific, impeding actors' abilities to generalize from it to dissimilar situations. *Tacit knowledge* refers to learned understandings that are difficult or impossible to verbalize (Polanyi, 1966; Nonaka and Takeuchi, 1995). Much of procedural knowledge is tacit or implicit and thus hard to codify.

Declarative memory refers to theoretical or abstract knowledge. It is the memory of facts, events, propositions, and principles. Declarative is more general than procedural

Table 4.2   Modes of organizational memory and knowledge

Concept	Definition
Organizational knowledge	Routines and competencies specific to an organizational activity system
Procedural memory/knowledge	Knowledge drawn from memory stored about specific routines and skills applied to familiar situations
Tacit knowledge	Knowledge that can be applied but that is difficult to verbalize
Declarative memory/knowledge	Knowledge drawn from memory that is theoretical or abstract, e.g. facts and events

memory and thus has a variety of uses. For example, knowledge of cost-accounting principles generalizes across a wide variety of industries and organizations. However, its value depends upon actors being able to use the right search algorithm to find what is needed in a specific situation. For example, an accountant must be able to recognize a 'cost' in service as well as manufacturing industries. Tacit knowledge of the conditions under which declarative memory should be invoked comes with maturity and experience.

The founding of a new organization often requires nascent entrepreneurs to *improvise*. As founders move deeper into the founding process, they must occasionally recall, develop, and apply knowledge under extreme time pressures (Baker et al., 2003; Moorman and Miner, 1998). The narrow time frame between conception and execution during founding compresses many activities that are stretched out over longer periods in established organizations. Managers often have the luxury of contemplating their options, whereas nascent entrepreneurs must act with little time for reflection. The short cycle between action and feedback provides many more opportunities for learning than managerial work in established organizations (Sitkin, 1992). During the improvisation process, occasions arise for blind variations and novelty, thus opening a window of opportunity for innovative organizational forms to emerge (Lant and Mezias, 1990).

Origins of knowledge

How do founders know what resources to pursue? Because most founders simply try to reproduce the forms most common in the populations they enter, much of the knowledge they require is widely available. They can obtain it from established organizations, industry experts, trade publications, newsletters, experience as an employee of an organization in the population, on-line databases, and early hires who have worked in the industry. We focus on three of the most likely sources of entrepreneurial knowledge: (1) previous work experience; (2) advice from experts; and (3) imitation and copying. We note the potential dangers involved in copying knowledge and also in sharing it.

Previous work experience

Nascent entrepreneurs can capitalize on knowledge gained and contacts made in their previous jobs. However, relying on previous experiences can also constrain their search for opportunities and limit the scope of the strategies they consider (Boeker, 1988; Romanelli, 1989; Ruef, 2002a). Labor market theories of human capital investments by workers stress the investment employees have made in their firm – and industry-specific knowledge (Becker, 1975). Nascent entrepreneurs only realize the full value of such investments if they capitalize on them by pursuing similar activities. Such knowledge may be less useful in other contexts. Previous work experience affects the knowledge available to founders in three ways: (1) through job-specific contacts; (2) through organization- or industry-specific knowledge; and (3) through the culture of an occupational sub-community.

First, existing networks of ties within and outside organizations are an important source of ideas about opportunities. Some work settings provide their incumbents with many opportunities to generate foundings (Romanelli, 1989: 218). For example, founders of innovative new high-technology ventures in Silicon Valley who were formerly employed in well-connected firms were more successful at raising outside funding than other founders (Burton et al., 2002). Knowing details about an individual's work unit may tell us not only if they will attempt a founding, but also which forms of organizations they are likely to create. Selection processes associated with particular jobs and organizational subunits filter the information and incentives available to potential entrepreneurs (Romanelli, 1989). People who work in specialized units stand at the crossroads of unique information on which they might capitalize to start their own ventures. Rao and Drazin (2002) found that executives with international stock fund experience stimulated the diffusion of new funds when they moved across mutual fund families.

Second, some research shows that owners tend to set up businesses in product or service lines similar to those in which they previously worked, serving some of the same customers. However, this tendency appears to vary across industries. In their research on innovative high-technology businesses in West Germany, Picot et al. (1989) found that most founders had previous work experiences in their own industrial sector. Not all studies have found evidence for direct replication of a founder's previous firm. Boeker (1988) examined the backgrounds of 51 founders of merchant semiconductor firms and the strategies they adopted when they founded their firms. He found that the organizing strategy of their former firm did *not* affect the founders' strategies – first mover, fast-follower, low-cost producer, or niche producer – but that an entrepreneur's functional background and training made a substantial difference.

Third, workers in occupational sub-communities that reach beyond the boundaries of specific organizations develop practices, values, vocabularies, and identities that are transferable to other contexts (Barley and Kunda, 2004). For example, ex-police officers often found detective and home security agencies (Van Maanen and Barley, 1984). Romanelli (1989: 221–222) argued that populations and communities bound the flow of information and incentives for people within them, with some quite isolated but others heavily interdependent with external actors. Interdependencies are often accompanied by access to information about potential entrepreneurial opportunities.

Experts

Advice from experts can substitute for direct experience. If novice entrepreneurs work with experts on solving problems, they gain access to the procedural knowledge held by the expert. Tacit knowledge, indeed, may only be brought to light in such relations. Working alongside an expert gives entrepreneurs a chance to practice on the expression of a routine, rather than its representation in books or training manuals. Seeking advice from predecessors within the same population encourages the replication of existing forms, and network connections thus help preserve the continuity of a population's competencies and routines. Baker et al. (2003) found that founders who responded quickly to opportunities reported by colleagues, suppliers, or customers were much more likely to found a firm in a familiar line of work than were founders who engaged in more systematic searches.

Owners seeking advice from experts in their industry often rely on their personal network, especially weak ties (Ruef, 2002a). About three-quarters of 217 business owners in a Research Triangle Area study in 1992 had sought expert advice within the past year, with about 40 percent asking five experts or more for advice (Aldrich et al., 1996). Women owners were just as aggressive as men in pursuing assistance. Ties to acquaintances, rather than ties within families, were the best information source for most owners. They turned mostly to people they knew, either through a work relationship or as a friend, and almost none paid market rates for the advice. Most rated the advice they obtained very highly, and about two-fifths said it had changed the way they organized their business.

Imitation and Copying

Founders are guided toward the reproduction of existing forms by knowledge obtained from experience, experts, and copying established organizations' routines and competencies. Imitation is not a simple process, however. Miner et al. (1999) found three distinct copying rules. *Frequency imitation* refers to founders copying the most common practices in the population they wish to enter. *Trait imitation* involves copying the practices of dominant or high-status organizations, regardless of their frequency in the whole population. *Outcome imitation* refers to copying practices that are perceived as successful when used by others. In mature populations, where environments are fairly stable, imitation is presumably a reasonable adaptation by founders to their situation. Miner et al. (1999) suggested, however, that the population-level consequences of individual copying practices are difficult to predict.

At the organizational level, four issues highlight some of the difficulties surrounding copying as a strategy for founders. First, procedural knowledge is easier to copy than declarative knowledge, especially when it has been externalized in training manuals, guidebooks, and performance programs. The tacit knowledge embedded in some procedures, however, defies simple transfer. Second, by copying routines and competencies from existing organizations, founders fail to explore other alternatives that might actually be better (Romanelli, 1999). Entrepreneurs who engage in outcome imitation are especially susceptible to the adoption of worthless managerial fads, given the success bias in their imitation strategy (Denrell, 2003; Strang and Macy, 2001). Exploring other alternatives, however, may not be possible for entrepreneurs forced to improvise under the time constraints of the founding process.

Third, as polythetic groupings, populations do not contain a single best way of organizing but rather a diversity of routines and competencies (McKelvey, 1982). Variety in existing routines poses a challenge to entrepreneurs whose insufficient declarative knowledge prevents them from making informed choices about what to imitate. Faced with overwhelming diversity, they may fail to recognize what does and does not work. Under such conditions, they might fall back upon frequency or trait imitation, solidifying the central tendencies in their population and increasing competitive intensity.

Fourth, copying existing forms from other populations can be dangerous for entre-preneurs because the selection forces operating in one population may not be present in another. For example, if copying occurs across national boundaries, differences in institutional infrastructures may render some routines and competencies inappropri-ate. In Sweden, entrepreneurs in the venture capital industry first looked to California's Silicon Valley for effective modes of organizing their firms. Almost all of the imitators' firms failed. Survivors and subsequent founders developed a distinctive Swedish approach, which proved more successful.

Tension inevitably exists between conformity via imitation and deviation via experimentation. Nascent entrepreneurs depend on sources of knowledge that often carry strong pressures toward conformity. For example, experts advise nascent entre-preneurs to sustain successful traditions within a population. In addition, local con-straints intensify the pressure on founders to borrow from existing forms. For example, resource providers treat new ventures that resemble old ones more generously than innovative ventures, as we discuss in Chapter 9. Paradoxically, the most informed and well-connected nascent entrepreneurs might have the greatest difficulty in breaking away. For outsiders to a population, ignorance of existing norms and practices may lead to the serendipitous adoption of deviant practices (Aldrich and Kenworthy, 1999). Many innovative organizations, of course, will be short lived.

Share knowledge or hoard it?

We noted that general entrepreneurial knowledge comes from many sources. However, specific entrepreneurial knowledge may be more difficult to find, making it exceptionally valuable. Entrepreneurs who discover or create valuable knowledge within a population face a dilemma. Should they codify their knowledge, turning tacit into explicit knowledge? In some industries, inventors seek patent protection for their innovations, thus gaining legal rights over their use. In other industries, innovators are more secretive because they fear that the public revelation of their work in the patent application will damage their competitive position. Procedural and declarative mem-ories are much easier to share within an emerging organization when they are codi-fied and made explicit, but such knowledge is also much easier for outsiders to copy.

Under conditions of competitive struggle, successful entrepreneurs have strong motives to hoard their knowledge (Campbell, 1982). Nascent entrepreneurs thus find their search for entrepreneurial knowledge complicated not only by uncertainty and information overload, but also by barriers deliberately erected to thwart them. If existing organizations withhold or disguise critical knowledge, copying from existing organizations becomes problematic. Nascent entrepreneurs will make many fatal organizing mistakes if they lack work experience within the population and access to expert advice. Poorly connected outsiders, in particular, will have lower rates of success-ful organizational foundings. Paradoxically, however, those that survive will also generate many of the most radically innovative organizational forms.

A countervailing force to entrepreneurial secrecy has arisen with the growth of print and on-line journals covering entrepreneurship and disseminating apparently successful recipes. By focusing on the exceptional practices in populations, rather than the most frequent, these sources encourage *outcome imitation*. For example, *Fast Company* and *Business 2.0* magazines publish articles on the 'best practices' of rapidly growing firms. Nascent entrepreneurs who use such sources may appear to avoid some obvious mistakes made by their less informed competitors, but they also suffer severe cognitive biases by focusing only on successful examples (Denrell, 2003). As Strang and Macy (2001: 162) demonstrated in their computer simulations, a consequence of imitation based only on success stories is 'a world of fad-like waves of adoption and abandonment.'

Selective use of knowledge is called the *representativeness heuristic* by cognitive psychologists, and refers to the willingness of decision-makers to generalize from small, non-random samples. People tend to ignore base rate information on the events they are assessing, and they underestimate the errors and unreliability inherent in small, unrepresentative samples (Kahneman et al., 1982). Busenitz and Barney (1997) compared 124 founders of young firms with 95 managers from two large corporations. Their research showed that new venture founders were more willing to rely on subjective opinions or simple rules of thumb in making decisions than were managers. When confronted with a lack of knowledge sharing, many nascent entrepreneurs will tend to over-generalize from personal experience. This is especially true for entrepreneurs from families with one or two self-employed parents or those who have held managerial positions (Aldrich et al., 1998). Under such circumstances, nascent entrepreneurs may believe that they have the capability of succeeding, in spite of the known odds against them.

Uses of knowledge

Nascent entrepreneurs need strategies for encouraging other people's beliefs in their competence and trustworthiness. If they have not previously been involved in forming a new organization, founders may lack credibility in the eyes of those to whom they appeal for resources. Accordingly, an 'entrepreneur must engineer consent, using powers of persuasion and influence to overcome the skepticism and resistance of guardians of the status quo' (Dees and Starr, 1992: 96). Lounsbury and Glynn (2001) call attention to 'cultural entrepreneurship' as a process of storytelling that mediates between the existing human, social, and financial capital possessed by nascent entrepreneurs and subsequent acquisition of resources. Because founders are pursuing many different resources at the same time, and some targets of their persuasive efforts will resist, pieces of the fledging organization will come together in a rather haphazard way.

Two uses of knowledge by nascent entrepreneurs enhance their chances of bringing together the resources needed by their ventures. First, founders can frame issues in ways that increase their credibility with others. Second, founders can use stories and other means of symbolic communication to assure others that the new venture is on the right track and actually has a future. These uses of knowledge highlight again the dilemma for founders of sharing their knowledge versus hoarding it. Sharing it through issue framing and stories may increase their following, but also reveal their proprietary knowledge to potential competitors.

Issue framing

Issue frames are important not only because of their psychological consequences, but also because of their value as legitimating and motivating symbols. Perceptions and evaluations of risk are highly subjective. The framing of an issue, rather than its actual content, often determines whether people see it as a foolish risk, especially in the absence of objective standards (Tversky and Kahneman, 1981). When external tests of reliability are unavailable, nascent entrepreneurs must find ways of simplifying and stylizing issues and giving them ritualized expressions (Hawthorn, 1988: 114). Noting that pioneers attract unfriendly critics, Lodahl and Mitchell (1980: 186) argued that innovative founders 'must create symbols, language, ritual, and organizational structures, not knowing to what degree they might support or subvert the intended innovations.' Founders who can behave as if the activity were a reality – producing and directing great theater, as it were – may convince others of the tangible reality of the new activity.

Issue framing can create new schemata with powerful psychological effects. Symbolic communication helps charismatic leaders transform members' beliefs, fostering a sense of commitment (Pettigrew, 1979). Charismatic leaders employ several specific rhetorical techniques to change members' beliefs (Fiol et al., 1999). First, charismatic leaders appeal to a common bond with followers, even when breaking established values, so as to appear trustworthy and credible. They do this through the frequent use of inclusive referents such as 'we' and 'us,' as opposed to 'I' and 'you.' Second, charismatic leaders frame issues using high levels of abstraction, thus fostering a degree of ambiguity around their innovative ideas. Similarly, Howell and Higgins (1990: 336) wrote of technology champions 'appealing to larger principles or unassailable values about the potential of the innovation for fulfilling an organization's dream of what it can be.' If founders frame their innovation broadly enough to encompass existing knowledge, they may appear more credible.

Some critics argue, however, that the rhetoric of 'leadership' and 'charisma' in the traditional entrepreneurship literature implies a more hierarchical structure to fledgling organizations than they actually possess, under-emphasizing the socially constructed nature of emergent organizations (Calâs, 1993). In the founding process, founders' intentions interact with those of others in the situation, especially those contributing resources, such as family, friends, and potential employees. Issue framing by founders is not simply an asymmetric imposition of one person's vision on powerless others. Given the small size and precarious status of fledgling organizations, unilateral actions by founders can be hazardous.

Stories and visions

Stories give nascent entrepreneurs the means to explain events without reference to external criteria, although institutional context often influences the efficacy of story telling (Lounsbury and Glynn, 2001). Founders can explain their actions without having to generate consensus on explicit criteria, and stories can subsequently form the currency of communications to a wider public. Leaders create encompassing stories that help people structure their experiences, and use their stories as a means of conveying their *vision* for the organization, attracting a wider following and developing legitimacy. An entrepreneur's vision, according to Pettigrew (1979: 577), represents the 'system of beliefs and language which give the organization texture and coherence.' In his study of the founding of a private British boarding school, Pettigrew (1979: 578) stressed the language used by the school's founder and the way his vision was communicated through stories: 'Visions may contain new and old terminology, sometimes using metaphors and analogies to create fresh meanings. Words can provide energy and raise consciousness.'

The validity of a story depends not just on a set of external criteria, but also on how well the story coheres and is free of contradictions (Fisher, 1985). A founding entrepreneur's 'truth' may well contradict the 'truth' people know. Stories can bridge the gap, by affirming the former without negating the latter. Howell and Higgins (1990: 336) concluded that successful introduction of innovations by technology champions depended on 'the articulation of a compelling vision of the innovation's potential for the organization, the expression of confidence in others to participate effectively in the initiative, and the display of innovative actions to achieve goals.' Gaining legitimacy is inherently a social process, requiring the cooperative efforts of more people than just founders and their creditors.

Summary

Nascent entrepreneurs are not clairvoyant. Lacking knowledge of the future, they must make educated guesses about what tactics will work and in what order to try them. Narrative strategies that persuade some potential employees and investors may baffle others, and founders themselves may be unable to make sense of the feedback they receive from their actions (Weick, 1995). Selection forces operate on the outcomes of actions, not their intended results. Lacking clairvoyance, nascent entrepreneurs must do the best they can, given their current understandings. Learning from trial and error involves frequent mistakes. Ambiguity in the feedback from their efforts makes it difficult for founders to decide what worked and what did not. Under conditions of complexity and uncertainty, most entrepreneurs succumb to social pressures and the security of imitating what others have already done. Thus, most foundings reproduce existing organizational forms, rather than breaking away to create innovative new forms. In Chapter 9, we examine startups that become the foundation of new populations.

Employees, capital, and other resources

Dominating all other statistics on new organizations is one inescapable fact: most new ventures begin small. Because initial endowments are critical to organizational survival, organizations that begin with few resources may be at high risk of early disbanding (Baum, 1996: 79–81; Fichman and Levinthal, 1991). At the same time, extensive resource support from outside constituencies may also impose risks. For example, Ruef (2002b) found that disbanding rates in a sample of business startups actually *increased* with external funding from investors, venture capitalists, and wealthy individuals. Entrepreneurs may have a durable commitment to their ideas and organization, but that commitment is not always shared by others. Information from nationally representative sources reveals that few resources, other than knowledge, are available to most new organizations.

Employees

Most businesses and non-profit organizations are very small when formed, and most change little, if at all, over their lifetimes. Thus, resource requirements at founding are fairly modest. Most firms never add more employees. Of the minority of firms that do grow, most add very few employees. Several studies, for example, found that only 3 percent of new firms added more than 100 employees as they aged (Duncan and Handler, 1994; Spilling, 1996). Archival records on business size show this result quite clearly.

Table 4.3   **Employment size of firms started in 1992**

Number of employees	Percent of all startups	Cumulative percent	Percent of all startups with employees	Cumulative percent
No employees	96.8	96.8	N/A	N/A
1–4	2.3	99.1	71.8	71.8
5–9	0.40	99.5	12.5	84.3
10–19	0.29	99.8	9.0	93.4
20–49	0.16	99.9	4.9	98.2
50–99	0.04	99.9	1.1	99.4
100+	0.02	100.0	0.60	100.0
Total percent	100.0		100.0	
Total number	1,761,475		56,328	

Source: Adapted from *Characteristics of Business Owners*, U.S. Department of Commerce, Bureau of the Census, 1992 (Washington, DC: USGPO), CB092-1, Table 14A, p. 118, and *Characteristics of Small Business Employees and Owners, 1997*, U.S. Small Business Administration, Office of Advocacy, 1997, http://www.sba.gov/advo/stats/ ch_em97.pdf Table 5.4

Using several data sources from the 1992 Characteristics of Business Owners census, we calculated the number of employees for all firms started in 1992. We included only businesses where the owner was also the founder, thus excluding businesses purchased from others or inherited. In Table 4.3, we present information on the distribution of business size in two ways: as a percent of all startups and as a percent of only those startups begun with at least one employee. Almost 97 percent of all businesses started with no employees and an infinitesimal fraction began with 100 or more employees, as shown in the second column. Of those startups that began with employees, about 72 percent had fewer than 5, and about 93 percent had fewer than 20 employees. Thus, even among firms that began with a workforce other than just the owners, most started very small.

The size of new firms varies substantially across industrial sectors. For example, a study of new Canadian firms between 1984 and 1994 divided the population into three industry clusters of about 70 industries each and examined minimum and maximum average firm starting sizes within each cluster (Baldwin et al., 2000). For the 'small' industry cluster, average startup sizes ranged from 0.6 to 11.1, about 11.2 to 36.3 for the 'medium' cluster, and between 36.9 and 1,590.1 for the 'large' cluster. Somewhat surprisingly, survival rates did not vary much by starting size.

Capital

Most founders begin their new ventures without much capital. If they need funding, they obtain it from their own savings, rather than outside sources. Using their own funds allows them to remain autonomous. However, they also start smaller and may be more vulnerable to competitive pressures than organizations with outside funding.

How much capital?

How much capital do nascent entrepreneurs need to start their businesses? Not very much, actually. In 1992, the Bureau of the Census conducted a special survey to ascertain the amount of original capital owners needed to start or acquire their businesses.

Table 4.4   **Starting capital requirements by size of firm, 1992**

Amount of original capital owner needed to start or acquire a business	Female-owned businesses (%)	Non-minority male-owned businesses (%)
None	29.9	22.6
$1,000–4,999	34.2	31.3
$5,000–9,999	7.7	10.5
$10,000–24,999	8.5	12.9
$25,000–49,999	4.5	6.3
$50,000–99,999	4.2	4.7
$100,000–249,999	2.6	3.2
$250,000–999,999	0.9	1.7
$1,000,000 or more	0.4	0.5
Not reported	7.3	6.4
Total percent	100.0	100.0
Total number	[5,888,883]	[10,114,456]

Source: Characteristics of Business Owners, U.S. Department of Commerce, Bureau of the Census, 1992 (Washington, DC: USGPO), CB092-1, Table 14A, p. 118.

The information is only for surviving firms, and thus excludes startups that disbanded before they could be surveyed. Thus, it undoubtedly overestimates the amount of capital with which businesses begin.

In Table 4.4, we show the results of the 1992 survey for female-owned businesses and non-minority male-owned businesses. Two points stand out. First, most owners required less than $5,000 to start their businesses – 54 percent of the men and 64 percent of the women. Second, only a small percentage required more than $100,000 – about 5 percent of the men and 4 percent of the women. Less than half of 1 percent of either group required a million dollars or more. Studies in Germany have found higher capitalization requirements, perhaps because of tighter government rules and regulations. For example, Albach (1983) reported that most founders in his study needed between $30,000 and $40,000, at 1983 exchange rates, to found their firms.

Most businesses thus begin without many employees or much capital. Founders in some sectors, of course, require a great deal of capital. For example, the high technology firms in Silicon Valley identified by the Stanford Project on Emerging Companies (SPEC) found that the average firm required about $2.5 million in startup funds (Burton, 1995). The 172 firms in the SPEC sample obtained outside investments ranging from $10,000 to $30,000,000. As fast-growth firms in the high-technology sector, they represent an extreme position in capital requirements.

Funding requirements are different for owners buying an established business, rather than starting a new venture. Some people become new owners each year without going through the full process of founding a new business, because they open a branch, subsidiary, or franchise of an existing business. They may also purchase or inherit an ongoing business founded by someone else. In the retail sector, franchises are capturing an increasingly large portion of revenues and in the late 1990s accounted for over a third of all retail sales (Bradach, 1998). Opening a branch, subsidiary, or franchise changes resource requirements drastically. The parent firm will provide support, and the potential franchisee must meet strict requirements established by the franchiser. As franchisers often require hundreds of thousands of dollars in entry fees and initial capital, access to such opportunities is restricted to people with substantial savings from previous jobs, business ownership, or other wealth.

Representative national data are hard to find, but apparently around one-quarter of the business population consists of branches or subsidiaries, in the United States and Canada. In the United States in 1982, about 20 percent of all establishments were owned by another firm (Small Business Administration, 1982). (Unfortunately, the SBA has not subsequently replicated the 1982 study.) In the Research Triangle Area of North Carolina in 1987, Aldrich et al. (1989) found that about 25 percent of the *new* establishments were branches or subsidiaries. Branches and subsidiaries are also an important component of the business population in Canada. In 1994, about 24 percent of the firms in the Vancouver Area and Lower Mainland of British Columbia were branches of other firms (Contacts Target Marketing, 1994). Across 320 3-digit Standard Industrial Categories, the proportion of establishments owned by other firms ranged from 0 to 100 percent.

In addition to becoming a new owner by setting up a subsidiary or franchise, owners can purchase an ongoing organization from its founder. Again, representative national data are hard to find, but from various community studies it appears that about one-quarter of all firms are owned by people who did *not* found them. For example, in a study of the Research Triangle Area, Aldrich et al. (1989) found that 28 percent of the independent businesses tentatively identified as 'new' in three sources were actually bought from a previous owner. In the Lower Mainland area of Vancouver, Canada, about 40 percent of firms with more than 5 employees in 1995 had been purchased as going concerns from a previous owner (Aldrich and Langton, 1998). Similar proportions of previously founded businesses were found in studies of the small business populations in portions of three United States cities – Boston, Chicago, and Washington, DC – and three English urban areas – Bradford, Ealing, and Leicester (Aldrich and Reiss, 1976; Aldrich et al., 1983).

Informal sources of capital: self, family, and angels

Most businesses start small because of the terms on which resources are available to them. Founders are often unsure of the market for what they offer and thus must begin with an exploratory probing of the market. Most owners do not borrow capital to start their businesses, either because they do not need it or because the terms that outsiders offer are unacceptable. Accordingly, founders mostly draw upon their own savings, as shown in Table 4.5. Information in Table 4.5 comes from the same survey that generated the information in Table 4.4, conducted by the Bureau of the Census in 1992 and is thus representative of United States' businesses in that year. (The percents do not add to 100 because of multiple mentions. Respondents could check more than one source, although few did.)

Most nascent entrepreneurs draw upon their own savings and personal assets in constructing their organizations. Most have not accumulated sufficient resources to give themselves much of a cushion in their early days. Financing through bank loans or investors can be difficult and disadvantageous for the small business owner for many reasons. Because small businesses are higher risk clients for potential financiers, lenders often compensate by increasing the financial costs associated with the loans, making this a less appealing path to gaining business capital in comparison to personal savings. In addition to the high costs of using financiers, small businesses also

Table 4.5   Sources of borrowed capital by sex of owner, 1992

Sources of borrowed capital	Female-owned businesses (%)	Non-minority male-owned businesses (%)
Spouse	1.3	0.8
Other family members	4.8	5.0
Personal credit card	2.6	2.5
Refinanced home/equity line	4.1	4.4
Other personal loan	4.9	6.8
Not reported	13.0	15.2
Did not need or did not borrow capital	72.2	67.9
Total percent	102.9*	102.6*
Total number	[5,888,883]	[10,114,456]

*Percents do not add to 100 because of multiple mentions – respondents could check more than one source.

Source: *Characteristics of Business Owners*, U.S. Department of Commerce, Bureau of the Census, 1992 (Washington, DC: USGPO), CB092-1, Table 16A, p. 134.

incur the cost of identifying potential financiers and undergoing bonding activities to ensure firm legitimacy. Furthermore, there is also evidence from research on home-based businesses, which comprise a large proportion of all new businesses, that few were eligible for bank loans (Jurik, 1998).

Although some economists have argued that liquidity constraints – lack of funds – inhibit people from attempting to start businesses, research does not support that argument. Using the PSED, Kim et al. (2004) found that neither the level of personal income nor wealth predicted which respondents would become nascent entrepreneurs. Indeed, many entrepreneurs find ways around their lack of funds. Many small business owners use financial 'boot-strapping' methods to decrease capital needs in the startup phase (Freear et al., 1995). These methods include relatives working below market salary, using owners' personal credit cards for business expenses, borrowing from relatives, withholding owners' salaries, taking on freelance assignments from other businesses, and leasing equipment rather than buying it (Winborg and Landstrom, 2000).

Very few founders receive any capital from their parents or other family members, as we noted earlier. Even when parental wealth is potentially available, it does not seem to make a difference in which people actually try to start businesses (Aldrich et al., 1998). Few women or non-minority men obtain funding from their families, as shown in Table 4.5. About 6 percent of men and women borrowed from spouses and other family members. Friends also played a minor role; building up debt on a personal credit card was just as likely as borrowing from friends. Inheritance of a family business is one route around lack of personal assets, but less than 10 percent of owners obtain their firms through inheritance (Aldrich et al., 1983, 1998; Aldrich and Reiss, 1976).

Within some ethnic communities, family members do supply a limited amount of capital to founders. For example, a study of Asian- and white-owned shops in three English cities (Zimmer and Aldrich, 1987) found that Asians obtained funding from family and friends to a much greater extent than whites. By contrast, the proportion using personal savings was not significantly different between the groups. For example, in Bradford, one-third of the Asian owners raised some capital through family ties, compared to one-tenth of the white owners. In the same city, 49 percent of the Asians but only 3 percent of the whites used capital from friends; in the other two cities, differences were smaller but still significant. Perhaps more importantly, Asians' greater access to a wider array of sources meant that no one source of funding predominated for them – on average, they obtained about one-third of what they needed from each source. By contrast, whites either relied heavily on their own savings or, for a small minority, on their families.

Social networks facilitating resource mobilization not only benefit subgroups within particular societies, but may also characterize entire societies (Peng, 2004). In their study of Taiwan's capital markets, Biggart and Castanias (1992) found a large proportion of people relying upon informal credit arrangements, rather than banks or other formal sources. They argued that Chinese social structure has extensive personalized networks of relations that provide an information-rich environment for risk assessments. In these personalized networks, social pressures limit defaults on loans by people who are struggling to make payments.

Business angels are affluent individuals who invest in business startups. Rather than investing their wealth in the stock market or with investment firms, they look for opportunities to invest directly in new ventures. They not only help fund a new business, but also provide expert advice and assistance to nascent entrepreneurs during the founding process. Observers have estimated that wealthy individuals provide the funding for many more startups than banks or venture capital firms. For example, Reynolds (2005) estimated that informal investors provided over five times as much funding to startups as did venture capitalists in 2002–2003. Business angels are more likely to invest in early stage ventures because they are willing to get actively involved in the business and to accept lower rates of return on their investments than venture capitalists. For example, in the United Kingdom, van Osnabrugge (1998) estimated that business angels had invested almost four times as much capital in early stage entrepreneurial firms as venture capitalists. Because business angels invest small amounts in each firm, van Osnabrugge calculated that they probably had invested in as many as 30 to 40 times more new businesses than venture capitalists.

Formal sources of capital

Banks and other lending institutions are reluctant to lend money to startups, except on terms that most nascent entrepreneurs find oppressive. Banks base their loan policies on their loss experience with previous loans in the same class, and thus their managers are aware of the high risks involved in startups (De Meza and Southey, 1996). Because of the high failure rates of startups, bankers demand extensive collateral and high interest rates from borrowers. Unlike most business angels, bankers conduct extensive *due diligence* on nascent entrepreneurs, involving background checks on the founders and a thorough assessment of the venture's financial prospects.

Banks face the classic problems identified by transaction cost economics and agency theory: *moral hazard* and *adverse selection* (Eisenhardt, 1989a). Borrowers pose a moral hazard to banks because they have strong incentives to conceal their shortcomings and overstate their competencies. The problem of adverse selection for lenders arises because the applicant pool for bank loans tends to contain the weaker ventures. New ventures that are strong enough to obtain financial commitments from private sources do not need bank funding and so do not apply for loans. Bank managers have difficulty evaluating the abilities of nascent entrepreneurs, who have every motive to hide their deficiencies and trumpet their strengths, especially given the factors of overconfidence and unwarranted optimism we discussed earlier. Banks must therefore offer terms to cover applicants who will, on the average, not do very well (De Meza and Southey, 1996).

Venture capitalists are also not interested in most new small firms (Gifford, 1997; Gorman and Sahlman, 1989). Startups have no track record on which to raise equity from public offerings, and until they build a record, they must rely on other funding sources. Studies show that formal sources are just not very important in explaining founding rates, even for technology-based organizations (Hart and Denison, 1987; but for an exception, see Delacroix and Solt, 1988). In recent years, venture capital has financed only a small proportion of startups in the United States. In 1995 there were 439 startup/seed venture capital deals. The number of startup deals peaked in 1999 at 813 deals, but then declined to only 184 startup/seed deals in 2003. Similarly, the amount of venture capital invested in young firms has followed a cyclical pattern. Total venture capital investments rose steadily in the 1990s, starting at under $3 billion in 1990 and reaching a peak of almost $106 billion in 2000, but they declined dramatically in the first few years of the current decade, to just over $18 billion in 2003 (PriceWaterhouseCoopers et al., 2004).

Founders have two external routes for realizing the wealth represented by the successful growth of their firms. First, they can take their firms public, through an initial public offering (IPO). Second, they can sell out to a larger firm. Both exit options are fairly rare, compared to the startup rate. The frequency of cashing out through taking firms public has been fairly low; in 1995, only 570 firms had an IPO. After the stock market crash of 2000, the number declined to only 86 in 2002 but then rose to 250 in 2004. Of the 3,186 firms that went public in the 1980s and had their company listed on a stock exchange, only 58 percent were still listed by the end of 1989 (Welbourne and Andrews, 1996: 894; Zeune, 1993). The other route to realizing substantial wealth involves being acquired by a larger firm, but that exit has also been difficult to achieve. Founders who were pursuing that dream faced long odds between 1990 and 1994, as the number of acquisitions of privately owned establishments only averaged a little over 20,000 per year (Small Business Administration, 1998). Instead of being acquired by a larger firm, most businesses that survive are sold to other owners, often through a *business broker*. Business brokers specialize in finding buyers for firms whose owners wish to realize the value of their business, retire, or enter another line of work.

The difficulty of benefiting from a startup by using these options does not discourage many nascent entrepreneurs, for three reasons. First, founders have many reasons for starting a business, only one of which involves *cashing out* – going public or selling the firm (Xu and Ruef, 2004). For example, women often express an interest in gaining greater flexibility in their lives through founding a home-based business (Brush, 1992). Second, information about IPO and acquisition rates is not terribly salient to most founders during the founding process, given the more pressing obstacles they face. Third, optimism and confidence in their abilities blinds some entrepreneurs to the small likelihood of their venture being one of the few to go public or be acquired.

Venture capitalists, and other investors, are probably as important for the mediating role they play in spreading knowledge of effective forms as for their role in funding startups. Moreover, as Podolny (2001) argued, the joint involvement of venture capital firms in entrepreneurial projects also conveys status, reducing the uncertainty experienced by others that seek to judge the quality of entrepreneurial efforts. In later chapters, we will return to the role of venture capital in funding new firms in emerging populations.

Summary

Some economists have puzzled over the seemingly irrational nature of entrepreneurs' perceptions of opportunities and subsequent decisions to enter self-employment, given the poor returns to human capital obtained by most self-employed people. Research on investment behavior (Thaler, 1994), as well as data on the true economic returns to self-employment and business ownership, raise questions about simple economic models of entrepreneurship. People seem to disregard cost–benefit calculations when they become entrepreneurs. For example, Hamilton (2000) showed that, on average, self-employed persons would have been better off economically as employees, and a more comprehensive study extended his results (Moskowitz and Vissing-Jorgensen, 2002). In contrast, sociologists have been more concerned with the social context in which entry occurs and the mobility opportunities presented by such entry.

Driven by diverse motives, entrepreneurs pursue goals that shift as some resources prove unattainable and others fall into their laps. Their ability to obtain resources reveals to entrepreneurs how they are evaluated by other people, and negative assessments cause many entrepreneurs to drop out of the process before they create a fully bounded entity. Others succeed in assembling what they need. In the process, they gain enough control over the required resources to protect them from other users.

Conclusions

We have emphasized two themes in this chapter, based on our interest in the evolutionary importance of variation. First, we presented a model of the process through which new organizations come into existence. We drew on principles from network analysis and social psychology to explain how the founding process unfolds. Rather than positing relatively fixed personal dispositions as antecedents to entrepreneurship, we focused on entrepreneurial learning that occurs during the founding process. Second, we considered explanations for the apparent tendency of most nascent entrepreneurs to replicate the routines and competencies in their population, rather than to break from tradition. Selection forces at the interpersonal, organizational, and population level constrain most variations into a reproduction mode.

Truly innovative startups are often the result of creative experimentation with new ideas by outsiders to a population. Previous work experience and advice from network ties affect nascent entrepreneurs' choice of domains for exploration, limiting their opportunities for radical breakthroughs. Indifference or ignorance of population routines and competencies may give outsiders the freedom to break free of the cognitive and cultural constraints on insiders. Improvisation during the founding process also provides opportunities for creativity and chance events, even by nascent entrepreneurs who believe that they are simply replicating dominant or successful forms in their populations.

Most nascent entrepreneurs begin with almost nothing but their intentions. Few have access to capital and most cannot afford employees. Thus, selection forces wreak havoc upon fledgling organizations. Some abandon the effort. Nevertheless, despite the many discouraging events nascent entrepreneurs encounter during the founding process, others receive positive feedback from their environments and proceed. Through support from their personal networks and the power of entrepreneurial heuristics, many persist and find ways around the obstacles. They also benefit from issue framing and selective use of symbolic communications and stories.

If, in spite of the odds, all the elements in the founding process converge, an organization begins to take shape. As the people dealing with the organization begin to treat it as an ecological entity, the new organization emerges as a social unit with a life of its own. Founders make commitments in the name of the new entity, deal with government agencies as a representative of it, and find that people act toward the organization as if it really exists. If coherence is *not* achieved, then the resources that were temporarily assembled slip back into the environment, potentially available to fill another nascent entrepreneur's needs. In the next chapter, we consider a key aspect of the founding process: the emergence of organizational boundaries.

Study Questions

1. Considering the startup activities mentioned in Figure 4.1, what types of environments are likely to encourage some to be pursued more quickly than others? When does the pursuit (or completion) of some of these activities pose a liability to an emergent organization?
2. It can be argued that both women and ethnic minorities are attracted to entrepreneurship due to prejudice they face in traditional employment relationships. However, rates of entry into entrepreneurial activity differ substantially for these groups (Reynolds and White, 1997), with women evidencing relatively low rates of entrepreneurship and ethnic minorities evidencing high rates. Develop a social network theory to account for this difference in entrepreneurial outcomes.
3. A robust finding in the literature on entrepreneurship and the life course is that the relationship between age and entrepreneurial activity tends to be curvilinear, with respondents around the middle of the age range being more likely to engage in startup activities than younger or older respondents (Sanders and Nee, 1996). Decompose this finding into specific variation in knowledge, resources, and social capital over the life course.

Exercise

1. Select an organization for analysis, using archival and/or interview data. Describe the events that created the organization. When did they occur? Who were the key entrepreneurs involved in the process? What do you know about their social network context and career background? Do these entrepreneurs appear to be 'innovators' or 'reproducers'?

5

Organizational Boundaries

From an evolutionary perspective, the development of organizational boundaries is important for four reasons. First, until organizations become bounded entities, selection pressures can only affect the direction of the founding process and not its ultimate outcome. A true test of the knowledge and resources assembled by founders occurs when an organization achieves standing as a population member. Second, organizations contribute to population dynamics only after they become fully-fledged units of selection. As bounded entities, they become actors that compete and cooperate with others. Third, after boundaries coalesce and activities begin, organizations become viable carriers of routines and competencies. They thus contribute to the reproduction of population-level knowledge and its diffusion. As new entities, they are potential sources of variation within populations. Fourth, after it emerges as an entity, an organization becomes another arena in which new routines and competencies can be generated, nurtured, and possibly copied by others. Every new organizational entity represents another test of an organizational form's fit with its environment, as well as an opportunity to modify the form.

In their struggle to build bounded organizational entities, founders and other participants face serious difficulties. In addition to mobilizing knowledge and resources and using them effectively, they must deal with two other problems. First, they must learn how to maintain organizational boundaries. Second, they must learn how to reproduce their portion of organizational knowledge. What they know and what they can do must endure from day to day, and over generations of newcomers. Preserving this knowledge requires that people play two contradictory roles in organizations: as *users* of what organizations offer through the resources they control, and as *supporters* of what organizations must do to reproduce themselves. From a user perspective, organizations are marketplaces of incentive exchanges and sites for negotiation over inducements and contributions. From a supporter perspective, organizations allocate incentives that constrain members' role behaviors according to some scheme greater than their own needs (Georgiou, 1973).

In this chapter, we examine the dilemma of people caught in these contradictory currents: *users* need to learn only the organizational knowledge serving their own interests, whereas *supporters* need to learn their part of the organizational knowledge that fully reproduces the organization's form. We pursue these themes by focusing on the processes by which new organizations create boundaries and become viable organizations by attracting, recruiting, and hiring applicants. We also focus on the construction of reward and control systems.

Boundary crossing is a way of life: matching organizations and members

Every morning, all across the industrialized world, people re-enact a familiar ritual. Millions of them get dressed, leave their homes, and set off on journeys to other locations, including factories, offices, and other distant work sites. On these journeys, a curious transformation occurs. Their activity rhythm shifts, no longer synchronized by household needs but driven instead by organizational compulsion. Many engage in a difficult struggle to balance the demands of work and family (Jacobs and Gerson, 2004). They try to shed their roles from home and replace them with new ones granting access to sites where most of their fellow travelers are not permitted (Ahrne, 1994). When they arrive at their destinations, most people head straight for a particular location at the work site, ignoring alternative paths. Some go to desks, others to work benches or assembly points. As they settle in, most begin working immediately, with no obvious commands to do so from anyone around them. They simply know what to do, and begin doing it. Computers are turned on, machines fine-tuned, and stacks of papers sorted into new piles. Some work in isolation, whereas others form teams and work cooperatively.

Behind this daily process lies a larger, longer-term selection process involving organizations and people looking for a match. When founders decide to hire workers, they begin a selective process of recruiting and retaining employees who seem likely to fit well with the organization. When people decide to seek work, they begin a process of successively trying different jobs until they find a reasonable fit with an organization. Most young workers try many short-term jobs until they settle into one long-term job. Voluntary associations go through a similar process of recruiting, retaining, and losing people, as they compete with other associations for members (Popielarz and McPherson, 1995).

Do organizations simply announce their boundaries to the world? If it were as simple as that, nascent entrepreneurs and founders would have an easy time constructing their organizations. Established organizations would simply expand or contract as conditions warranted, without regard to their environments. Instead, new organizations struggle to establish and maintain their boundaries. In this chapter, we focus on one part of this struggle, examining the interactions between founders and members in new organizations as they carry out the activities upon which their resource flows depend. We concentrate on selectivity in hiring processes and the development of organizational role systems, rather than newcomer socialization, which we cover in the next chapter. Although socialization of new members plays a key role in boundary formation, socialization processes typically operate on a highly-filtered stream of initiates. Selection forces thus simplify newcomer socialization practices.

Two models of organizational coherence: users and supporters

Given the large-scale boundary crossings occurring each day, what holds organizations together? Organizations coalesce as entities when nascent entrepreneurs gain control over resources and shape them into ongoing exchange relations. If intentions, resources, and boundaries converge, an entrepreneur's activities take on sufficient coherence so

Table 5.1   The Janus principle: two models of organizational coherence

	Associative	Social systemic
Members' relations to organization	Users	Supporters
Role of authorities	Mediate incentives	Allocate incentives
Norms of exchange	Negotiated	Generalized

that the people dealing with the organization began to treat it as an ecological entity, a social unit with a life of its own. Emergence as a recognized entity secures a tentative place for an organization in a population, but its persistence depends upon the continual replication of its routines and competencies. Replication, in turn, depends upon what members do. The category of *member* includes paid and unpaid employees, participants in voluntary associations, officials in government agencies, and others whose working life is subject to organizational control. Sociologists have described the place of members within organizations as *organizational roles*, but this term captures only one side of members' orientations to organizations.

The Janus principle: modes of member orientation

Members participate in organizations in *two* senses: as *supporters* of activities sustaining an organization's needs, and as *users* of organizational resources pursuing their own needs. We can reduce all models of members' orientations to these two basic models, as shown in Table 5.1. Swanson (1971) called the first the *social systemic model* and the second the *associative model*. The social systemic model treats organizations as social systems, sustained by the roles allocated to their participants. Members' roles and the incentives offered within the system mold their behaviors toward supporting the larger whole. The associative model, by contrast, treats organizations as associations of self-interested parties, sustained by the rewards that autonomous participants derive from their association with the organization (Dow, 1988; Georgiou, 1973). These two views have a venerable heritage in the social sciences, particularly in social exchange theory (Blau, 1964; Ekeh, 1974). Despite subtle variations, all perspectives on organizations ultimately use one of these models, or combine the two in some way.

In the associative model, the role of authorities is to mediate *negotiated exchanges* between self-interested users. The power of members hinges on their relations with other members, as well as their place in the organization's opportunity structure. In the social systemic model, the role of authorities is to allocate incentives from within their places in the organizational hierarchy. Members are committed to *generalized exchange*, in which contributions are not directly linked to personal benefits, and they draw power from organizationally allocated roles. The associative model implicitly treats organizations as at constant risk of dissolution, jeopardized by negotiations gone awry. The social systemic model implicitly treats organizations as fairly stable entities, with norms of generalized exchange keeping self-interested members in check.

Authors using an associative model often write as if organizational roles were optional for members. If role behavior were totally voluntary, then compliance with authoritative directives would be a matter of individual discretion. However, as Arrow (1987: 233) noted, 'people just do not maximize on a selfish basis every minute. In fact, the system would not work if they did. A consequence of that hypothesis would be the end of organized society as we know it.' Social systemic models posit that organizations cannot be sustained by self-seeking individualistic behavior alone. Reproduction requires supporter behavior too, or else an organization's resources might be squandered.

Authors using a social systemic model often write as if the reproduction of organizational routines and competencies occurs automatically, regardless of members' orientations. However, organizational authorities pursuing this line of control pay a price in substantially increased control costs. Authorities who routinely neglect users' interests increase the likelihood of disquieting reactions, such as exit and voice (Hirschman, 1972). Even though *silence* is probably the modal response to neglect, exit and voice occur often enough to raise the costs of organizational maintenance for many unresponsive organizations (Aldrich, 1979: 232–242). Thus, authorities' efforts at maintaining organizational boundaries typically involve activities that acknowledge members' interests as well as those of the organization.

We use the term *supporter* to refer to members' behaviors, not their emotional state. Being a supporter carries no necessary implication of emotional commitment to an organization. Commitment, satisfaction, and other affective orientations to an organization are empirical questions, contingent upon job, work group, firm, and industry characteristics (Kalleberg and Griffin, 1978; Lincoln and Kalleberg, 1990). Similarly, the concepts of *supporter* and *social identity* are related but not identical. Identifying with an organization means that people perceive themselves as psychologically intertwined with the fate of a group, without necessarily identifying with the group's goals, or internalizing all its values and attitudes (see Kreiner and Ashforth, 2004, for an expanded model of organizational identification). We use the term 'supporter' specifically to cover organization-sustaining *behaviors* that are not linked to self-interested outcomes. Becoming a supporter does not mean 'becoming a better person,' but rather becoming a person who supports the in-role behaviors of other members.

Constructing members

Organizations must work with the materials made available to them by their environments, turning them into organizationally useful resources. Members – employees, volunteers, and other participants – are arguably the most critical resource, given the flexibility and creativity they bring to organizations. Not all organizations, of course, take advantage of the potential inherent in their human resources. Employers increasingly offer temporary or contingent work, rather than full-time and permanent employment, leading to concerns about low pay and a lack of benefits (Kalleberg et al., 2000). As a result, many members resist the notion that they are, in fact, 'resources' for any specific organization (Barley and Kunda, 2004). Most people are members of more than one organization, thus generating competition for their time (McPherson, 1983; Popielarz and McPherson, 1995). New organizations, in particular, face difficulties in obtaining adequate human resources.

Except for 'total institutions' (Goffman, 1961), members of most organizations have some control over their entry, and thus raw power and naked coercion are ruled out as methods for constructing members. Even though most people in capitalist societies must work for wages or salaries to sustain themselves, and are thus wage-dependent

(Perrow, 1991), they are formally free to choose their employers and to change jobs. Similarly, most organizations have a substantial amount of control over the entry and exit of members, and therefore deal with only a subset of all possible members (Aldrich, 1979: 223–228). Member control and organizational control interact to present organizations with entrants, but members' potential contributions are only fully realized when they accept – at varying levels of commitment – organizational roles.

Recruitment: new organizations and new members

Early decisions about which people to hire, how their jobs are structured, and how new members interact have lasting consequences for new organizations (Baron et al., 1999). Studies of emerging organizations show that most do not grow, as we note in Chapter 7. Of those that do grow, most grow opportunistically, rather than by following a pre-set plan. Opportunistic growth, if not tempered by practices fostering supporter orientations among members, threatens the coherence of new organizations. Growth tends to increase horizontal and vertical complexity in organizations, creating a major administrative challenge for managers (Blau, 1970). Increasing complexity generates units and interest groups that may develop objectives at odds with those of the founders and leaders. Organizational coherence depends upon founders achieving a balanced mix of supporter and user orientations among the recruits that remain with their organizations. Becoming part of a bounded entity is not just something 'done to' members, however. In many respects, members are fully compliant in the process, as we will explain in the next chapter.

Founders recruiting their first employee face a situation that has received little attention in the human resource management (HRM) literature. 'Most of the strategic human resources management research has been conducted with cross sections of large, established organizations, while targeting the practices of their human resource departments' (Welbourne and Andrews, 1996: 892). That literature concentrates almost entirely on older medium- and large-sized firms, with a few exceptions (e.g. Aldrich and Langton, 1998; Baron et al., 1999). Authors typically take for granted the existence of a human resource professional. For example, Rynes and Barber (1990), in their review of the literature on applicant attraction strategies, implicitly assumed that organizations have an HRM professional staff, even though some of their propositions were clearly applicable to smaller and newer organizations. Thus, writings on HRM are only partially applicable to the genesis of a small firm.

Human resource practices are among the last activities formalized in growing firms. O'Reilly and Anderson (1982: 7) collected survey data on 127 firms in the Los Angeles area and found that 'the personnel function in firms of fewer than 300 employees was either nonexistent or rudimentary.' They followed up this pilot study with a survey of 143 Fortune 500 firms. Based on the combined sample of 290 firms, they concluded that 'firms with less than 1,000 employees typically have no separate personnel function unless there is an extensive legislative burden, rapid growth, or special circumstances such as being a subsidiary of a large firm. In these circumstances, the personnel function is almost invariably a bureaucratic one with no influence. Only when there are more than 2,000 employees does the personnel function appear to develop to the point that college-trained personnel officers are employed' (O'Reilly and Anderson, 1982: 11). In Welbourne and Cyr's (1999) study of firms that had initial public offerings (IPOs) in 1993, the median firm was six years old and employed 341 people. Only 9 percent of the firms reported they had a vice president of HRM, and another 15 percent had someone doing HRM who reported to a top officer of the firm.

Thus, founders and a few trusted employees usually shoulder the responsibility for recruitment in new organizations. Based on their study of high-tech startups in Silicon Valley, Baron and his colleagues (1999, 2001) proposed three common criteria for recruitment: (1) recruitment based on technical skills and experience needed to accomplish immediate tasks; (2) recruitment based on cultural fit with the new organization; and (3) recruitment based on long-term potential. *Skill-based selection* of new employees most closely matches the well-known ideal-type of bureaucracy, as described by Weber (1978), but also requires the most extensive capabilities in human resource management. Given their lack of HRM personnel, many startups fall back on simple assessments of *cultural fit*, often relying on socio-demographic homophily, as described in Chapter 4. Thus, founders and managers tend to recruit people similar to themselves, and organizations tend to attract people who believe that the organizations' other members have similar attitudes and interests. Finally, because new organizations explore many paths before choosing one, some founders employ ambiguous criteria for recruitment. They try to forecast the *long-term potential* of new members while simultaneously considering their emergent organization's short-term needs.

Creating a core workforce

Startup founders face an immediate issue of what proportion of their employees to hire as part of their permanent workforce versus hiring them under other contractual arrangements (Pfeffer and Baron, 1988). If firms are trying to minimize their fixed costs, they have a number of options. First, they may split their workforce into a core of workers who are (nearly) guaranteed permanent employment and another set of workers who are explicitly temporary. Second, they can contract for some of their employees through a temporary help agency, externalizing the costs of recruiting, record keeping, and so forth, but incurring possible transaction costs. Third, they can structure their operations so that some can be contracted out to other firms, including professional services such as advertising and legal affairs, and support services such as mailing and maintenance. Fourth, if they are available, owners may hire children, spouses, and other kin for below-market wages, although family members apparently constitute a small minority of a startup's workforce (Aldrich and Langton, 1998). If they take on any paid workers, most firms hire permanent employees.

Deciding what proportion of the workforce to hire into the core of the new firm involves several tradeoffs. The smaller the core workforce, the lower the fixed overhead expenses and thus the more flexible the firm can be if it runs into cash-flow problems, as many startups do. However, supplementing a small core workforce with temporary and leased workers carries costs for new firms. Hiring a small core workforce means that temporary and leased employees gain knowledge that permanent workers would otherwise learn. Thus, many of the benefits of learning by doing are lost. Temporary and part-time employees are likely to remain 'users' in their orientation to the organization, lessening their interest in supporter-like behavior. Employees pick up a great deal of implicit knowledge that they will have no stake in passing on if they are not in the core (Polanyi, 1966; Shaiken, 1986).

Continually hiring new employees to replace the departing temporary employees also lowers organizational stability, as new employees disrupt organizational knowledge (Carley, 1991). Consequently, the available evidence suggests that most founders concentrate on hiring full-time employees. For example, Aldrich and Langton (1998) found that only 14 percent of the 229 firms in their Vancouver sample began with part-time employees. According to transaction cost arguments, asset-specificity should predict which individuals are recruited as core members (David and Han, 2004). In their analysis of the PSED data set, however, Xu and Ruef (2006) found that specialized skills and ideas failed to predict which members of a startup's assistance network would become core organizational members. Founders apparently used other criteria, such as personal familiarity and local knowledge, in deciding whom to employ permanently.

The labor market for new firms

Given that many older workers have found jobs that are a good match for them, the most readily available recruits for new organization will be disproportionately young. Individuals enter the labor force in their late teens or early twenties. They remain in it until reaching retirement age or becoming disabled. Depending on their occupations, people may thus be in the labor force for three to five decades, although many interrupt their careers with spells of other activities, such as unemployment, child rearing, or further education and training (Rosenfeld, 1992). The majority of the workforce will not find lifetime employment with a single employer. Although for the entire workforce, median employee tenure was approximately four years in January 2004, it was only 2.9 years for workers aged 25 to 34. Older workers averaged much longer tenure: 9.6 years for workers aged 55 to 64 (U.S. Department of Labor, 2004a). About half of all workers aged 45 and older had been with their current employer for 10 years or more, compared to only one-quarter for workers aged 35 to 44. The association between age and job tenure is thus quite strong.

Volatility in organization–employee matching derives from many factors, including new workers coming into the labor force, workers leaving current jobs to find new ones, retirements, and organizational foundings and disbandings. Indeed, Carroll et al. (1992) estimated that organizational foundings, disbandings, and mergers cause at least 25 percent of all job mobility in the United States. For example, in the California savings and loan industry over a 20-year period, foundings increased the mobility of managers between firms by about 13 percent (Haveman and Cohen, 1994). New organizations often recruit employees in labor markets where mobility is quite high, and they add to the turbulence by actions such as hiring workers away from other organizations (Phillips, 2002).

For a variety of reasons, then, people in the United States change jobs rather frequently. Representative data on job changes come from the National Longitudinal Survey of Youth (NLSY), which interviewed men and women in 1979 who were 14 to 22 years old and then followed them until 2002 (U.S. Department of Labor, 2004b). Over that 24-year span, the average person held ten jobs, with more than two-thirds of the jobs held during the first half of the period, when workers were aged approximately 18 to 27. Even as they aged, however, workers continued to change jobs frequently, with people aged 33 to 38 holding an average of 2.5 jobs. The lack of lifetime employment reflects considerable volatility in the labor market, produced by many forces.

Volatility in labor markets is higher in the United States than most other industrialized nations. For example, workers change employers less frequently in Germany and Japan than in American (Carroll and Mayer, 1986; Shirai, 1983). A study of Japanese workers found that an average male worker held about six jobs over his working life (Hashimoto and Raisian, 1985). Using retrospective job history data from a 1975 study, Cheng (1991: 166) estimated that 'an average male Japanese worker who started working at age 16 and continued until age 65 would have made four employer changes and one intrafirm job shift.' In Germany, a much higher proportion of the labor force is unionized than in the United States. Workers also enjoy legal protections against dismissal that are not available to U.S. workers. Consequently, workers in Germany, as well as other European nations, are much more strongly tied to their employers than workers in the United States.

Turbulence in the labor market and the strong tendency for older employees to stay with their current employers strongly affect the mix of user and supporter orientations within new and growing organizations. Many of the potential employees available to new firms are relatively youthful and inexperienced, and they approach organizations with a strong user orientation. The relatively small number of older workers who are available to new firms will have left jobs in which they had developed comfortable routines and expectations about what constitutes a 'job.' For younger workers, accumulating several years of seniority at a new firm means much less than it does to older workers. Thus, younger workers, in the early stages of their work careers, are much less attached to their employers than older workers (Krecker, 1994). However, younger workers do have a stake in building good reputations in job-related networks (Campbell, 1988; Granovetter, 1995).

Searching for new members: formal versus informal search

Founders of new ventures use a mix of formal procedures and informal searches, such as recruiting through social networks (Aldrich and Langton, 1998). Depending on the methods chosen, founders may have difficulty achieving a balance between user and supporter orientations in their workforce. They face added pressures because, unlike established firms, they are often recruiting employees for positions that have never been filled. Position descriptions, as well as job expectations, may be difficult to articulate. In this section, we consider two key features of recruiting: what are the consequences of hiring strangers, and to what extent will using social networks reduce reliance on strangers? In conjunction with some recruiting criteria, such as hiring for cultural fit, organizational coherence is facilitated by selection through social networks and blending processes in small groups. However, they do not assure it.

First, young firms face a central concern: how many *strangers* should they recruit? What fraction of the workforce will be unknown to one another? The more strangers hired, the greater the problem of molding a coherent organization. Hiring many strangers, for example, raises the potential for opportunism and purely instrumental behavior by recruits, thus lowering organizational coherence (Williamson, 1994). Boundary maintenance is tenuous for organizations because relations between organizations and members are inherently ambivalent, and neither can fully know the other (Smelser, 1998). Selecting agents use as much information as they can manage, but uncertainty remains. Moreover, until entrants are inside their organizations, they cannot fully know what membership is like. Consequently, sorting and re-sorting goes on continuously, through termination, quitting, and other forms of exit (Stewman, 1988).

As organizations recruit more strangers, uncertainty increases because of imperfect knowledge on both sides of the employment relation. 'The information workers hold about the value of a prospective job is highly imperfect because certain properties of jobs … are difficult to assess in the absence of actual employment' (Halaby, 1988: 12). To the extent that workers have incorrectly anticipated what a job will be like, a new firm may incur increased recruiting and retention costs (Jovanovic, 1984). Founders can lower their costs if they search in markets they already know. As we noted in the previous chapter, some nascent entrepreneurs start organizations in populations with which they are familiar because of previous employment or other contacts. If they recruit members via these same contacts, they increase their chances of finding people with relevant competencies.

When firms begin recruiting strangers, they must consider additional institutional requirements, such as creating job advertisements that resemble those already familiar to job seekers. In Baker and Aldrich's (1994) research on new firms in the Research Triangle Area of North Carolina, owners hired strangers on an impersonal basis, typically through newspaper advertisements or college recruiting offices. A startup firm's first job descriptions were created to advertise an opening and were very simple. The advertised jobs tended to be relatively standard ones used by other firms in the industry, which made them understandable and legitimate to people reading the advertisements (Aldrich and Fiol, 1994). Unlike the amorphous early senior positions that founders filled with persons already known to them, relatively junior jobs tended to be fairly well defined and required a set of skills that founders could describe concretely.

Second, just as *social networks* play a critical role in founding organizations, they also influence the recruiting of new members. Strong ties to kin make them a likely target for early recruiting and thus family members will be called upon to fill in when the work becomes overwhelming. The spouses of married owners typically contribute at least some unpaid labor to the business (Zimmer and Aldrich, 1987). Typically, however, few extended family members are in a position to aid founders (Aldrich and Langton, 1998). Young children can only work when they are not in school, and older children are not available because they are beginning their own careers. Most small and medium-sized business owners, in fact, say they do not want their children to follow them into the business because of the long hours, low returns, and high risk (Aldrich et al., 1983).

Most social network recruiting takes place through weak rather than strong ties, as shown in studies of job search (Granovetter, 1995). For example, roughly three out of five male respondents in a study of the Albany-Schenectady-Troy area of New York in 1975 used personal contacts to find their first jobs. A similar proportion also used personal contacts to find their most recent jobs (Lin et al., 1981). Ensel (1979) replicated these findings, and he also found a strong same-sex basis in the job-finding process: men were especially likely to use other men as a link to new jobs. Campbell (1988), in her 1984 study of the Research Triangle Area of North Carolina, also detected evidence of gender-bias in how people use networks to find jobs.

Some job applicants gain advantages when using intermediaries in their job search. In research conducted in a large globally diversified financial services institution, Fernandez and Weinberg (1997) found that applicants for jobs in the bank who were referred by current employees were more likely to obtain interviews and more likely to be hired than non-referred applicants. However, subsequent research has raised questions about the benefits of contacts for job outcomes. Using survey data collected in the early 1990s from samples in four cities in the United States – Atlanta, Boston, Detroit, and Los Angeles – Mouw (2003) found that the possession of social capital did not improve occupational attainment or even the probability of using contacts for job searches. Some effects on wages were apparent in Mouw's results, although these are likely to be spurious, reflecting the unmeasured impact of homophily when the acquaintances of successful job seekers are other successful individuals.

Recruitment through networks and word of mouth generates members about whom something is already known. Fernandez and Weinberg (1997) found that the advantages gained by referred applicants were partially due to pre-screening by current employees, who could judge whether an applicant would fit the bank's criteria. Naturally, many firms do not rely on pre-screening to the same extent: the major advantage gained by referred applicants in this particular study followed from the bank's desire to give current employees a sense of empowerment by taking their recommendations seriously. Under conditions of uncertainty, recruiters thus gave referred applicants the benefit of the doubt over whether to interview them. As a consequence of listening to employees' suggestions regarding hiring, social obligations were reinforced between 'newly hired workers and the employees who have recruited them' (Fernandez and Weinberg, 1997: 899). Under these conditions, members become more receptive to the supporter orientation upon which organizational coherence depends.

Increasing coherence

Selection forces within emerging organizations tend to reduce their internal variability, thus increasing coherence by making them more homogeneous. For example, Mouw (2002) found that employers who relied on referrals from their employees had job applicants who closely resembled their current employees, thus perpetuating racial homogeneity within firms and racial segregation across firms. The effect was substantial: when he controlled for the spatial location of firms, employers' use of employee referrals reduced the probability of hiring a black worker by 75 percent in firms that were less than 10 percent black. Hiring via social networks thus tended to reinforce workforce homophily. Similarly, in a study of immigration and labor market conditions in Los Angeles, Waldinger and Lichter (2003) found that extensive reliance on network recruitment tended to heighten organizational boundaries through social closure.

Building on Pfeffer's (1983) model of organizational demographics, a number of studies have shown that relative heterogeneity not only lowers levels of social integration, but also increases turnover. For example, in a study conducted between 1979 and 1985 on 20 work groups in a large convenience-store chain, O'Reilly et al. (1989) found that heterogeneity in tenure lowered within-group social integration. Low group-level integration led to higher turnover rates. Heterogeneity in age did not affect group-level integration, but it did raise turnover rates, and members who were distant in age from an otherwise homogeneous group also left at higher rates. Campion et al. (1993) found that heterogeneity in the background and expertise of work teams negatively affected team effectiveness. In their study of ten towns in Nebraska, Popielarz and McPherson (1995) found that the highest exit rate from voluntary associations occurred among those who were dissimilar from the rest of the group or who felt the pull of other potential group memberships.

MTV – Music Television – is a particularly interesting example of an organization whose effectiveness apparently depends upon age-homogeneity produced by a constant inflow of employees in their early twenties. 'When you are in your early twenties and are working for MTV, you carry in your brain, muscles, and gonads a kind of mystical authority that your bosses don't possess' (Seabrook, 1994: 66). MTV's audience is primarily 18 to 24 years old, and youth in this group are called 'the demo,' a shorthand term for 'demographics.' When MTV was founded, in 1981, the average age of employees was about 25. In the intervening years, despite the efforts of founders and members to preserve the youthful demography of the organization, the workforce aged. Nonetheless, in 1994 the average age of all MTV workers was still only 29. Workers over 30 began to feel uneasy in this culture, and organizational cohesion was preserved by their leaving to take jobs with other television networks or advertising agencies, where they found people in their own 'demo.'

The research we have reviewed suggests that new and small organizations benefit substantially from recruiting practices that attract and retain people who are already at least minimally receptive to the controls they will face as organizational members. New organizations achieve relative homogeneity through various selection practices, allowing their founders to focus on issues other than human resource management. Although homogeneity may have salutary effects on members' abilities to get along with one another, it limits internal variation and may impair an organization's ability to respond creatively to changing environmental conditions. To date, researchers have tested ideas from the organizational demography model on large, well-established organizations, such as universities and Fortune 500 companies. Applying the principles of organizational demography to new firms is a logical, though recent, extension of the model (e.g. Baron et al., 2001). Indeed, we would expect that turnover among members would have a much greater effect in new organizations because much of what people have learned has not yet become embedded in rules and routines.

Evolution of organizational role structures

As founders work with their early hires and organize the processes of producing goods or services, two developments occur that affect boundaries. First, an elementary *division of labor* emerges, because job structures and roles grow in concert with the evolution of organizational routines and competencies. Second, an *organizational form* emerges from the interaction of members within internal and external constraints as they deal with specific selection pressures. From the perspective of individual organizations, an organizational form refers to a patterned social interaction between members that sustains organizational knowledge and orients participants to a common identity. We examine the dynamics of an emerging division of labor below, and take up the construction of organizational forms in the next chapter.

Emergence of a division of labor

The vast majority of new businesses start small, as we pointed out in Chapter 4, with founders working alongside employees to move the organization toward viability. More than nine out of ten start with fewer than 20 employees, and more than two-thirds start with fewer than five employees. Early days are chaotic: founders work long hours, have a hard time delegating activities, and resist formalizing role assignments or job titles. Kimberly (1980: 29) described how the dean of a newly founded medical school worked 16- to 18-hour days, trying to build a reputation for the innovative nature of his school. Kaplan (1994) told of working straight through weekends as he fought to keep his young firm alive. In the uncertain atmosphere of a startup, an organization's structure bears only a remote resemblance to the pictures painted in management or human resource textbooks.

Idiosyncratic jobs

Out of the chaos, some founders succeed in creating order, but many do not. For the startups that achieve coherence, actions taken during this early period create a legacy that may persist long after the events precipitating them. 'Tasks' and 'activities' become formalized as roles and job titles, and if an organization survives, future members will be recruited for jobs that emerged under these formative conditions. Many of the jobs created during a firm's early days are *idiosyncratic jobs*, defined as 'jobs created around individual people, rather than in the abstract' (Miner, 1992: 195). Idiosyncratic jobs may be created by the founders or management to make a place for a promising recruit, or they may be created by employees who carve out new jobs as their organization struggles to adapt its activities to its niche. Early idiosyncratic jobs, and by inference the processes which affect their creation, have important and long-lasting effects (Baker and Aldrich, 1994; Miner, 1987, 1991).

Idiosyncratic jobs often emerge as new organizations put together their initial team. For example, a high-tech startup firm in Washington recruited a senior-level engineer from among local applicants. That engineer's wife was subsequently recruited to perform a variety of duties until a new job could be created especially for her, as her specialty was systems analysis. Having been alerted to her talent through word-of-mouth (in this case her husband), she was hired without a job description and worked in accounting until the organization's systems capability became more formalized. Her supervisor told her that she had superior talent, and while the job function was not there immediately, she should 'bear with them' until they were able to create a job for her. New firms often have the structural flexibility to allow for this type of recruitment and to grow via the accumulation of idiosyncratic jobs.

The effect of idiosyncratic jobs on a new organization's division of labor depends, in part, on two factors. First, early hires may be senior or junior level employees, with differing degrees of responsibility. Second, the scope of the tasks assigned to employees may be broad or narrow. Some employees are hired as *generalists* and given broad latitude in their jobs, whereas others are hired as *specialists* and take on jobs that are more limited. To illustrate the consequences of early hiring decisions, we review some findings from the study of two knowledge-based industries in the Research Triangle Area mentioned earlier (Baker and Aldrich, 1994). The study suggests certain conditions under which a new organization's role structure changes.

Founders in the two industries – environmental consulting, and computer education and training – tended to hire very senior and very junior employees. By contrast, they hired very few employees at middle levels. This practice had consequences for the different ways in which idiosyncratic jobs emerged at junior and senior levels. Early employees were hired through informal recruiting – word-of-mouth or personal networks – and were given senior jobs with general responsibilities. Rather than hiring specialists, founders intentionally hired generalists who had substantial experience in their industries and were willing to accept relatively undefined positions. Some generalists were explicitly hired with the idea that they would eventually become department or division heads if the firm expanded, and all were hired because they needed little additional training to begin doing their jobs.

Some organizations grew beyond the point at which the founders and their early hires could cope with the work. In such cases, founders turned to hiring people for relatively junior jobs that were fairly well defined and required a set of skills they could concretely describe. Founders explicitly attempted to hire the most junior strangers they could find who could do the job satisfactorily. Such potential employees needed to posses only the elementary skills necessary to do the least complex set of tasks in the firm. Hiring for well-defined positions brought some clarity to an organization's role structure, but that was not the reason given for the hires by founders. Instead, they mentioned gaining control over costs and the need to avoid building 'hierarchy' and levels of middle management into their firms.

Hiring generalists early on, through informal channels, and specialists later, through more formal channels, created a *demographic gap* in the firms, with very senior people at the top and very junior people at the bottom. The small companies had few people in mid-level positions, and few junior specialists were being trained to move up into middle positions. Like most small organizations, the firms lacked employee development and management training programs. Therefore, junior employees were not being prepared to take on managerial responsibility. Consequently, if a firm expanded further, outsiders were hired to fill its middle management positions.

Senior hires tended to play somewhat diffuse general organizational roles, rather than filling specifically-defined jobs. Senior people were brought into new firms based on particularistic criteria, personal acquaintance, and trust. Most *joined* the firm in a very general sense, rather than coming into a pre-defined position. As the roles of the early senior hires coalesced into more clearly defined patterns, they became idiosyncratic by definition, as they evolved around the particular talents of the person in the job. Similarly, Miner and Estler (1985) described a process of *accrual mobility* among staff employees at a large California research university. As people accumulated responsibility and knowledge well beyond the normal growth of their roles, their jobs evolved into new positions. Their new responsibilities stretched their career path horizons further into the future.

Three conditions sometimes led to idiosyncratic jobs being created around junior employees: high employee turnover, sudden growth spurts, and managerial delegation of autonomy. First, voluntary turnover was quite high in these young firms: many more people quit than were fired. When someone quit on short notice, founders were often forced to assign their job tasks to another employee, even combining two jobs into one, and in the process, they discovered employee skills that had gone unnoticed. Second, sudden growth spurts sometimes gave junior employees an opportunity to take on more responsibilities, as not enough new members could be hired from outside and senior members were overwhelmed by the increase. Junior employees could then be allowed to keep the new responsibilities they had added to their old jobs. Because growth was unpredictable and uneven, founders were unable to plan when junior employees would get such chances. Third, as Miner (1992) noted, if given enough autonomy, employees sometimes take the initiative in constructing their own idiosyncratic jobs, based on their unused skills and their opportunistic matching of these skills to emergent task requirements. Such opportunities were often found in the early days of the firms studied, as founders neglected formalizing job definitions in the interests of getting on with the work.

The evolutionary significance of junior idiosyncratic jobs

Idiosyncratic jobs increase internal variability and give organizations a chance to take advantage of hidden employee skills, thus adding to their stock of organizational knowledge. Many employees have skills that are not formally required by their job descriptions. As members gain experience in their jobs, their understanding of organizational knowledge deepens and becomes more cognitively complex (Chi et al., 1988). As they become more experienced, they begin to see that specific tasks, previously seen as separate, are actually interrelated. Hidden skills, previously untapped, come to the surface. They also may begin creating more encompassing conceptual categories for activities. New categories allow them to recognize holes in their organization's competencies. Experience, then, gives members a more analytic understanding of how their jobs fit into the overall activity system.

Consequently, organizations that allow the creation of idiosyncratic jobs around junior employees may become better aligned with their environment. Founders' abilities to create abstractly-defined jobs are limited by their imperfect understanding of existing routines and competencies and how they relate to environmental contingencies. Jobs defined by founders may not reflect the tasks a firm needs to accomplish. The more that organizations and their environments change, the lower the probability that founders' initial definitions will reflect current needs. Were jobs created solely on the basis of internal selection criteria, organizations would eventually lose touch with their environments.

By contrast, allowing idiosyncratic jobs to evolve and displace or supplement previously-defined jobs unlocks the creative potential inherent in members' abilities to learn. An organization might thus be able to exploit relevant employee skills that were concealed in an old job assignment. Indeed, organizations that focus too rigidly on defining expectations around specific jobs, rather than larger organizational needs, run the risk of discouraging variation that could benefit them. Welbourne's (1997: 15) research suggested that large bureaucratically structured organizations encouraged employees to work on their own jobs at the expense of 'working for the overall good of the company.' Some theorists have labeled such company-regarding activities *organizational citizenship behavior* (Morrison, 1994), insofar as members engage in behavior that goes beyond what is formally required.

Summary: emergence of a role structure

In new organizations, most of the routines and competencies needed are borrowed from other organizations, thus ensuring the population's reproduction. However, many will also have to be produced, on the spot, by knowledgeable members responding to immediate contingencies (Schön, 1983). Organizational knowledge and new roles emerge from these situated responses, and boundaries become more salient to organizational members. A new organization's division of labor thus emerges not just from pre-planning by founders, but also from the accumulation of responses to organizational problems encountered during the startup phase. As Sitkin (1992) observed, a series of small losses will keep organizational members in a learning mode and blunt any feelings of complacency. Organizations thus learn from their experience during the founding process. Idiosyncratic jobs are an important part of this process, together with members who are willing to take on tasks not falling within their formal job descriptions. Organizational structures that allow or encourage variation promote the production of new knowledge, but variability poses a threat to organizational coherence until internal selection criteria are established (Carley, 1991).

Organizational reward and control systems

In capitalist societies, most people work for a living. To attract and hold members, organizations must reward them with an income and other inducements. New organizations usually adopt the reward and control systems common in their populations, but organization-level variations are possible. HRM texts are a compendium of useful information regarding reward systems in established organizations, but they tend to overlook the special circumstances facing new organizations. In new organizations, growth by adding members may increase the tension between user and supporter orientations. In the associative model, founders need to structure reward systems to appeal to members as users, who are seeking personal benefits from their affiliations. In the social systemic model, founders need to create control structures that protect the coherence of their organizations by turning members into supporters. Understanding organizational evolution thus requires that we investigate how organizations manage the tension between user and supporter orientations.

What are reward and control systems?

Reward and control systems must include procedures for: (1) evaluating the performance of members; (2) rewarding or compensating them, not only for their direct job performance but perhaps also for other, more indirect contributions to the organization; and (3) controlling and directing workflow (Edwards, 1979). These systems vary widely across different organizations, and are empirically quite diverse. In their typology of incentive systems, Clark and Wilson (1961) noted three common approaches to rewarding organizational members. Some organizations rely on *material* incentives, such as salary, equity, or benefits. Others stress *purposive* bases of attachment to the organization, fostering commitment to collective goals and pride in challenging work. A third set of organizations build *solidary* networks in the workplace, believing that a primary source of attachment for many members is friendship with their colleagues and a sense of personal belonging.

Systems of control are equally diverse, as emphasized by Baron and colleagues (1999) in their study of Silicon Valley high-tech startups. Managers in some firms engage in *direct* oversight, stressing relatively continuous supervision of their workforce. Others depend on *formal* oversight, emphasizing conformity to procedures that organizational members believe are legitimate. Because both of these systems of control can lead to considerable administrative overhead, many startups rely instead on *peer culture*, where organizations exercise control through the informal socialization of new employees. Finally, managers in some startups do not believe that norms of control are transmitted within those organizations at all, but rather are imported with the recruitment of new employees, given their internalized norms and formal education. This leads to a *professional* system of control, akin to that found in architectural firms, medical groups, universities, and similar organizational forms.

Table 5.2   **Ideal-types of organizational membership models**

Membership model	Recruitment	Rewards	Control structure
Autocracy	Skills	Material	Direct
Bureaucracy	Skills	Purposive	Formal
Commitment	Fit	Solidary	Peer Culture
Star	Potential	Purposive	Professional
Engineering	Skills	Purposive	Peer Culture

Source: Adapted from Baron et al. (1999).

On the surface, the combination of different systems of reward and control seems to lead to a large, and bewildering, set of options for developing the formal boundaries of emergent organizations. Indeed, these options are expanded further when different criteria for the recruitment of new members are added to the mix, as discussed earlier in this chapter. Among startups, however, these membership models often cluster into a relatively small set of ideal-types (Baron et al., 1999), as shown in Table 5.2. The model of *autocracy* draws inspiration from Taylorism and scientific management, promoting recruitment based on skills, attachment based on material rewards, and direct supervision of the workforce. The model of *bureaucracy* matches the ideal-type emphasized by Weber (1978), entailing meritocratic recruitment, attachment based on purposive rewards, and a control structure characterized by rationalized rules. Both of these membership models tend to draw relatively rigid organizational boundaries that separate the personal and organizational lives of their members.

Organizational boundaries tend to be more permeable in the remaining membership models. The model of *commitment* recruits members based on cultural fit, provides solidary rewards, and builds on peer socialization as a means of control. In studying direct-selling organizations (DSOs), such as Amway, Biggart (1988) found that a commitment model tended to be preferred in the absence of a clear boundary separating DSOs and family units. In other contexts, such as universities, the challenge to organizational boundaries arises from the prior professional socialization of members. The *star* model of membership often develops in these cases, advocating recruitment based on long-term potential, purposive rewards, and a control structure based on internalized professional norms. A final ideal-type of organizational membership tends to be associated in particular with regions such as Silicon Valley, which have an agglomeration of skilled and mobile employees. Dubbed the *engineering* model, it recruits based on technical skills, applies purposive rewards, and relies on peer culture as a control structure.

Reward and control systems can strengthen organizational coherence, if they promote a supporter orientation among members and reduce turnover. Changes in membership models can prove especially disruptive in this respect (Baron et al., 2001). For young companies, personnel instability disrupts organizational knowledge if it still resides in individuals rather than in rules and routines. By contrast, if an organization has evolved to the stage where established routines and competencies codify selection criteria, turnover may have little effect on performance. Indeed, turnover may actually increase opportunities for learning in established organizations by disrupting existing patterns of communication and bringing in new knowledge (March, 1991).

Organizational reward and control systems are linked to the wider society through their fit with institutionalized norms and values regarding legitimate work practices

(Dobbin et al., 1993; Kelly, 2003; Selznick, 1969). The social context of the times constrains workplace authority at the organizational level and affects the extent to which workers perceive a reward system as legitimate. In the United States, workers' attachment to their jobs is affected by a process in which 'workers grade governance practices and calculate authority costs by reference to a belief in legality' (Halaby, 1986: 646). Workers in the United States bring to their jobs a set of expectations about what principles should guide an employer's reward, discipline, and other practices. Guiding principles include universalism (equality and fairness), due process, and non-arbitrary evaluations of achievement.

For new organizations in the United States, these principles are an institutional constant in the short run and a feature of the American landscape to which all new organizations must adapt. As Selznick (1969) noted, an endogenous normative order develops over the long term within organizations that *reflects* a nation's labor laws. However, the internal order can also *influence* the laws, if opponents bring labor disputes before industrial tribunals and the courts. In addition to national norms, values, and regulations, organizations must also attend to the principles followed in their populations. For example, industries vary in the extent to which they use negotiation, arbitration, and mediation systems to settle workplace disputes (Kochan and Osterman, 1994). Organizations vary in how well they convince workers that they conform to legitimate principles, and lack of conformity constitutes one more selection pressure on new organizations.

Even if organizations follow general societal norms, they must also confront a problem that occurs in any situations where benefits or burdens are distributed. Do members perceive the system as just, in a distributive and procedural sense? 'Evaluations of the fairness of the resulting distributions are the purview of *distributive justice*, whereas *procedural justice* focuses on the fairness of the processes leading up to the distribution' (Hegtvedt and Markovsky, 1994: 257). For example, in the Research Triangle Area of North Carolina, the CEO of a rapidly growing medical services firm bemoaned the pressures he faced in trying to keep up with the human resource needs of his firm. The firm was growing too rapidly to promote from within, because young employees had not yet acquired the experience needed to fill middle-management jobs. Consequently, the owner brought in outsiders to fill jobs in which they managed insiders who had been with the firm since its startup days. Persons passed over by this policy were confused and resentful over their treatment by a founder they had previously perceived as fair-minded. Their concepts of procedural justice had been violated (Hegtvedt and Markovsky, 1994). Haveman and Cohen's (1994) study of career mobility in the savings and loan industry indicated that outsiders moving into the industry filled many managerial jobs in newly founded firms. Their results suggest that many of the young firms in that industry faced similar issues of fairness and justice.

Systems for allocating rewards

Aside from the basic distinction of material, purposive, and solidary incentives, we must also consider the system of allocating rewards. Two dimensions are particularly important in new organizations because of their effects on the user/supporter orientation of members. First, they can be contingent or non-contingent on performance. Second, they can be based on individual or collective characteristics. *Contingent rewards* are based on individual, group, or overall organization-level performance,

Table 5.3   *Bases on which job rewards can be given: two dimensions*

Rewards are	Policy level	
	Individual	Collective
Contingent on Performance	Individual's performance e.g. productivity bonus	Group/unit's performance e.g. gain sharing
Non-contingent	Membership benefits e.g. salaries based on job description	Collective benefits e.g. annual cost of living increase

whereas *non-contingent rewards* are benefits that flow simply from affiliation with an organization or from being in a particular status in an organization. *Individual rewards* are based on a specific individual's characteristics or performance, whereas *collective rewards* are based on a total unit's characteristics or performance. They may be given at the group, team, or organization level.

In Table 5.3, we have cross-classified these dimensions to produce a two-by-two table, with an example for each cell. Two complications tend to affect the choice of systems for allocating rewards. First, contingency theories of organizations argue that the degree of member interdependence built into the reward system should match that of the task structure (Hackman, 1987). However, as we noted in the last chapter, founders draw on many sources in constructing their organizations, such as personal experience, industry-wide practices, and borrowing and imitation from practices observed in other industries. Accordingly, task structures and reward structures are not always in harmony, raising the issue of potentially disruptive conflict (Welbourne and Andrews, 1996).

Second, *technological separability*, or the difficulty involved in monitoring individual productivity, complicates the assessment of workers' contributions (Alchian and Demsetz, 1972). If task interdependence is very high, founders will be unable to separate the individual contributions of members (Williamson, 1981). Under these circumstances, contingency theory advocates creating a matching collective reward structure. For example, the issue of monitoring of individual productivity arises in startups with diverse knowledge bases and founders who lack the technical expertise to understand thoroughly all aspects of the business (Baker, 1995). Under such conditions, founders may have to rely on collective reward structures, regardless of the task structure. However, monitoring is less of a problem in small and emergent organizations, where founders are closely involved in most aspects of their activities, than in the large organizations typically studied by industrial economists and HRM theorists.

Contingent-individual rewards focus members' attention on their own contributions, and can be tailored to fit each member's circumstances. However, such rewards might also raise the salience of a user orientation and create a competitive atmosphere within an organization, perhaps heightening employees' perceptions of intra-organizational inequality. For example, in 1997, about 13 percent of the common stock of the 200 largest U.S. firms was reserved for contingent rewards to their executives (Morgenson, 1998). Such rewards raise managers' equity in firms and thus may spur them to higher performance, but they may also harm morale among the excluded employees. Competition among members inhibits the cooperation needed in an organization's early days, when routines and competencies are still being worked out. Individual rewards that are based on performance may also suppress members' interests in their non-job activities and lower their interest in pursuing variations that benefit their team or group (Welbourne, 1997).

Contingent-collective rewards are also performance based, but they focus on achievements at a team or group level, providing members with inducements to cooperate to improve their collective lot. Welbourne (1997: 17) noted that *gainsharing* and other contingent-collective plans 'reward teamwork, entrepreneurial behaviors, and organizational-based behaviors.' Gainsharing involves paying a bonus to all employees in a business unit when the unit achieves higher productivity or some other target. A 2003 survey of American workers found that access to contingent-collective rewards was much less widespread than access to non-contingent rewards, such as medical care and retirement benefits (U.S. Department of Labor, 2004c). For example, only 5 percent had access to a profit-sharing bonus and only 11 percent had access to stock options. Benefit availability varied substantially by firm size, with 18 percent of workers in firms of 100 or more having access to stock option plans, compared to only 4 percent of workers in smaller firms.

In contrast, startups in the past few decades have made such benefits more widely available to their employees. For example, Welbourne and Cyr (1999) found that 37 percent of the firms in the sample of IPOs from 1993 had incentive stock option plans for all employees, 28 percent had stock purchase plans, 7 percent had employee stock ownership plans (ESOPs), and 12 percent had profit sharing. None of these plans had a significant association with changes in stock price.

Large Japanese firms have proved particularly adept at designing team-based incentives (Lincoln and Kalleberg, 1990; Nonaka and Takeuchi, 1995). They reward employees for suggestions that improve team productivity and, when times are good, pay large year-end bonuses. The principles they use are also applicable on a smaller scale (Weber, 1994). If problems of shirking or free-riding can be overcome, such contingent-collective rewards enable an emergent organization to preserve a team-learning orientation among its members.

However, founders still face the issue of whether to treat groups, teams, or the entire organization as the collective for purposes of rewards. The more inclusive the unit chosen, the greater the likelihood that members will focus on organizational performance, rather than their own unit (Welbourne and Gomez-Mejia, 1995). Offsetting that principle, larger units tend to encourage free-riding and shirking. Research on free-riding and cooperation has found that greater cooperation in groups is associated with small size, high visibility of individual efforts, and high feelings of personal responsibility by group members (Wagner, 1995). In new organizations, the first two conditions are typically present. For the third condition, founders manipulating task interdependencies can amplify feelings of personal responsibility.

Non-contingent individual rewards are benefits members receive because of their organizational position, rather than their performance. In new organizations, founders may give themselves a bigger office or a company car. They sometimes offer ownership to early hires rather than late hires, as an incentive to join early. *Non-contingent collective rewards* are typically given to all the members of a new organization, such as Friday afternoon parties, weekend retreats, and markers of organizational identity, such as baseball caps and T-shirts. They can also be material, such as annual cost of living increases. Established firms in the United States offer a wide variety of such benefits to their employees: for example, retirement, medical care, life insurance, disability benefits, and even child care. However, access is strongly associated with full versus part time status, by unionization, firm size, and industry (U.S. Department of Labor, 2004c).

Purely collective rewards make salient the supportive role that all members play in a new organization. Welbourne and Andrews' (1996) research on 136 non-financial firms with IPOs in 1988 found that the highest survival rate was for firms that placed a high value on human resources and used organization-based employee rewards. Indeed, competition with established firms puts strong pressure on new firms to offer such rewards. If replicated on other populations and in other periods, their research strongly supports a selection argument based on the resources startups devote to HRM issues.

Contradiction and complexity

In practice, organizations will have some mix of the four types pictured in Table 5.3. Consequently, several contradictory incentives will emerge in a new organization's operations, producing complex, inconsistent demands that founders and members will have to meet, however imperfectly (Boettger and Greer, 1994). For example, founders may offer generous individual-level rewards as a way of inducing extremely ambitious persons to join, but then also offer collective-level rewards to bring them together as a team. Individual and collective level incentives may interact in unforeseen ways, as Wageman (1995) discovered in her research on service technicians at the Xerox Corporation. Using a quasi-experimental design, Wageman showed that group rewards had no independent effect on cooperative behavior, but they did motivate members of already highly task-interdependent groups to perform well.

Contradictory policies may create stress for some members, as illustrated in Tracy's (2004) study of the ambiguities facing correctional officers in jails and prisons. Correctional officers must be respectful of inmates, but at the same time on their guard against suspicious activities. They must make an effort to nurture inmates on the road to rehabilitation and yet not be seen as becoming personally involved with them. Officers must also maintain a consistent stance toward correctional institutions' rules while also exercising professional discretion. Finally, they must depend on their colleagues for support, but not become so dependent that they cannot act autonomously. Tracy argued that officers' abilities to cope with the resulting role ambiguities and tensions depend upon how they frame the dilemmas they face. In particular, if the institution allows members to step back from the paradoxes and reflect on them, recognizing them for what they are, they may gain enough understanding to develop effective coping strategies.

Because they have little chance of completely reconciling the dilemmas generated by rewards based on different premises, organizational members in surviving organizations develop tactics to handle the tensions. They serially attend to conflicting goals, buffer radically inconsistent demands, and simply ignore some things for a while (Weick, 1991). Contending with divergent viewpoints may even lead to creative, non-traditional solutions to the problems an organization faces. Wageman's (1995: 173) research showed that 'individual's preferences came into congruence over time with the kinds of tasks and rewards they experienced.' On a larger scale, Baron and colleagues (2001) found that high-tech startups adopting membership models that deviate from the ideal-types shown in Table 5.2 experience lower turnover when they subsequently adopt one of these models than startups shifting between ideal-types. Organizations that preserve contradictory policies may thus gain an adaptive advantage in changing environments.

Formalizing reward and control systems

Founders probably have only a limited amount of time in which to establish an organization's policy regarding job rewards. If left untouched, early practices will accumulate into an implicit set of priorities, and consequently founders will discover that the emergent system has become firmly established. As in most other features of organizational life, the emergence of stable internal selection criteria poses a difficult problem for founders who subsequently wish to change organizational practices (Baker and Aldrich, 1994; Baron et al., 2001). Organizations that begin with an emphasis on individual rewards may have a very hard time switching to collective rewards, and vice versa. Individually focused reward systems direct employees' attentions to their own responsibilities and careers, perhaps at the expense of the group or overall organizational goal. Collectively focused reward systems emphasize a teamwork orientation, but may lead to shirking and a loss of individual initiative if not implemented consistently.

Organizations with a bureaucratic membership model typically use job descriptions to direct the work of employees, and then judge employees by how well they measure up to the job description. However, new and small organizations rarely create job descriptions, unless they are needed to advertise for job candidates. Internally, owners and managers mostly ignore such descriptions. As we have already noted, role structures often evolve in unplanned ways in new organizations, and consequently they have unclear or ambiguous job descriptions, and a very open appraisal process. Premature formalization of its reward and control system may limit a new organization's capacity for flexibility in the face of changing environmental conditions.

Conclusions

We began this chapter by noting four reasons that evolutionary theory pays attention to the development of organizational boundaries. First, organizations face different selection pressures than nascent entrepreneurs, and until organizations become bounded entities, the outcome of the selection process cannot be judged. Second, organizations must become bounded entities before they can contribute fully to population dynamics. Competition and cooperation in industrial economies tend to occur between organizations, not their founders. Third, routines and competencies are kept alive within the boundaries of organizations. Without the shelter afforded by boundaries, bundles of routines and competencies cannot coalesce into organized action. Fourth, organizations not only keep alive their population's knowledge, but also transform it. New organizations are testing grounds for innovative routines and competencies.

Many organizations never achieve coherence as bounded entities, and others achieve it temporarily, only to lose it again. Founders and members who succeed in constructing strong organizational boundaries still face many obstacles. Their survival depends, in part, on the extent to which members become supporters, as well as users. Organizational boundaries can be made more or less salient, depending upon how an organization structures its membership model, including recruiting, reward, and control systems. New organizations benefit substantially from recruiting members through social networks, as they thus attract people who are already somewhat receptive to the pressures they will face as organizational members. Through such practices, organizations achieve relative homogeneity, allowing their founders to focus on other issues.

Study Questions

1. The contrast between users and supporters generates very different images of the conditions under which individuals will offer assistance to one another in the workplace. For the user orientation, there are strong expectations of reciprocity ('I'll scratch your back, if you scratch mine'), while the supporter orientation relies on norms of indirect exchange ('what comes around, goes around'). Identify organizational conditions under which each type of social exchange becomes more likely.

2. The appearance and disappearance of idiosyncratic jobs calls attention to organizational jobs as possible units of variation, selection, and retention. What theoretical and methodological advantages arise in applying an evolutionary approach to job roles, as opposed to other types of routines?

3. Our discussion of membership models has primarily focused on the perspective of founders/managers seeking to maintain organizational boundaries. Review the models shown in Tables 5.2 and 5.3 from the perspective of other organizational members. What models are most likely to contribute to member satisfaction? What contingencies affect the relationship between membership models and member satisfaction?

Exercise

1. Consider the issue of membership boundaries in the formal organization you selected for analysis in Chapter 4. How would you describe its membership model? Has that membership model changed over time? Why, and with what consequences?

6

Organizational Forms

Founders spend a considerable portion of their time hiring employees and allocating roles, especially in high-growth firms. Organizational roles also emerge through the creation of idiosyncratic jobs. Through frequent interaction, members learn their roles, their portion of organizational knowledge, and how to use such knowledge. Eventually, they develop shared understandings that facilitate the reproduction of organizational routines and competencies. Comprehending this process requires consideration of developments in the fields of social cognition, reference groups, attribution theory, and related domains. Together, these fields emphasize the power of social processes in bringing new organizations' boundaries to life. Without boundaries, organizations themselves cannot be units of selection.

In this chapter, we present a view of organizational knowledge as grounded in interaction between members and in the cognitive schemata they use. We build on the concept of schemata developed in Chapter 4 and examine how shared schemata develop among organizational participants. Schemata influence the kinds of variation generated and create an organization-specific selective retention system. Founders and members may borrow from existing schemata in their population as well as generating new elements out of their own experience. As a result, an *organizational form* emerges: a set of rules that patterns social interaction between members, facilitates the appropriation of resources, and provides an internally and externally recognized identity for an organization. Some organizational forms, such as the membership models described in Chapter 5, help strengthen the boundaries of organizations; others, such as 'network' forms of organizations (DiMaggio, 2001), may challenge typical conceptions of organizational boundaries.

Views of organizational forms

Organizational forms provide taken-for-granted templates for structuring activities in modern society. Although common labels for organizational forms – such as 'universities' or 'hospitals' – imply a well-established, intuitive understanding of these constructs, considerable debate exists regarding the theoretical basis for defining organizational forms. Two dimensions are useful in distinguishing among perspectives on organizational forms, as shown in Table 6.1. The vertical dimension considers the extent to which the definition of an organizational form is seen as objective or subjective in

Table 6.1   Theoretical approaches to defining organizational forms

Focus with respect to role of perception	Focus with respect to organizational boundaries	
	Internal	**External**
Objective	*'Blueprints'* (Hannan and Freeman, 1977; McKelvey, 1982; Pentland and Rueter, 1994)	*'Resource Niches'* (Hannan and Carroll, 1995; DiMaggio, 1986)
Subjective	*'Organizational Identities'* (Albert and Whetten, 1985; Martin, 2002)	*'Cultural Codes'* (Pólos et al., 2002; Zuckerman, 1999)

character, while the horizontal dimension considers whether the definition relies on internal organizational attributes or processes external to the boundaries of organizations.

Traditional approaches to defining organizational forms have generally emphasized processes that occur within the boundaries of organizations. Insofar as organizational knowledge and routines are seen as having an 'objective' existence – that is, somewhat independent of the perception of observers – this suggests that organizational forms can be defined in terms of basic *blueprints* for transforming inputs into organizational products or responses (Hannan and Freeman, 1977: 935). In this respect, some commentators call attention to a subset of 'dominant competencies' that are especially important to particular organizational forms (McKelvey, 1982), while others are interested in a more comprehensive inventory of the routines employed in an organizational setting (Pentland and Rueter, 1994). Taken literally, the blueprint conception of forms implies that the fundamental features of organizations are specified *a priori*, rather than emerging as organizations interact with their environments.

Other organizational theorists treat the relative level of consensus on organizational form as an empirical question, even when viewed from the internal perspective of members. This leads to a subjective definition of organizational forms in terms of *identities*, revolving around the members' sense of who 'we' are (Albert and Whetten, 1985; Kreiner and Ashforth, 2004). Following analyses of organizational culture (Martin, 2002), this approach argues that multiple strands of meaning run through most organizations as they evolve into bounded forms. Although an emphasis on identities may seem to underscore the uniqueness of organizations, students of organizational culture point out that such claims are typically paradoxical, since notions of identity often draw on standardized cultural templates found in the surrounding society (Martin et al., 1983). The concept of an organizational 'form' can capture this internal redeployment of standardized cultural templates.

In this chapter, we address these internal definitions of organizational forms, first considering the knowledge required to sustain formal blueprints for organizational activity and then addressing the often contested organizational culture and identities that evolve in the process. We emphasize the role of forms in structuring individual organizations to show how abstract notions, such as 'blueprints' and 'organizational identities,' are made manifest. Notably, this emphasis differs markedly from the level of analysis employed in other studies of forms, which address features of organizational populations as a whole (Carroll and Hannan, 2000).

In later chapters, we call attention to definitions of organizational forms that focus on processes outside the boundaries of individual organizations. One alternative perspective moves the locus of perception from organizational members to external audiences, defining forms in terms of *cultural codes* that allow the audience to classify organizations and sanction deviance from their categorical schemata (Pólos et al., 2002; Zuckerman, 1999). The other external perspective emphasizes the material, rather than cultural, context of organizations. Accordingly, organizational forms are defined in terms of their *resource niche*, consisting of the 'social, economic, and political conditions that can sustain the functioning of organizations that embody a particular form' (Hannan and Carroll, 1995: 34; DiMaggio, 1986). For example, charter school founders must meet the strict requirements specified in the laws of their states (Renzulli, 2005). Because these definitions call for a sophisticated understanding of the environment confronting organizations, we defer explicit treatment of them until Chapter 9.

Organizational form and routines

From an internal perspective, an organizational form emerges as members' activities begin to involve them more deeply in shared routines. Behaviors and interpersonal relations, not just cognition, catalyze the process of constructing organizational knowledge, as Blau's (1955) study illustrated. Procedural knowledge learned via interaction with others may remain tacit, rather than becoming verbalized as declarative knowledge. In social psychology, investigators have used laboratory experiments to study people's abilities to verbalize their understandings of why they take particular actions. Such research shows that people are able to respond to situations without necessarily having access to the mental or cognitive processes that produced the actions (Berry and Broadbent, 1984). Members may recognize what they should do, but not be able to explain 'why.' Lack of access to those parts of the brain dealing with multiple criteria processing also means that people often lack insight into their own decision-making processes (Lichtenstein and Fischhoff, 1977). Nevertheless, they can participate fully in the routines that help define an organizational form.

Research Illustration 6.1 Routines as a Foundation for Organizational Forms

Brian Pentland's field studies convey a sense of the processes through which members collaborate in constructing an organizational form, seen as a blueprint for transforming organizational inputs into responses. Pentland (1992; see also Pentland and Rueter, 1994) conducted a participant observation study of two software support hotlines at the firms DBI and AP – both pseudonyms – in which technical support specialists responded to customer calls. By collecting detailed information on the routines adopted by support specialists, Pentland sought to understand how organizational members *enact* organizational knowledge (Weick, 1995), learning jointly, rather than separately.

Following Goffman (1967), Pentland identified a 'move' as a unit of analysis in social interaction, involving actions and reactions under the control of participants and meaningful to them.

Customers triggered moves when they called for help. Specialists had to deal with the problem themselves, get help from others, or give the problem to others to deal with. At DBI, specialists dealt with about 32 percent of the calls themselves; at AP, specialists dealt with about 60 percent themselves. The rest were handled collaboratively by either getting help or giving the problem away. As selected moves accumulated, they built up the organizations' role and competence structures. In turn, these structures constituted the organizational forms at DBI and AP, constraining the moves that members could make.

Role structures (Pentland called them 'ritual structures') constituted the social requirements for talk/interaction between members, and between members and customers. Competence structures constituted the explicit and implicit distributed knowledge available to specialists, because of their participation in the community of practice with other specialists. Even though the units' work involved many exceptions, frequent interruptions, and appeared non-routine to outsiders, a set of organizational routines evolved that produced a high degree of regularity in behavior (Pentland and Rueter, 1994). Indeed, contemporary perspectives on routines highlight their ability to handle exceptions (Feldman and Pentland, 2003). Organizational knowledge involved not just the abstract declarative memory needed to solve problems, but also the set of shared understandings generated and retained as situated practices. Procedural memory was meaningful because of the context in which members played out their roles.

Structure evolved via the accumulation of variations selected as members tried to solve problems. Problems evoked responses. If the responses solved the problems, the responses then became part of an organization's knowledge. Lave and Wenger (1991: 29) echoed this theme in their description of how learners participate in established communities: 'the mastery of knowledge and skill requires newcomers to move toward full participation in the sociocultural practices of a community.' When the practices become standardized, they support a consistent view of an organization's form and sense of identity among its membership.

These field studies of technician support lines raise a number of interesting substantive issues. Pentland studied established rather than new organizations. Although the social-psychological dynamics he identified fit well with the view of organizational emergence we proposed in the past several chapters, additional research is required to understand concretely how selection and retention mechanisms favor the survival of some routines and the elimination of others. This empirical exercise seems more straightforward in the case of written rules and routines, involving declarative knowledge (e.g. March et al., 2000), rather than routines based on procedural knowledge. The analytic role of individual cognitive orientations and the collective memory of organizations also warrant further consideration. As individuals, technicians contributed to the construction of their own identity as members of their organization, thus making salient their supporter role. As interacting participants, technicians contributed to the construction of a blueprint defining an organizational form.

Organizational forms and the interdependence of members' schemata

A variety of variation and selection processes shape patterns of social interaction in new organizations. Such processes include: (1) information search routines; (2) modifications of members' cognitive schemata; (3) growing interdependence around shared information; and (4) pressures toward a homogeneous outlook among members.

Together, these processes speed the production of a coherent organizational form and create relatively homogeneous clusters of members. Over time, they also sharply delimit the boundaries of surviving organizations from their surrounding contexts.

Offsetting these developments are political processes in which homogeneous clusters turn into interest groups and coalitions. From the perspective of members as users, such groups frequently attempt to impose their own interpretations on the rest of the organization. In the struggle over organizational resources, interest groups and coalitions may close off their ranks to outsiders or seek allies among them (Pfeffer and Salancik, 1978). Moreover, conflict, creativity, and deviance can generate alternative threads of meaning that can become the basis for differentiated and fragmented organizational knowledge. We explore the issue of diversity within organizational cultures after discussing the four processes shaping members' schemata.

Information search routines

People are constantly seeking information within organizations. In uncertain situations, they may perceive a gap in their knowledge and thus seek more information. If they have arrived at a tentative solution to a problem, they may seek information to validate their interpretation. As they interact, members acquire knowledge about each other's skills. When it is widely shared, members can rely on this information while doing their jobs. Wegner and Wegner (1995) called this pool of shared information a *transactive memory system*. In addition to knowledge needed to perform their tasks, members also seek information for self-enhancing reasons, such as to confirm that they have taken the correct action, or that others positively evaluate them (Ridgeway et al., 1998). Members are thus drawn to one another in ways that reinforce their interdependence. An organization's network of interpersonal ties enhances cooperative action and prepares members to deal more effectively with crises (Krackhardt and Stern, 1988).

Modification of cognitive schemata

As members interact in situated organizational forms, their participation shapes their *cognitive schemata*, and they learn organizationally biased ways of dealing with the world. Schemata – cognitive structures of organized knowledge – are generated from early socialization experiences and from interactions with others throughout a person's life. They develop as people begin generalizing from experiences they accumulate with incipient categories of people and events. Schemata become habitual and implicit taken-for-granted ways of perceiving the world and categorizing it.

Habitual behaviors, which require no interpretation or decision making, can be contrasted with other kinds of behaviors which do require interpretation. In their research program, Wood and colleagues (Wood et al., 2002; Wood and Quinn, 2005) call the former 'reflexive' and the latter 'reflective' to emphasize the differences between thoroughly learned responses to situational cues versus responses that must be generated in the moment, as situations are assessed. Many studies show that well-learned habits seem impervious to intentional change, as long as people encounter similar situations that evoke the habitual behaviors. The underlying predispositions for the habit are not easily overridden unless someone's attention is explicitly called to the habit.

Table 6.2   Organizational knowledge and member schemata

Concept	Definition	Example
Organizational knowledge	Routines and competencies that are specific to an organizational activity system and embedded in its internal selection processes	Routines for handling customer reports of computer software problems
Cognitive schema	Cognitive structure that represents organized knowledge about persons, roles, and events	
• *Person schema*	Knowledge about a person or a particular type of person	Belief that customers are technologically unsophisticated
• *Role schema*	Behaviors expected of people in a particular social position	Expectation that managers will demand employees work overtime to solve problems
• *Event schema*	Expected sequence of events in a situation	Anticipation that a difficult case goes first to a specialist before being sent to a supervisor
Cognitive heuristic	Problem-solving techniques that reduce complex situations to simpler judgmental operations	Rule of thumb that says 'ignore technical manuals more than 6 months old and call a technician instead'

Even then, the habit tends to win out over intentions, as Wood and her colleagues have shown in a series of ingenious experiments (Wood and Quinn, 2005).

Cognitive schemata growing out of members' participation play an important part in organizational knowledge. (See Table 6.2 for definitions and examples.) Howard (1994) identified three types of schemata, according to their content: person, role, and event schemata. *Person schemata* encompass particular persons and types of people, including oneself. For example, some people associate the category of 'leader' with 'men' (Calâs, 1993). *Role schemata* refer to behaviors expected of people in particular social positions. For example, Lounsbury (2001) found two distinctive role schemata for the staffing of college recycling programs: one based on the creation of new, full-time positions filled by activists, the other entailing part-time work added to the existing work roles of environmentally ambivalent employees. *Event schemata* describe expected sequences of events in familiar situations, thus encompassing a major portion of a person's procedural knowledge. For example, event schemata influenced the 'moves' identified by Pentland and Rueter (1994) at the software support hotline office. Role schemata guide members in choosing others with whom to coordinate their behaviors, and event schemata make concerted actions possible when they are integrated with others' actions.

Growing interdependence on shared information

Organizational knowledge is context dependent. Its value arises from being used inside organizational boundaries, where it has relevance. In that respect, organizational knowledge is another heuristic for members to use in solving problems (Kahneman et al., 1982). *Cognitive heuristics* – problem-solving techniques that reduce complex situations to simpler judgmental operations – can become specific to an organizational form, or even an individual organization. Organization-specific heuristics create an idiosyncratic view of the world. Orlikowski and Yates (1994: 542) coined the term *communicative genres* to refer to 'socially recognized types of communicative actions – such as memos, meetings, expense forms, training seminars – that are habitually enacted by members of a community to realize particular social purposes.' As templates for action, such genres mold a member's behavior in organizationally specific ways.

As a guide to action, the value of organizational knowledge often depends on others being present to apply and validate the knowledge. Cues from co-workers shape workers' perceptions of their jobs, such as beliefs about the scope of members' ethical responsibilities to their organizations (Thomas and Griffin, 1983; Trevino and Victor, 1992). Members use role schemata as a cue for who has valid knowledge for them and use event schemata as a cue for what action to take next. Person schemata help members choose others with whom to interact. Talking with co-workers on the job about what they are doing and why spawns much of the shared knowledge in organizations (Boden, 1994; see also Blau, 1993). Pentland's (1992) study, for example, showed that information was kept alive by how it was accessed, shared, and refined collectively, as members talked about how to solve problems.

A great deal of organizational knowledge is also shared across organizations with the same organizational form. Members from one organization will find many familiar competencies and routines in other organizations. Argote and her colleagues have conducted studies of organizational learning curves in shipyards, truck factories, petroleum refineries, and pizza stores (Argote, 1993; Argote and Epple, 1990; and Argote et al., 1990). They have paid particular attention to the transfer of learning across organizational boundaries. In a study of 36 pizza stores operated by 10 different franchisees, they found evidence that knowledge acquired through learning by doing transferred across stores owned by the *same* franchisee (Darr et al., 1995). For example, one store discovered a better way of arranging pizza boxes next to the ovens, so that fewer steps were required and fewer pizzas dropped. This boxing innovation quickly spread to the other stores owned by the same franchisee, with the knowledge spread via phone calls, personal acquaintances, and meetings. However, despite their ultimate ties to a single national corporation, knowledge was not transferred across stores owned by *different* franchisees. Communication and exchange of information across different franchisees was too low to permit effective transfer of knowledge. The same boundaries that render organizations coherent can thus also block useful external knowledge.

Pressures toward homogeneity

Organizational knowledge is meaningful to members because, to a great extent, their schemata are shared. However, internal pressures toward homogeneity of belief may damage the value of organizational knowledge. Campbell (1969) argued that, over time, activities within organizations come to have more and more of an internal relevance, relaxing the fit between an organization and its context. In small groups, the likelihood that members will move toward greater homogeneity of belief grows when they already share much in common (Stasser et al., 1989). When members hold similar information in common, 'they are more likely to share and discuss this information than to attend in a focused way to non-shared information' (Rosenwein and Campbell, 1992: 131). Consequently, members are biased toward sampling shared information, and tend to ignore non-shared information. Depending on the interaction structure within an organization (Friedkin, 1999), the views of the majority may be amplified by this frequency-dependent bias and those of the minority further suppressed, reducing intra-organizational variation.

When selected routines and competencies are embedded in a web of social affiliations, the power of organizational knowledge intensifies. The web of affiliations conveys not only cognitive knowledge but also emotional knowledge, such as affection and hatred, envy and suspicion, and trust and distrust. Mumby and Putnam (1992: 470) asserted that managers attempt to *close off* the expression of emotions in organizations or channel them to suit organizational purposes. However, in many of the studies they cited – such as Rafaeli and Sutton's (1990, 1991) research on check-out clerks, criminal interrogators, and bill collectors – emotion management tactics were actually developed and shared by the workers as part of their community of practice, rather than by managers. The tactics were thus emergent, rather than imposed, practices. Experimental research also suggests that managers and members may implicitly favor displays of some emotions, such as anger, even when they are not normatively sanctioned features of organizational routines (Tiedens, 2001).

Summary of organizational forms and knowledge

In new organizations, founders interact with members in adopting an organizational form. New members are entering relatively small organizations, and in some cases their contributions play a major role in shaping the cognitive schemata held by other participants: an organizationally biased way of dealing with the world emerges from the integration of local knowledge with routines and competencies imported from their population. Subsequent organizational schemata organize experience and guide action, as a division of labor and an organizational role structure emerge from founders' plans and the evolution of idiosyncratic jobs. Once developed, routines are resistant to change, not only for organizational reasons but also because they simplify members' lives (Gersick and Hackman, 1990).

Paradoxically, rapid learning of organizational knowledge by new members can actually lessen an organization's fitness by producing *premature closure* on suboptimal routines (March, 1991). Closure on routines may embed unresolved problems in organizational practice, making subsequent adaptation difficult (Tyre and Orlikowski, 1994). Conversely, the entry of new members may prevent premature closure if they are slow learners. In organizations with powerful pressures toward a homogeneous outlook, a recruit can be a conduit of new information from the environment. The longer these new members maintain their deviance from accepted practices, the greater the likelihood that they will influence others and cause the diffusion of new practices. By contrast, if new members quickly adopt the majority's outlook, new external information will be lost in a short time. Premature convergence on a satisfactory routine may thus preclude future movement toward better routines (Bruderer and Singh, 1996).

Nonetheless, intraorganizational variation persists in many organizations, regardless of external influences and the homogenizing influence of the competencies and routines encoded in an organizational form. Organizational learning cannot completely eradicate people's schemata that are based on their personal dispositions and career histories. In addition, the tension between user- and supporter-orientations within organizations never completely disappears, even in total institutions (Goffman, 1961). When pockets of members coalesce around alternative user interests, variability increases. The selection pressures we reviewed in this chapter and in Chapter 5 can create organizations that exhibit substantial coherence, but few become truly monolithic. Multiple threads of meaning persist, nourishing alternative understandings and potentially fostering organizational flexibility. They also sustain ambiguous interpretations of organizational routines and competencies. We turn now to a closer examination of the issue of organizational cultures and their composition.

Construction's consequences: organizational culture

People's lives in organizations depend on their sense-making abilities. During the early days of new organizations, diverse threads of meaning permeate and link strands of activities. These intertwined threads create an organizational culture that blends competencies, routines, member understandings, and identities. Many theorists have claimed that a strong organizational culture can be a source of competitive advantage for organizations, e.g. Fiol (1991). Many organizations, of course, do not succeed in building a coherent culture and thus evidently increase their risk of disbanding. For new organizations, organizational coherence is a major accomplishment.

What model of organizational culture should we adopt in characterizing this accomplishment? Almost all studies and conceptual musings on organizational culture are based on well-established, ongoing organizations. Such entities do quite well in reproducing their organizational forms on a daily basis (see the essays in Frost et al., 1985, 1991). Studies of these organizations usually find intertwined threads of meaning that ring true. Thus, most researchers have had the luxury of observing construction's consequences, rather than the construction process itself. For example, Schein (1990) offered a structured and hierarchical definition of organizational culture, with artifacts resting on the surface, basic assumptions involving taken-for-granted beliefs serving as bedrock, and espoused values sandwiched in-between. For emerging organizations, however, we need a perspective on organizational culture and identity that fits with the evolutionary model of variation and selective retention.

Meyerson and Martin (1987) developed such a perspective in their attempt to capture the diversity of models describing organizational culture. They proposed three different views of organizations and cultural change, and labeled them *integration*, *differentiation*, and *fragmentation*. The first posits that organizations have unitary cultures, the second assumes multiple cultures, and the third begins with the assumption that fixed cultures do not exist. (We might think of them as the mono-culture, multi-culture, and messy-culture views.) In Table 6.3, we show the essential features of each view.

Table 6.3   **Organizational culture: three threads of interpretation**

	Integration	**Differentiation**	**Fragmentation**
Consensus	Organization-wide	Only within clusters	Fluctuating across issues
Consistency	High	Low	Fluctuating
Sources of change	External events or managerial directives	Inter-group conflict	Individuals and groups
Focus	Narrative, rituals, artifacts	Behavior, routines	Cognition, behavior
Identity	Central, enduring, distinctive	Contested, multifaceted	Unclear, transitory, opportunistic

Martin (2002: 121) argued that the three views represent different ways of *thinking about* organizational cultures, thus locating them in an observer's subjective outlook. She also noted that members of an organization themselves 'often find one of these three perspectives easier to understand and use, making it their personal "home" perspective.' Following this line of argument, we prefer to see them as three simultaneous but different threads of interpretation that flow through organizations. Members can engage in more than one interpretation, depending on schemata and situational cues. They may do this serially or even simultaneously, generating the kinds of ambiguities identified by Meyerson (1991b). Thus, all three threads of understanding may be present in one organization, especially in its early days. Martin (2002: 121) noted that 'sometimes most members of a culture share a home perspective; sometimes they do not. In time, home perspectives of both researchers and culture members may change.' Even well-established organizations can carry the threads of all three views, as Hylmo and Buzzanell (2002) demonstrated in their analysis of workers' feelings about telecommuting at the Federal Systems Integration and Management Center. We think Martin's scheme advances our understanding by capturing the cultural dynamics within emergent organizations. In particular, we stress that the adoption of an organizational form as an evolutionary outcome does not necessarily imply a unified view of organizational culture.

Integration view of culture

The *integration* view emphasizes consistency and organization-wide consensus. In this view, organizational culture is composed of shared values and perceptions, while organizational identity describes the central, enduring, and distinctive features of that culture (Albert and Whetten, 1985). This definition emphasizes those cultural manifestations that can be interpreted as consistent with, and reinforcing, one another. For example, Fine (1984: 239) pointed out that the term 'organization structure' has a special meaning in the interpretive perspective: 'a relationship among members, produced and created so that the organization becomes constitutive of the members' provinces of meaning.' An emergent organizational form can be associated with a consistent set of interpretations about how to respond to specific organizational problems. In its strong version, this view implies an organization-wide unity of orientation among members. Pressures toward consensus may stem from powerful leaders (Trice and Beyer, 1991), intensive and inclusive interaction between members, and members using privileged organizational positions to enact strong symbol systems (Stevenson and Bartunek, 1996).

Meyerson and Martin labeled this the 'integration view' because it assumes that almost all members share the same taken-for-granted interpretations, with nearly identical schemata. 'Culture' therefore constitutes an arena of clarity, a clearing in the jungle of meaninglessness (Wuthnow, 1987). Cultural elements are assumed to have a single, dominant interpretation. Typically, although not necessarily, leaders or top managers initiate the interpretation (Clark, 1972; Ouchi, 1981). The unitary organizational culture view focuses on unifying myths, symbols, and ceremonies in organizations, and their consequences for participants and organizations. For example, McDonald's (1991) analysis of the Los Angeles Olympic Organizing Committee (LAOOC) showed that it used stories, jokes, rituals, celebrations, and other ceremonies to create a rallying point for members. Some models of organization give great weight to leaders' roles in taking action on collectively valued purposes, crediting them with creating community and organizational coherence (Selznick, 1957). As we argued in Chapter 4, founders' visions are most critical in the early days of a new organization, during the mobilization of resources and the recruitment of members (Baron et al., 1999).

A weak version of the integration argument does not assert that organizations achieve total unity, but rather that founders/managers play a central role in whatever meaning systems emerge in organizations. The rules and guidelines created by founders channel information, resources, and member discretion. Thus, founders draw attention to conflicts among differing norms, values, beliefs, and visions, and raise the salience of certain issues, which members then act upon. This weak version probably describes the dynamics of many emerging organizations. For example, it fits the picture painted by Martin et al. (1985) of a young firm in which the employees interpreted many key events within the framework of the founder's views and objectives. Issues concerning the firm's rapid growth – from 200 to 700 employees in one year – were described in ways congruent with the founder's perspective. The weak version of the integration view shades over into the second view offered by Meyerson and Martin: organizational culture as differentiated.

Differentiation view of culture

The *differentiation* view of organizational culture posits a lack of consensus on some issues across organizational sectors or clusters, coupled with consensus within subcultures. When differentiation affects core features of the organizational culture, organizational identity itself becomes seen as multifaceted and contested. Researchers employing this view emphasize that various cultural manifestations directly clash with each other, such as the different feelings about time held by research versus production departments (Lawrence and Lorsch, 1967). For example, research departments work with projects of long duration and prefer to leave space for the unexpected, whereas production departments work with daily quotas and abhor unexpected developments. To the extent that different clusters of shared values and meanings are found in distinct subunits, they mark the existence of discrete subcultures. Clusters of members with local-supporter orientations would be found in their own units, but not cutting across an entire organization. Members' user orientations, when focused upon their subunit's goals, exacerbate cross-unit struggles (Van Maanen and Kunda, 1989).

How do such differences arise? When organizations are small, selective recruiting and hiring practices often produce members whose characteristics closely resemble those of current members. However, increases in size make simple reproduction more difficult. Early hires often become senior generalists and subsequently are less involved in later hires. The specialized tasks taken on by later hires, and the evolution of idiosyncratic jobs, can create distinct domains of organizational knowledge that are difficult to share or even explain to other members. Technological differentiation of tasks in organizations relying on very diverse knowledge can generate distinctively different beliefs between organizational subunits. Later, if founders create separate divisions or departments, differentiation can become enshrined in organizational recruiting, promotion, and reward systems. Groups within organizations may even become primary groups for their members, as Martin et al. (1985) noticed in the startup firm they studied. To the extent that communities of reference emerge within subgroups, relations with the larger organization may become problematic. Under such conditions, organizational reproduction sustains differentiation rather than integration.

Because researchers using this view are highly cognizant of discrepancies across subunits, they have often adopted an associative perspective on members to interpret their findings (Young, 1989). Misunderstandings and communication failures are sometimes the cause of conflict in organizations, but deliberate distortions of meanings and withholding of information are also strategies to gain power (Welsh and Slusher, 1986). Coalitions may form around powerful members whose goals unite a subgroup and set it apart from other groups (Cyert and March, 1963).

In the new, small organizations discussed in this chapter, role differentiation is fairly low in an organization's early years. By contrast, in the larger organizations that many culture researchers have studied, multiple sources of differentiation exist and most members have trouble identifying with the whole organization. Instead, they focus their identity and commitment on their local peer group, on their own division, on their occupational group, and so forth. Larger organizations must then cope with the fragmentation of meaning that their complexity introduces, creating separate islands of sense-making within the larger structure. In turn, the separate islands exacerbate struggles for control of resources. For example, Thomas (1994) discovered such struggles in his research on conflict between engineers and others involved in manufacturing process innovations. He found that most people were acting on situations from the perspective of their own occupational groups and their own unit's position within the organization. Quite often, a sizable gap separated lower-level workers' understandings of what they were doing from what top corporate executives were thinking.

The social-psychological consequences of multiple viewpoints co-existing within an organization can be profound, encouraging members holding minority views to speak out and increasing internal variation. We have pointed out the strong pressures toward homogeneity within organizations and the resulting construction of members with a similar outlook on practice. However, the presence of subunits with viewpoints at odds with the majority may foster an atmosphere in which dissension emboldens members into offering views that challenge current knowledge. Research on dissent within small groups has found that the expression of minority viewpoints tends to stimulate complex thinking, problem solving, and an active search for more information (Nemeth,

1995, 1997). Exposure to minority views also generates many original solutions to problems, regardless of whether the views are 'correct.' If divergent viewpoints are protected within a subunit that supports and encourages its members, internal organizational variation is enhanced. Increased variation, in turn, raises the odds of organizational adaptation to changing selection criteria.

Fragmentation view of culture

The *fragmentation* view – the third cultural view – posits that intrinsic and inescapable ambiguities exist in all organizational cultures. A lack of clarity, multiple meanings and beliefs, and weak organizational leadership may produce complex and chaotic situations. Under such conditions, cultural manifestations are subject to divergent interpretations and organizational identity tends to become transitory and subject to opportunistic definition. What is consistent according to one person's view may be inconsistent according to someone else (Martin and Meyerson, 1988). Whereas the unitary view presupposed consensus as the order of the day, the fragmentation view sees consensus as ephemeral and fluctuating across issues, individuals, and organizational life cycles (Meyerson, 1990, 1991b). Disagreement sharpens members' understandings of current situations, but they cannot reach consensus without anchors of meaning within subgroups. Culture is *not* the island of clarity within a jungle of meaninglessness – it is the jungle itself (Martin, 2002).

Researchers using the fragmentation view have focused on more ordinary behaviors and on the meaning embedded in routine transactions (Boden, 1994), whereas researchers using the unitary culture metaphor have tended to focus on the fixed or formal genres of folklore studies, examining narratives, rituals, and artifacts (Martin, 1982). Fragmentation researchers conduct unstructured interviews, do field work and participant observation, and collect archived information (Aldrich, 1972; Kleinman and Copp, 1992). Trethewey's (1999) field study of the Women's Social Services Organization in an American Midwestern community uncovered multiple paradoxes and ambiguities, such as client selection procedures that led staff members to choose mostly self-sufficient people for 'help.' From this viewpoint, the expressive side of participation is as important as the task-related side, because bounded or cognitive rationality governs a great deal of organizational behavior: people behave in ways that seem appropriate at the time (March, 1981).

Dependence on an organization can lead to ambivalent feelings toward it (Smelser, 1998). The more free people are to enter and exit relationships, the more one-dimensional their feelings, e.g. totally positive or negative. But, when people are locked in, committed, and unable to exit easily, they develop simultaneously strong positive and negative feelings. Their loyalty leads them to care a great deal about the organization, but their inability to exit nurtures potent negative feelings about it. For example, entrepreneurs who have built successful companies face a dilemma. Having built a large firm, many find that the thrill is gone and they are free to move on, to initiate another startup effort (Dobrev and Barnett, 2005). However, they may also feel a strong sense of obligation to the vision they championed and the employees they recruited. Their ambivalence may render them unable to make a decision.

Smelser's argument suggests that ambiguity will be a central feature in the culture of organizations that have high member commitment. Meyerson and Scully (1995:

586) coined the term 'tempered radicals' to refer to members who 'identify with and are committed to their organizations, and are also committed to a cause, community, or ideology that is fundamentally different from, and possibly at odds with the dominant culture of their organization.' Their ambivalence makes them critical of both the status quo *and* change that is too radical. Ambiguity will be tempered by their option to exit, but because the least committed will leave first, ambiguity will actually increase in shrinking organizations.

The fragmentation view probably gives too much weight to members' positions as users in organizations and not enough weight to their roles as supporters. Martin's jungle metaphor evokes images of under-socialized actors struggling under chaotic conditions in new organizations. Fine (1984) offered a slightly less Hobbesian image in his description of the *negotiated order* view. Fine's view assumes that change is inevitable and continuous, though often slow. Individuals and groups continually adjust to new situations, and where interpretations clash, no agreement may be possible. When disputes over meanings stop organized action, resource exchanges break down, threatening organizational survival. If this occurs repeatedly, organizations disband and their resources dissipate. Thus, we would expect a higher rate of disbanding among emergent organizations that experienced sustained ambiguities surrounding the core of their organizational knowledge.

Organizational permeability

Organizational cultures do not develop in isolation from the surrounding society, and organizations are not closed self-referential systems. Thus, we need to put the three views of organizational culture in a sociocultural context. Cultural norms and values permeate organizational boundaries via the personal history each member brings to an organization and via the reproduction of practices from the surrounding society. The greater the permeability of organizational boundaries and the availability of alternative interpretations, the higher the likelihood of cultural fragmentation and ambiguity within organizations.

Organizations are sites for the *reproduction* of cultural norms and practices, but they also *generate* cultural norms and practices (Swidler, 1986; Wuthnow, 1987). As creative initiators of fads and fashions, organizations may act as agents for the genesis and diffusion of innovations from one field to another (Strang and Soule, 1998). Occasionally, organizational forms become holding areas for the preservation of ideas whose time has not yet come, but soon might. For example, colleges and universities often preserve obscure languages and esoteric academic specialties that have no popular or commercial support. Similarly, one defense of public spending on art museums rests on the argument that 'they help to define the national heritage and are integral to a people's awareness of their cultural attainments, historical past, and sense of worth' (Blau, 1995: 87). Art museums have also been the focus of intense struggles between Popular Culture and High Culture, as commercialized notions of value have penetrated organizations seeking more public funding.

Two examples of the permeability of organizational culture involve the reproduction of norms and practices involving *age* and *gender*. First, with respect to *age norms*, universities are particularly good sites to observe the influence of societal norms regarding age-appropriate behavior. Universities are also interesting sites for observations of gender-based practices, because they are the primary location where middle-class youth meets potential mates in the United States (Elder, 1969; Mare, 1991; Scott, 1965). Colleges and universities were much more insulated from trends in popular culture in the 19th century and through the early 20th century than they are today. College traditions were easily replicated over generations of students when their recruitment base was limited to youth from a particular social class, race, or gender (Horowitz, 1987; Story, 1980). Many colleges had initiation rituals for freshmen and traditional songs. Student associations such as fraternities and sororities perpetuated local customs. Substantial regional differences existed between sub-populations of colleges, such as between the Ivy League schools and Midwestern universities (Clark, 1970; Karabel, 2005).

A host of changes, beginning in the 1960s, broke down the barriers between colleges and the wider society, and between sub-populations of colleges. First, the *in loco parentis* norms that turned college administrators into surrogate parents declined. College youth was thus freed to engage in whatever behavior age peers off campus enjoyed. Second, social movements, such as those supporting the civil rights movement and opposing the Vietnam War, began recruiting on college campuses, drawing students into society-wide conflicts. Finally, the proliferation of state-funded campuses and the greater availability of government-guaranteed student loans greatly expanded the student population. Colleges and universities grew rapidly, creating more heterogeneous student populations.

By the 1980s, college cultures no longer reflected the inheritance of internal tradition, but rather the projection of contemporary late-adolescent culture onto college and university campuses (Moffat, 1989). Today, intelligent young people with free time on their hands and minimal adult involvement in their activities populate colleges and universities. Whereas adult supervision had played a major role in directing students' activities in 19th century colleges, today's college youth enjoys nearly unfettered control over how they spend their time. Currents of popular fads and fashion – in musical tastes, dress, films, and language – sweep through the college-age population, on and off campuses. Moffat's (1989) field study at Rutgers University in the 1980s found that students spent surprisingly little time on academic pursuits. Two decades later, a national survey of over 34,000 students at 200 colleges and universities found students' allocation of time had not changed much (UCLA, 2003). Faculty members are mostly irrelevant in the lives of ordinary students. The very permeable nature of college boundaries has produced a low rate of culture replication over generations of students, with colleges serving as one more site for the intensification of popular culture.

Second, with respect to *gender norms*, values and practices in the surrounding society manifest themselves in work-related organizational norms and practices. Gherardi (1994: 599) argued that 'the symbolic order of gender is maintained, reproduced, and culturally transmitted by ceremonial work whose rules are defined by the "good manners," customs, and etiquette of a particular organizational culture.' Within organizations, men and women engage in ceremonial work that gives proper representation to the attributes and behaviors expected of their own gender, and they expect that others will do the same. Sexual harassment represents an extreme form of gender-typed behavior, but there are also lesser forms, such as in work assignments.

Some organizations encourage gender-stereotyped role allocations and behaviors, whereas others discourage them. Organizational policies are a crucial intervening factor between external norms and values and how employees deal with each other (Kanter, 1977). For example, a participant observation study of a Subaru automobile manufacturing plant in the Midwest found that it failed to eliminate gender differences on the factory floor, even though it had tried to eliminate hierarchy. By allowing sex-typed job assignments and male domination of within-group activities, societal gender patterns re-emerged within the plant (Gottfried and Graham, 1993). Gender-neutral practices were not sustainable, because the company was not systematic enough in its efforts to buffer employees from societal norms regarding gender relations.

Two norms are especially pernicious, as Charles and Grusky (2004) documented in their large-scale study of sex segregation in ten countries. One, which they termed *gender essentialism*, entails a belief that men are more suited to perform certain kinds of occupational tasks (especially manual ones) than women, leading to a 'horizontal' segregation of occupations. The other, which they termed *male primacy*, entails a belief that men are more competent or better-suited to positions of authority, leading to a 'vertical' segregation of occupations. Sex segregation regimes differ significantly across organizations and nation-states, and Charles and Grusky (2004) suggested that parameters assessing the prevalence of these norms can account for much of the variation.

Gender relations permeate some organizations in spite of norms and ideologies that attempt to screen them out (Acker, 1990; Buzzanell, 1995). For example, Kleinman (1996) showed that traditional gender relations between men professionals and women staff persisted in an organizational form that was specifically constructed as an alternative to hierarchical social relations in the wider society. The Wellness Center was built on norms opposing the non-holistic practices of modern health care, with members stressing norms of concern for each other's personal welfare and integrity. Nonetheless, the male professionals consistently got the lion's share of organizational resources and avoided doing 'menial clerical work.' Pierce (1995) noted similar gender-based inequalities in the law firms she observed. Working as a participant observer, she found that some of the men lawyers routinely ignored rules of civility in dealing with women staff and that gender-based stereotypes infused role relationships.

Implications for organizational evolution

All views of organizational culture assume that people's lives in organizations depend on their sense-making abilities (Fine, 1984). Treated as multiple threads of meaning within organizations, however, Martin's three conceptions of culture diverge in their implications for organizational evolution. The unitary culture view posits a collective order in which values and perceptions are widely shared. By contrast, the differentiation and fragmentation views propose that interacting groups and individual members make accommodations to what they perceive as an external, even foreign, order. To the extent that an organization's culture is unified, change will mainly occur at the level of the entire entity, rather than within subunits. The greater the unity, the higher the likelihood of organization-wide change. In stable environments, such changes might disrupt an organization's ability to obtain needed resources. Unity can also lead to efficiency gains, however. Thus, which distinct mix of unitary, differentiation, and fragmentation cultural threads is selected ultimately depends on their fit with specific environmental conditions.

The differentiation paradigm focuses on inter-group conflicts as sources of change, as individuals shift group allegiances or coalitions change. From this view, changes can occur in piecemeal fashion, as conveyed by the notion of *loose coupling* in organizations

(Aldrich, 1975; Weick, 1976). Institutional and ecological theories have generally taken an integration perspective, although on a different level of analysis than most interpretive researchers. The theories have treated organizational forms and their surrounding environments as unitary objects, containing a single view of what is legitimate. In this respect, the fragmentation and differentiation views, carried to their extreme, contain a major challenge to the ecological and institutional perspectives, for how can organizations be institutions if they have multiple or ambiguous cultures? If organizations do not cohere as unitary entities, then the 'object' or 'target' of selection by external forces is no longer clear.

Conclusions

Together, founders and members of new organizations develop or adopt organizational forms. Boundaries become more salient as the contrast between organizational activities and surrounding environments deepens. Boundaries also come into sharper focus as reward systems succeed in reinforcing organizationally-focused member orientations. Sharing knowledge through a community of practice thus increases organizational coherence. Only when bounded entities emerge can selection pressures change the organizational composition of populations.

The evolutionary model treats the ongoing production of internal organizational processes as a major influence on the coalescence of organizational boundaries. Organizational boundaries are not sealed, because cultural norms and practices, institutional requirements, and flows of people permeate them. Thus, although we have stressed the internal development and self-maintenance of an organization's form in this chapter, we will also emphasize the embedded nature of organizations in larger social systems in the remaining chapters.

Organizational emergence is marked by organizational boundaries coming into focus. With definite boundaries, an organization is no longer merely an aggregation of individuals. In their organizationally defined roles, people now constitute an entity that differs radically from the accumulation of individual self-interests. In this respect, there may be an asymmetry in members' orientations to their organizations: their options have narrowed, their careers have been altered, and new identities have been constructed. They do not need to renegotiate their relationship to their organization each day. Members have learned a great deal and have begun to take it for granted. We have described the social construction of organizational identity in a way that emphasizes outcomes favorable to an organization, with supportive behavior following from a variety of social processes. However, we have not meant to imply an over-socialized view of membership, in which people are simply role-takers and role-fillers rather than self-conscious actors (Granovetter, 1993). Organizational changes do occasionally occur: ideas can change, creative insights might blossom, and taken-for-granted worlds may be overturned.

Creative moves by members often generate unforeseen consequences, including organizational transformations. Thus, the adoption of an organizational form does not imply absolute uniformity in organizational structure, knowledge, beliefs, and routines. Multiple threads of meaning often run through perfectly viable organizations. An organization's survival depends upon the daily reproduction of *enough* of its routines and competencies to, at a minimum, keep its resource exchanges in balance. Organizational survival also depends upon the availability of *enough* internal variability to permit it to cope with uncertainty. How much variability is *enough* is contingent on many factors, some external and others internal, with the contingencies varying by organization, population, community, and historical period.

Study Questions

1.   How does the approach employed by students of organizational culture differ from that employed by students of organizational knowledge and routines?
2.   An emphasis on procedural knowledge or the subjective perceptions of organizational members implies a conception of organizational forms that is reducible to the cognitive and affective processes of individuals. Develop an argument against this version of methodological individualism, while focusing exclusively on processes within organizational boundaries.

Exercises

1.   The definition of an organizational form is inherently multidimensional, possibly subsuming such features of an organization as its membership model, its processing activities, its legal structure, its model of funding, its positioning in product/service markets, or its 'branding' identity. Develop a research design that: (1) adequately captures variation in organizational forms along multiple dimensions; and (2) identifies what dimensions are most salient to participants.
2.   Describe the culture of the organization you selected for analysis in Chapter 4. Use each of the perspectives outlined in Table 6.3, first providing a view of the culture as integrated, then differentiated, and, finally, fragmented. What data sources inform each account? What theoretical and empirical biases does each perspective introduce?

7

Organizational Transformation

In organization studies, a polemical debate has raged around the issues of adaptation and selection within organizations, populations, and communities. If organizations seldom change or adapt to their environments, as early population ecology arguments suggested, then organizational foundings are the principal source of variety in populations. Similarly, if populations seldom adapt or only do so in small increments, then new populations are the source of diversity in communities. In this controversy, proponents of organizational inertia have been skeptical of claims that organizations not only react to environmental changes, but also alter their structures in adaptive ways. After almost two decades of research, however, even ecologists admit that organizations can and often do change, sometimes in quite radical ways (Barnett and Carroll, 1995), although the risks of such transformation can be considerable. Advocates of strategic choice, in turn, have noted that organizations often face formidable obstacles to their own transformation (Boisot and Child, 1988).

Just as theories of a lifetime fixed personality have given way to theories of life-long socialization in social psychology (Elder and O'Rand, 1995), so too have organization theorists adopted a more contingent and time-based view of organizational change. In 1979, Aldrich (1979: 160) argued that 'environmental selection processes set the limits within which rational selection among alternatives takes place. Prior limits and constraints on available options leave little room for maneuvering by most organizations, and strategic choice may be a luxury open only to the largest and most powerful organizations.' Today, rather than framing transformation as an either–or issue, we suggest considering the conditions under which change occurs. Posing the question in this manner requires a definition of transformation and specification of a period in which it occurs.

Previous chapters have been concerned with the process by which organizations come into being and achieve coherence as entities. Now, we take the existence of organizations as given and examine their possible transformation. We begin with a definition of transformation as a major change occurring along three possible dimensions: changes in goals, boundaries, and activities. To qualify as transformations, changes must involve a qualitative break with routines and a shift to new kinds of competencies that challenge existing organizational knowledge. Next, we frame the study of transformation in terms of variation, selection, and retention, and then illustrate the argument using selected empirical studies. We point out that the evolutionary framework calls our attention to several dimensions of the transformation process, such as the extent of member involvement. Finally, we consider the conditions under which transformation disrupts organizations and the paradoxical nature of disruptive events. Disruption may increase variability in ways that facilitate adaptation to changing environments, but it may also pose a threat to organizational coherence and survival.

Explaining transformation at the organizational level

A transformation is a change, but not all changes are transformations. To gain generality and consistency, a theory of transformation needs to focus on a clear set of identifiable changes. However, organizational theorists have had great difficulty finding a generic classification scheme for organizations and organizational changes (Scott, 2003). Given the diversity of contending theoretical perspectives and research designs, no general scheme has won approval from the community of scholars. Moreover, attempts at generic taxonomic schemes in the past have produced rather arid abstractions that are difficult to relate to specific organizational practices (McKelvey and Aldrich, 1983). For example, a proposed distinction between core and periphery features won some popularity but showed little empirical power when used in studies of organizational change (Baum, 1996: 101).

Using a definition of organizations as involving three dimensions – goals, boundaries, and activity systems – obviates any simple one-dimensional scheme for classifying transformations. By examining content changes within each of these three dimensions, we show the many opportunities for selection forces to make their weight felt. We do not prejudge which dimension is most critical to organizational coherence. Using the three dimensions also gives us concepts that are part of a larger approach to analyzing organizations. By linking transformation to founding conditions, the growth of organizational knowledge, and development of organizational forms, an evolutionary approach has the potential to unify studies of organizational change and stability.

Three dimensions of transformation

We define *transformation* as a major or substantial change in organizations and classify types of transformations along the same dimensions as those used to define organizations: goals, boundaries, and activity systems. Theorizing about transformation involves a decision on the meaning of 'substantial' and 'major' organizational change. We can classify the importance of changes by examining whether they involve an entire organization and by weighing the value of the resources involved. For example, one indicator of a transformation might be that it overturns existing organizational knowledge and makes relevant new routines and competencies. Judging whether new knowledge has become relevant requires that we study organizations over time, and

Table 7.1   Organizational transformation: three dimensions

Definition	A transformation is a major change in an organization involving a break with existing routines and a shift to new kinds of competencies that challenge organizational knowledge.

Three dimensions along which transformations occurs:

Goals	Major changes in domain claimed or in breadth of products and services

Examples:
- Changes in the domain claimed, e.g. conversion of hospitals from public to private ownership (Scott et al., 2000)
- Changes in the breadth of an organization's goal, e.g. S&Ls entering the market for direct investments in real estate (Haveman, 1992)

Boundaries	Expansion or contraction involving members or other organizations

Examples:
- Expansion of boundaries, e.g. corporations diversifying through conglomerate mergers (Davis et al., 1994)
- Contraction of boundaries, e.g. corporations divesting themselves of unwanted business units (Davis et al., 1994)

Activities	Changes in an organization's activity system that have a major effect on organizational knowledge

Examples:
- Changes in administrative systems, e.g. corporate adoption of the multi-divisional form (Fligstein, 1985)
- Changes in human resource management systems, e.g. the bureaucratization of personnel relations in startups (Baron et al., 1999)
- Major technological innovations, e.g. the adoption of computerized tomography scanners by radiology departments (Barley, 1990)

this requirement poses stringent methodological demands on investigators. Table 7.1 provides a summary list of definitions and examples for this section.

Goals

Organizations, unlike other social units, have distinct objectives in the sense that we can usually observe members engaged in collective action toward a target. For all but a handful of organizations, survival is a generic goal and thus we cannot use it to classify types of changes. Similarly, for almost all business organizations, profitability is a long-term generic goal. Being universal, it also does not allow us to distinguish between change outcomes. Organizations not oriented toward profitability usually frame their goals in language emphasizing a purposive or solidary outcome, e.g. improving the physical fitness of youth or providing occasions for like-minded people to socialize (Clark and Wilson, 1961). Researchers have sought a classification scheme general enough to encompass organizational diversity, and thus have turned to the nature and scope of the niche or domain in which organizations acquire resources. Two types of goal transformations have figured prominently in studies: (1) changes in the domain claimed by an organization, e.g. a market or target population served; and (2) changes in the breadth of an organization's goal, especially changes from specialism to generalism. Some investigators have been interested primarily in goal changes themselves, whereas others have been more interested in the consequences of goal changes for organizational survival.

Boundaries

Organizational boundaries can be transformed in two ways: by expansion or contraction. Organizations may expand their boundaries to take in other organizations, such as through mergers and acquisitions. They may also take in other types of members, such as when the YMCA expanded to take in members of all ages and religions (Zald and Denton, 1963), or traditionally men-only golf clubs were forced by legislation and law suits in the past decade to take in women (Vanderpool, 2001). Among studies of business firms, the most common types of boundary transformations have probably been mergers, acquisitions, and divestitures, even though they involve only a very small fraction of all US organizations. We discuss them in detail in Chapters 8 and 10. Organizations may contract their boundaries by shedding organizational units, as in divestitures, or they may contract via member expulsions, as occasionally occurs when political movements *purge* members (Staggenborg, 1989) or major corporations practice *downsizing* (Budros, 1997). The impact of boundary changes depends on the scope of the expansion or contraction, relative to an organization's initial size, and on how rapidly it occurs. Depending on their scope, an organization's boundary changes may affect other organizations in its population.

Activity systems

Activity systems in organizations are the means by which members accomplish work, which can include processing raw materials, information, or people. Activity systems consist of bounded sets of interdependent role behaviors that are contingent upon the techniques used. Small changes in activity systems are probably a daily occurrence in most organizations, and existing routines accommodate such changes. Thus, not all changes are transformations. Executive succession, for example, represents a turnover within an authority structure, rather than a transformation, to the extent that it occurs within the rules accepted within an organization (Cannella and Lubatkin, 1993). However, non-routine succession, such as top executives being forced out before reaching retirement age or apparent heirs being passed over for outsiders, may signal a major corporate restructuring (Haveman, 1993b; Cannella and Shen, 2001).

We can classify transformations in activity systems, such as technological innovations, by the scope and depth of their influence. Researchers have extensively researched three types of transformations over the past several decades. First, investigators have studied changes in administrative systems, such as the adoption of total quality management (TQM) programs (Sitkin et al., 1994; Westphal et al., 1997) and changes in corporate forms (Fligstein, 1990). Second, studies have analyzed changes in human resource management systems, such as the growth of employer-sponsored child care in response to changes in tax law (Kelly, 2003) or bureaucratization of personnel relations in startups (Baron et al., 1999). Third, research has focused on technological innovations that have organizational consequences, such as the adoption of information technology by professional organizations (Barley, 1990). Information technology includes such things as computerized medical diagnostic equipment, computer-aided design, teleconferencing, and corporate intranets.

How frequently do transformations occur?

Transformation, as currently conceptualized, only takes on meaning if we assume that relative inertia constitutes the normal state of organizational life. A state of relative inertia would obtain if small fluctuations and minor departures from established routines occurred within an overall pattern of activities that faithfully reproduced an organization's form, keeping it in alignment with a static environment. As we noted in Chapter 3, Hannan and Freeman (1977) made this assumption the cornerstone of their initial formulation of the population ecology approach, and re-affirmed it in subsequent work (e.g., Hannan and Freeman, 1984, 1989). They argued that organizations tend to be favored by society for their reliability and accountability. These properties are most likely to be found in highly inert organizations, exhibiting stable routines and structures.

Several other perspectives we reviewed in Chapter 3 are not as explicit as population ecology. Nonetheless, they also advance an image of organizations as facing strong internal and external inertial pressures. For example, in the institutional and resource dependence perspectives, *transformation* is implicitly defined as a substantial departure from established routines and competencies. From these perspectives, the departure threatens an organization's coherence and possibly its existence. Some theorists have argued that the observed tendency of young organizations to disband at a higher rate than older ones – labeled the 'liability of newness' in Chapter 4 – actually reflects the failure of new organizations to 'establish effective routines or stable exchange relations' (Baum and Amburgey, 2002: 307).

Research suggests that the assumption of inertia is well founded. Most organizations do not grow very much after they are founded. Growth is *not*, then, a natural outcome in the life course of most organizations. Longitudinal studies of representative samples of for-profit firms in the United States have found that only about 15 percent or so add a significant number of employees after they are founded (Duncan and Handler, 1994; Reynolds and White, 1997). Research in other nations shows similar results. For example, a Norwegian study of 200,000 establishments active in 1989 found that only a small proportion had grown significantly by 1993 (Spilling, 1996). In England, Storey (1994) followed a cohort of new firms for ten years. He found that 4 percent of them accounted for about 50 percent of the net new jobs generated by the cohort.

Among businesses that grow, a small number of large, publicly traded, incorporated firms have attracted the attention of organization and management theorists. These larger organizations constitute the circumscribed set over which debates have raged about adaptation and strategic choice. Shortcomings in previous research on organizational change further limit our understanding of transformation because of unrepresentative samples and cross-sectional designs. Our knowledge of the *process* of transformation mostly comes from small-scale case studies, ethnographies, and field studies.

Three aspects of transformation frequency

In particular, three aspects of transformation frequency have drawn special attention. First, from an historical perspective, researchers have theorized about the relative likelihood of major transformations across different populations within a community. We take up that question in Chapters 9 and 10. Second, within populations, investigators have studied the frequency of transformations. Third, in related investigations, researchers have asked whether some organizations are more likely to undergo repeated occurrences than others. Generally, changes that follow a regular cycle, periodicity, or rhythm as part of the normal ebb and flow of organizational life are not treated as transformations.

To calculate the relative frequency of organizational transformation, we need information on the number of changes and the period during which they occurred. Given this data, we can investigate two important empirical questions about the *rate of change* within organizational populations. First, what types of transformations are likely to occur least frequently (or with the greatest amount of disruption)? Second, to what extent is aggregate change in the population accounted for by transformations on the part of individual organizations versus by ecological events affecting the composition of the population as a whole, e.g. foundings and disbandings?

As a theoretical response to the first question, Hannan and Freeman (1984) proposed a hierarchy of organizational attributes, rank-ordered in terms of structural inertia. In particular, they suggested that the goals of an organization would be more inert than the formal structure defining organizational boundaries and that, in turn, the formal structure would be less amenable to transformation than organizational activities and technology. Despite the significant evolutionary implications of the proposed hierarchy of structural inertia, it has more often been assumed than investigated. The reason for this neglect may be methodological. Although the argument for differential inertia in organizational features appears straightforward, the direct comparison of raw rates of change is not. An analyst's conclusions may vary according to the choice of indicators. For example, should we conceptualize organizational boundaries in terms of membership or connections among organizational units? Moreover, we may observe high aggregate rates of change in populations, even for truly inertial attributes, because new organizations replaced older organizations, not because existing ones were transformed.

To resolve this dilemma, organizational researchers have begun to conceptualize structural inertia in a population as the amount of variation in changes explained by organizational transformation versus the amount explained by ecological events. For instance, in a longitudinal study of hospitals in the San Francisco Bay area, Scott and his colleagues (2000: 106–109) found that 82 percent of the changes in outpatient services and 51 percent of the changes in size were accounted for by transformations. However, transformations accounted for only 40 percent of the aggregate changes in ownership. Hospital founding and disbanding events were the major factors accounting for ownership change. The progressive reduction in variation explained by transformation provides empirical support for Hannan and Freeman's (1984) hierarchy of structural inertia among organizational goals, boundaries, and activities, respectively.

Some transformations occur only once, and are unlikely to be repeated. For these *non-repeatable* events, we can ask whether the transformation occurs earlier or later than it does in other organizations at risk of change. However, no meaningful statistic on a single organization's frequency of change can be computed for unique events. It is all or nothing. For example, over the past century, single-sex women's colleges that were transformed into co-educational institutions did not switch back to single-sex education (Studer-Ellis, 1995a). Most *repeatable* transformations apparently occur infrequently, although – with some exceptions – investigators have seldom reported systematic information about their actual rate of occurrence in individual organizations.

Frequent transformations may establish a momentum for change that increases the likelihood of future transformations (Amburgey and Miner, 1992; Jansen, 2004; Kelly and Amburgey, 1991). For example, some American corporations have pursued very aggressive boundary expansion strategies, appearing to gain momentum as they acquired other firms. Most of the 50,229 mergers and acquisitions announced in the United States between 1998 and 2003 were one-time offers. However, 23 companies made 20 or more merger and acquisition offers over that period, accounting for about 2 percent of all offers. Some firms were extremely aggressive: General Electric made 242 offers, Century Business Services, Inc. made 94 and United Rentals made 74. We return to the topic of mergers in Chapter 10.

More generally, studies have found that the likelihood of organizational change increases with the number of prior changes of the same type. Organizations may develop routines and competencies that make them particularly adept at certain kinds of changes. Organizational members may come to prefer well-known kinds of changes, regardless of whether they are appropriate to a situation (Levitt and March, 1988). Support for the principle of repetitive transformation has been found in studies of: the U.S. airline industry, Finnish newspapers, large U.S. corporations in diverse industries, wineries in California and Missouri, and bank holding companies in the United States (Amburgey et al., 1993; Amburgey and Dacin, 1994; Baum, 1996: 101–103; Delacroix and Swaminathan, 1991; Stoeberl et al., 1998). The results of these studies suggest that the effect may decay with elapsed time from the last change. Thus, the momentum eventually vanishes (Ginsberg and Baum, 1994).

Evolutionary explanations at the organizational level

The same processes that make organizational coherence possible in the day-to-day reproduction of an organization's routines and competencies also impel the transformation process. In previous chapters, we have invoked the mechanisms of variation, selection, retention, and struggle to explain the foundings of organizations and the development of their organizational form. Therefore, we offer only a brief review of the mechanisms now, showing their application to the study of transformation. After reviewing them, we examine the extent to which transformation processes involve a high proportion of members. Table 7.2 provides a summary of definitions and examples for this section. We do not include 'struggle' in the table because it implicitly underlies all organizational life under conditions of limited resources.

Variation

Variations in activities provide the raw materials from which selection processes cull those that are most suitable, given a set of consistent selection criteria. The higher the frequency of variations, whether intentional or blind, the greater the opportunities for change. Within organizations, most purposeful variations occur as intentional responses, when organizational members actively attempt to generate alternatives and seek solutions to problems (Cyert and March, 1963; Greve, 2003). Because they draw on existing organizational knowledge, these actions usually replicate the current organizational

Table 7.2   *Transformations: evolutionary explanations at the organizational level*

Variation	The greater the frequency of variations, the greater the opportunities for transformation.
	• Level of variation dampened by internal selection criteria favoring inertia
	• Level of variation increased by institutionalized experimentation, incentives to innovate, official tolerance of unfocused variation, and creative enactment of organizational practices, especially group-based action.
Selection	Changes in selection criteria open avenues for new practices.
	• Internal selection criteria not linked to environmental fitness may be realigned
	• External discontinuities may trigger changes in selection pressures, such as changes in competitive conditions, government regulations, or technological breakthroughs.
Retention	Transformations are completed when knowledge required for reproducing practices is embodied in an organizational form. Retention by:
	• individuals and groups
	• structures, policies, and programs
	• networks.

form. Organizational reproduction, indeed, depends on members using problem-solving behavioral or cognitive routines that have worked in the past. Intentional variations that lie outside current practices are mostly overlooked, ignored, or negatively sanctioned, as are blind variations that occur independently of selection pressures. Nonetheless, potential sources of variation that break with routine are ever present (Aldrich, 1979: 75–105).

Variations from routines are important because they generate and sustain the variety that would otherwise disappear due to pressures to conform. In Chapter 2, we described several sources of intentional and blind variation in organizations. *Sources of intentional variation* within organizations include: (1) programs of experimentation and imitation; (2) incentives for innovative behavior; and (3) tolerance of unfocused variation.

First, managers might intentionally experiment by creating research and development programs, such as a rule setting aside a certain proportion of the budget for innovative activities (Mezias and Glynn, 1993). Organizations may foster innovations by creating competitions between work groups with recognition as a symbolic reward. Organizations may also introduce intentional variation through outside consultants, who often play a role in spreading new managerial practices such as total quality management (Sitkin et al., 1994). Second, an organization might offer various incentives to employees, such as allowing managers to create spin-offs in which they have an equity stake (Garvin, 1983). Managers might build incentives for innovative activities into employees' job descriptions. Third, official tolerance of unfocused variation or 'playfulness' allows members to make minor departures from routines without fear of sanctions (Burgelman, 1984; March, 1981).

Sources of blind variation include: (1) the everyday variation generated by members fulfilling their roles as organizational participants, involving trial and error learning, misunderstandings, and idle curiosity; and (2) collective action taken in response to situations not covered by current organizational knowledge. Roy (1953) described machine operators in a piecework system playing games to make the time pass quickly and to flaunt their disdain for management. The shop foreman was clearly aware of what was going on, but tolerated the games because the workers made their production quota. Many everyday variations are generated by members creatively enacting organizational practices, involving imitation, mistakes, conflicts, passion, misunderstandings, and surprises (Weick, 1995). Powerful variations are also often generated when members of a work group, organization, or population take collective action to fix a problem. For example, collective action may be provoked when one faction in an organization decides that another faction has strayed from the organization's original goals (Breines, 1980).

Interorganizational relations may serve as a conduit for information about the practices of others (Gulati and Gargiulo, 1999; Mizruchi, 1996). Researchers have divergent opinions regarding whether the consequences of network ties are intended or blind. Some researchers argue that such relations simply allow managers to learn about and copy successful practices. Other researchers assert that imitation is a socially conditioned response to uncertainty. Interlocks with previous adopters have been found to increase the likelihood of a firm adopting a golden parachute plan (Davis, 1994), poison pill defenses against takeovers (Davis, 1991), the multidivisional form (Palmer et al., 1993), and engaging in acquisition activity (Haunschild, 1993). Not all studies report that interlocks have effects. A study of the 1982 elections found no association between interlocks and campaign contributions (Burris, 1987), and another found no association between interlocks and merger activity (Fligstein and Brantley, 1992). Mizruchi (1996: 288) summarized this research by arguing that the findings 'support the argument that the behavior of firms is socially embedded.' However, the process by which network ties lead to changes in organizational action will remain unclear until researchers conduct more process-oriented research (Mizruchi, 1996).

Is organizational variation associated with age and size? Researchers are not sure. Organizational ecologists initially argued that organizational age was negatively associated with a propensity to change. They posited that selection forces favor accountability and reliability and that older organizations would thus be more inert than younger ones (Hannan and Freeman, 1984). Some theorists argued that larger organizations are more inert than smaller ones, because of higher levels of formalization and internal homogeneity, the growth of vested interests around current arrangements, and often the security of a dominant position in their environment (Aldrich and Auster, 1986). For example, Haveman (1993a) noted that large savings and loan associations in California did not need to adapt in response to the deregulation that occurred at the end of the 1970s. They held back because they reaped economies of scale from their current operations, in which they dominated the traditional real estate mortgage market. Accordingly, the medium-sized firms, which were the most flexible, entered the new markets more quickly than the largest firms.

To counter arguments about the liability of aging, some organizational learning theorists have argued that older and larger organizations are more fluid, with more resources that can be deployed in the interests of change (Cyert and March, 1963). Resource dependence theorists maintained that, as organizations grow larger, their market power increases with the resources available to them (Pfeffer and Salancik, 1978). With more resources, they are not so closely bound by their exchange partners and can ignore developments that might crush smaller competitors. To date, research findings have been mixed. For example, Zajac and Kraatz (1993) found that larger private liberal arts colleges were more likely to add programs than smaller ones, but Studer-Ellis (1995a) found that larger private women's colleges were more likely to resist converting to co-education than smaller ones. Baum (1996: 101–104) reviewed 18 studies of age and size dependence in rates of change and argued that any conclusions were premature. He suggested that researchers needed to focus more on the organizational processes underlying the association between age, size, and change, a sentiment echoed in recent efforts at formalizing the relationship between change and disbanding (Hannan, 1998). We will take up this issue again in the next chapter.

Selection

Consistent *selection* criteria generally promote organizational reproduction by differentially selecting certain types of variations. Accordingly, when selection criteria shift, some variations that previously proved more beneficial than others are no longer positively selected. An avenue thus opens for new practices. In competitive environments, changes in the terms on which resources are available may create new selection pressures, generating changes in internal diffusion, imitation, promotion, and incentive systems. Internal selection systems that were previously irrelevant or not tightly connected to environmental fitness may be realigned.

Evolutionary explanations of transformation emphasize *external* catalysts to change because evolutionary processes, as described in Chapters 4 to 6, create internal selection systems promoting persistence rather than change. First, frequent interaction between members leads to positive reinforcement of interpersonal actions encouraging stability and compatibility. Second, current internal selection criteria may continue as vicarious representatives of past external criteria that are no longer relevant. Daily reproduction makes members more proficient at their practices and thus more likely to continue using them. Hence, explanations of organizational transformation typically begin with a search for a discontinuity that has undercut support for existing selection criteria, such as a change in competitive conditions, new government regulations, a turnover in leadership, or a technological breakthrough.

Deregulation in the 1980s in industries such as airlines and trucking reshaped competitive conditions and pushed many firms to adopt new strategies. For example, deregulation in the savings and loan industry exposed firms to withering competition for which many executives were unprepared (Haveman, 1993a). New, more aggressive managers took over many firms, transformed their strategies, and began acquiring weaker organizations. Haveman's research also cast light on the association between organizational growth and the extent to which inertia burdens large organizations. Pressures for inertia accompanied growth in the S&L industry, but growth also brought external opportunities for change. In the next chapter, we explore at greater length the genesis of shifts in organizational environments propelling changes in selection pressures.

Retention

Retention mechanisms for selected variations embody the third evolutionary process. Retention occurs when selected variations are preserved, duplicated, or otherwise reproduced so that the selected activities are repeated on future occasions or the selected structures appear again in future generations. As we argued in previous chapters, stability in the structure and activities of individual organizations has been a central focus of sociological theory, as well as organizational analysis. Classic social theory located stability either in socialized individuals who had internalized all they needed to know as inhabitants of social systems, or in structures of exteriority and constraint that severely limited individual discretion. Organization theorists have worked with a similar dichotomy, with some emphasizing individual commitment and organizational identity and others focusing on externalization and various forms of subtle control (Perrow, 1986). Granovetter (1985) argued for a more contingent position, in which local social relations embed people in networks that constrain but do not wholly determine their behavior.

Individuals can carry retained variations to the extent that members give up or suspend their individuality while engaged in organizational activities. Researchers have found, for example, that commitment, satisfaction, and other affective orientations to an organization are contingent upon job, work group, firm, and industry characteristics (Kalleberg and Griffin, 1978; Lincoln and Kalleberg, 1990). Retained variations may be embedded in organizational structures. Documents and files embody past practices, specialization and standardization of roles limit members' discretion, and centralization of authority and formalization of duties not only limit discretion but also make the members accountable to higher authorities. Finally, retention may be embedded in networks of social relations when members' role responsibilities and trust bring about practices that reproduce organizational knowledge. Networks of relations with powerful institutional actors may provide a *transformational shield* for organizations, buffering them against selection pressures that would otherwise induce or provoke change (Fischer and Pollock, 2004; Miner et al., 1990).

Successful transformations are not complete until the knowledge required for maintaining the new form becomes embedded in new routines. When the new form becomes a taken-for-granted aspect of everyday life in the organization, its legitimacy is assured. Organization cultures in which integration tendencies dominate will undoubtedly have an easier time completing transformations than those where differentiated or ambiguous strains are stronger, as we noted in Chapter 6. However, organizations where differentiated or ambiguous strains are strong probably generate more variations. They thus increase their chances of creating opportunities for change.

Examining the three dimensions of transformation

To portray transformation processes, we have chosen cases illustrating each of the three dimensions: goals, boundaries, and activities. Because we focus on the organizational level of analysis in this chapter, we sought cases that provided richly detailed information on an organization's form. Accordingly, most are based on intensive fieldwork, observation, or extensive use of archival materials. Table 7.3 lists the dimensions and cases discussed in this section.

Goals

Organizational researchers in the decades after World War II wrote splendid monographs on goal transformation in non-business organizations, public agencies, and

Table 7.3   **Case studies of transformation processes**

Dimensions	Examples
Goals	• Change in goal breadth: the remaking of three liberal arts colleges – Reed, Antioch, and Swarthmore (Clark, 1972).
	• Change in domain: the conversion of single-sex colleges to co-education (Studer-Ellis, 1995a, 1995b).
Boundaries	• Boundary contraction resulting from conflict: the Chicago Women's Liberation Union and Chicago Now (Staggenborg, 1989).
	• Disbanding as an alternative to transformation: Students for a Democratic Society 1962–1969 (Breines, 1980).
Activities	• Culture clash in a human resource management system: a Japanese firm in Italy (Botti, 1995).
	• Technological innovation and power relations: information technology's consequences (Barley, 1990; Burkhardt and Brass, 1990).

social movements, such as the Tennessee Valley Authority (Selznick, 1949), the Women's Christian Temperance Union (Gusfield, 1963), and the YMCA (Zald, 1970). Because the authors were typically writing in an 'exposé' mode, they often framed their stories as quasi-tragedies in which an organization's original goals were betrayed (Perrow, 1986). These studies not only documented major changes in goals, but also offered rich descriptions of the processes through which organizations were transformed. Authors wrote few case histories on unsuccessful organizations, although a few comparative case studies have contrasted 'successful' with 'unsuccessful' transformation. Because of potential bias in selection of cases, we must be cautious in drawing strong inferences from such work. Most instances of unsuccessful transformations are documented in population-level studies, albeit without a rich description of the process itself.

Two kinds of goal changes have drawn a great deal of attention from researchers: changes in goal breadth and changes in domains. A consistent theme in studies of goal breadth changes has been competitive pressures on organizations to find new resources. Organizations that specialize in a limited range of products or services occasionally encounter conditions preventing them from acquiring enough resources. Under pressure, many adapt by undergoing a transformation from *specialism* to *generalism* (Zald and Denton, 1963). By offering a wider range of products and services, generalists appeal to the diverse segments of a heterogeneous population and compensate for the inadequate support in their original niches. The Planned Parenthood Federation evolved out of the Birth Control Foundation in the 1940s by adopting a broader set of programs, and the American National Red Cross survived the crisis of increased governmental intervention in disaster relief by adopting its highly successful national blood donor program.

We have chosen two cases of changes in goal breadth and domain to illustrate three key themes: (1) changing external circumstances often trigger initial variations; (2) retention forces inhibit many efforts to transform organizations; and (3) organizational forms play a major role in the implementation of transformations. The first case is Clark's (1972) study of three distinctive American colleges, and the second is Studer-Ellis' (1995a, 1995b) study of the conversion of women's colleges to co-education.

The remaking of a college

Clark (1972) studied the transformations of three small private colleges – Reed, Antioch, and Swarthmore – from narrow goals to more encompassing ones. He depicted the development of an *organizational saga*, which is an historically grounded collective understanding of an organization's core goals and values. Clark showed how the growth of distinctive sagas influenced the life course of each college. Reed College was founded in Portland, Oregon, in 1910 by a young president who wanted to build an organization unencumbered by custom and tradition. From the start, the president stressed his desire for an academically pure college, an American imitation of Oxford's Balliol College, and he recruited a like-minded faculty. By contrast, Antioch College, founded in the 1860s, was in decline and disarray when Arthur Morgan began his attempt to transform it in the 1920s. His plan for Antioch involved academic study, off campus work, and community participation. Swarthmore differed from the other two in that it did reasonably well after its founding by Quakers in the 1860s, but was nonetheless judged ready for reform by a new president in 1920. He pushed for a modified Oxford honors program that included special seminars and exams given by visiting scholars to seniors.

In each case, a president committed to a new vision of higher education introduced transformation into a college. As Clark (1972: 180) noted, 'Strong sagas do not develop in passive organizations tuned to adaptive servicing of demand or to the fulfilling of roles dictated by higher authorities.' However, he did not attribute the transformations solely to the presidents' efforts. Instead, he pointed out that the changes were only expressed in practice when faculty members became committed to them. 'In committing themselves deeply, taking some credit for the change and seeking to ensure its perpetuation, [the faculty] routinize the charisma of the leader in collegial authority' (Clark, 1972: 181). As Weber (1947) argued, the routinization of charismatic authority concludes when a founder's vision is firmly entrenched in a rationalized organizational form. Members with supporter orientations no longer need centralized direction to carry out their duties.

At the two colleges where leaders perceived a need for reform, leaders approached transformation in different ways. At Antioch, financial and staffing difficulties, as well as problems in recruiting students, weakened the old organizational structure. Thus, little support existed for retaining it, and the new president and his followers easily pushed it aside. Swarthmore was not experiencing a similar crisis and so the transformation occurred in incremental steps and took longer. Reed College was founded with goals supported by faculty and students, and succeeding presidents were strongly committed to the founding president's vision. The unifying strength of their shared values enabled them to reject challenges to the organization's goals by new change-oriented presidents in the late 1930s and the early 1950s.

Retention processes played a key role in the staying power of the distinctive new goals at each college. Faculty, students, alumni, and outside supporters contributed to the persistence of new organizational goals, despite changing external conditions. Clark (1972: 181) found that faculty supporters of the transformations 'replaced themselves through socialization and selective recruitment and retention.' The internal selection system thus became a vicarious representative of past selection criteria, reflecting the president's and senior faculty's goals. Although the potential always exists in colleges and universities for multiple cultures to spring up around student and faculty interests, no such divisions occurred at Reed, Antioch, or Swarthmore. 'All three student bodies steadily and dependably transferred the ideology from one generation to another. Often socializing deeply, they helped produce the graduate who never quite rid himself of the wish to go back to the campus' (Clark, 1972: 182). All three colleges were more liberal than their peer institutions, and their alumni felt a special responsibility to protect their boundaries from conservative forces in the larger society.

Competitive pressures on single-sex colleges

In contrast to the heroic imagery of three elite liberal colleges and the staying power of their transformations, the story of women's colleges in the United States – another historically important organizational form – contains mostly melancholy overtones. Women's colleges were well established in the United States by the end of the 19th century and enjoyed continued growth until the 1960s, when almost 300 were still active. However, environmental changes in the 1960s put increasing pressure on women's colleges to enroll men, turning many into co-educational colleges (Studer-Ellis, 1995a). A huge expansion in publicly funded colleges and universities created stiff competition with women's colleges for students. Normatively, the civil rights' and women's movements were unsympathetic to separate educational spheres for men and women. Moreover, men's colleges increasingly adopted co-education, adding to the competitive pressure on single-sex women's colleges.

By 1990, 108 women's colleges had changed their domains to include men, thus becoming co-educational, leaving only 66 four-year women's colleges still operating in the United States. The remainder of the original population of colleges had simply disbanded. Larger and older private women's colleges were most able to resist the selection pressures toward goal changes, whereas publicly funded colleges were not (Studer-Ellis, 1995a). We could view transformation from a single-sex to a co-educational college not only as a domain change, but also as a move away from specialism and toward generalism. Other moves toward generalism occurred in US liberal arts colleges between 1972 and 1986. Many expanded their curricula: 63 percent of the 276 liberal arts colleges that had no business programs added a business major, and 28 percent of the 169 colleges that had no graduate programs added some (Zajac and Kraatz, 1993: 95).

Studer-Ellis (1995b) studied two cases of women's colleges deciding whether to remain single-sex or switch to co-education. He showed that Vassar and Smith colleges went through lengthy periods of struggle, involving intense negotiation and bargaining with alumni and other interested parties, before making decisions on whether to transform themselves into co-educational institutions. The two colleges provide an excellent opportunity for application of the comparative case method, as they are similar in many respects and yet the outcome of the process was different. They were founded within a decade of each other – Vassar in 1865 and Smith in 1875 – and enrolled similar numbers and types of students. Both are Seven Sisters colleges and are considered on a par with the formerly all-male Ivy League colleges, and both are located in the Northeastern USA.

What selection and retention forces confronted those who might have championed co-education at each college? Studer-Ellis (1995b) noted three constraints on transformation that differed across the two colleges. First, Smith College's charter very explicitly bound it to follow its founder's wishes and promote 'the higher education of young women,' and the state legislature in Massachusetts could use this language to block transformation attempts. Vassar, by comparison, had a much less restrictive charter and its board of trustees was more willing to take the risk of creatively interpreting their founder's wishes. Second, Smith College's students, faculty, and alumnae treated its single-sex status with reverence, whereas the Vassar community was more pragmatic. With its traditional status elevated to near-mythic standing, Smith College retained a very strong link to its past.

Third, Smith College is located in the Pioneer Valley area of Western Massachusetts, home to four other major colleges and universities, and so opportunities for alliances and joint ventures blunted the urgency of enrolling male students as a strategy for increasing diversity and raising revenues. Vassar, by contrast, was located in Poughkeepsie, New York, near three lower-status co-educational colleges and universities that were not viable partners for alliances or partnerships. Accordingly, Vassar had fewer options in responding to the selection pressures facing single-sex colleges. In 1969, Vassar adopted co-education as an official policy and admitted men to its freshman class the following year, whereas in 1973 Smith explicitly reaffirmed its policy of remaining a woman's college and remains one today.

We have reviewed several richly detailed case studies to illustrate three themes in evolutionary explanations of goal transformations. First, transformations in goals are often a response to changing external selection pressures, including not only a deteriorating resource base and shrinking niche, but also the declining legitimacy of an organization's current goals. Internally generated attempts at renewal or revitalization that are not responses to external pressures also occur, but we believe that they occur much less frequently. Second, transformational agents must overcome forces of selective-retention that reproduce an organization's current form, a lengthy and time-consuming process. All the examples we described unfolded over a period of years, and they seem unlikely to occur again in the life of these organizations. Deciding whether a transformation has occurred sometimes requires that we follow organizations over a lengthy period, as we noted in discussing the definition of transformation. Third, although the examples all involved presidents as champions of goal change, the studies also show that changes were only fully implemented when the organizational form was transformed. To the extent that changes disrupt current understandings of organizational knowledge, goal transformations are a potential threat to the reproduction of routines and competencies.

Boundaries

Boundary transformations may involve expansion or contraction. Management and strategy researchers have been especially concerned with mergers and acquisitions, often from a transaction cost economics perspective (Williamson, 1994). They have also studied the consequences of mergers, such as what happens to top management after a merger (Walsh, 1988). Sociologists have also studied mergers, but mostly from an historical perspective at the population level (Davis et al., 1994; Stearns and Allan, 1996). Organizations occasionally shed whole units, as in divestitures by large firms, but the most common form of boundary contraction involves layoffs or expulsions of members. Member turnover is common among business and non-profit organizations, and routines have usually been developed to deal with such boundary-crossing activity.

Some large-scale turnover goes beyond routine, however. Mass layoffs, associated with plant closings or relocations (Fernandez, 1997), and mass expulsions, typically associated with ideological or purposive changes in organizations (Skocpol, 1979), are consequential enough to be called transformations. For example, in the late 1970s, the United States' auto industry experienced such severe economic problems that by the end of 1980, firms laid off over 300,000 workers – about one-third of all auto-workers. New factions that take over political parties, unions, and social movements occasionally embark on large-scale purges of opposing factions (Michels, 1962). In choosing examples for this section, we picked several concerned with contraction because they clearly illustrate the link between external selection pressures and organizational transformation.

Conflict and contraction

Boundary contractions are sometimes rather dramatic events, especially within social movements. Conflict often leads to member expulsions, as contending factions struggle for control of an organization's goals and boundaries. Two social movement organizations founded in the same year in Chicago vividly depict such conflict. Staggenborg (1989) studied the Chicago Women's Liberation Union (CWLU) and Chicago Now, two women's movement organizations founded in 1969 in the same political environment but with different boundary-maintaining processes. The CWLU was an autonomous, socialist-feminist organization, committed to women's liberation and a broader 'liberation framework' that encompassed many radical issues of the times, including opposing imperialism, capitalism, and racism (Staggenborg, 1989). Chicago Now was a chapter of the National Organization for Women that devoted its energies to issues of sex discrimination in employment. Chicago Now focused on a narrower agenda than the CWLU, concentrating on equal rights and opportunities for women, rather than on broader political goals.

As a multi-issue organization, the CWLU attracted an extremely heterogeneous membership, and its decentralized structure and informal procedures made coherent, unified action extremely difficult. Although the resulting structure kept the CWLU true to its ideology of participatory democracy, it also made decision making problematic and follow-through impossible. The CWLU never achieved financial stability or a formalized division of labor. Chicago Now, by contrast, followed national guidelines. The chapter had formal bylaws and a formalized and centralized structure. As a result, Chicago Now 'was decidedly more successful than the CWLU in creating a stable organization capable of mobilizing impressive financial resources as well as activists for specific projects' (Staggenborg, 1989: 79). Initially, Chicago Now pursued the interests of activist members willing to form committees, but gradually it exerted central control over committee formation. Only those issues voted as high priorities by the entire chapter were allocated to committees for further action. By contrast, the CWLU pursued many issues simply because a committed group of members showed an interest in them.

Tight control over membership criteria made Chicago Now a fairly exclusive organization, with paid staff and membership committees having responsibility for boundary maintenance. Chicago Now staff worked hard at involving members in chapter activities, with weekly work sessions in which members wrote letters, made phone calls, and carried out other supportive activities. In contrast, loose control over membership criteria in the CWLU made it a very inclusive organization, with ambiguous boundaries and heterogeneous membership. The CWLU's open, inclusive nature left it vulnerable to 'the ultimately devastating problem of takeover attempts by left-sectarian groups' (Staggenborg, 1989: 84). Groups with radical goals saw the CWLU as an organizational resource they could turn to their own purposes. Infiltration by outside groups was possible because permeable organizational boundaries permitted almost anyone to participate in the organization's activities. In 1975, the October League, a left-sectarian group, succeeded in forming chapters within the CWLU. They proceeded to attack the CWLU's fundamental goals by arguing against 'feminism' as a goal and in favor of more overtly political aims. However, the remaining independent women in the organization still formed a majority of the steering committee. They voted to purge the sectarians from the CWLU in a vote that was subsequently upheld by the membership. Bitter conflict raged throughout the last few months of 1975. The organization was so weakened by the conflict that it disbanded shortly thereafter. Chicago Now, on the other hand, was still active in 1989, the last year of Staggenborg's study.

Disbanding as an alternative to transformation

Another social movement case study describes an organization that fiercely *resisted* a transformation process that would have changed its goals. In 1969, the same year that the CWLU and Chicago Now were created, another radical social movement organization disintegrated. Students for a Democratic Society (SDS) was founded on the principles of the Port Huron Statement of 1962, which called for participatory democracy allowing individuals to participate equally in all of the decisions affecting their lives (Breines, 1980). SDS had extremely ambiguous boundaries, as 'SDS recruited members neither to a political position nor to an organization, and, as a result, *became* what its members, always changing, were' (Breines, 1980: 424). SDS was so decentralized and grassroots oriented that it never coalesced as a formalized organization. Thus, no authoritative membership criteria were ever enacted. 'Around the country, activists acted and functioned politically with little regard for what the SDS National Office or specific leaders suggested ought to be done' (Breines, 1980: 423). The movement *was* the point, local leaders insisted, and they celebrated SDS's anti-organizational ideology. As in the CWLU, members fought over whether to compromise the organization's radical anti-hierarchical ideology in favor of a more formalized action-oriented structure. Ultimately, the members of SDS chose dissolution rather than giving up their intertwined organizational and political goals.

A central theme emerges from these case studies of boundary transformation. To the extent that formalized recruitment and selection processes are created during the founding process, prospects for radical boundary transformation are lessened. Organizations continually struggle with external selection pressures that limit access to the resources they need, including members. Structures and practices that maintain selectivity over membership entry and exit are another example of a *transformational shield* against radical change. Such forces are more likely to be invested with symbolic meaning in membership-based organizations, such as political parties and social movements, than in business firms. However, any organization with ambiguous boundaries or a low degree of control over them is susceptible to transformation, and this category includes many young and small businesses.

Activities

The third category of transformation is perhaps the most heterogeneous, as 'activities' cover a wide spectrum of possibilities. In this section, we review two types of transformation: changes in human resource management systems, and technological innovations that have organizational consequences. In the studies we have chosen, transformations affected entire units – a Japanese transplant in Italy, an American high-technology firm, a federal agency, and a radiology department in an American hospital – but mainly their activity systems, not their goals or boundaries.

Culture clash

Richly detailed ethnographic studies account for most of what we know about the *speed* of transformation processes in organizational activities that fall short of goal or boundary changes. Botti (1995; Botti and Bonazzi, 1994) described the case of Nipponware, a Japanese transplant that manufactured zippers, established in 1970 in Borgarolo, Italy. The original Japanese managers did not want to disrupt the Italian way of organizing semi-skilled factory work. Therefore, they left shop-floor organization in the hands of the Italian foremen. The Italian foremen, coming from a culture where close relations with one's superiors represented power-dependence relations (Emerson, 1962), cultivated the Japanese top management at the plant and subtly blocked any efforts to install 'Japanese-style' management in the plant. The Italian-style organizational form, based on patrimonial relations, remained intact. Japanese top managers in the plant, coming from a culture where close relations with one's subordinates represented reciprocal ties of obligation and responsibility (Jacoby, 2005), assumed good faith on the foremen's part and allowed the plant to retain patrimonial-style work relations. In short, Japanese managers misinterpreted the Italian workers' user orientations to their superiors as supporter orientations, and the Italian workers had no incentive to change. When Japanese managers were rotated through the plant, from Japan, they made few efforts to change things, and indeed would not have known how.

The system was stable for 17 years, maintained by a growing market for the plant's products and non-interference by the parent firm. Changing competitive conditions, in 1987, brought radical changes in the product market and caused the parent firm to examine the plant more closely. Close scrutiny of the plant exposed its severe competitive inefficiencies and production problems, and forced it into a transformation effort that took five years. The transformation process received a boost when a local Italian manager, aided by American consultants, read company documents and made several visits to Japan. Based on his observations in Japan, he realized how much his plant had forsaken the parent company's actual plans for their subsidiaries. His efforts at change finally succeeded when he dismissed the established Italian foremen and promoted his own people into positions of responsibility. By disrupting the established organizational form, he was able to create a new system of practices that was more in accord with the parent firm's system. In this case, then, the transformation took years at a pace best described as leisurely.

New technologies

Transformations in activity systems sometimes involve changes in organizational knowledge caused by the introduction of new technologies that radically alter organizational practices. Henderson and Clark (1990) examined the impact of structural innovations in technology-based industries in the United States. They considered how innovations may change the way the components of a product are linked together but leave the core design concepts intact. Thus, the basic organizational knowledge supporting the product remains valid, but the architecture of the product has been changed. The changes enhance some competencies but destroy others. For example, the development of the jet engine 'initially appeared to have important but straightforward implications for airframe technology. Established firms in the industry understood that they would need to develop jet engine expertise but failed to understand the ways in which its introduction would change the interactions between the engine and the rest of the plane in complex and subtle ways' (Henderson and Clark, 1990: 17). Somehow, Boeing's engineers grasped this dilemma, whereas engineers at Douglas and other established airframe manufacturers did not. With this change and subsequent success on other fronts, Boeing eventually dominated the industry.

Henderson and Clark's (1990) case study of the photolithography industry showed that firms new to the industry consistently outperformed established firms in exploiting innovations. When they tried to introduce radical innovations, incumbent firms were significantly less productive than firms new to the industry (Henderson, 1993). Why do some organizations fail to recognize potential architectural innovations when they arise? Lacking clairvoyance, organizational members can only judge the magnitude of an innovation, not its consequences. Unlike component changes, which are usually obvious, architectural changes are more subtle and difficult to spot.

Changes in power and status relations

Two other field-based, longitudinal studies of how new technologies affected organizational structures reveal the pacing of changes in power and status relations. Burkhardt and Brass (1990) collected four waves of data over a 15-month period in a federal agency in which a new computer system was adopted that made distributed processing capabilities available to all employees. (The study was apparently carried out in the late 1980s, although no dates were given in the article.) Within three months, early adopters of the new computer system had increased their centrality and power in the agency, but employees who were already powerful prior to the technological innovation retained much of their influence in the new system. Barley (1990) observed changes in role relationships resulting from the introduction of a potentially competence-enhancing technology: CT scanners. Based on his year-long observational study of two radiology departments in 1982–1983, he described 'technically occasioned social change as a series of reverberations that spread across levels of analysis much like ripples on the surface of a pond' (Barley, 1990: 70). During the year in which the new technology was being implemented, older radiologists whose competencies were tied to older technologies lost out to younger radiologists with greater knowledge. Technologists who had suffered from inferior status under the old system became more integrated into the new role system because of their technical expertise and closer working relationships with radiologists using the new technology.

We highlight three themes in the cases of activity changes we have reviewed. First, analysts should be very attentive to the level of analysis in transformation studies. In the Italian firm and the aircraft manufacturer, transformation represented a major change because the whole set of role relationships within firms was affected. For the other two studies of units within larger organizations, the changes put at risk the unit itself, but not the entire organization, which might have been disturbed but not fatally damaged if the innovations had failed. Second, the pace and speed of change are highly contingent on the source of variation and the strength of opposing forces. If powerful champions introduce variations, then transformation can proceed rapidly. If a resistant organizational form impedes variation, transformation is slowed or even blocked completely. Third, transformations in activity systems can modify role relations and change the distribution of intra-organizational power and influence. Several studies demonstrated that transformation in the role relationships of organizations could occur within a matter of months through a mandated technological change.

Summary of three dimensions

We have identified three types of transformations, based on the content of changes: changes in goals, boundaries, and activities. We used detailed case studies focusing on change processes to highlight some issues that deserve more attention. First, the examples show that transformations in goals, boundaries, and activities often overlap. For ease of analysis and exposition, we separated the three dimensions, but they are clearly interdependent. For example, when Vassar adopted co-education as an official policy in 1969 and began admitting men, it had to adapt by making changes in many of its practices. The CWLU's inability to control its boundaries also affected the goals it could pursue. Thus, organizational transformations that begin in response to selection pressures on goals or boundaries may well ramify into all aspects of an organization.

Second, the length of the period over which some transformations unfold places severe demands on research designs. The cases we reviewed involved much more than simply counting the occurrence of events. Instead, understanding what the events meant to participants required archival and field research. Third, because the investigators deliberately chose cases in which 'something happened,' we cannot use them to estimate the likelihood of similar transformations occurring elsewhere in their populations. The cases illustrate the need for studies of the frequency and intensity of everyday variations in organizations. Without baseline information on ordinary variation within organizational forms, we face great difficulty in judging the true strength of inertial forces in organizations. Just as organization studies researchers now recognize the need to pay more attention to entrepreneurship and organizational emergence, so too should research be designed to systematically monitor routine background variation in organizations.

Fourth, many of the cases showed that transformation was accompanied by conflict. Some members and groups fought to retain their existing practices, whereas others welcomed the changes. Powerful champions played a major role in several cases, acting as *organizational entrepreneurs* to push their positions (DiMaggio, 1988, 1991). Their intentions often clashed with those of other interested parties. Groups and cliques also were involved, illustrating the relevance of Martin's (2002) perspective on organizational culture. We suggested using the notion of three intertwined threads of meaning in organizations as a way of assessing an organization's propensity for conflict. When unified interpretations dominate an organization's culture and its boundaries are strong, transformation faces a smoother road than when a differentiated culture exists in an organization with weak boundaries. For example, consider the difference between the experience of the Chicago Now chapter and the Japanese transplant in Italy.

The extent of member participation in transformation activities

Organizational reproduction involves most members, by definition, but what about transformation? Is the transformation driven by top-down or bottom-up processes, are many members involved in the decisions, and are only insiders involved? Strategic choice and top management team theories of organizational change typically imply that an elite group within an organization makes the decisions leading to transformation (Child, 1972; Eisenhardt, 1989b). So strong is the assumption of limited participation that researchers rarely seek evidence for wider participation. Theories of planned variation as a cause of organizational change also assume that managers typically control the transformation process (Miller and Cardinal, 1994). In discussing shortcomings in the resource-based view of the firm, Montgomery (1995: 264) noted that 'research on strategy content hinges on optimism and has a history of blocking or marginalizing insights that might challenge managerial authority ... it overemphasizes the power of managerial prerogative.'

Social movement theorists, by contrast, have called attention to the processes whereby lower-level members and outsiders can challenge and transform organizational forms (Zald and Berger, 1978). Given the option of exit, movements within organizations can be effective even when owners or managers disenfranchise members. For instance, former slaves challenged the wage plantation form that appeared in the aftermath of the American Civil War and forced landowners to offer alternative forms of agricultural tenancy (Ruef, 2004). What seems crucial to the viability of such bottom-up processes of organizational transformation, therefore, is not just the extent to which organizational forms are participatory, but also whether changes in legal and regulatory contexts empower organizational members.

The legal and regulatory context of ownership

Whether extensive member involvement occurs depends fundamentally on the structure of ownership and control of organizational assets. For businesses, a legal and regulatory framework determines who has the authority to use organizational assets, as well as who has the right to delegate such decisions to others (Edelman and Suchman, 1997). In the United States, businesses can take one of three basic legal forms: sole proprietorships, partnerships, and corporations. Corporations can be privately or publicly held, with a board of directors, a chief executive, and other officers. The corporate form exists in all industrialized economies, although nations vary in the legal regulations governing forms of business organization. In proprietorships, partnerships, and closely held private corporations in the United States, owners have nearly absolute discretion, and employees' involvement in transformations will depend upon authorization, delegation, and power sharing by owners (Russell, 1985). Family members, as partial owners, are often involved in major decisions. As we discussed in Chapters 5 and 6, in *new* and *small* firms, employees may also substantially affect the development of an organizational form.

A board of directors governs publicly held corporations with a fiduciary responsibility to an organization's stockholders. A variety of rules circumscribes top management's discretion over the use of assets (Mizruchi, 1982). The directors, in law, are obligated to prevent reckless use of a corporation's assets, such as ill-advised mergers and acquisitions. In practice, directors in the past often neglected such responsibilities. Despite law suits brought by disgruntled stockholders, new professional association standards, new federal laws, and Securities and Exchange Commission regulations instituted during the 1980s (Espeland and Hirsch, 1990), ongoing problems of governance and oversight continue to stir debates about the efficacy of corporate directors (Hermalin and Weisbach, 1998).

Employees play a very limited role in most US publicly held corporations with regard to major decisions (Cole, 1985). New models of personnel and labor relations have appeared regularly since the end of World War II without fundamentally changing the power balance between employees and top management. In particular, schemes that attempt to transform organizations by substantially increasing employees' participation have waxed and waned over the past few decades (Osterman, 1994). Some employee participation programs, including schemes that give workers a share in gains made through productivity improvements, appear to raise firm performance (Weber, 1994). For example, Hatcher and Ross (1991) collected survey data from employees at an auto parts manufacturing firm before and after implementation of a gain-sharing plan. Their results indicated that grievances and product returns decreased significantly after the plan was implemented, and concern for teamwork, performance, and quality also increased. Despite such studies, reporting the positive effects of gain-sharing plans, very few firms have actually adopted these human resource management innovations (Weber, 1994).

A similar fate has befallen another human resource innovation: small-group activities. In the United States, managers mostly ignored small-group activities, whereas they were enthusiastically embraced in Sweden and Japan. Cole (1985) analyzed why industrial firms in the United States failed to adopt small-group activities as enthusiastically as Japan and Sweden in the 1960s and 1970s. He identified three factors. First, in the United States, national labor market conditions produced a large pool of unemployed workers, easily allowing employers to replace dissident workers. Second, the lack of national organizational champions – such as trade associations – for the innovation left advocates without an organizational resource base. Third, unions gave the new programs only lukewarm support. The failure of gain-sharing plans and small-group activities to diffuse widely in business populations reminds us that other organizations do not automatically imitate effective variations.

As McCaffrey et al. (1995: 619) noted, 'the principles *undermining* participative systems are embedded deeply in society, and are valued more highly than the prospective benefits of such systems.' Many initiatives toward greater employee involvement were brought forward in the past few decades, including quality of working life (QWL) and team-based management, but almost all such programs still sharply delimit the authority delegated to workers or presume that workers will take on additional work tasks (Weber, 1994). For example, Appelbaum and colleagues (2000) noted that 'high performance work systems' often require workers to assume coordinating responsibilities and develop new interpersonal skills. In his review of the literature on high-performance work practices, Baker (1999) concluded that most of them seldom hurt and sometimes helped organizations, while often helping members. Vallas's research on the United States' paper industry between 1999 and 2001 illustrates the limits of such programs (Vallas, 2003). He found that new work practices involving team initiatives and continuous improvement failed when centralized control did not allow autonomous local adaptation and when management's rigidly instrumental logic trumped the normative logic of greater worker participation.

The legacy of participatory organization is more established internationally. Many countries in Western Europe enacted legislation in the 1960s and 1970s giving workers a formal role in corporate governance, including seats on the boards of large firms (Stephens and Stephens, 1982). For example, in Germany, major decisions such as relocations and layoffs involve works' councils made up of employee representatives. Beginning in 1991, the European Union (EU) endorsed initiatives promoting greater employee participation and ownership, and a series of EU directives in 1994 through 1997 paved the way for European-wide expansion of employee rights. In 2004, the EU's proposed first constitution explicitly directed member states to work towards a coordinated strategy for employment. The new constitution required that all national employment policies be consistent with the EU's broad economic guidelines. As of 2005, the proposed constitution had yet to be ratified.

Membership-based organizations

Collectivist organizations represent a more significant opportunity for members to influence organizational transformation (Rothschild, 1979; Rothschild and Whitt, 1986). From their founding, collectivist organizations stress member involvement in all aspects of management, based on a strong participatory-democratic value system. Organizational norms emphasize rotation through office, sharing of organizational knowledge, and consensual decision making. Such conditions blunt oligarchic tendencies, and significant transformations require most members' participation. Some economic cooperatives operate on similar principles, such as the Mondragon cooperatives in the Basque region of Spain (Johnson and Whyte, 1977), which spin off new ventures if a business unit grows too large for effective participatory-democratic principles.

In voluntary associations and non-profit organizations, the extent of member involvement in transformations depends upon the organization's charter or constitution and the extent to which it has avoided *the iron law of oligarchy*. Michels (1962) argued that all mass-based organizations – political parties, unions, voluntary associations – were susceptible to the iron law of oligarchy, which is the tendency toward tyranny and unresponsiveness by leaders toward their membership. Michels, a German sociologist writing in the decade prior to World War I, observed strong oligarchic tendencies in the German Social Democratic Party and the socialist parties in France, Italy, and elsewhere. These parties were ideologically committed to the extension of democracy to the working class, and yet in their own internal structures they were highly undemocratic.

Rather than completely devoting their actions and resources to achieving the manifest purposes of their organizations, the leadership was concerned with defending itself in office and preserving its position against internal challengers. Michels' analysis of oligarchy was the stimulus to Lipset et al.'s (1956) study of union democracy in the International Typographical Union (ITU), an exceptional case that Michels' law did not seem to fit. *Union Democracy* stands out as a classic work in organizational sociology precisely because the high level of membership participation it depicted is so rare. However, the ITU was not able to sustain the structure observed by Lipset et al., according to a follow-up study conducted in the 1980s (Stratton, 1989). Analyses of contemporary samples of unions suggest that contingencies such as organizational boundaries and administrative routines explain only limited variation in democratic goal formation (Jarley et al., 1997).

Despite leaders' and members' strong efforts, Michels' law seems as relevant to organizations of today as it was almost a century ago, because many membership-based organizations are run by a small faction of highly committed leaders (Knoke, 1990). Nonetheless, Voss and Sherman (2000) argued that a bureaucratized structure does not always doom unions to oligarchy. In their study of the potential for revitalization in the Northern California chapters of three international unions, they found that some chapters overcame the iron law of oligarchy and adopted new organizing tactics. Revitalization was most likely when the national union leadership initiated and supported local change, when a local chapter had experienced a political crisis, and when local leaders had activist experience *outside* the union movement. Left unsaid in their analysis, however, was the question of how frequently such conditions obtain in the wider community of unions and other voluntary associations. We suspect such occurrences are rare.

Consequences of transformation

Transformations are dramatic events, introducing discontinuities into an organization's life, but are they also necessarily disruptive, beyond their effect – by definition – on goals, boundaries, and activities? Weick (1995) argued that interruptions in organizational routines – shocks produced by unexpected, disconcerting, and inexplicable events – disrupt the communication activities that are the lifeblood of organizations, triggering intensified efforts at sense-making. Might transformations actually improve an organization's performance if it gains effective new routines and competencies or revitalizes the old ones? Organizational ecologists have been explicitly concerned with transformation's effect on organizational survival, whereas other investigators have typically not made a distinction between the transformation they studied and any concurrent or subsequent disruptions. Ideally, to determine the effects of a transformation, we should analytically separate the disruption imposed by the change 'process' itself and subsequent consequences resulting from the 'content' of the change (Barnett and Carroll, 1995).

Transformation's potentially harmful consequences were explicitly addressed in Hannan and Freeman's (1984) model of structural inertia. They posited that structural transformations are disruptive in the short run, but may improve an organization's life chances in the long run. In the short run, confusion in the implementation of routines and challenges to organizational knowledge raises the risk of organizational reproduction going awry. However, if an organization successfully creates new routines that reproduce the new form, then its chances of survival may improve. Some studies have confirmed their predictions, such as Amburgey et al.'s (1993) historical study of Finnish newspapers. Content changes altered the institutional status of papers in Finland in the mid-19th century, especially if they were political papers. Changes also required newspapers to modify their routines for collecting news, thus bringing about changes in their organizational knowledge (Amburgey et al., 1993). Content changes had a disruptive effect on the newspapers, and the changes were increasingly disruptive as the newspapers aged.

However, other investigators have not found any harmful effects from transformations. For example, Zajac and Kraatz (1993) found no serious disruptions when liberal arts colleges added programs in response to environmental changes. Similarly, in their study of transformations in the US airline industry from 1962 to 1985, Kelly and Amburgey (1991) found that none of the changes was disruptive enough to affect the likelihood of an airline surviving. In his review of 11 studies that investigated the association between organizational change and failure, Baum (1996: 104) noted various methodological problems with many studies. He concluded that 'any conclusions drawn at this time would thus be premature.'

The effects of transformation may not be uniform across different categories of organizations and different kinds of outcomes. For example, Haveman's (1992) study showed that some kinds of transformation could negatively affect survival chances, whereas others had no effect. She explicitly looked for the disruptive effects of organizational transformation in her study of California savings and loan institutions (S&Ls). Between 1978 and 1982, legislators passed three federal laws and one state law that altered the rules for California-based S&Ls, provoking a spate of transformations. The new laws substantially loosened regulatory constraints, opened new markets, and provided the S&Ls with opportunities to expand beyond their original domains. Haveman argued that changes away from the S&Ls' traditional market – residential mortgages – into new domains could be classified by the extent to which serving new markets taxed an S&L's initial competencies and thus potentially lowered its survival chances. She examined the similarity between seven new markets and the original domain served by S&Ls along three dimensions: clientele, products, and technology. She found that the more closely related the new domains were to the old, the better an S&L's chances of performing well and surviving.

Short of fatal consequences, other possible disruptive effects of transformations include a loss of power and status by some members and groups in an organization, interruptions in careers, and a spillover from one kind of transformation into another. Some accounts of life in corporate America paint a picture of political intrigue and in-fighting so all-encompassing that transformations would seem to have little chance of making any difference in the turmoil (Kunda, 1992). Such studies are undoubtedly biased toward firms that have attracted attention precisely because they are such interesting cases. Nonetheless, the case studies we reviewed earlier support some of their findings, which found that intraorganizational relationships were often disrupted by transformations.

Career consequences of transformations may involve members being forced to seek work in other organizations or even to switch careers altogether (Walsh, 1988). Haveman and Cohen (1994), in their study of the S&L industry in California between 1969 and 1988, found that mergers meant not only job loss for managers made redundant in takeovers, but also movement to non-banking careers. They found that mergers led to moves between S&Ls for about 43 percent of the managers and to exits from the industry for about 21 percent of them. By contrast, the slow bureaucratization of personnel functions among large US firms, induced by federal regulation in the 1940s, helped create a new career track for human resource professionals (Baron et al., 1986).

The disruptiveness of transformations depends, in part, on their speed and size, and so these three dimensions are clearly interdependent. Field-based studies have usually emphasized the unruly aspects of transformations, but investigators probably selected such cases because they were good sites for studying disrupted organizations. For businesses, patterns of ownership and control limit widespread member involvement in initiating transformations, although the extent of their participation affects whether planned changes are implemented successfully. Membership-based voluntary associations and non-profit organizations would seem more likely candidates for widespread participation in major events, but research has found little evidence that more than a handful of members take part in such fateful decisions.

Conclusions

Transformation involves a major change in an organization over time and represents a substantial variation, planned or unplanned, that has been selected and retained. Variations may arise through institutionalized experimentation, incentives offered to members, organizational tolerance of unplanned variation, and many other sources. Selecting forces may be internal (e.g. managers and members) or external (e.g. market forces and government regulations). The selected variations represent a discontinuity in organizational life and a break from the normal reproduction of organizational routines and competencies. Retention of changes involves alterations in an organization's routines such that the newly transformed organization is reproduced over time.

Transformations in goals, boundaries, and activities take place against a background of the daily reproduction of routines and competencies that perpetuates organizational forms more or less untouched. Seen from this perspective, the incidence of transformations reported in large-sample studies is quite low, perhaps even rare. The speed with which transformations are completed, once initiated, is also unclear, given the paucity of large-sample studies. Case studies show, however, that we can probably measure the pace of change for most transformations in months and years, not days or weeks. Speed and pacing during transformation are important because a lengthy process may put an organization's resources at risk, and organizations without slack resources may not survive the process.

Transformation is significant for organizational evolution for three reasons. First, an organization that cannot change in fundamental ways will constantly be at risk, if its environment is evolving and it cannot keep pace. Second, if most organizations in a population are constrained from undergoing significant transformation, then that population will persist in evolving environments only through the founding of new organizations that are better suited to the changing context. If, however, some organizations are transformed and survive, their routines and competencies represent variations that have been selected and retained. If the new routines and competencies spread through imitation, borrowing, or other forms of diffusion, other organizations in the population that adopt them will also survive. Existing organizations will thus sustain the population. We return to this issue in Chapter 10. Third, if a substantial fraction of the organizations in a population is unable to make the transformations necessary to evolve in tandem with the environment, and new organizations do not replace them, the population itself may be doomed. Indeed, new populations regularly challenge existing ones, as we discuss in Chapter 9. To the extent that organizations in a challenged population remain inert, a new population has an easier time making a place for itself.

Transformation processes, then, provide a clue as to whether foundings of new organizations or changes in existing ones will drive the development of populations. Transformations in which boundary expansion occurs can produce population distributions in which a decreasing fraction of the population controls an increasing proportion of the resources available. By contrast, boundary contractions, on a sweeping scale, may increase the level of competitive intensity in a population as smaller, more focused organizations compete with one another. How frequently transformations occur in a population, whether they are reversible, and whether some organizations are more likely than others to experience repeated occurrences, tells us whether organizations are likely to keep up with changing environmental conditions. If transformations are rare and the probability of any particular organization experiencing one is low, the co-evolution of organizations and environments becomes increasingly unlikely. Instead, long-term evolution will be a result of the rise and fall of entire populations.

Study Questions

1. Under what internal and environmental conditions is structural inertia a desirable property of organizations? Under what conditions is structural inertia an undesirable property?
2. Recent interest in organizational transformation has emphasized the 'cascades' of change in other attributes and units that may be set off by an initial transformation (Hannan et al., 2003). Using the basic dimensions of goals, boundaries, and activities, develop a set of empirical hypotheses that explain when (and how) transformation in one dimension is likely to affect the others.
3. Albert Hirschman (1972) described 'exit' and 'voice' as two basic strategies that members and external stakeholders could use to transform unresponsive organizations. When are members and other stakeholders most likely to employ the 'exit' strategy, abandoning an organization (or its products) for other alternatives? When are they most likely to rely on 'voice', expressing their dissatisfaction to management or other authorities?

Exercise

1. Describe previous transformations in the organization you have chosen for analysis in Chapters 4 to 6. To what extent have the goals, boundaries, and/or activities of the organization been affected? What was the extent of member participation in these changes? What were the consequences of the changes, seen in both 'process' and 'content' terms?

8

Organizations and Social Change

Organizational transformations occur within historical and geographical contexts. Some transformations are dramatic, one-of-a-kind historical events that are earth shattering in their implications, such as those accompanying cataclysmic wars and revolutions. For example, after the Meiji Restoration in 1868 established a new political order, development-oriented officials in Japan looked to Western Europe for institutional models (Westney, 1987). As a result, Japan's public sector – the financial system, the police, the postal system, the military, and so forth – was transformed along the lines of those of France, England, and Germany. Other transformations have modest individual effects but great cumulative significance. For example, personal computers not only increased the efficiency of information processing in individual offices, but also made possible the growth of electronic data exchange systems between organizations. Transformations, then, involve significant social, economic, and political changes, especially when they sweep across entire populations.

All transformations are time-dependent processes. To gain full appreciation of their significance, organizational transformations must therefore be placed within their historical context (Isaac and Griffin, 1989). In this chapter, we present a framework for classifying and interpreting historical transformation processes. We begin by reviewing life cycle, teleological, and dialectical models from an evolutionary perspective. We suggest substituting the concept of *life course* for *life cycle* as a way of avoiding the deterministic implications denoted by the term 'life cycle.' Next, we argue that to study population-level transformations, we must embed our explanations in an historical context. We borrow from population demographers a conception of history as comprising age, period, and cohort effects. We present a simple framework for making *history* a key feature of an evolutionary explanation, rather than 'time.'

The life cycle metaphor: developmental and stage models

Many accounts of transformations are implicitly based on a life cycle model. They not only use an organization as their unit of observation, but also construct their explanations at the organizational level. Two models of change follow a pure life cycle metaphor: developmental and stage. We begin with them, as the life cycle metaphor has been a very powerful image in organizational studies, particularly in the strategy, marketing, and product development literature. In these models, 'time' is viewed from the perspective of a focal organization, and 'age' represents accumulated experiences.

Life cycle models are not limited to organizations as units of analysis. In organizational ecology, the density-dependence model is a life cycle theory with a population as the unit of analysis, rather than an organization (Carroll and Hannan, 2000). In young populations, increases in density cause large increases in legitimacy and small increases in competition. In older populations, an increase in density causes small increases in legitimacy and large increases in competition. As we discuss in the next chapter, theorists predict that these processes result in a particular pattern of change in founding and disbanding rates.

In most developmental and stage models, theorists posit that organizations confront certain generic problems as they age, such as how to produce goods or services, market them, and account for the costs of production. Managers and members then respond with generic solutions, such as increasing an organization's complexity, formalization, and delegation (Pugh et al., 1968). In pure form, these models focus heavily upon internal processes, viewing all organizations as if driven by a common dynamic. Cross-field borrowing can generate insights, but if used uncritically, these models may mislead theorists into too facile an equation of human development and organizational development. We thus urge caution in applying life cycle models to organizations.

In their comprehensive review of 63 identifiably separate stage models of organizational growth between 1960 and 1996, Levie and Hay (1998) concluded that such models had made no progress toward the goal of predicting patterns of organizational growth. Indeed, they argued that stage models persisted in spite of repeated failures to confirm them empirically. As we review the features and shortcomings of developmental and stage models, we discuss how they could be replaced by taking account of insights from the evolutionary approach. We summarize the various models in Table 8.1.

Developmental models

Most theories of organizational founding and growth are developmental, rather than evolutionary. Developmental approaches assume that change occurs in a cycle of emergence, growth, maturity, and decline. In this process, maturation represents a realization of the potential inherent in organizations when they were founded (Greiner, 1972; Van de Ven and Poole, 1995). The specific contents of the stages are 'always mediated by the immanent logic, rules, or programs that govern the entity's development' (Van de Ven and Poole, 1995: 515). The natural unfolding of organization structures and processes flows from the forces that all organizations face, and the timing or pacing of events has a natural rhythm which participants create but which also constrains them (Gersick, 1991, 1994). From this perspective, the principles of organizational emergence and

Table 8.1   **Historical models of organizational change**

I. Life cycle metaphor	'Time' is viewed from the perspective of a focal organization. 'Age' represents accumulated experience. Assumption: Organizations encounter generic problems as they age.
Developmental model	Life cycle model in which an organization changes on the basis of the potential inherent at its founding.
Stage model	Life cycle model in which organizational change proceeds in stages during which members must solve new problems.
Metamorphosis model	Variation on the stage model in which change occurs in discontinuous stages provoked by a mismatch with context.
II. Non life cycle models	'Time' is viewed from the perspective of the length of problem-solving sequences. 'Age' represents a series of cycles. Assumption: Organizations can achieve 'progress'.
Teleological model	Model in which an organization's 'purpose' drives organizational actions.
Dialectical model	Model in which change is a never-ending shift between confrontation and temporary reconciliation.
III. Evolutionary models	'Time' is viewed from the perspective of organizational context. 'Age' represents accumulated experience in historically-specific environments.Assumption: Builds on previous models and adds elements of ambiguity and uncertainty.

growth are similar for *all* organizations. The principles can be learned by investigating the natural history of existing organizations.

An evolutionary approach is much more contingent, as it assumes that organizations do *not* follow a fixed path of development. Instead, external events interact with an organization's own actions to drive the pace, pattern, and direction of change. Organizational problems occur in response to changing situations, rather than in a predetermined order. Although all organizations face similar fundamental problems of organizing, their histories – the timing, sequencing, and intensity of changes – are rooted in the selection forces they experience. For example, in their analysis of 645 small business cases developed at universities in Michigan, Ohio, and South Carolina, Dodge et al. (1994) found that the level of competition faced by firms was a much more important cause of problems than their life course stage. Similarly, Ruef's (2005) study of 532 business startups found that the timing of some activities, such as the announcement and delivery of a new product or service, was strongly influenced by the competitive environment that each firm faced.

From an evolutionary perspective, organizational changes must be linked to particular environmental conditions, such as geographical context and national boundaries. Generalizations should be historically grounded and limited to the domain of organizational forms sampled. Rather than positing fixed developmental sequences, without regard to environmental circumstances, evolutionary theory contains multiple *if-then* statements. Organizational change is algorithmic, not developmental. Arguments take the contingent form of 'If organizations encounter particular environmental circumstances, then particular consequences follow.'

Stage and metamorphosis models

Stage and metamorphosis models are variations on the developmental and evolutionary models. Stage models assume a developmental sequence, but modify the developmental model by asserting that an organization pauses at various steps, during which founders, managers, and members might take adaptive actions (Bartunek and Betters-Reed, 1987; Kamm and Nurick, 1993). Metamorphosis models may use either developmental or evolutionary foundations and then build on them by postulating that changes are provoked when structures are mismatched with environments (Starbuck, 1965). In developmental formulations, the key to survival turns on successful internal restructuring. Metamorphosis models posit that change occurs abruptly and in discontinuous bursts, rather than gradually and smoothly.

Some misinterpretations presume that evolutionary models *only* posit smooth, incremental changes in organizations. Actually, all evolutionary models have in common the absence of a strong *a priori* notion of a fixed pace at which changes occur. Evolutionary formulations emphasize the interaction of external selection with internal variation, with change proceeding at a pace set by the intersection of organizational and external forces. Thus, a metamorphosis model can be treated as a special case of a more general evolutionary model. However, over the long run, most changes in organizations are probably small and incremental, rather than large and monumental, as we noted in Chapter 7.

Non life cycle models: teleological and dialectical

Van de Ven and Poole (1995: 520–521) identified two models of change that they contrasted with life cycle and evolutionary models: teleological and dialectical. Teleological models treat change as 'a cycle of goal formulation, implementation, evaluation, and modification of goals based on what was learned by the entity. This sequence emerges through the purposeful social construction among individuals within the entity.' Dialectical models of change propose that 'conflicts emerge between entities espousing opposing thesis and antithesis that collide to produce a synthesis, which in time becomes the thesis for the next cycle of a dialectical progression.' A pattern of confrontation and conflict between opposing entities sets a dialectical cycle in motion. Reconciliation is always temporary, never permanent.

Teleological and dialectical models may be partially incorporated within the framework of evolution, rather than treated separately as competing alternatives. *Teleological models* propose that goal setting by individuals and organizations leads to purposeful variations as well as selection criteria. In turn, the evolutionary approach reminds us that actors' goals reflect the influence of particular social locations in time and space. *Dialectical models* propose that organizations exist 'in a pluralistic world of colliding events, forces, or contradictory values that compete with each other for domination and control' (Van de Ven and Poole, 1995: 517). The evolutionary approach explores the historical origins of such oppositions.

Adding evolutionary ideas to life cycle and non life cycle models

The evolutionary approach builds on life cycle models by adding room for human agency, ambiguity, and uncertainty (March and Olsen, 1976). In contrast, developmental models suggest that internal forces dominate firms, implying that managers and members have few choices to make. Stage models of development allow more room for choice, but only within the confines of an unfolding natural history. Commenting on life cycle theories, March (1994: 49) argued that the language of life cycle theories implies a set of nearly inevitable outcomes and destinations. By contrast, evolutionary models allow much more latitude for choice and chance.

An organization's trajectory of development results from the interplay of its actions with environmental resources and constraints. Although members might intend a certain course, interaction with their environment may take them on a different journey. The case studies of organizational transformation in three American colleges, discussed in the last chapter, showed that presidential intentions were only one of several forces generating an organizational saga. For example, Arthur Morgan's plan for Antioch College focused on the short-term goal of returning it to solvency, but he also initiated a program of off-campus study that became an enduring model followed by many other colleges. Thus, we wish to avoid the deterministic and linear implications of the term 'life cycle.' Instead, we borrow the term *life course* from the field of human development and family studies. This concept explicitly links the evolutionary approach to research domains using social psychological and learning models of change.

Framed in life course terms, we no longer view 'time' in evolutionary models solely from a focal organization's perspective. Organizations emerge in evolving environments that preceded them and will outlive them. Ambiguity and uncertainty arise because organizations move through their life course in a population context, in which their survival and transformation depend on other organizations' actions. Organizations struggle to keep or expand their place within a population and, in turn, a population struggles within a community of populations. Organizational members strive to make sense of their evolving worlds, but they must work with the sense-making schemata made available by their historical period. Understanding how and why their world changes is a major task of evolutionary theories, and we turn now to a three-part historical framework.

Three components of an historical framework

Max Weber explicitly framed his writings on organization and bureaucracy in historical terms. Many authors since then have called for approaches to organizational analysis that emphasize broad historical implications (Hinings and Greenwood, 2002). However, surveying the results of avowedly historical analyses, Abbott (1992: 429) argued that Weber's concerns for 'action and process have largely disappeared from empirical sociology.' A kind of *narrative positivism* has taken over as the dominant method for dealing with time and temporality. Although Abbott was critical of recent efforts to construct historical explanations, he also recognized the diversity of approaches across social science sub-fields. In this chapter, we borrow some ideas from historical

Table 8.2 **Three components of an evolutionary-historical framework for understanding organizational change**

Age effect	Changes produced by processes inherently associated with duration of existence. For example, decay of a founder's initial enthusiasm for a project.
Period effect	Changes produced by historical events and forces that have a similar effect on all organizations, regardless of age. For example, deregulation of financial markets applied to all savings and loan financial institutions.
Cohort effect	Changes produced by historical events and forces that have a different effect on organizations of different ages. For example, wartime shortages of essential resources may weaken younger organizations but have little effect on older ones.

demographers and life course theorists who have developed a framework that explicitly incorporates history in analyses of social change (Isaac and Griffin, 1989). Mindful of Abbott's criticisms, we point out some potential pitfalls in such borrowings.

Historical influences may be classified into three types of effects: cohort, period, and maturation or aging, as shown in Table 8.2. *Aging or maturation effects*, as defined by demographers, describe the secular process of aging. For example, organizations might become less flexible as they age. To avoid the anthropomorphic and developmental implications of the term 'maturation,' we will use 'age' and 'aging' to refer to organizations growing older. A *cohort effect* occurs when historical events have a differential impact on younger versus older organizations. For example, wartime shortages might seriously weaken younger organizations but have little effect on older ones. A *period effect* occurs when historical events have similar consequences on different age cohorts. For example, wartime demands on organizations to rationalize production processes might affect all firms equally.

In Figure 8.1, we show the three effects in graphic form, with organizational age on the vertical (y) axis and year of founding on the horizontal (x) axis. Successive cohorts of organizations labeled A through H are shown as parallel lines, starting on the horizontal axis and running diagonally to the upper right corner of the figure. Dashed lines with arrowheads at the top represent each cohort. Organizations founded in the same year, e.g. cohort A in 1955, make up a group that moves together through time, experiencing historical periods while they are all of the same age. For example, all surviving organizations in cohort A experienced the period of heightened government regulations in the early 1970s (Vogel, 1973). Other cohorts, e.g. B and C, also experienced the same regulations, but organizations in them were 5 and 10 years younger, respectively, than cohort A.

Through a detailed investigation of a particular population's history, researchers try to identify periods of significant changes in selection forces. In Figure 8.1, we have identified two periods – I and II – for the purposes of illustrating the concept. We demarcate Period I by two political events, beginning with Lyndon Johnson's election to the U.S. Presidency in 1964, and ending with the conclusion of his term in 1968, when the

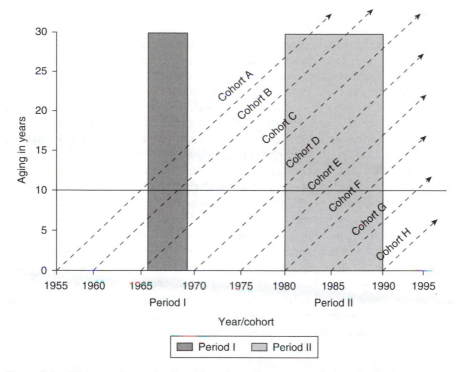

Figure 8.1   History and organizational transformation: age, period, and cohort

Democratic Party 'New Deal' coalition was shattered and he decided not to run for re-election. His term in office was marked by a major expansion in government programs, foreign and domestic, affecting a large proportion of organizational populations in the United States. For example, Johnson's 'Great Society' policy poured millions of dollars into urban renewal and anti-poverty programs, such as model cities and youth-oriented local government agencies (Moynihan, 1970; Warren et al., 1974). Community action organizations prospered, as did public agencies dealing with urban problems. Period II is demarcated as the decade of the 1980s, following Davis et al.'s (1994) claim that the era represented a period during which norms regarding corporate diversification were transformed. The bracketing years for the period were inferred from actual changes in corporate behavior, rather than from any single sociopolitical or economic event.

The age of an organization at any year in Figure 8.1 can be read off the vertical axis, by tracing from the cohort arrow to the age scale at the left. For example, ten years of aging is represented by a dashed line, drawn from the '10' on the age scale across all the cohorts. Surviving members of any cohort that reach the dashed line have all lived through ten years of events, and we could superimpose all the cohort arrows onto one line to emphasize the equivalence in duration of their experiences. However, organizations of different cohorts lived ten years through different historical periods, and thus comparable ages in organizational life courses might still involve quite dissimilar accumulated experiences. We develop these ideas in the following sections.

Age effects

Transformation, by definition, is associated with organizational age, for if organizations don't age, they can't change. But, is it true that organizations can't age unless they change? Three positions have been staked out regarding transformation and aging. First, the stage and metamorphosis models of organizational life cycles we reviewed earlier implicitly assume that change occurs naturally in aging organizations, as they encounter and solve generic problems (Selznick, 1949). Transformation, in this sense, constitutes an integral part of the aging process. At this level of analysis, 'time' runs on a universal clock, rather than being historically situated. This means, for example, that stage and metamorphosis models implicitly treat one year in the 19th century as equivalent to one year in the 20th century. Problems are problems, regardless of the century in which they are encountered.

Second, theories of strategic choice, organizational learning, and other models positing adaptive organizational behavior assume that transformation is possible as organizations age, but not inevitable. With transformation seen as contingent, rather than intrinsic to the aging process, theories of choice and learning propose organizational characteristics that facilitate or impede transformation as organizations age. Accordingly, aging by itself is not the critical factor in transformation. Rather, aging creates learning opportunities for organizational members, who can then make choices, carry on past practices, or explore new ones (March, 1994).

Third, some classical writings in organizational sociology, as well as early ecological models, contended that organizations ossify with age. Merton (1957) argued that long-term occupants of organizational roles take on a 'bureaucratic personality' that turns them into members more concerned with means than ends and stubbornly resistant to change. Initial statements in organizational ecology assumed that aging depends on organizational inertia, because environmental selection favors organizations that display reliable and accountable structures (Hannan and Freeman, 1984). Thus, as organizations age and experience external selection processes, the surviving organizations are those that retain the most stable structures. Older organizations, consequently, undergo significant transformation less often than younger ones. Of course, 'inertia' in this context does not mean complete lack of change, but rather that an organization maintains a consistent course of action and predictable orientation to its environment.

Despite the theoretical plausibility of the structural inertia model, Baum (1996) found little empirical support for it. He reviewed almost two dozen studies of organizational change and found that after appropriate controls were introduced, particularly for contemporaneous organizational size, no clear pattern emerged. Even separating changes into the categories of 'core' and 'periphery,' as suggested by Hannan and Freeman (1984), did not clarify the studies' findings. Ranger-Moore (1997) and Hannan (1998) suggested two explanations for the mixed results from past studies.

First, heterogeneity across different organizational populations restricts investigators' abilities to generalize. Global models may hide the extent to which populations experience very different environments, particularly populations subject to severe regulatory pressures or rapid technological change. Ranger-Moore (1997) recommended that investigators replicate their research across populations with different histories, such as comparing populations that experienced constant turbulence versus those experiencing mostly periods of tranquillity. Second, as Hannan (1998) noted in a formalization of age-dependent processes, multiple mechanisms may be implicated simultaneously as organizations age, including imprinting effects from different stages of an organization's or population's history, the rise and decline of resource endowments, the development of capabilities and positional advantage, as well as structural inertia. These mechanisms can give rise to various liabilities of newness, adolescence, obsolescence, or senescence (Barron et al., 1994; Fichman and Levinthal, 1991; Ruef, 2002b; Stinchcombe, 1965).

Failure to include key organizational and contextual factors thus limits a study's ability to detect the effects of aging. In a study of adaptations to changing market conditions among non-federal hospitals in California, Ruef (1997) included controls for organizational size and population density, as well as period effects. The study avoided some problems that have plagued earlier analyses, but it nonetheless covered only the period from 1980 to 1990. Ruef's analysis showed that relative structural inertia increased with organizational age. However, because organizations that disbanded before 1980 were not included and only one decade was covered, he had to be cautious in drawing inferences about the effects of aging. By contrast, when Ranger-Moore (1997: 917) studied the life insurance industry over a longer period of time, he found that the effect of age varied dramatically by historical period.

Population and community context of aging

The evolutionary model views aging not only as an organizational-level process, but also as occurring within two other contexts: populations and communities. First, an organization ages within a population that is also aging. Second, a population ages within a community of populations. Thus, an historical approach to understanding transformation must take account not only of an organization's accumulated experiences, but also of the extent to which its population's aging may affect its life chances. For example, being a young organization in an emerging population means something quite different from being a young organization in a mature population (Barnett et al., 1994; Ingram and Baum, 1997). New organizations in mature populations compete with organizations that have already weathered the competitive storms and thus have gained organizational knowledge that new organizations lack.

If aging were all that mattered in organizational transformation, then the slanting parallel lines in Figure 8.1 could be collapsed onto one line or superimposed on one another. Accordingly, we could write simply of a generic aging process. However, such an approach ignores the historical importance of periods and cohorts, such as the possibility that aging through the 1960s had different consequences for transformation than aging through the 1980s. We turn now to a consideration of the historical context within which aging occurs.

Period effects

A period effect is an historical discontinuity that has a similar impact on all organizations or organizational members in a population, without regard to their ages. By explicitly identifying historical periods, analysts imply that 'underlying causal regularities themselves differ across temporal contexts' (Griffin, 1992: 407). Investigators recognize period effects by observing abrupt breaks in the continuity of social, political, economic, and normative trends in a society. Many 'periods' become salient to organizational analysts because historians and journalists, with the benefit of hindsight, create labels for such periods. For example, in 20th-century America, the 1930s were 'the depression years' (Elder, 1999), and the early 1980s were the era of market-oriented 'regulatory reform' (Scott et al., 2000).

Period effects give direction to a narrative analysis of organizational evolution, ordering events by their chronology (Aminzade, 1992). Identifying periods gives observers a way of conceptualizing one-time events, while emphasizing the common features of all organizations in a population. For evolutionary analyses, we concentrate on identifying periods of historical events that affect populations of organizations, rather than with a specific organization's life course. For example, Aldrich and Staber (1988) argued that the processes governing the founding of business interest associations differed substantially between the periods *before* and *after* the 1933 National Industrial Recovery Act (NIRA). The NIRA legitimated many new forms of business interest associations and temporarily boosted their founding rate.

Choosing which years constitute a 'period' reveals a potential problem with historical analyses, because narrative analysis not only relies on events occurring serially, in a chronology, but also tends to emphasize unique events (DiMaggio, 1994). Marking discrete segments in history as 'periods' is thus fraught with potential arbitrariness. Different observers view the same events from diverse perspectives on their significance. In practice, analysts create period labels on the basis of their research objectives and working hypotheses. For example, in her analysis of the higher education publishing industry between 1958 and 1990, Thornton (2004) used three techniques to identify periods. She interviewed industry participants to obtain oral histories, read newspaper and magazine accounts of that era, and examined graphical plots of trends in various industry statistics. Based on her investigation, Thornton identified two periods – editorial and market – during which patterns of industry control differed, resulting in different patterns of acquisition and leadership succession. In their study of the health care field after World War II, Scott and colleagues (2000) employed archival research, factor analyses of historical indicators, and sensitivity analyses to identify three major periods with distinctive institutional logics. They found that the early era of professional dominance, characterized by autonomous physicians and community-oriented hospitals, was replaced in the 1960s by an era of federal involvement, with increased participation by the national government in funding and regulation. During the 1980s, this period, in turn, gave way to the current era of market orientation, with an emphasis on managed care and competition.

In the following research case study, we consider yet another example of period effects that reflect profound institutional transformation, examining Li and Walder's (2001) study of changing patterns of Communist party recruitment in China over a half century.

Research Illustration 8.1   Elite Recruitment and Social Change in China

Using retrospective life histories of a representative sample of adults in urban China, Li and Walder (2001) sought to explain the evolution of Communist party recruitment, beginning in the era of Mao Tse-Tung in 1949 and ending in 1996, following extensive party reforms. The outcome of interest involved the selection mechanism guiding entry into the party and the individual characteristics it favored. To analyze historical changes in recruitment, Li and Walder partitioned the study into three time periods, based on the occurrence of political events: (1) the Mao era (1949–1977), coinciding with a program of 'counter-selection' that sought to improve the mobility of individuals from working-class and peasant backgrounds; (2) an early reform era (1978–1987), which followed preliminary shifts in party policy following soon after the death of Mao; and (3) a late reform era (1988–1996) that culminated in a program of 'technocratic' selection favoring the promotion of well-educated individuals.

The evolution of elite recruitment in China from 'counter-selection' to 'technocratic' selection was tested more formally by noting temporal variation in rates of Communist party entry among adults in the sample. During the Mao era, respondents from 'red' backgrounds (those whose fathers were elite administrators, party members, Red Army soldiers, martyrs, and the like) were more than twice as likely to be recruited into the Communist party as those lacking such backgrounds. By the late reform period, however, the effect of a 'red' background had dropped dramatically, only increasing elite recruitment of those respondents by 25 percent.

With respect to the educational background of the respondents, an opposing trend was noted. Under Mao, the effect of a college education generally did not improve the chances of Communist party recruitment significantly (although this depended to some extent on the career stage of an individual). By the late reform period, on the other hand, a college education resulted in dramatic (eight- to nine-fold) increases in elite recruitment, suggesting broad support for a shift to 'technocratic' selection criteria.

Li and Walder's study illustrates the importance of period effects in evolutionary analysis as well as some of the methodological difficulties they may introduce. Variation, selection, and retention mechanisms are unlikely to be static, tending to change according to the dictates of the social, economic, and political environments that confront organizations. Period effects are well-suited to capture these temporal variations, but they also tend to be operationalized with historical hindsight and may be defined arbitrarily. To combat such tendencies, investigators can judge the robustness of different period specifications by conducting sensitivity analyses. Thus, Li and Walder (2001: 1391) found that their late reform period generated clearer contrasts to Mao's program of 'counter-selection' than the early reform period. They posited that the disruptive effects of the Cultural Revolution produced an early reform period in which party organizations were being rebuilt and clear patterns of sponsorship were less likely to be observed.

Types of period effects
Four classes of period effects have been investigated in organizational studies: (1) political events and change in regimes; (2) legal and regulatory policy changes; (3) shifts in societal norms and values; and (4) changes in resource availability not otherwise due to any of the previous three changes. Below, we review each and present several brief examples. A word of caution is in order. The interpretation of period effects must take into account the substantial accumulation of historical products that current actors and observers take for granted, such as nation-states, political regimes, and cultural patterns. Theories treating states and regimes as self-interested actors are especially vulnerable to interpreting contemporary events without regard to the historical constraints laid down by the past.

Political events
Robins (1987), in his critique of transaction cost theory, argued that analysts need to make a distinction between social and political conditions existing at a given time and

place, and the economic/organizational processes unfolding within that sociopolitical framework. Thus, in criticizing the priority Williamson (1981) gave to transaction cost economizing, Robins argued that the history of the 19th century was not really a story of hierarchy displacing markets. Instead, social and political centralization created the conditions making large-scale commerce and manufacturing possible.

Changes in political leaders or governing parties sometimes bring about substantial changes in organizational environments, as we illustrated in summarizing Li and Walder's (2001) study of changes in Chinese party recruitment following the death of Mao Tse-Tung. Shifting national political currents are also often associated with changes in populations of organizations that are not exclusively political in purpose. In the United States, charter schools proliferated after the 1991 charter school legislation in Minnesota (Renzulli and Roscigno, forthcoming). In Ireland and Argentina, political events played a major role in the founding and disbanding of newspapers (Delacroix and Carroll, 1983). Similarly, Amburgey et al. (1993) argued that content changes in Finnish newspapers were worthy of study because they reflected the way in which political legitimacy and other resources were mobilized (see also Dacin, 1997). They studied content changes in all 1,011 newspapers published in Finland at any time between 1771 and 1963. Although many Finnish newspapers provided general coverage of the news, almost half were either affiliated with a political party or adopted an independent political stance. In addition to papers specializing in political content, a smaller proportion covered the economy, religious news, and other non-political topics.

Legal and regulatory events

Legal and regulatory actions, a second type of period effect, often change the institutional framework for populations (Leblebici et al., 1991). They may create new legal categories, impose requirements, or offer incentives that change organizational practices. Officials rarely apply laws and regulations in a straightforward manner (Suchman and Edelman, 1996: 932). Instead, ambiguity, ignorance, and interaction between regulators and the regulated cause a form of 'collective construction of compliance.' Accordingly, outcomes often evolve in unforeseen ways (Vaughan, 1996). A reciprocal relation between regulators and targets confounds the treatment of laws and regulatory actions as period effects, given the initially indeterminate nature and magnitude of the effect. Moreover, such interaction means that the legal environment evolves continuously rather than discretely during the period when compliance is constructed. For this reason, Suchman and Edelman were implicitly critical of modeling legal effects with simple before-and-after dummy variables.

Some regulatory changes affect not only a single population but also an entire community of populations. Federal legislation in the United States substantially strengthened the long-term trend in the 20th century toward the expansion of due process rights for employees aimed at eliminating inequality among groups defined by race, color, religion, sex, or national origin. The Civil Rights Act of 1964 and the Equal Employment Opportunity Act of 1972 created national legislation and agencies to administer and enforce the rights of groups, defined in the law, to equal treatment by employers. Around the same time, worker rights were also being expanded with respect to employee safety and benefits, as reflected in the Occupational Safety and Health Act (OSHA) of 1970 and the Employee Retirement Income Security Act (ERISA) of 1974.

Using a stratified random sample of 279 organizations from California, New Jersey, and Virginia, with data gathered in 1985, Dobbin and Sutton (1998) examined when affirmative action, health and safety, and benefits offices were adopted. With the possible exception of OSHA, the legal period effects served as a significant stimulant to the creation of these offices. By the mid-1980s, over a quarter of the organizations had health and safety offices, a third had benefits offices, and around 40 percent had affirmative action offices. The latter trend was especially dramatic, because no EEO/AA offices were established prior to the 1964 Civil Rights Act.

Aside from stimulating changes to existing organizational forms, legal and regulatory events may lead to the emergence of new forms. Regulatory changes in Japan, after World War II, created an environment in which some firms were able to create highly effective vertical business network structures, or *keiretsu* (Edwards and Samimi, 1997; Gerlach, 1992). Vertical keiretsu are usually confined to one industry, in which a lead company focuses on a comparatively small number of activities with a limited set of other firms. Williamson (1985) argued that possible opportunistic behavior by subcontractors makes such inter-firm dealings problematic. However, in Japan, a small set of large firms was able to create an inter-firm structure in which opportunism was suppressed. In the 1970s, when Japanese automobile manufacturers were pressured by the United States to limit their exports to America, they responded by setting up similar networks of production facilities within the United States (Florida and Kenney, 1991). Japanese parts manufacturers followed the auto plants to the American mid-west and recreated the vertical supply networks that they had developed in Japan.

Many theorists have attributed this Japanese corporate success to enduring cultural values, norms, and sociopolitical factors. In contrast, Edwards and Samimi (1997) argued that the rise of successful vertical *keiretsu*, such as Toyota, was an historically specific response to a set of temporary conditions. In Japan, government policies in the 1950s changed the business environment such that large firms such as Toyota and its smaller subcontractors had strong incentives to cooperate, rather than engage in simple mutual-benefit exchanges. Government controls on foreign exchange made it difficult for firms to buy what they needed from overseas, and controls on foreign investment effectively banned foreign firms from producing in Japan. Other controls forced Japanese firms to seek foreign technology licensing agreements and one-way technology transfer. Vertical *keiretsu* thus arose during a comparatively brief period in Japan's modern history when selection forces were favorable – from shortly after World War II until the early 1960s – and none has appeared since then (Edwards and Samimi, 1997: 499). Firms attempting to copy the vertical *keiretsu* form have been unable to replicate it.

Shifts in norms and values

Shifting cultural currents represent a third period effect. In turn, these can be differentiated into: (1) period effects where the agents of change were highly visible, involving social movements; and (2) period effects where the cultural forces at work were subtle and specific agents of change were difficult to detect.

Social movements and moral crusades sometimes engender abrupt shifts in norms and values that change entire organizational populations (Gusfield, 1963). For example, Clemens (1993: 791) argued that women's groups 'helped to create a new system of political institutions' in the early decades of the 20th century. Two examples of important social movements involve single-sex colleges and shareholders' rights movements. The decline of women's colleges between 1960 and 1990 was hastened by strong normative pressures from the civil rights' and women's movements against the acceptability of separate facilities (Karabel, 2005; Studer-Ellis, 1995a). By 1996, the few remaining state-funded single-sex colleges for men – the Citadel, VMI – were under intense pressure to change, as normative support for single-sex education had all but evaporated in the United States. Similarly, shareholders' rights groups changed the behavior of many US firms between 1984 and 1994. Pressure from social movement activists arguing for share-holder rights forced many big American corporations to adopt investor relations depart-ments (Rao and Sivakumar, 1999).

Even though some social movements do not succeed in their primary purpose, they might generate more subtle forms of cultural change. Between 1929 and 1934, Southern textile workers in the United States were mobilized through the emergence of new media, such as radio, and musical genres, for example the folk protest songs produced by mill musicians (Roscigno and Danaher, 2004). The labor mobilization culminated in the Labor Day walkout of 1934, the largest in U.S. history. Although the textile strike lasted only three weeks before being squashed by mill owners, traces of the working-class songs nonetheless persisted in subsequent social movements, such as the protest music of the 1960s.

Shifts in norms and values may also occur without explicit social movements. Along with legal and regulatory events, changing norms regarding appropriate corporate behavior influenced the pattern of mergers and acquisitions over the past four decades in the United States. The rise of the 'firm-as-portfolio' model of corporate growth in the 1960s sanctioned corporate expansion through diversification into products unrelated to a firm's core business (Fligstein, 1990; Weston et al., 1990). Chief executives were encouraged to think of firms as bundles of assets analogous to the stocks investors hold in their portfolios. An executive's job was to allocate corporate resources across the var-ious strategic business units in a firm, picking winners and losers, without regard to the particular products or services of the units. Return on investment was what mattered most, not what the businesses actually produced (Espeland and Hirsch, 1990). Throughout the 1970s, the largest U.S. firms adopted portfolio planning and engaged in a flurry of unrelated acquisitions, and levels of corporate diversification increased sub-stantially. By the early 1980s, this same view of corporations made it possible for corpo-rate raiders, investment bankers, and management consultants to lead takeover attempts that broke up conglomerate firms into their component parts and sold them off.

In the 1980s, a new, much narrower conception of appropriate corporate bound-aries replaced the older, much broader view (Davis et al., 1994: 563–564). Indeed, organizational boundaries and the very definition of an organization itself were at the heart of the changing nature of corporate mergers in the 1980s, calling into question American managers' traditional conception of a corporation. The 'organization as body' naturalizing analogy supplanted the 'organization as portfolio' analogy and sup-ported the notion that organizational boundaries marked off real entities from one another. Conglomerate mergers fell out of favor – were *deinstitutionalized* – and in a changed regulatory climate, horizontal mergers once again flourished. Managers were advised to focus their activities on a core business, specialize in what they know best, and contract out unrelated activities to other firms. The changed conception of appro-priate boundaries was captured in such phrases as the 'networked organization' and the 'virtual corporation' (DiMaggio, 2001). Corporations that grew through internal expansion, as well as those that acquired competitors or suppliers, still fit the traditional idea of a coherent entity with a discernible core.

By way of comparison, conglomerate expansion was still the norm in Thailand in the 1980s, as financial conglomerates supported the efforts of their industrial conglomerate clients, and government policies favored firms that were involved in import substitution and rural development activities. In contrast to the adversarial relation between large firms and the state in the United States, the state in Thailand was very active in soliciting corporate involvement in its economic development plans (Suehiro, 1992). In the industries chosen for export promotion and development, government policies favored large over small firms. Whereas the 'organization as body' analogy seemed natural for the United States, in Thailand, as in other Asian nations, businesses relied more on family networks, 'stressing the importance of relational bonds as organizational principles' (Pananond, 1995: 21). For example, the leaders of the five largest conglomerate groups shared the same clan association or dialect group. Thus, the normative trends that de-legitimated the conglomerate form in the United States were culturally specific and did not have any effects in Thailand.

Changes in resource availability

A fourth type of period effect involves dramatic shifts in resource accessibility. Sudden swings in resource availability may produce rapid changes in their environment for populations, thus opening up avenues for growth or forcing drastic economizing measures. Political, legal-regulatory, technological, and normative shifts may initiate such periods, but they may also arise because of the population's own actions, as well as through exogenous events (Brittain, 1994). Natural disasters and rapid demographic swings, such as sudden changes in birth and death rates, can also change the conditions of existence for populations. We focus on the example of rapid technological innovation, as investigated by Tushman and Anderson (1986). We describe it briefly here and cover it extensively in the next chapter.

How frequently do organizational transformations alter the composition of populations? Pinpointing discontinuities and classifying them as competence-enhancing or destroying requires detailed historical knowledge of a population. Tushman and Anderson (1986) hypothesized that technological changes within a product class are characterized by long periods of incremental change, punctuated by discontinuities. For the cement industry, founded in the early 1870s in the United States, Anderson and Tushman (1990: 610) identified two competence-enhancing and three competence-destroying technological innovations over the next 90 years. For the container glass industry, they identified two instances of each type of discontinuity between 1893 and 1956, and for flat glass, one competence-enhancing and three competence-destroying innovations from about 1900 until the early 1960s. Finally, for the minicomputer industry, founded in 1956, there were two competence-destroying innovations and then one competence-enhancing innovation over the 24 years of observations.

They expected that competence-enhancing discontinuities would be associated with fewer entries and more exits, and that the opposite pattern would prevail for competence-destroying innovations. Their expectations were supported for competence-enhancing but not for competence-destroying innovations. Competence-enhancing innovations strengthened the positions of established firms and thus apparently discouraged foundings in the cement and airline industries. In the facsimile transmission industry between 1965 and 1992, a similar process occurred, with the competence-enhancing shift from analog to digital technology lowering the founding rate, although the rate increased as the effects of the innovation wore off (Baum et al., 1995).

Although Tushman and Anderson were careful to note the limitations of their purposely chosen sample, three points stand out. First, all three industries they studied experienced *both* kinds of discontinuities – competence-enhancing and destroying. No industry was untouched. Second, in a typical year, technological changes were incremental rather than discontinuous. Incremental change favors the replication of an organization's existing routines and competencies, but perhaps sets the stage for a serious surprise later.

Third, a more complete understanding of why entrants usually do better than incumbent firms at introducing radical innovations needs to consider not only the impact of new organizational knowledge but also the strategic issues involved. Henderson (1993) noted that neoclassical economic theory predicts that entrants to an industry do well because they have greater strategic incentives to invest in radical innovation than do incumbents. In contrast, organization learning theory predicts that entrants do well because they are not burdened with the obsolete routines and competencies of incumbent firms. Separating these two effects will require complex research designs of the kind used by Henderson (1993) in her study of the photolithographic alignment equipment industry and Tripsas (1997) in her study of the typesetter industry.

Cohort effects

Cohort effects occur when events within a period differentially affect organizations within successive founding cohorts, as defined by year. Unlike a pure period effect, which affects all organizations within a population regardless of their ages, a cohort effect depends upon *when* an event occurs within the life course of an organization. In ecological analysis, a classic example of a cohort effect is *density delay*, which occurs when population density during an organization's founding subsequently affects its life chances (Carroll and Hannan, 1989). Organizations founded in times of high population density and fierce competition may be pushed to the margins of their niche, scrambling for resources they need. If these conditions persist, organizations are forced to compromise, perhaps by hiring less-experienced workers or purchasing inferior equipment. Consequently, they may face a life-long liability that makes them weak competitors. When they encounter harsh conditions, these weakened organizations may not survive, whereas younger or older organizations, founded in different periods, will pass through the difficult times. Although Carroll and Hannan (1989) and subsequent researchers (Dobrev et al., 2002; Ruef, 2006) have found support for density delay, not all studies have replicated these results (Aldrich et al., 1994; Lomi and Larsen, 1998). We return to this issue in Chapter 10.

How frequently does an organization's age interact with a period effect to produce a cohort effect? Because most investigators have not framed their research in these terms, we can only speculate about the role cohort effects play in organizational evolution. However, a re-examination of the four classes of period effects reviewed above provides some hints of how cohort analyses might be carried out in the future. After discussing how cohort effects might interact with period effects, we describe a case where changes in a single cohort of organizations eventually spread across all cohorts: the multi-divisional organizational form.

First, changes in governance structures and political regimes may benefit younger, less-well-established organizations by weakening connections between older organizations and the political elite (Stinchcombe, 1965). Wars and political revolutions often promote new political leaders who have no loyalties to the existing elite (Carroll et al., 1988). After the defeat of Germany in 1945, the four Allied Powers moved swiftly to remove all Nazis from power. Government officials were chosen with one criterion in mind: having been anti-Nazi. Later, in East Germany, the Soviet Union applied another test: evidence of commitment to a socialist or communist organization. As in the case of Maoist China, these new recruitment and selection policies substantially changed the social composition of the bureaucratic class in East Germany, as many more officials than before were chosen from the agricultural and working classes (Hardin, 1976; cf. Li and Walder, 2001).

Second, legal and regulatory changes often have selective effects on younger versus older organizations. For example, during World War II the United States War Production Board substantially changed the regulatory environment for locomotive producers. When diesel locomotives first appeared on the horizon early in the 20th century, managers of two steam locomotive producers – Baldwin and Lima – very strongly opposed the notion that diesel power would ever displace steam (Marx, 1976). Even when General Motors introduced the first diesel-electric passenger engine in 1934, and then followed up five years later with a diesel freight locomotive, the two firms remained committed to a 'steam' strategy. Perhaps a follower or late adopter strategy might have worked, eventually, were it not for the abrupt onset of World War II. The two laggard firms were dealt a mortal blow when the War Production Board issued an order that assigned production quotas for the locomotive industry. General Motors was given the exclusive rights to produce diesel freight engines because it had the only proven design. Baldwin and Lima never recovered.

Third, shifts in norms and values have more diffuse effects on organizational populations, unless moral crusaders or social movement organizations manage to solidify their gains through political or legal actions (Clemens, 1997; Wuthnow, 1987). Whether such events have age-specific consequences is difficult to foresee. Several studies suggest that population decline through reversal of fortune is pervasive rather than age-specific. For example, at the end of the Cold War, the number of peace-movement organizations in the United States declined (Edwards and Marullo, 1995), and in the late 1970s, the alternative organization movement faded away (Rothschild and Russell, 1986). Nonetheless, if selected members of a cohort survive a turbulent period, they become carriers of a rather precious cargo – the norms and values of an earlier era – and sympathetic constituencies may undertake heroic efforts to keep them afloat. The NAACP seemed to benefit from such support during a leadership and funding crisis in 1995–1996, as it struggled to recover from nearly 20 years of inactivity and recurrent crises (Smith, 1996).

Fourth, density delay is an example of how sudden swings in resource availability may produce rapid change in the carrying capacity for a population, differentially affecting organizations because of their ages. Technological innovations of a competence-enhancing kind may also have cohort-specific effects because such innovations may be easier for younger firms to adopt than older ones. By contrast, competence-destroying innovations favor entirely new cohorts of firms rather than existing ones. In the photolithographic alignment equipment industry, for example, waves of new entrants took over from leading firms after each competence-destroying innovation (Henderson and Clark, 1990). In their study of airlines, cement manufacturers, and the minicomputer industry, Tushman and Anderson (1986) found that existing firms initiated almost all of the competence-enhancing innovations, whereas firms new to the industry pioneered competence-destroying innovations.

Competence-destroying technological change does not inevitably lead to the destruction of existing firms, however. In an analysis spanning over a century of change in the typesetter industry, Tripsas (1997) identified three waves of competence-destroying technological innovations: 1949, 1965, and 1976. She found that existing firms responded in each case by investing heavily in the new technologies, but their products were consistently inferior to those introduced by firms new to the industry. Nonetheless, in two of the three waves, existing firms survived the technological onslaught because they possessed valuable *specialized complementary assets* (Mitchell, 1992; Teece, 1986). Some had a specialized manufacturing capability, some controlled a strong sales and service network, and others owned a proprietary font library. Depending on the characteristics of the innovation, some assets retained their value and allowed existing firms to survive the new technological wave.

Cohort effects that spread

Changes in the form of large U.S. corporations are an example of a transformation that arose in a single cohort of organizations but then rapidly spread across all cohorts of firms. In his classic study of large firms' adoption of divisional structures, Chandler (1962) argued that territorial expansion and product diversification placed an intolerable strain on the old unitary structure (U-form) of large corporations. In response, Du Pont, General Motors, Jersey Standard, and Sears Roebuck adopted divisional structures (M-form) in the 1920s. According to Chandler (1962: 2), the divisional form was a strategic response to the competitive pressures facing the large firms: a general office planned, coordinated, and appraised the work of a number of operating divisions and allocated to them the necessary personnel, facilities, funds, and other resources (see Freeland, 2001, for a critique of this argument). The executives in charge of divisions were responsible for their division's financial results and success in the marketplace.

At first, the multi-divisional form (MDF) was not widely copied by other large firms, but it now constitutes the dominant form. In 1929, only 1.5 percent of the 100 largest non-financial firms in the United States had adopted the MDF, but by 1979, 84.2 percent of the 100 largest firms had adopted it (Fligstein, 1985). Over the decades since 1929, established and newly emergent large firms have been equally likely to adopt the MDF, and neither corporate size nor age has apparently influenced such transformations. Fligstein (1985: 388) identified three conditions affecting which firms were transformed: (1) pursuing a multi-product strategy; (2) being in an industry where the firm's competitors had already adopted MDF; (3) and having a CEO with a sales or finance background (Fligstein, 1990).

Fligstein's findings are open to several interpretations, depending upon which theoretical perspective one adopts. Copying from other firms in the same industry could be seen as a form of mimetic isomorphism under conditions of uncertainty (DiMaggio and Powell, 1983), or it could be seen as a process of population-level learning. *Population-level learning* means a systematic change in the substance and mix of routines and competencies in a population arising from that population's experience (Miner and Haunschild, 1995). Mimetic isomorphism implies that firms will adopt the practice, regardless of its efficacy, whereas population-level learning implies that firms pay attention to whether the practice works. Amburgey and Dacin's (1994) analysis of the 262 largest U.S. mining and manufacturing firms between 1949 and 1977 strongly confirmed that pursuing a multi-product strategy increased the likelihood of a firm's adopting MDF. Palmer et al. (1993) reported similar results from their analysis of 105 large corporations active between 1963 and 1968. Thus, a type of transformation that began in the 1920s, when two large firms adopted it, became a standard feature of large firms' structures by the 1980s. From a cohort-specific practice, MDF evolved into community-wide organizational knowledge.

A methodological caution

If periods have varying consequences for organizational transformations, depending on an organization's age, then models of organizational evolution must include such effects. In the age, period, and cohort scheme of Figure 8.1, definitional dependence among the three concepts renders their separate effects unintelligible, *unless* non-linearities are involved. If their effects are merely linear and additive, then knowledge of any two of the three historical effects automatically generates the third effect. For example, assume that the effect of aging is monotonically linear – each year of advancing age has the same consequences – and that the effect of Period I is the same for all organizations. In this case, the difference between cohorts A, B, and C is simply the difference in their founding years (their ages). Knowing 'age' and 'period' would generate the 'cohort' effect. Similarly, at the beginning of Period II, the differences in surviving organizations attributable to age would be the differences in founding years and the periods they had experienced.

When we probe more deeply into theories of organizational transformation, however, we rarely find an assumption of simple linear relations. For example, models of organizational disbanding and aging usually assume that the protective effect of age increases at an increasing rate, rather than at a constant rate. Researchers, moreover, often fail to realize that they must make theoretical assumptions about age, period, and cohort effects when they study historical processes. Ecological analyses stand out as being much more explicit about such decisions. Complicating matters immensely, age, period, and cohort effects often interact with other factors to make generalization difficult.

Conclusions

Organizations are embedded within populations of like organizations and communities of dissimilar populations. Evolutionarily significant transformations are those that occur across many organizations within a population, that spread within particular cohorts of a population and fragment it, or that spawn new populations. Accordingly, the evolutionary perspective gives greater weight to widespread transformations than to changes occurring within isolated organizations, no matter how large or important they might seem. At the population level, waves of transformation evidently appear infrequently but have potentially significant effects, especially if they are competence-destroying or change population diversity. For example, the wave of conversions of single-sex colleges wiped out most of the women's colleges in the United States and the multi-divisional form completely displaced older corporate forms.

Diversity in populations and communities, from an evolutionary perspective, arises from the continuous variations introduced into populations through the intersection of age, period, and cohort effects. At any given moment, a population includes organizations that have experienced different periods because they were founded in different years. If, as they age, organizations move through predictable courses in their structures and activities, then organizations of the same age will resemble one another, regardless of period. If, as they move through historical periods, organizations become imprinted with the events of those eras, then organizations whose accumulated experiences include the same periods will increasingly resemble one another, regardless of age.

Some periods have had similar effects on all organizations, whereas others have had age-specific effects. If the effects of an historical period are contingent on the ages of the organizations affected, then neither age nor period by themselves will be enough to help us understand similarities. Instead, each cohort in a population will accumulate unique experiences that mark them off from other cohorts, and their evolution will be path dependent in the extreme (Arthur, 1989). At the limit, idiosyncratic historical trajectories will make the transfer of organizational knowledge across cohorts impossible.

Transformation thus occurs within an historical context in which some forces conspire to drive organizations apart, whereas others move organizations toward a common set of routines and competencies. Will organizations in a population converge on a dominant design, with selection pressures keeping variations within a narrow range? Or, will diversity remain high, as innovations, competition, cooperative alliances, and other factors generate variations that are favored by beneficial period and cohort effects? From an evolutionary viewpoint, the ability of populations to adapt to changing environments depends on organizational diversity. Accordingly, evolutionary analysis devotes substantial energy to understanding transformation's role in promoting or reducing diversity, in the face of historical forces.

Study Questions

1. Many studies of organizations are either cross-sectional in character or only address relatively short time periods, thereby missing the early years of organizations or organizational populations. What are the methodological limitations of such research designs?

2. The effects of age, period, and cohorts can be divided further into *contemporaneous* effects, which pertain to the impact of conditions on an organization at a given point in time, and *imprinted* effects, which pertain to the impact of conditions on an organization from a given point in time and onward. Thus, a *contemporaneous* cohort effect from the Civil Rights Act may have had a disproportionate influence on newly founded organizations during the mid-1960s, while an *imprinted* cohort effect would have continued to influence those same organizations during the following decades. Identify other empirical examples where it would be important to invoke this distinction.

3. In this chapter, we have emphasized the impact of social context on organizational change, assessed through historical time 'clocks'. Another type of 'clock' that could be linked to organizational outcomes is the personal history of key members, such as founders or top managers. Develop a set of hypotheses that relate age, period, and cohort effects from the life histories of founders/managers to the organizations they help run.

Exercise

1. What age, period and cohort effects have played an especially important role in the development of the formal organization you have analyzed in previous chapters?

9

Emergence of New Populations of Organizations

Organizational communities consist of diverse populations that occupy different niches and use a mix of general and population-specific routines and competencies. In the short run, we observe a fairly stable set of populations, depending on the rate at which new organizations replace disbanding ones. However, this placid image can deceive us. Populations appear and disappear with some regularity. Given a long-enough period of observation, almost all populations show an inverted-U shaped growth pattern, with numbers of organizations rising and falling as a population ages. In this chapter, we examine the social processes surrounding the emergence of new populations, from the founding of pioneering ventures through to the early stages of population growth. We also examine conditions surrounding the period when the form proliferates and the population becomes established.

By what process do new populations emerge? We know that organizational forms reflect the knowledge and resources available to nascent entrepreneurs during a specific period, as discussed in Chapters 6 and 8. Competencies and routines used in organizing are also culturally embedded and historically specific. Thus, populations founded in different eras embody different organizational forms (Stinchcombe, 1965). Analytically, organizational populations and forms reflect a simple definitional duality. Populations consist of organizations that are alike in some key respects; an organizational form embodies the key features that allow observers to identify whether an organization belongs to a particular population. From the perspective of subjective approaches to defining organizational forms, as discussed in Chapter 6, the study of population emergence never involves simply 'counting' the first appearance of an organization that has discovered effective new competencies and routines. It also entails an understanding of the socio-cultural rules that lead observers to differentiate that organization's form from those of its contemporaries (Pólos et al., 2002).

In this chapter, we concentrate on the growth of new populations, rather than the opening of new markets. New markets may emerge within existing markets and be exploited by so-called *de alio* entrants – either existing organizations that already serve similar markets or new ventures sponsored by existing organizations (McKendrick et al., 2003). For example, Barnes and Noble was a well-established bricks-and-mortar company when it created a new venture to enter the on-line book business. By contrast, our interest lies in wholly new populations formed by nascent entrepreneurs who carve out a niche by constructing independent organizations. For example, Amazon.com, one of the first on-line book sellers, was started as an entirely new entity. Such independent ventures cannot rely on existing institutions to provide external support and therefore face especially acute problems of learning and legitimacy.

Definitions: populations, learning, and legitimacy

Studying populations of organizations is of broad interest to many social scientists, inviting considerable diversity in terminology and analytic approaches. Economists often want to understand what organizations might compete with one another in providing products or services. Policy analysts might investigate which aggregates of organizations will be affected in similar ways by regulation or other governmental policies. Sociologists might want to consider what organizations could draw on a common identity, norms, and set of routines. More generally, researchers analyze the emergence of new organizational populations because such populations (and the forms they embody) offer a repository of solutions to societal needs and problems.

In this section, we consider a series of issues that must be addressed in an analysis of the emergence of organizational populations. Because few theorists have examined the emergence of populations and forms, our argument is necessarily speculative on some points. First, we consider the empirical issue of identifying organizational populations and timing when they come into existence. Second, we define the resource constraints that affect the development of organizational populations. Third, we recognize that the founders of the first ventures in a new population operate in situations with few, if any, precedents. Thus, they must learn about new markets and develop the organizational knowledge to exploit them. In addition, they often face situations in which potential members and resource providers question their legitimacy. Although learning and legitimacy are only two of several factors influencing whether a population successfully grows beyond a few pioneers, they constitute major constraints over the time span covered by evolutionary arguments and are thus worthy of concentrated attention.

Identifying organizational populations

The duality of organizational forms and populations raises the empirical issue as to how easily any given organization can be mapped to a form. In practice, forms tend to be defined referentially, on the basis of common labels applied to organizations in industry censuses, trade directories, newspapers, phone books, and other archival sources. However, as Ruef (2000) noted in his analysis of the health care field, this exercise in labeling may be subject to a number of difficulties. First, common labels for organizational forms, such as 'hospitals,' can subsume a diverse set of organizations which, by some criteria, should be divided into more fine-grained categories (e.g. *general* hospitals as opposed to *specialized* hospitals). Second, some hybrid organizations could, in theory, be mapped to multiple organizational forms. For example, the Juvenile Psychopathic Institute, an organization that appeared in early 20th-century America, combined elements of child health services and education with criminal correction.

Third, observers may apply common labels to 'quasi-forms,' organizational arrangements perceived as having separate identities without being truly independent. Such quasi-forms often appear when the existence of a market predates the emergence of an organizational form. For example, despite the size of the established world market for disk arrays – data storage subsystems connecting hard disk drives – there is still limited recognition of disk array producers as an autonomous organizational form (McKendrick and Carroll, 2001). Even though two trade associations represent disk array technology users, many observers do not acknowledge disk array producers because they lack what McKendrick and colleagues (2003) termed 'focused identities' in this market. A significant number of producers are *de alio* entrants, with origins in a diverse set of industries. A lack of focus is also apparent in the geographic distribution of disk array producers, spread across the United States between Silicon Valley, Boston's Route 128 corridor, and other high-tech regions. More generally, a lack of focused identity poses difficulties for researchers trying to identify organizational populations, especially in the early years of a form's emergence.

Other issues in the identification of populations are more semantic than operational. We sometimes use the terms organizational 'population' and 'industry' interchangeably. Industrial economists typically associate 'industry' with patterns of consumption, whereas organizational ecologists associate 'population' with sets of potential competitors in a production system (Hannan and Carroll, 1995: 29–30). In practice, ecologists often use the same data source as economists and just change the label. Nevertheless, the term 'population' seems preferable for a number of reasons. Many voluntary and public sector organizations do not fit easily under the label of an 'industry,' and neither do any pre-industrial organizational forms. By contrast, we readily identify colleges, grocery stores, and craft guilds as comprising *populations* of organizations. In this book, we use the term *population* most of the time, but we also use the term *industry* in some cases, e.g. in referring to the 'auto industry.'

Timing the emergence of populations

Before considering *what* social conditions engender or constrain the emergence of new organizational populations, we must attend to the issue of *when* a population (and corresponding form) can be said to exist. Because population emergence is a process, observers often have difficulty in identifying discrete points of origin. For instance, the concept of a health maintenance organization (HMO) in the United States can be traced back as far as the Marine Hospital Service, which began providing prepaid medical care in 1798 (Freeborn and Pope, 1994). A number of prepaid group practices proliferated between the late 1920s and the 1940s, including the Ross-Loos Clinic of Los Angeles, the Health Insurance Plan of New York, and Kaiser Permanente in Oakland. Nevertheless, the term 'health maintenance organization' was only coined in 1970 and definitive regulatory endorsement did not occur until 1973, with the passage of the HMO Act (Scott et al., 2000). By most accounts, then, the HMO form emerged over many decades.

Precise efforts to time the origin of populations depend largely on how scholars conceptualize organizational forms. As we discussed in Chapter 6, some perspectives emphasize processes occurring within organizational boundaries, whereas others stress processes that occur beyond the organizational level. Perspectives calling attention to internal processes typically rely on key exemplars of 'pioneer' organizations to identify a population's emergence. For instance, many analysts of the HMO population trace its origins back to 1945, when Kaiser Permanente opened its enrollment to the general public. Objective definitions of the organizational form could emphasize routines such as Kaiser's enrollment of individuals in a specific geographic area under per capita payment arrangements, whereas subjective definitions could emphasize the sense of organizational identity within Kaiser as it rebelled against the constraints of 'orthodox' medicine (Caronna and Scott, 1999). Thus, a new organizational population begins whenever observers see culture or material practices within a pioneering organization as sufficiently novel to cause a break with previous forms.

External perspectives on form emergence consider processes beyond individual organizations, such as regulatory initiatives, technological breakthroughs or patents, social movements, and the development of labels for organizational forms in public media sources (Ruef, 2000). The particular marker utilized may depend on the technical and institutional pressures facing an emerging population (Scott and Meyer, 1983). For organizational communities subject to strong institutional and technical pressures, such as health care, utilities, and banks, regulatory markers often prove important in marking the emergence of new populations. When only technical pressures predominate – as in many areas of large-scale manufacturing – innovations or patents may serve as the most useful timing markers. Conversely, populations subject to strong institutional and weak technical pressures, such as schools and churches, can be tracked through the rise of social movements that advocate one form or another. For forms that are subject to neither strong technical nor institutional pressures, the initial identification and naming of new organizational forms in public media sources may be the most suitable marker of population emergence.

Resource constraints

Substantial variability exists across organizational populations in elapsed time from the first startups to population stability, as Klepper and Graddy (1990) demonstrated. Their study of industry growth found that some industries went from origin to stability – defined as the year when the number of firms reached a peak and remained more or less the same for a few years – in only two years, whereas others took over 50. The average was 29 years and the standard deviation was 15, illustrating an enormous range of variation in the time required for industries to establish themselves. What conditions in new populations generate such variation?

Available resources determine an environment's carrying capacity and set a limit on *population density*: the number of organizations competing for the same resources in a limited space. An environment's *carrying capacity* – the number of organizations it can support – for a newly forming population cannot be known in advance. Instead, carrying capacity is only revealed as organizations of the new form carve out their niche in the face of competition from established forms, institutional constraints, and other forces affecting the terms on which resources are available (Brittain, 1994). In practice, this means that we only know the level of carrying capacity after it has been reached and a new population's numbers have stabilized or shrunk.

As we discussed in Chapter 6, one common perspective on organizational forms visualizes them by thinking about their resource *niche*, defined as a distinct combination of resources and other constraints that are sufficient to support a population. A new population must carve out a space for itself, within the community of populations, either by creating a new niche or by invading an already-occupied niche. Competition between populations for the same space is captured by the distinction between 'fundamental' and 'realized' niches. A *fundamental niche* represents the full range of conditions under which a population could be sustained. However, if other organizations compete for the same resources, then the population may be confined to the realized niche (Podolny et al., 1996: 685). A *realized niche* is the 'restricted environmental space in which a population can be sustained even in the presence of competing populations of organizations' (Hannan and Carroll, 1995: 34). In most cases, a population's realized niche is smaller than its fundamental niche because of competitive interactions with other populations.

The balance a new population achieves between competition and cooperation vis-à-vis other groups of organizations ultimately determines its boundaries. Members learn and respond to constraints and opportunities as they strive to construct a population's boundaries. Their struggle is very much a collective effort, although not necessarily a collaborative one. Indeed, in the early days, founders might struggle with each other to set a direction for the new population, as we discuss later. Thus, we do not argue that explicit strategic intentions drive all of the collective actions benefiting a population. Nonetheless, when achieved, legitimacy and population level knowledge become resources that cloak the foundings of all organizations in the population, regardless of their individual characteristics (Rao, 1994).

Learning and legitimacy constraints

Founding rates are lower and disbanding rates are higher when organizational populations are young and small (Carroll and Hannan, 2000). As a population grows, the pattern of low founding rates and high disbanding rates in its early years is followed by a gradual increase in founding rates and a decrease in disbanding rates. What contextual factors discourage potential founders and undermine the survival of new organizations? Two factors seem particularly important: (1) lack of effective organizational knowledge; and (2) lack of external legitimacy for the new activity. In Chapter 4, we discussed the sources and uses of organizational knowledge by nascent entrepreneurs and we build on that discussion in this chapter. Because the issue of population-level legitimacy has not received much attention in previous chapters, we define it and give examples before presenting our main arguments.

With regard to legitimacy, Hannan and Freeman (1989) synthesized arguments from institutional and ecological theory. They argued that a pattern of low founding rates and high disbanding rates exists because organizations in new populations initially lack external legitimacy. As a population grows in size, its legitimacy increases. Their strongest arguments were based on findings from organizational populations with chronic problems of sociopolitical opposition and repression, e.g. labor unions and newspapers (Delacroix and Rao, 1994). In response to early criticisms, Hannan and Carroll (1992) proposed a more general model, addressing legitimacy issues stemming from a lack of knowledge and understanding.

Forms of learning and legitimacy

Two problems confront nascent entrepreneurs in new populations. First, they must discover or create effective routines and competencies under conditions of ignorance and uncertainty. When the number of organizations in a new population is small, organizational members must learn new roles without the benefit of role models. Second, new organizations must establish ties with an environment that might not understand or acknowledge their existence (Stinchcombe, 1965). In an initial exploration of these issues, Aldrich and Fiol (1994) used the term *legitimacy* to cover both problems. However, for analytic purposes in this chapter, we have separated problems into *learning* and *legitimacy* issues. Although clearly intertwined, taken separately the two concepts highlight the extent to which the principles in this chapter build on the concepts developed in previous chapters.

After presenting an overview of the two issues, we examine the strategies pursued by founders as they cope with learning and legitimacy problems and opportunities. We highlight the knowledge involved in founding new organizations and emphasize the agents involved: entrepreneurs, industry associations, and other collective actors. We treat learning primarily as a cognitive issue and examine it together with cognitive legitimacy. In Table 9.1 and our subsequent discussion, we have thus grouped learning and cognitive legitimacy under the heading of 'cognitive strategies.' A second dimension of legitimacy – sociopolitical – is broken into two sub-categories of moral and regulatory (see Table 9.1).

Learning: the diffusion of organizational knowledge

Some of the knowledge used in new populations exists in the form of scientific laws and regularities that can be discovered by organizational experimentation. For example, in technology-based industries, applied research and development activities focus on turning basic scientific knowledge into commercial products or services (Murmann, 2003). In non technology-based populations, some of the knowledge used can be enacted through an arbitrary but creative recombination of existing knowledge. Thus, fads and fashions in cultural industries – music, theater, the arts, and so forth – spring from new ways of looking at existing knowledge. Some beneficial knowledge may even already exist in the form of well-understood and legitimated models that can simply be copied. The more that founders deviate from established forms, the more challenging their task of developing new knowledge.

We noted in Chapter 4 that nascent entrepreneurs develop their own organized knowledge structures through experience, and they use those structures as templates – schemata – to give information form and meaning (Walsh, 1995: 281). In established populations, entrepreneurs benefit from pre-existing templates from which they can choose the most suitable. However, in new populations, beneficial templates are scarce. Instead, pioneering entrepreneurs must learn new schemata. For example, joint agreement on a dominant design enables technology-based populations to push ahead with their expansion, whereas disagreement discourages potential entrepreneurs from entering. Without the development of a broad knowledge base for the population, low founding and high disbanding rates will stymie population growth.

Table 9.1 Strategies facilitating the growth of new populations

Level of analysis	Cognitive strategies		Sociopolitical strategies	
	Learning	Cognitive legitimacy	Moral legitimacy	Regulatory legitimacy
Organizational	Create knowledge base through experimentation	Link new ventures to the past via narrative and identity development	Build on local networks of trust	Avoid entanglement with government agencies as long as possible
Within-population	Deepen a knowledge base by encouraging convergence around a dominant design	Collaborate to create recognized and standardized organizational form	Foster perceptions of reliability by mobilizing to take collective action	Present a united front to political and government officials
Between-population	Spread knowledge base by promoting alliance and third party activities	Draw on taken-for-grantedness of existing populations with similar identity	Develop a reputation of a new activity as a reality by negotiation and compromise with other industries	Co-opt government agencies as allies against competing populations
Community	Solidify a knowledge base by creating linkages with established educational curricula	Fit categorical requirements of independent certifying institutions	Embed legitimacy by organizing collective marketing and lobbying efforts	Embed the population within the political system via PACs and hiring of former government officials

A new population's growth also depends upon the extent to which its potential audience learns more about it. What is the expected value of a new population to the various constituencies it affects (Suchman, 1995: 578)? Customers, suppliers, creditors, employees, and others need to learn the basic facts about a new population before they can form judgments concerning their own involvement in it. For example, the diffusion of knowledge to potential customers about personal computers in the 1970s and 1980s facilitated the spread of PC use in homes and businesses, and helped spawn many startups. Knowledge about a new population must thus diffuse not only to nascent entrepreneurs, but also to their intended audience or market.

Legitimacy: cognitive and sociopolitical

We adopt Suchman's (1995: 574) inclusive definition of *legitimacy* as 'a generalized perception or assumption that the actions of an entity are desirable, proper, or appropriate within some socially constructed system of norms, values, beliefs, and definitions.' Suchman proposed a three-part typology of types of legitimacy – pragmatic, moral, and cognitive – but we depart from his suggestion in subsuming his category of 'pragmatic' under our concept of organizational learning, and in subsuming 'moral' under sociopolitical legitimacy (see also Aldrich and Fiol, 1994; Scott, 2001). As Suchman pointed out, the concept of sociopolitical legitimacy refers to all cultural regulatory processes, whereas 'moral' is limited in scope to conscious assessments of right and wrong. We thus employ a two-part typology: cognitive legitimacy and sociopolitical legitimacy, and divide the latter into moral and regulatory elements.

Cognitive legitimacy refers to the acceptance of a new kind of venture as *a taken for granted* feature of the environment. The highest form of cognitive legitimacy exists when a new product, process, or service is accepted as part of the sociocultural and organizational landscape. When an activity becomes so familiar and well known that people take it for granted, time and other organizing resources are conserved, 'attempts at creating copies of legitimated forms are common, and the success rate of such attempts is high' (Hannan and Freeman, 1986: 63). From a producer's point of view, cognitive legitimacy means that new entrants to a population are likely to copy an existing organizational form, rather than experiment with a new one. From a consumer's point of view, cognitive legitimacy means that people are committed users of a recognized product or service.

Sociopolitical legitimacy refers to the acceptance by key stakeholders, the general public, key opinion leaders, and government officials of a new venture as appropriate and right. It has two components: *moral acceptance*, referring to conformity with cultural norms and values, and *regulatory acceptance*, referring to conformity with governmental rules and regulations. Clemens (1993: 771) noted that 'the adoption of a particular organizational form influences the ties that an organized group forms with other organizations.' Indicators of conformity to moral norms and values include: the absence of attacks by religious and civic leaders on the new form; and heightened public prestige of its leaders. For example, in the 19th century, the life insurance industry was initially vilified by the clergy and church leaders as profaning the sacredness of life (Zelizer, 1978). Indicators of conformity to governmental rules and regulations include: laws passed to protect or monitor the population; and government subsidies to the population. For example, the passage of the Wagner Act in 1935 gave special status under federal law to unions that conformed to federal guidelines. Government approval was a symbol of a long struggle for regulatory legitimacy, waged first by craft and then industrial unions.

Cognitive strategies

Cognitive issues – lack of organizational knowledge and low levels of legitimacy – rather than sociopolitical issues are probably the most pressing issues facing founders of entirely new activities. As Delacroix et al. (1989: 247) noted, in capitalist nations, firms benefit from a 'diffuse belief that profit-seeking activities are valid, unless otherwise specified.' Though it may be legally validated in the form of a legal charter, an entirely new activity often begins with low levels of knowledge, depressed cognitive legitimacy, or both. Either of these problems may be an obstacle to population growth, and unless they are overcome, not much will happen. Without widespread knowledge and understanding of their activity, entrepreneurs may have difficulty maintaining the support of key constituencies. Potential customers, suppliers, and sources of financial resources may not fully understand the nature of the new venture, and potential employees may view jobs in the new population with a mixture of skepticism and distrust. To succeed, founders must find strategies to raise the level of public knowledge about a new activity to the point where people take it for granted (see Table 9.1).

Given the absence of information and prior behaviors, pioneering founders begin at the organizational level by creating a knowledge base in their own organization. Early on, they might also struggle with founders of other organizations in their emerging population. With regard to cognitive legitimacy, they cannot base initial trust-building strategies on objective external evidence. Instead, they must concentrate on framing the unknown in such a way that it becomes believable. In the following discussion, we weave together the issues of learning and legitimacy, given the degree to which they overlap in new populations.

Organization-level cognitive strategies

The fundamental rules of organizing are widely diffused in all modern societies. Beginning with these basic templates, founders of ventures in new populations use feedback from their experimental forays to guide their actions. If they were simply trying to reproduce the forms most common in familiar populations, they would find knowledge widely available. However, heavy reliance on traditional sources would make their efforts competence-enhancing, rather than competence-destroying (Tushman and Anderson, 1986). Instead, innovative founders break with tradition in generating variation.

Lawless and Anderson (1996) coined the term *generational technological change* to describe innovations that represent a significant advance within a technological regime, taking place during periods of incremental change, and which can thus be adopted by existing firms. Competence-enhancing innovations may make it easier for ambitious employees to leave their employers and replicate established organizational forms. However, they would then have to compete with established organizations, a prospect that undoubtedly dampens entrepreneurial spirits. By contrast, competence-destroying innovations pose major problems for existing firms in mature populations, because inflexible routines and competencies may prevent adaptive change. Several studies have reported that new entrants were more likely than incumbent firms to take advantage of disruptions caused by competence-destroying innovations. Indeed,

Anderson and Tushman (1990) argued that established firms find it very difficult to adopt competence-destroying innovations.

By definition, competence-destroying discontinuities typically require that new forms of organizations produce or implement the new product, service, or process. For example, as we noted in the last chapter, waves of new entrants took over from leading firms in the photolithographic alignment equipment industry after each competence-destroying innovation (Henderson and Clark, 1990). Kulicke and Soffa introduced the first commercially successful aligner, in 1965, and dominated the very small market until 1974, when Cobilt and Kasper replaced them. Perkin-Elmer, GCA, and Nikon followed them in rapid succession. 'In nearly every case, the established firm invested heavily in the next generation of equipment, only to meet with very little success' (Henderson and Clark, 1990: 24).

Given their origins in new and untested organizational knowledge, pioneering new ventures face critical problems of cognitive legitimacy. How do pioneering entrepreneurs gain such legitimacy? They must find ways of convincing others to trust them, in spite of their risky undertaking. Trust is a critical first-level determinant of founding entrepreneurs' success because, by definition, little evidence exists regarding their new activity. In Chapter 4, we described how entrepreneurs use their social network ties to mobilize resources. Use of strong ties and network brokers will be especially important to founders of pioneering ventures. Founders can use the connections of third parties to certify their reliability and reputation, as well as drawing on their own social skills for securing cooperation based on interpersonal relations (Baron and Markman, 2003; Kramer and Cook, 2004).

Entrepreneurs can take advantage of the inherent ambiguity in interpreting new behaviors by skillfully framing and editing their behaviors and intentions vis-à-vis the trusting parties. Lounsbury and Glynn (2001) stressed that entrepreneurs not only draw on tangible stocks of human, social, and financial capital, but also deploy narratives that highlight or downplay the distinctiveness of new ventures, depending on the cognitive legitimacy of their organizational form. Founders can emphasize those aspects of their ventures and their own backgrounds that evoke identities that others will understand as risk-oriented but responsible. Podolny (1994), for example, noted that in the highly uncertain world of junk bonds, the status of the third-party underwriting firms affected perceptions of quality much more than in the highly certain world of investment grade bonds. Founders can emphasize the continuity between the innovative new activity and those activities familiar to their customers, employees, creditors, and others.

Within-population cognitive strategies

Within-population processes constrain the emergence of new populations by structuring the immediate environment of new organizations. Two problems confront pioneering ventures in new populations. First, founders must create and spread useful organizational knowledge. Under some circumstances, founders can imitate others who develop effective routines and competencies. Convergence on a dominant design then eases the way for new entrants. Second, founders must somehow obtain collective agreement on standards and designs so that the population becomes a taken-for-granted reality by its constituents. Without accepted standards and designs, population boundaries will be ambiguous and organizational knowledge fleeting. Foundings will be inhibited and disbandings will be frequent.

Organizations founded after a new population has achieved some stability benefit by vicariously learning from early successful foundings (Delacroix and Rao, 1994). This holds true, in particular, when entrepreneurial activity tends to be geographically concentrated, allowing entrepreneurs to draw on local networks of friends and acquaintances (Sorenson and Audia, 2000). Under such conditions, organizational knowledge is widespread and easily accessible. Nascent entrepreneurs can serve an apprenticeship with an established owner, read accounts of successful organizations in local publications, take courses at a community college, and attend trade fairs. For example, managers and owners of 17 firms in a geographically concentrated Scottish knitwear industry visited one another, talked with the same set of buying agents, read the same trade publications, and shared a common vocabulary for what they were doing (Porac et al., 1989). They constituted an identifiable cognitive community responding in similar ways to their perceived markets. In contrast, the earliest founders in new populations have no such advantage.

Early on, founders within a population implicitly compete to have their approach taken for granted, appealing to potential customers, investors, and others to accept their version. Organizations attempting to copy a new activity, while starting-up, are in a difficult position because poorly understood activities are only imperfectly imitable (Barney, 1986; Reed and DeFillippi, 1990). Much of the knowledge of a new population is implicit, held by the founders and their employees in uncodified form. Such tacit knowledge is often complex, making it hard for others to identify causal relations (Nelson and Winter, 1982). Knowledge tied to a particular organization creates relationships that are difficult for others to duplicate. Thus, until entrepreneurs come together around a reduced set of accepted standards or designs, pioneering founders will inevitably make frequent mistakes.

Imitation and dominant designs

The lack of convergence on a *dominant design* – an agreed-upon architecture and set of components constituting a product or service – in new populations constrains the perceived reliability of founding firms by increasing confusion about what standards should be followed. Not only must founders convince skeptics of their organization's staying power, but they also must fend off organizations offering slightly different versions of their products and services, creating confusion in the minds of constituents. During the period following a radical innovation, an era of ferment may arise in which struggles occur between contending designs. The era of ferment ends when a dominant design emerges for the core subsystem. An era of incremental change follows (Anderson and Tushman, 1990). Convergence toward an accepted design is facilitated if new ventures find it easy to imitate pioneers, rather than seek further innovation, and when users see evidence of *demand-side increasing returns*, where the value of a design increases with the number of other users (Arthur, 1989; Saloner et al., 2001). For instance, video cassette recorders, computer software, and yellow page listings all become more useful when other users tend to rely on the same standard.

Chance events, as well as aggressive actions by small groups of firms, can play a key role in the evolution of a population where new technologies display demand-side increasing returns. If the adoption of a technology permits adopters to gain experience and perhaps improve it, then seemingly insignificant events may give one form of the new technology an initial advantage that competing technologies cannot overcome. The fortunate technology steals a march on the competitors, improves more rapidly, and thus appeals to a wider set of potential adopters, enjoying still more chances to improve. 'Thus, a technology that by chance gains an early lead in adoption may eventually "corner the market" of potential adopters, with the other technologies becoming locked out' (Arthur, 1989: 116). The process is *path dependent* because the population's growth depends upon a unique series of historical events. The path cannot be retraced, nor can it be easily deflected by subsequent events.

Path dependence can be illustrated with two well-documented historical cases, showing how an early-established technology gained such an overwhelming advantage that subsequent potentially superior technologies were locked out: the design of typewriter keyboards, and conflict over alternating versus direct current. The QWERTY keyboard layout now universally used in the United States was developed to overcome a mechanical problem plaguing early typewriters. The layout is arguably inferior to later versions, such as Dvorak's, but its rapid early adoption gave it a locked-in advantage that has never been overcome (David, 1985). Networks of electrical power generation developed in a more complex fashion, with a lock-in advantage gained as established networks obtained coordination economies that could not be overcome (see Hughes, 1983, for a cross-national comparison of this process). Some sociologists have argued, however, that the early push toward the dominant design in this population – central station electric systems with AC current – occurred primarily due to personal friendships and conflicts among key industry participants, such as Thomas Edison, J.P. Morgan, and Samuel Insull (Granovetter and McGuire, 1998).

Implicit agreement on a dominant design, common standards, and the inter-firm movement of personnel increase the level of shared competence. In the early days of the automobile industry, fierce competition occurred between electric, steam, and gas powered manufacturers. Early automobile manufacturers almost always began with undercapitalized firms, as established financial institutions would not risk their assets on an unproved product, with no clear market (Rao, 1994). Entrepreneurs entered and exited the population at a high rate. By 1902, competition ended and gasoline-powered vehicles became the dominant design, partly as a result of their superiority in car rallies. Almost all foundings from that point on were based on the gasoline engine, not other power sources. As the prevalence of these forms increased, they gradually assumed a taken-for-granted nature. In research on the hotel industry, Baum and Ingram (1998) also found that successful organizational designs diffused throughout a population. Imitation and borrowing from early successful foundings spread knowledge of new activities beyond their point of origin and contributed to convergence on a dominant design (Baum et al., 1995).

Imitation and interorganizational relations

A new venture's ability to imitate others depends on whether knowledge is protected by legal instruments – patents, copyrights, and trade secrets – and on whether the innovation is codified (Teece, 1987). If an innovation cannot be legally protected and it involves a product or process whose nature is transparently obvious to outsiders, others may freely copy the innovation. By contrast, if the innovation can be protected and its nature is difficult to understand, except through learning by doing, others are unlikely to imitate it (Arrow, 1962; Dosi, 1988). Such conditions can exacerbate discord over a dominant design.

Sponsors – firms that produce the original designs – may cling tightly to their proprietary interests in a technology or design, or they may allow it to spread freely (David and

Greenstein, 1990). Effective knowledge, when widely diffused, reduces imperfect imitation and lowers disbanding rates. Technological change within a design might still occur, even when a new population settles on a dominant design (Iansiti and Khanna, 1995). The selection and retention of a dominant design may simply shift the competition to alternative technological trajectories within the design, rather than ending the period of ferment and experimentation surrounding competition between competing designs.

In technology-based industries, dependence upon a common set of technological antecedents introduces a strong element of inertia into organizational strategies (Podolny et al., 1996: 664–665). Cooper and Schendel (1976), in their study of seven cases of technological substitution, found that new technologies took from 5 to 14 years to surpass sales of existing technologies. In four of the seven cases, sales of the existing technologies actually continued to expand after the new technology was introduced. Eventually, as competition follows guideposts laid down by a dominant design, a new population's legitimacy is no longer in doubt, but its technological future remains open.

Populations with imitable innovations are more likely to generate collective action than populations with difficult-to-imitate innovations. If founders with imitable products or services perceive that their innovations are leaking to competitors and potential new entrants, they gain a strong incentive to cooperate on stabilizing conditions in the population. By contrast, firm-centered actions are likely to *increase* under conditions of inimitability, as founders are able to protect their core competencies from being widely diffused. Such fiercely competitive individual strategies hinder a united collective front by a population.

Trust and interorganizational relations

Trust within a population may arise from patterns of collective interaction over the long term that build strong ties between organizations (Uzzi, 1997). In such cases, the number of ties involving trust does not depend on strictly dyadic interaction, but instead reflects a collective understanding of the situation. For example, Larson (1992) studied four high-growth firms whose relationships with other firms were characterized more by in-depth coordination and collaboration than pure instrumental exchange and competition. Larson argued that formal contracts were less important than informal agreements among firms, based on their history with one another. Long-term relationships, based on trust and understanding, created partnerships in which there was a lack of explicit control and monitoring devices between firms. Incentives for economic action were jointly set, rather than being based upon formal buyer–seller relationships.

Uzzi (1997), building upon earlier studies, conducted a field and ethnographic analysis of 23 women's dress firms in the New York City apparel industry. Although the firms often engaged in straightforward economic exchange relationships, they also depended very heavily on embedded relationships. Trust, rather than the 'calculated risk' favored by transactions cost economics, smoothed transactions between firms. Fine-grained information transfer allowed the spread of tacit knowledge across firms. Building on their underlying social relationships, they also were able to use joint problem-solving arrangements.

Collective action and business interest associations

Population-level collective action facilitates both learning and legitimacy. Initial collaborations between organizations begin informally, in networks of inter-firm relations, but some later develop into more formalized strategic alliances, consortia, and trade associations (Powell, 1990). New-to-the-world innovations tend to be pursued by a handful of parallel, independent actors, as Van de Ven and Garud (1994) found in their study of the cochlear implant industry. People come to know one another through personal interaction and through traveling in similar social/technical circles, such as attending the same industry conferences and technical committee meetings. This small handful of actors can generate social networks that, in the aggregate, result in population-level collective action.

Trade associations are associations of organizations in the same population that formulate product/process standards via trade committees and that publish trade journals. They also conduct marketing campaigns to enhance the population's standing in the eyes of the public and promote trade fairs at which customers and suppliers can gain a sense of the population's stability. Trade associations are *minimalist organizations* – able to operate on low overhead and quickly adapt to changing conditions – and founded more easily than, for example, production organizations (Halliday et al., 1987). An industry champion often steps forward as a catalyst to an association's founding by volunteering to cover the costs of running the association until it recruits enough members to gain a stable dues base. Typically, the largest firms in an industry do this, and they are well represented on the association's board of directors. Many trade associations, following the example of state bar and other voluntary associations, operate out of the offices of member firms in their early years. Law firms representing the largest firms in the industry administer many smaller trade associations.

Trade associations and other inter-firm entities play a critical role in helping founders promote a population's cognitive legitimacy by raising its standards to a taken-for-granted status (Aldrich and Staber, 1988). In the United States, they collaborate on standard setting with the National Institute of Standards and Technology, an agency of the Technology Administration under the Department of Commerce. For example, the Semiconductor Equipment and Materials Institute (SEMI), founded in 1970, devoted considerable resources to creating technical specifications for its industry. In 1973, silicon vendors were following several thousand specifications, creating chaos in the industry. 'Despite the initial opposition of semiconductor manufacturers, a SEMI standards committee defined and publicized specifications for emerging three-inch wafer lines. By 1975, more than 80 percent of all new wafers met SEMI specifications' (Saxenian, 1994: 49).

Trade associations can increase the rate of population-level learning. In the United States in the 1980s, as the population of independent-power producers emerged, its trade associations held conferences at which 'best practices' were discussed (Sine et al., 2005). They also circulated reports about technical issues that entrepreneurs consulted before building new plants. In Japan, associations have played a very active role in linking their members to developments overseas. They have created libraries of foreign language publications and established databases of patents and scientific reference manuals. Japanese trade associations have also sent delegations overseas to study research programs in firms, laboratories, and public agencies (Lynn and McKeown, 1988). U.S. trade associations, by contrast, have been fairly passive with regard to overseas research and development, except for a few industries, such as iron and steel.

Trade and occupational associations can also constrain new population growth when they try to protect the status quo against new populations threatening their resources. For example, teachers' unions, such as the National Education Association and the American Federation of Teachers, opposed the creation of charter schools and were able to undermine their legitimacy by challenging their efficacy. They managed to slow or weaken the adoption of charter school legislation in many states. However, after state legislators passed laws enabling charter school foundings, these associations had little effect on subsequent foundings (Renzulli, 2005).

Because collective action benefits all organizations, regardless of their own contributions, new populations face the classic problem of free riders not participating in collective activities (Moe, 1980; Olson, 1965). *Free riders* benefit from the efforts expended by their peers but do little or nothing themselves to advance those efforts. Trade associations, and other collectivities of organizations that survive, generally maintain organizational discipline against free riders in two ways. First, they provide strong incentives for members to contribute and not defect. Paralleling the case of rewards for members within individual organizations, as we discussed in Chapter 5, incentives fall into three categories. *Material incentives* can be offered to members, such as earning a certification sticker or logo that can be displayed on a product or in advertising. *Solidary incentives*, such as the intangible rewards resulting from associating with others at trade fairs and other sociable occasions, are inexpensive and easy to provide. *Purposive incentives* are the intangible rewards resulting from achieving a worthwhile cause, as in ideological oriented social movements. For example, Snow et al. (1986: 477) noted that as a social movement grows, it generates 'interpretive frames that not only inspire and justify collective action, but also give meaning to and legitimate the tactics that evolve.'

Second, organizational collectivities create a compliance structure for monitoring, detecting, and sanctioning defections. Dissension within a population generally hampers the ability of an industry champion – typically one of the larger firms – to form coalitions promoting the entire population (Bolton, 1993). The most effective compliance structures generally involve government regulations that require all organizations in the population to follow the same standards and practices. For example, the National Highway Traffic Safety Administration requires all automobiles sold in the United States to meet certain emission and passenger safety standards. The federal government thus plays the role of monitor and enforcer of standards, freeing auto manufacturers' resources for other uses.

Aside from the problem of free-riding, collective action in a population can also be threatened by the existence of multiple associations representing different standards or interests. *Interest associations* may accentuate divisions in populations, as they compete for organizational members, symbolic resources, and dominance of an organizational field (Galvin, 2002). In the field of U.S. collegiate athletics, for instance, the National Association of Intercollegiate Athletics (NAIA) was founded in 1938 in opposition to the National Collegiate Athletic Association (NCAA), which had proven to be exclusionary toward lower-status schools (Washington, 2004). In response, the NCAA slowly expanded its membership among small colleges, forming a second athletic division in 1952, instituting a small college tournament in 1957, and giving membership to historically black colleges by the 1960s. By redefining their goals and membership criteria, interest associations such as the NCAA may thus seek to provide a common basis of cognitive legitimacy and learning in a population, while fending off threats from competing interest groups.

Between-population cognitive strategies

Inter-population processes – the nature of relations between populations, whether competing or cooperating – affect the distribution of resources in the environment and the terms on which they are available to entrepreneurs. New populations are, in a sense, surrounded by established populations, and thus are highly vulnerable to attack. Organizations in established populations that feel threatened sometimes attempt to change the terms on which resources are available to emerging populations by questioning their efficacy or conformity to the established order. Even after a new population grows into a recognized entity, organizations in other populations may withhold recognition or acceptance of it. The greatest risk to the emergence of a new organizational form occurs when it displays an identity that is similar to existing forms with a high population density, as Ruef (2000) found in his study of the U.S. health care field. However, cognitive legitimacy may be enhanced if similar forms only have low or moderate density, allowing entrepreneurs in the new population to build on the reputation and recognizability of their predecessors.

Business interest associations and political action groups that organize across population boundaries facilitate population-level learning and cognitive legitimacy. For example, in 1943, a diverse group of 25 California electronics manufacturers formed the West Coast Electronics Manufacturers Association (WCEMA) in response to the War Production Board's (WPA) announcement of a cutback in defense contracts awarded to west coast firms. The WCEMA – later renamed the Western Electronics Manufacturers Association (WEMA) – lobbied the WPA for a larger share of defense contracts. They argued that a disproportionate share was going to eastern firms, such as Raytheon and General Electric. In the 1960s, WEMA concentrated its efforts on the smaller entrepreneurial firms in Silicon Valley, and 'sponsored seminars and educational activities that encouraged the exchange of ideas and information, including management training sessions on subjects ranging from finance and technology marketing to production and export assistance' (Saxenian, 1994: 47). WEMA eventually expanded outside of California and was renamed the American Electronics Association (AEA) in 1978. The WCEMA's transformations into the WEMA and the AEA illustrate the advantages of cross-population organizing efforts, as well as the flexibility of minimalist organizations.

As in the case of collective action within populations, not all efforts at cross-population organizing succeed in promoting joint standards or a common public policy position. When the largest firms in cross-population alliances disagree, they may impede convergence on a common standard. For example, throughout the 1980s, computer and software manufacturers, software users, and other interested parties struggled over Unix standards for technical workstations, an industry with over $10 billion in sales by 1990 (Axelrod et al., 1995). Bell Laboratories developed the original Unix operating system during the 1960s, and subsequently software developers wrote more than 250 versions. An early attempt to develop a common standard, the X/Open group, failed when two large firms – AT&T and Sun Microsystems – pulled out and announced their own effort to develop a system that would be available under proprietary license to others. Seven major firms, including IBM and DEC, formed an alternative coalition – the Open Software Foundation – and eventually recruited nine full sponsors. AT&T and Sun responded by forming Unix International, an alliance of ten firms. Both alliances eventually released their own commercial versions of Unix.

As this example illustrates, large firms play a crucial role in mobilizing other firms to join a standard-setting coalition, and conflicts between them can fragment alliances.

Organizations in established populations that feel threatened by a newcomer may undermine a new venture's cognitive legitimacy through rumors and information suppression or inaccurate dissemination. Sometimes a low level of cognitive legitimacy may be an advantage for a new venture, such as when established organizations do not treat the activity as a serious threat. However, it is a detriment when older, competing firms spread rumors that a product or technology is unsafe, costly, or of inferior quality. For example, early mail- and phone-order computer supply stores in the United States were highly specialized, selling mainly to people very knowledgeable about electronics who were building or modifying their own equipment. When the population began to grow rapidly in the 1980s, selling to 'amateurs,' traditional walk-in stores argued that mail- and phone-order firms did not provide after-sales service and thus were an inferior form.

Similarly, health maintenance organizations (HMOs) confronted bitter opposition from traditional physician practices, which argued that HMOs violated customary expectations about effective physician–patient relationships, and thus delivered inferior services to patients. Physicians fought HMOs through a national organization, the American Medical Association (AMA), as well as state associations. They found a powerful ally in the American Association of Retired Persons (AARP), which argued that HMOs shortchanged senior citizens. HMOs grew slowly until other organizations, such as large insurance companies, intervened on their behalf and the institutional context of health care became oriented toward cost-cutting (Scott et al., 2000; Wholey et al., 1993). HMOs also organized their own powerful associations, such as the American Association of Health Plans and the Group Health Association of America, an association including most of the HMOs in the United States. On a methodological note, if HMOs had been successfully suppressed at an early stage in their development, this example may never have come to our attention. We return to this issue of success bias at the conclusion of this chapter.

Community-level cognitive strategies

Community-level conditions affect the rate at which a population grows by affecting the diffusion of knowledge about a new activity and the extent to which it is publicly or officially accepted. If founders have pursued effective trust-building and reliability-enhancing strategies within their emerging population, and have established a reputation vis-à-vis other populations, they have laid the groundwork for attaining legitimacy at the community level. If not, then population survival becomes much more problematic. At this level, founders are no longer working as isolated individuals. Instead, many vehicles for collective action are involved: industry councils, cooperative alliances, trade associations, and others (see Table 9.1).

Established populations enjoy an enormous benefit via the institutionalized diffusion of knowledge about their activities. The 'social space' (Delacroix and Rao, 1994) a population has achieved in a society is sustained, in part, by widespread understanding of how it fits into the community. In the beginning, organizations in the new population are too rare to create the critical mass needed to raise a new population's level of public understanding. Reporters, newspaper and magazine editors, and other mass media gatekeepers are unfamiliar with the terms needed to describe the activity, and their depiction may be inaccurate. Thus, potential entrepreneurs may be seriously misled if they rely on such reports, and mistakes in imitating the new activity will be common (Phillips, 1960).

The role of colleges and universities in diffusing knowledge

Educational institutions create and spread knowledge about dominant competencies (Romanelli, 1989), thus putting resources in the hands of potential founders. To the extent that specific competencies underlie particular populations, the activities of educational institutions may increase the diversity of organizational communities. Universities, research institutes, and associated programs not only conduct research but also train persons who can exploit the latest research products. Dean Frederick Terman of Stanford University's Engineering School promoted close and reciprocal ties between Stanford and local industry in the 1940s, helping to build an inter-dependent network of technical scholars. Educational institutions also 'formalize and centralize information by establishing courses and degree programs that train students in basic competencies. Once technologies are understood, and stabilized and identifiable jobs (e.g. computer engineer) emerge in a population, colleges and universities take over much of the training of skilled personnel' (Romanelli, 1989: 230). Historically, the growth of national educational systems has spurred founding rates by spreading generalized competencies that give nascent entrepreneurs the necessary skills to succeed (Nelson, 1994).

In the United States, new organizations regularly establish partnerships with community and technical colleges, often at the request of local economic development agencies that crave the venture's job generation possibilities. Educational institutions, especially vocationally and professionally oriented ones, base their training on curricular materials prepared by mass-market-oriented publishing houses. Without an accepted vocabulary or conceptual framework, writers and editors face serious difficulties in devising manuals and textbooks. Because educational institutions are conservative in their curriculum development, a new population must achieve a fairly high degree of self-organization before curriculum materials will be written especially for them.

Superconductor research was well underway in the United States before universities began putting science/industrial ceramics sequences into their applied sciences and engineering curricula. In the early 20th century, the rise of chemical and aerospace engineering as disciplines within universities benefited the chemical processing and aircraft industries because the disciplines 'served as a locus of research as well as a training ground for future engineers' (Rosenkopf and Tushman, 1994: 414). Shan et al., (1991: 82) noted that early in the history of the biotechnology industry in the United States, 'there was only a limited supply of scientists with Ph.D.s and other specialized training so essential for an NBF [new biotechnology firm].' Eventually, as career prospects in the industry became known, more recruits were attracted and the supply of scientists improved.

New populations must either build on the competencies already supported by educational institutions or find ways to encourage the provision of new ones. In technology-based industries, the basic research on which firms draw has often been generated in university laboratories a decade or more before it was commercialized (Link and Bauer, 1989). For example, the basic ideas for cochlear implant devices were developed in the late 1950s and early 1960s, almost two decades before the ideas were fully commercialized. Thus, firms such as Nucleus and 3M had an already developed pool of scientific expertise from which they could draw consultants and employees (Van de Ven and Garud, 1994). The growth of the Internet and the World Wide Web will increase the amount of information available to nascent entrepreneurs searching diligently for new opportunities. Accordingly, we speculate that the founding rate of information-technology-based firms will probably increase in the early decades of the 21st century, despite the dot-com 'bust' at the end of the 20th century.

Legitimacy through certifying institutions

In the first few decades of the industrial revolution in the United States, fledgling industries were disadvantaged by the lack of independent agencies and institutions that could certify their legitimacy (Zucker, 1986). The population of organizations that could certify trust and reputation grew slowly, spurred on by trade associations, a growing consumer movement, occasional government commissions, and the rise of a commercial market for independent assessment of firms and products. The growth of independent consumer watchdog organizations was a result of battles between organizational entrepreneurs with very different cultural conceptions of how consumers could be protected from inferior and unsafe products. As Rao (1998) documented in his case study of Consumers Research and Consumers Union, some founders of consumer watchdog organizations saw them as impartial scientific testing bodies, whereas others wanted an aggressive consumer movement that would challenge irresponsible companies. Under attack from critics and facing a changed economy as a result of wartime developments, Consumers Union 'slowly ceased to be an engine of political, social, or moral activism and reinvented itself as an impartial testing agency' (Rao, 1998: 944). In addition to non-profit groups such as Consumers Union, commercial firms evaluating products and services have also flourished.

Following the lead of Consumers Union, many special-purpose organizations now provide independent rating services for firms in established populations. Examples include guidebooks from Michelin and Zagat for the restaurant industry, A.M. Best and Moody's for insurance, J.D. Powers for the automobile industry, newspaper film reviews for movies, and certified public accounting firms for incorporated businesses in general (Rao et al., 2003; Hsu and Podolny, 2005; Han, 1994). Of course, some organizations gain more than others do when a population's legitimacy is strengthened, as Rao (1994) found in his study of the early years of the American automobile industry. As the auto industry struggled for acceptance, firms that won victories in reliability and speed competitions were more likely to survive than those that did not win. Thus, these firms enjoyed a boost to their own legitimacy that went beyond the generalized legitimacy bestowed upon the entire auto industry by such competitions.

Analyses of certification processes sometimes risk conflating the cognitive dimension of legitimacy (how recognizable is an organization or form?) with the sociopolitical dimension (do third parties feel that organization or form is legal and appropriate?). In his study of securities analysts, Zuckerman (1999, 2004) sought to separate the cognitive dimension by assessing the valuation and volatility of stocks for firms that did not match conventional industry-based classifications. Firms not consistently covered by a homogeneous set of analysts suffered an 'illegitimacy' discount, leading to decreases and higher volatility in stock market returns. For the community of publicly traded corporations, securities analysts thus operate as powerful arbiters of categorical conformity to cultural codes.

Cognitive strategies: summary

Entrepreneurs in new populations face the twin problems of a lack of effective organizational knowledge and a low level of cognitive legitimacy. As with all new ventures, they begin at the organizational level by constructing a knowledge base and identity within their own organization, but with much more experimentation than in reproducer organizations. They must frame their activities not only around their own ventures, but also within their emergent population, as they respond to inquiries and pressures from potential employees, clients and customers, suppliers, creditors, and others. As organizations in a population carve out their niche, collective action through trade associations, industry councils, and other groups brings population boundaries into sharper focus.

When a population's boundaries intersect those of other populations, the clash between them makes salient how populations differ from one another. Interaction with key constituents also helps define a population's boundaries. Recognition by public agencies and vocational training programs and certification by private and non-profit organizations lends an aura of legitimacy and credibility to a new population. In time, if the population survives, it gains a taken-for-granted status in the organizational community. However, for many populations, issues of moral acceptance and regulatory approval impede their growth. We now turn to those issues.

Sociopolitical legitimacy strategies

Sociopolitical legitimacy is the acceptance by key stakeholders, the general public, opinion leaders, and government officials of a new venture as appropriate and right. Sociopolitical legitimacy has two components: the moral value of an activity within cultural norms, and acceptance of an activity by political and regulatory authorities. Founders must find ways of adapting to existing norms and laws or changing them. In the process, they may have to fend off attacks from religious and civic leaders, and find ways of raising the public image of the population. Through strategic social action, entrepreneurs attempt to construct new meanings that may eventually alter community norms and values. Social contexts, from this perspective, not only represent patterns of taken-for-granted meaning, but also sites within which the construction of new meaning takes place. By founding innovative ventures – the first stage in creating new populations – entrepreneurs initiate the process of reconstruction.

Organization-level sociopolitical strategies

At the organizational level, few founders face serious moral legitimacy issues in established capitalist societies because entrepreneurs have a presumptive right to create new ventures. Nonetheless, some new organizational forms provoke public resentment or even condemnation. For example, the life insurance industry in America was initially condemned as a vulgar commercialization of the sacredness of life (Zelizer, 1978). In the past several decades in the United States, the toxic waste disposal industry, the nuclear power industry, biotechnology, on-line pornography, and family planning clinics have been attacked as immoral and a threat to certain cherished values. By themselves, individual founders can do little to overcome the moral deficiencies attributed to them. Gaining moral legitimacy requires collective rather than individual action, as we argue in the following sections.

Organizations seeking moral legitimacy must be wary of appearing cynical or self-interested, because moral calculus rests on a communal rather than an interest-based foundation. Nonetheless, Suchman's (1995: 580–582) proposed typology of four forms of *moral legitimacy* does suggest the general outlines of a strategy for new populations. *Consequential legitimacy* rests on a claim that an organization produces a public good, such as better health care or a cleaner environment. For this dimension, founders need to associate their organizations with prevailing public tastes. Given the abstract level at which norms regarding the public good are pitched, organizational goals can be framed in equally abstract language. *Procedural legitimacy* depends on an organization using socially accepted techniques to generate its products or services. In situations where outputs are difficult to evaluate, procedures might be the only observable activities. For example, charter schools may claim procedural legitimacy because they are 'following the mandated curriculum,' even though student test scores remain abysmally low.

Structural legitimacy stems from organizations displaying the proper form expected of organizations in their population. For example, does a school employ a guidance counselor and social worker? Clearly, for new populations, the form itself is still in flux. Thus, *mimetic isomorphism* – copying the most common or highly valued structure in the population (DiMaggio and Powell, 1983) – is not an option. Instead, founders have an opportunity to create what structures come to be perceived as legitimate. Finally, *personal legitimacy* depends upon the charisma of organizational leaders. Because charisma is unstable and difficult to institutionalize, its long-run value to an organization is questionable (Nelson, 1993). For new ventures, however, charisma plays an important role in mobilizing resources in the absence of personal assets or experience.

New organizational forms that are firmly embedded in local networks of trust in their communities begin with a reservoir of moral legitimacy not available to others. In the early 20th century, the emerging population of credit unions in the United States benefited from network ties among early members that diffused information to potential new members (Barron, 1995: 148–149). A related form, mutual savings and loan associations, began as 'friendly societies' in Pennsylvania in the 1830s (Rao, 1989). Founded on networks of interpersonal trust, they drew their members from local ethnic neighborhoods and were staffed by officials drawn from the membership. With the goal of enabling members to build their own homes, their structures were simple and officials' actions easily monitored.

In the 1880s, by contrast, entrepreneurs failed when they attempted to create national mutual savings and loan associations by establishing branches and employing agents to recruit members who were strangers to one another (Bodfish, 1931). However, by the turn of the century, changing norms and values had undermined the older forms of thrift institutions. 'The rise of a transient and heterogeneous population [in California] and the bureaucratic spirit that attended Progressivism contributed to the downfall of thrifts based on mutuality and enforced effort and the rise of thrifts celebrating bureaucracy and voluntary effort' (Haveman and Rao, 1997: 1644).

Regulatory legitimacy and the role of government

One of the most common complaints voiced by owners of businesses in established populations in the United States concerns the overly intrusive role of government in what they perceive as their internal affairs (Vogel, 1973). Historically, however, the relationship between government and the economy has been much weaker in the United States than in other industrialized nations. In the United States, firms enjoy considerably more autonomy vis-à-vis the state and organized labor than in Western Europe and Japan. In contrast to the continental European context and in spite of legislation such as the Sherman Act (1890), the American state was largely an agency for industrial development until well after the turn of the 20th century (Roy, 1981, 1997). Three factors inhibited the growth of a strong central state: rapid economic growth, a large number of small enterprises, and the recurring discovery of new domestic markets, helped along by westward expansion. However, state power and state intervention eventually increased, and government became a force that businesses could neither completely dominate nor totally ignore.

Since the 1960s, independent consumer and environmental interest organizations have emerged in the United States to challenge the private business sector. The new organizations have enjoyed increased access to the political process, regardless of which political party holds power. Moreover, in the 1970s, business perceived itself challenged by a large number of increasingly sophisticated government agencies, staffed with public bureaucrats who were perceived as highly sensitive to the demands of non-business interest groups. In that climate of elevated political conflict and debate, the regulatory process became even more politicized. Since then, interest group activity has notably expanded, responding to the increased involvement of state and local governments in economic and social affairs (Gray and Lowery, 1996; Schlozman and Tierney, 1986).

Nascent entrepreneurs, building organizations with little or no precedent, are not terribly well placed to win regulatory approval. Studies show that most founders of new firms avoid entanglement with government bureaus and officials as long as possible. They delay filing social security papers and state unemployment insurance forms for their employees, and put off filing income tax returns and applying for business licenses until they can no longer avoid such actions (Aldrich et al., 1989). Such delays, often lasting several years, reflect founders' uncertainties about whether a bounded entity really exists yet. Despite the existence of some templates for legal establishment (Khandekar and Young, 1985), its timing remains hard to predict (Ruef, 2005). Delays also reflect founders' recognition that government agencies are only dimly aware of *new* firms. We suspect that most founders of new organizational forms follow this same strategy, with the exception of highly regulated populations, such as biotechnology or charter schools.

Within-population sociopolitical legitimacy

Collective action constitutes the foundation of sociopolitical strategies for population-level action. As we argued in discussing cognitive strategies, the key events affecting the emergence of new populations as stable entities involve the formation of other types of organizations (Delacroix and Rao, 1994). Gaining moral legitimacy for a new population involves altering or fitting into existing norms and values, something individual organizations lack the resources to accomplish. Similarly, winning legal and regulatory acceptance generally requires campaign contributions, political action committees, lobbying, and other costly activities beyond the reach of individual organizations. Thus, early in a new population's growth, sociopolitical issues will have to be addressed by interorganizational action.

Sociopolitical approval – especially regulatory approval from governmental agencies – may be jeopardized if collective action fails. Failure to agree upon common standards leaves a new population vulnerable to illegal and unethical acts by some of its members. Such actions may bring the entire population into moral disrepute and jeopardize its legitimacy. In contrast, mobilization around a collective goal may enable new populations to shape the course of government regulation and perhaps even win favorable treatment. As Edelman and Suchman (1997: 489) noted, organizations and associations are not only subjects of the law but also help shape it. If early founders succeed in creating an interpretive frame that links a new population to established norms and values, later founders will easily mobilize support.

The example of the Information Industry Association, representing the pay-per-call industry in the United States, shows how associations may attempt to solicit their own regulation to ward off more drastic action by government. The nascent pay-per-call information services industry (using 900-prefix phone numbers) was growing rapidly until it ran into regulatory legitimacy problems in the early 1990s. Small startup firms used the 900-prefix numbers to sell jokes of the day, credit card information, telephone sex, and other services for which they charged high prices. They used the billing services of regular local telephone companies and often concealed or misrepresented their billing practices. Problems arose because the small but highly profitable industry lacked uniform standards and consistent government oversight. U.S. Sprint and other phone companies decided to stop carrying most pay-per-call services because of consumer complaints and difficulties in collecting from customers who disputed their bills. The industry formed the Information Industry Association, a trade association that lobbied for uniform federal regulations. However, the conflict badly weakened the industry (Andrews, 1992).

Populations that succeed in creating a strong organization to represent their interests may use their position to block the way for alternative organizational forms. Populations that not only solicit favorable treatment from the state but also cloak themselves in moral legitimacy are especially blessed. For example, funeral home owners in the United States enjoyed great success for many years in controlling state regulation of the industry (Torres, 1988). Locally owned homes controlled most state boards regulating the industry by playing on the twin themes of local control of business and respect for the sacredness of their practices.

For almost a century, state boards blocked alternatives to traditional means of disposal of the dead, opposing crematoriums, burial societies, and chain-owned funeral homes. Following the wishes of the locally owned funeral homes, state boards imposed requirements that were intended to exclude alternative forms, such as: prohibiting corporate ownership; requiring that all establishments be fully equipped; prohibiting establishments from sharing equipment; and requiring that all establishments employ a full-time embalmer. Their actions kept the founding rates of technically superior alternatives very low, almost totally suppressing the emergence of competing populations. Only when changing political currents in the 1980s began to favor deregulation did regional and national chains gain the upper hand.

Between-population sociopolitical legitimacy

New populations are vulnerable to attacks from other populations that may jeopardize their sociopolitical legitimacy. Established organizations in affected populations often strongly oppose the rise of new ventures seeking to exploit similar resources, and try to block them at every turn, including calling into question their compatibility with existing norms and values. They usually do not challenge entrepreneurs' generic rights to create business or non-profit organizations – such rights are assured in most Western political democracies – but rather resist the creation of organizations that threaten their niche. In addition to questioning the cognitive legitimacy of a new population, as we discussed earlier, established populations may mount an effective opposition by inducing legal and regulatory barriers against the threatening newcomer.

The emergence and growth of new populations thus partially depend on the severity of attacks from established populations that may resist encroachment. In discussing cognitive strategies, we noted that established organizations might raise doubts about a new activity's efficacy. In addition, they may also question its conformity with societal norms and values, and thus change the terms on which resources are available to emerging populations. Beyond recognition, new populations need reliable relationships with other, established populations. If they achieve legitimacy, tacit approval in the form of economic transactions is more likely.

If a new population faces overt sociopolitical conflict with an established population, a trade association or industry council is probably required to mobilize the newcomer's strength. In zero-sum conflicts between newcomers and incumbent populations, compromise may be impossible. However, many inter-population relations involving moral and regulatory acceptance involve issues of education and negotiation rather than zero-sum conflict. For example, new biomedical and health care industries only survive if they can convince third parties – insurance companies and the government – to pay the costs that patients cannot bear, such as for CAT scans or cochlear implants. Thus, firms in the population must cooperate to educate and influence these third parties to include the product or service in their payment reimbursement systems (Van de Ven and Garud, 1994). *Moral* arguments for technology-intensive patient care emphasize the health care system's obligation to do all it can for the quality of human life, and *regulatory* arguments stress equitable treatment of citizens covered by government and private insurers.

Cooperation across population boundaries gives associations and other collective bodies a stronger power base from which to operate politically. By aggregating their resources, umbrella organizations wield greater sociopolitical influence, although at the cost of increasing internal heterogeneity. In this clash of the strategy of influence versus the strategy of membership, umbrella associations choose greater membership. However, as a consequence, they sign up only a small fraction of all the potentially eligible membership. In the United States, only the very largest firms belong to the Business Roundtable, the Conference Board, and the Council for Economic Development. Mid-sized and smaller firms join associations such as the United States Chamber of Commerce, the National Federation of Independent Businesses, and the National Association of Manufacturers.

Cooperative action by such heterogeneous business interest groups has changed the organizational landscape. Labor and consumer interest groups enjoyed a period of great success in the late 1960s and early 1970s, resulting in several landmark pieces of legislation: the Equal Employment Opportunity Act, the Occupational Safety and Health Act, and the Environmental Protection Act (Dobbin and Sutton, 1998; Hoffman, 2000). Business interests fought back in the 1970s through the creation of new groups and the revitalization of established associations. Between 1974 and

1981, collective action by the unified business community resulted in initiatives such as the Labor Law Reform Bill and the defeat of the proposed Federal Consumer Protection Agency (Akard, 1992).

We again see the paradox of individual versus collective benefits: pioneering ventures that solicit or accept cooperative relations with established populations may succeed to such an extent that followers – so-called 'second movers' – enter the fledgling population with lower costs and thus drive the pioneers out of business (Jovanovic, 1982). Osborne Computer, for example, was a pioneer in bundling other manufacturers' software with its products, but did not survive some costly marketing blunders that gave other firms a chance to surpass it. At the population level, however, such cooperation is often essential for survival. Our argument is evolutionary, not functionalist. Efforts at cooperation do not guarantee that it will be achieved. The evolutionary model says only that *if* cooperation emerges in a population, *then* that population will gain a selective advantage, to the extent that it overcomes problems of internal coordination and external legitimacy.

Community-level sociopolitical legitimacy

Lack of community-level support for new populations may undercut their efforts to secure sociopolitical approval. Most new forms of business enterprise have enjoyed at least moral and regulatory tolerance of their existence (Delacroix et al., 1989; Zucker, 1989). Nonetheless, this apparent easy success is counterbalanced by many occasions on which support has not been forthcoming or has been lost. The first newspaper editor in the United States was jailed (Delacroix and Carroll, 1983), and many forms of inter-business alliances were ruled illegal in the 19th century (Staber and Aldrich, 1983). Resistance to technological innovation during the Industrial Revolution in England and France came from intellectuals who opposed innovation on moral and philosophical grounds, as well as from people with a vested interest in the current technology. Mokyr (1992) attributed greater British success in industrial development to stronger government support for innovation than in France.

Today, low sociopolitical legitimacy still constitutes a barrier to many potential business activities. For example, new schemes for burning or burying toxic waste often clash with U.S. communities' norms about local control over land-use decisions (Levine, 1982). Citizens protest that *procedural legitimacy* has been violated because their views were not solicited when officials made important decisions about waste disposal. A similar public controversy in the 1940s and 1950s dogged attempts by chemical firms manufacturing fluoride to convince local community officials to purchase fluoridation systems for their public utilities (Coleman, 1957). Firms tried to hire lobbyists with local connections and formed 'citizen's groups' backing proposed schemes. In the final decades of the 20th century, the tobacco industry was particularly effective at disguising its sponsorship of local community groups that opposed smoking-control legislation.

In the 1960s and 1970s, alternative organizations faced legitimacy barriers that hampered their ability to recruit members and compete with mainstream businesses (Rothschild, 1979). Similarly, organizations that wished to convert to employee ownership were initially perceived as challenging fundamental economic values in American society (Rothschild and Russell, 1986). They were viewed as *structurally illegitimate* because they rejected hierarchy, formalization, and a division of labor based on expertise and training. Nonetheless, alternative organizations enjoyed some moral legitimacy for a brief period as proponents created organizations such as free schools, medical clinics, and newspapers. However, that period ended when various legislative initiatives promoting cooperative banks and worker ownership failed in successive sessions of Congress.

Cross-national differences in cultural norms and values mean that some activities are morally suspect in one society but not another. The emerging biotechnology industry in Germany has faced more severe sociopolitical legitimacy problems than its American counterpart. During the mid-1990s, an analyst at a major German bank noted that 'Biotech is almost nonexistent within Germany ... the public is still very much against it, so German companies find they have to go abroad, to the U.S. or Japan' (Nash, 1994: C1). In addition to federal regulatory barriers, local elected officials in Germany were hostile to biotechnology laboratories in their communities. Environmentalists, such as the politically powerful Green movement, spearheaded public opposition to genetic technology research and production. Sociopolitical opposition, combined with the traditional conservatism of the German business community, resulted in only 17 biotechnology companies in Germany in 1994, compared with about 1,200 in the United States. 'Public suspicion of biotechnology in Europe has led many European chemical and pharmaceutical firms to establish research laboratories in the United States and to develop research, development, and other alliances with American firms' (Ryan et al., 1995: 346–347).

Even if they do not raise issues of moral legitimacy, new populations whose activities and long-term consequences are not well understood may have trouble in winning approval from cautious regulatory agencies. In the 20th century, U.S. firms in the fledgling biotechnology industry, which based their technologies on manipulation of DNA, faced a major hurdle in winning FDA approval of their testing procedures (Ryan et al., 1995), a case we consider again in Chapter 11. New populations whose production technologies may put workers at risk have to win approval from state and federal OSHA offices, although such offices are so under-funded that their monitoring efforts are not likely to threaten most non-complying firms (Draper, 1991).

Sociopolitical strategies: summary

In addition to problems of inadequate organizational knowledge and a low level of cognitive legitimacy, organizational entrepreneurs in new populations face problems of moral and regulatory legitimacy. We have emphasized that cognitive issues are paramount for most new organizations in the early days of a new population, but sociopolitical issues will arise whenever new activities break cultural frames or run afoul of governmental laws and regulations. Founders try to convince key constituents that their ventures are appropriate and right, given existing norms and laws. They attempt to co-opt religious and civic leaders and raise the public image of the population. New organizations acting on their own rarely win sociopolitical legitimacy. Instead, founders make common cause with other organizations within their emergent population. Collective action through trade associations, industry councils, and other groups allows a population to speak with one voice. Collective action also brings population boundaries into sharper focus.

Table 9.2   Examples of new populations that encountered collective action and legitimacy problems

Population	Problem	Outcome
Auto industry in 1890s	Competing designs for power source	Victories in road rallies gave gasoline power an advantage
Biotechnology industry in the 1970s–1990s	Public anxiety and tight government regulation	Extremely lengthy FDA approval process, shortened by political action in early 1990s
Pay-per-call telephone information industry in 1980s and 1990s	Lack of uniform standards and self-monitoring	Government regulation of population

Conclusions

Given the organizational, intra-population, inter-population, and community conditions facing pioneering founders in new populations, different strategies are called for than those used by founders in established populations. Strategies for generating and sustaining new organizational knowledge and legitimacy are as interrelated as the hierarchical contexts that spawn them. Gaining the trust of stakeholders within and around the organization provides a basis from which to build a knowledge base via cooperative exchange with other similar organizations. Such strategies, in turn, make it easier for member organizations to organize collectively and to build a broad reputation of their population as an enduring reality. After a dominant design and standards are set within a population, its boundaries come into sharper focus as new entrants are judged on conformity to the institutionalized order. An established reputation also facilitates the co-optation of institutional actors, ultimately improving a population's chances of achieving effective collective action and legitimacy.

The period during which a new population emerges deserves more theoretical attention, because the struggle to carve out a niche involves such strong forces that the events of that period may be forever imprinted on the organizations that persist (Stinchcombe, 1965). Indeed, the model of population growth implicit in Table 9.1 points toward a new activity pattern that eventually harmonizes with its interorganizational and community-level environments. As a settled member of the community, the new population takes its place as a defender of the status quo. However, based on the examples given, many promising new activities clearly never realize their potential, because founders fail to develop trusting relations with stakeholders, succumb to opposing populations, and never win external support.

In Table 9.2, we list some of the examples used in this chapter as a reminder that population survival and growth are often problematic. The automobile industry was hampered by competing designs for power sources, and victories by gasoline-powered vehicles in certification contests helped push the industry toward a single dominant design. Biotechnology firms faced lengthy and expensive scrutiny from government agencies, but increased political power in the 1990s shortened the process. The pay-per-call information industry, by contrast, incurred increased government regulation as a result of its dubious practices and lack of uniform standards. Thus, understanding the learning and legitimacy constraints facing founders of new ventures helps us understand the forces contributing to and constraining population variety in organizational communities.

The models laid out in this chapter highlight three issues. First, as we noted in Chapter 4, researchers often attempt to distinguish between new organizations that copy well-known practices in their population and truly innovative new organizations, pioneering practices without precedent. However, such distinctions almost always occur within the context of studying an established population. Limited attention has been paid to the possible origins of a new population. Investigators thus conflate two very different kinds of innovation events that pose very different problems for entrepreneurs: innovating within an institutionalized context versus striking out into uncharted waters, where population boundaries are not yet secure. Future research needs to separate these two forms of innovation. In the next chapter, we focus on foundings and disbandings within *established* populations.

Second, the debate in the ecological-institutional literature over 'legitimacy' has focused, in part, on the issue of left-truncation of a population's history (Baum and Powell, 1995; Hannan et al., 1995). Is data on the population available from its earliest days, when foundings were just beginning to be observed? Left-truncation of data – not having the early years of a population's history available – can lead to misspecification of models and biased conclusions regarding the pattern of population growth. However, such debates overlook a more serious form of selection bias (Miner, 1993). To the extent that we study only populations that survived long enough to make their mark upon the usual sources of archival information, we overlook the unsuccessful ones. Groups of organizations that struggled and did not succeed in building a new population provide the best historical record for testing our ideas about the social context of population formation.

How can we avoid a bias against populations with truncated histories? Just as evolutionary theorists have made us aware of the danger of focusing our research attention on cross-sectional studies of surviving organizations (Aldrich, 1979: 56–61), so too must we become aware of our tendency to focus on surviving populations. Investigators must pay more attention to economic and business history, written not at the level of case studies of individual firms, but rather at the level of eras and epochs. Economic theories of industry creation focus narrowly on the risks and economic tradeoffs that characterize new industry entry decisions (Klepper and Graddy, 1990; Winter, 1984) and give little weight to the social context within which those decisions are embedded. Which activities have attracted entrepreneurs, speculators, investors, and others, only to lose out when support was not forthcoming from key stakeholders, relevant populations, and other forces? The business press serves as a good source of information on new activities that attract attention because they challenge traditional populations, fail in spectacular fashion, or otherwise make short-run news.

Third, when we identify a new population's genesis, research needs to focus intensively on its early years. Researchers now routinely collect information on fairly complete life histories for many populations, but only for such generic events as foundings and disbandings. In addition to these key events, we also need to collect information on patterns of contact between the entrepreneurs who founded early ventures, and especially on any efforts they undertook to create vehicles for collective action (Granovetter and McGuire, 1998). We also need information on how other groups of organizations – possible competitors, regulatory agencies, local governments, and so forth – responded to the first new ventures in a fledgling population. Again, social historians, cultural anthropologists, business historians, and others can enrich our understanding of the early days of a new population.

Study Questions

1. Mechanisms supporting the development of new populations – such as learning, cognitive legitimation, and sociopolitical legitimation – are often hard to measure empirically. To what extent can (and should) organizational theorists proxy these mechanisms through more visible indicators, such as interorganizational imitation, population density, and ties to powerful interest groups? What other proxies might be used?

2. The concept of *path-dependence* reminds us that we must be on guard against viewing existing dominant designs in a population as having the best 'fit'. Using the variation-selection-retention framework, describe social contexts within which inefficient designs are most likely to come to dominate an organizational population.

3. The examination of mechanisms leading to the emergence of new populations is often premised on the assumption that diversity in organizational arrangements produces desirable outcomes for society as a whole. Present arguments that both support and counter this assertion.

Exercises

Choose an organizational population for historical analysis and answer the following questions:

1. Discuss what you know about 'pioneer' organizations that served as early instances within this organizational population. Who were the key entrepreneurs involved in those organizations? Describe what you know about their backgrounds. What were the entrepreneurs trying to accomplish? What obstacles did they face?

2. Describe the historical processes that created the population. To what extent did pioneer organizations collaborate (or compete) for the sake of resource mobilization? Were there scientific, technological, or intellectual breakthroughs that were critical to the emergence of the population? Were any trade associations formed? Did organizations in the population face early regulatory challenges? At what point did the population achieve name recognition in the public media? What early examples of good and bad press can you identify?

10

Reproducing Populations: Foundings and Disbandings

Why should we be concerned about the *rate* at which organizations are founded and disbanded in a population? From an evolutionary perspective, we offer two reasons. First, given typical disbanding rates, especially in a population's early years, a population would grow slowly or not at all unless new organizations were added. Many populations have disappeared from the organizational landscape in the past century, as studies by population ecologists and economic historians have documented (Ruef, 2004; Schmookler, 1962). Second, disbandings may be a clue to the selection forces affecting populations. By observing which kinds of organizations are selected out and which survive, subsequent entrants might be able to identify favored forms and ascertain which selection criteria are at work. They may use such information to improve their fitness, relative to prior generations, refreshing the population.

Although most newly founded business organizations are small and short-lived, they nonetheless constitute a major source of volatility and potential innovation in mature populations. For example, Dunne et al. (1988: 503) examined 387 four-digit SIC manufacturing industries over a span of five census periods: 1963, 1968, 1972, 1977, and 1982. They found that on average, '38.6 percent of the firms in operation in each industry in each census year were not producing in that industry in the previous census.' Of these new entrants, about 55 percent were new firms creating new plants, rather than existing firms diversifying their products. Their analysis excluded the bottom 1 percent of the firms in each industry; if those firms were included, the entry rates would increase by approximately 10 percentage points. By replacing disbanding and exiting organizations, foundings preserve a population's viability and sustain its place in a society.

In the previous chapter, we focused on the emergence of new populations. New organizations in new populations are certainly critical to the long-run growth and diversity of organizational communities. However, most foundings and disbandings are commonplace events that add and remove organizations from established populations, rather than new ones. In this chapter, we focus on these ordinary foundings and disbandings, taking the initial emergence of the population as given. We emphasize two factors affecting the rate at which new organizations emerge and disband: entrepreneurial knowledge and intentions, and entrepreneurial access to resources. We concentrate on the population level of analysis and on societal level forces affecting populations. In Chapter 11, we will examine the coevolution of diverse organizational populations within a community context.

Definitions: rates of organizational foundings and disbandings

We defined foundings in Chapter 4 as occurring when founders mobilized sufficient resources to create a coherent bounded entity. Just as we used the term *foundings* rather than 'births' to convey a sense of the process-driven, emergent nature of organizational creation, so too we used the term *disbandings* to avoid the finality of terms like 'death.' Organizations cease to exist for a number of reasons. For example, in businesses, owners retire, fulfill their expectations, run out of patience or money, or find more interesting things to do. It appears that relatively few cause losses to creditors when they disband, which is the financial definition of 'bankruptcy.' Historically, researchers have relied on the Small Business Administration's estimate that bankruptcies cause a small proportion of all business terminations (Small Business Administration, 2003). However, Lawless and Warren (2005) argued that official statistics vastly undercount business bankruptcies because small business owners often mingle personal and business assets. The problem stems from current reporting practices by the Administrative Office of the U.S. Courts, which apparently encourage owners and lawyers to classify many business bankruptcies as personal. Owners may also plan some bankruptcies strategically to avoid legal liabilities or obligations to employees and other stakeholders (Delaney, 1992). In voluntary associations, members and leaders may decide that they do not like their lack of recognition, become disillusioned with oligarchical leaders or uncooperative members, or find better uses of their time. Whatever the reason, disbandings are everyday events.

When organizations disband, the dissolution of their boundaries releases resources back into the environment. The freed resources – members, equipment, a fixed site, inventory, and other assets – then become available for other organizations, although the high costs of retraining and reuse may leave workers unemployed and sites abandoned. The term 'disbanding' captures this aspect of organizations' final days, as intentions, resources, and boundaries become disconnected. From coherence, a disbanding organization sinks back into incoherence and disorganization, and disappears as an evolutionary entity. The odds of disbanding are strongly linked to an organization's size and moderately related to its age, as we noted in Chapter 8.

Rate of founding refers to the number of organizations added to the population in a given unit of time, relative to the number that already exist. Calculating this rate requires that we identify the population at risk for such events, thus forcing us to be clear about population boundaries. For example, if 10 organizations are founded over a 12-month period in a population that already numbered 100 at the start of the year, the founding rate is 10 percent for that year. In the United States and the European Union, founding rates of businesses over the past decade have, in fact, been about

10 percent per year. High founding rates, of course, do not guarantee that populations will grow. Population growth depends on the balance between foundings and disbandings, as well as other entries to and exits from a population. For example, population members are occasionally transformed – such as by merger and acquisition – into something else. Growth in a population may also be stimulated by *de alio* entries from existing organizations in other populations (McKendrick et al., 2003).

Rate of disbanding refers to the number of organizations that disband in a given unit of time, relative to the number that already exist. If aggregate founding and disbanding rates are about equal, populations will stabilize. If the founding rate is higher than the disbanding and other exit rates, populations will grow. Occasionally, disbanding rates rise substantially above founding rates, and populations actually shrink, as happened to Japan's manufacturing sector in the mid-1990s (Japan Small Business Research Institute, 1995). High founding rates are sometimes matched by high disbanding rates, as in populations of neighborhood restaurants, and so the population only holds its own. Indeed, restaurants represent a type of business in which disbanding rates decline only slightly as organizations age.

In Chapter 4, we focused on the immediate situation of potential founders and examined the emergence of new organizations at the entrepreneurial level. In the last chapter, we examined the emergence of new populations. Now, we apply the evolutionary approach to the population level, considering three questions about variations in rates of foundings and disbandings in established populations. First, what factors affect how nascent entrepreneurs learn about opportunities and gain access to resources? Second, what factors discourage entrepreneurs and reduce the level of resources available to them? Third, what impact do the actions of other organizations have on founding and disbanding rates? We consider the social and political conditions that affect cultural expectations about the likelihood of succeeding in a population.

Other vital events: mergers and acquisitions

Organization studies and strategy scholars have paid a great deal of attention to mergers, acquisitions, and divestitures over the past three decades. Beginning with Pfeffer's (1972) pioneering studies of resource dependence and mergers, researchers have investigated mostly the causes and occasionally the consequences of such interorganizational events (see Casciaro and Piskorski, 2005, for a recent analysis). They are certainly dramatic events, often involving a struggle for control over millions of dollars in corporate assets. For example, in the United States, a wave of mergers and acquisitions (M&A) in the 1990s radically altered the organizational landscape in certain sectors, such as in banking and finance. However, the number of M&A events is relatively small, compared to the number of foundings and disbandings. Their economic impact is difficult to estimate, given the way government agencies report economic information in the United States.

First, as with foundings and disbandings, we calculate rates of M&A events by identifying an underlying population at risk for the event. The *merger and acquisition rate* refers to the number of organizations that disappear as independent entities because they merge with or are acquired by other organizations, relative to the number active in that period. For businesses, the appropriate denominator to use in calculating such rates is not always clear. To maintain consistency with other rates, we could include only those organizations actually at risk of being merged or acquired. Thus, we might exclude most sole proprietorships and many partnerships because they are small and have low levels of assets. Even among incorporated firms, many are unattractive merger or acquisition candidates because they have little prospect of growth and lack proprietary assets that would be of value to another firm. Not all proprietorships and partnerships are small, however. In addition, some promising young firms with low levels of revenues and assets are acquired for their potential, especially if they have developed a promising innovation. Excluding them may thus unreasonably shrink the population at risk.

How extensive is M&A activity among small and large firms? In the 1990s, the U.S. Bureau of the Census developed a new database, using the Longitudinal Establishment and Enterprise Microdata (LEEM) file (Small Business Administration, 1998), but it was subsequently abandoned. An early report from that project, focusing only on 1990, 1994, and 1995, provided information for a more comprehensive view of M&A events in the United States than previously available. Among the 5.5 million establishments with employees in 1990, 3.8 million were still active and had employees in 1994. Of those surviving establishments, about 2.6 percent had been acquired by another firm at some point during the period 1990 to 1994, yielding a yearly rate of about 0.5 percent. The targets of acquisition activity were primarily establishments belonging to larger firms. Among establishments in 1990 belonging to firms with fewer than 20 employees, only 0.7 percent were acquired. Among establishments belonging to firms with 20 to 99 employees, 3.8 percent were acquired, and for establishments belonging to firms with 100 or more employees, 8.7 percent were acquired. The establishments acquired from firms with 100 or more employees over this period represented about 7 percent of all the employment in such firms, as of 1990.

We downplay M&A activity in this chapter because it disproportionately affects large (particularly, publicly-traded) companies, rather than all members of an organizational population. We also know that M&A events tend to be distributed very unevenly across organizational populations. According to the LEEM data, for example, the most active sector was finance, insurance, and real estate, in which 6.4 percent of all 1990 establishments that survived to 1994 was acquired. These acquisitions represented about 12.1 percent of 1990 employment in the sector. Fourteen 4-digit SIC code industries had more than 1,000 establishments acquired, and in the top four industries, more than 4,000 establishments were acquired: eating places, national commercial banks, state commercial banks, and grocery stores (Small Business Administration, 1998: 14).

We present these figures to make a simple point. Mergers and acquisitions can have a major impact on competitive conditions in a selected set of industries, especially banking and finance in the past decades (Haveman and Cohen, 1994). Because so many entrepreneurs and organizations depend on the financial services industry, the effects of M&A in that sector have spread to other populations. Over the life course of most populations, however, foundings and disbandings dwarf the impact of M&A on population growth and decline. The conservative calculations we have presented above show that the rate of M&A is very low, relative to foundings and disbandings. In recent years, about 0.5 percent of all establishments have been acquired by other firms. The economic impact of M&A, however, is unquestionable and clearly deserves more attention from organization studies.

Conducting research on M&A events from an evolutionary perspective requires that we link data on these events to changes in competitive dynamics within populations.

Table 10.1   Population dynamics: basic definitions

Founding rate	The number of organizations added to a population during a specified unit of time, relative to the number already in the population
Disbanding rate	The number of organizations that disband in a population during a specified unit of time, relative to the number already in the population
Density	The aggregate number of organizations in a population
K or carrying capacity	The maximum density that an environment can support
Population mass	The aggregate size of all organizations in a population
Density dependence	The dependence of population processes, such as foundings, on the level of population density
Density delay	Level of population density at the time an organization is founded affects its subsequent life chances
r or intrinsic rate of increase	Rate at which a population would grow in the absence of external competition and resource constraints

Unfortunately, publicly available data often do not fit population boundaries identified by researchers. Matching data from government and commercial sources with information on trade associations, industry councils, and other possible markers of population boundaries represents one possible research strategy.

Intra-population conditions

Foundings and disbandings depend, in part, on conditions endogenous to a population, and thus we focus first on population dynamics and population density. *Population dynamics* include the numbers of prior foundings and disbandings in a population. They affect subsequent events because of their effects on the resources available to organizations and on the intentions of founders and managers. *Population density* is usually defined as the number of organizations in a population, even though it seems to imply that a population's size is being compared to the level of resources available to support it. In organizational ecology, *rate dependence* is defined as the dependence of a process on the rate of previous processes, such as foundings and disbandings. A companion term, *density dependence*, refers to the impact of a population's size on subsequent events, such as foundings and disbandings. Table 10.1 lists definitions for the terms covering basic population dynamics.

Population growth – increase in density – results from the changing balance between two events: founding rates and disbanding rates. These events, in turn, are a function of two underlying constraints: an environment's *carrying capacity*, labeled **K**, and the natural or *intrinsic rate of growth* of the population, labeled **r**. The intrinsic rate of increase is the hypothetical rate at which a population would grow, in the absence of constraints imposed by competition with other users of its resources. The rate of increase depends on the balance between foundings and disbandings, and it

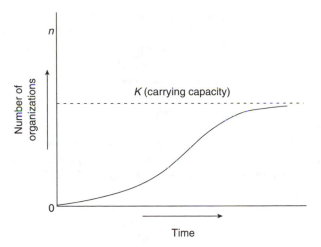

Figure 10.1   **Growth pattern of a population of organizations, assuming fixed organizational size and limited resources**

changes over time as the legitimacy of a population increases. As we noted in Chapter 9, **K**, the carrying capacity for a population, cannot be known *a priori*. Instead, **K** is revealed as the organizations within a population carve out their niche within the organizational community.

If we make some simple assumptions about the intrinsic rate of increase of a population and about how carrying capacity affects competition within a population, we can generate an expected pattern for population growth (Aldrich, 1979: 63–66), as shown in Figure 10.1. Typically, standard ecological models assume populations grow rapidly at first, proceeding exponentially but then tapering off as the population approaches its carrying capacity. Hannan and Freeman's (1989) theory of the competitive and institutional processes involved in population growth, discussed in the last chapter, added further complexity to the model. They built a density dependent model of population growth by positing that founding and disbanding rates vary over the life of a population. We will review the density dependent model in the subsequent section.

The S-shaped growth pattern shown in Figure 10.1 can be formalized in a common logistic growth function:

$$dN/dt = rN[(K - N)/K]$$

In this equation, **N** is the population density, or the number of organizations in the population at any given time, and **r** is the intrinsic rate of growth in the population. **K** is the carrying capacity for the population, and **dN/dt** is the change in the number of organizations for a given unit of time. At the beginning, density is low, and environmental resources are available for exploitation. The population grows rapidly because the growth term **r** dominates the equation. Foundings increase faster than disbandings and the population expands as it exploits the resources in its niche. As growth occurs, and **N** increases, the carrying capacity term **K** begins to dominate the equation because more organizations are competing for a fixed pool of resources. Disbanding rates begin to offset founding rates. After a high level of density has been reached, net additions drop off as the population approaches the carrying capacity of its environment. When density reaches **K**, **N** stabilizes.

Our simple analysis of intra-population processes may be extended through a number of refinements, as we discuss below. First, in the logistic model, only contemporaneous population density drives population growth. The model does not consider prior foundings, disbandings, density-dependence, and the lag structure of these processes. Second, all organizations in a population are treated equally, in terms of their niche location and competitive intensity. However, most recent treatments of population evolution allow for segregating processes, which differentiate organizations by niche, geographic location, or size (Carroll and Hannan, 2000). Third, the model assumes that carrying capacity for a population is constant. In reality, exogenous factors, such as shifts in the demography of consumers, and endogenous factors, such as collective mobilization on the part of entrepreneurs, also affect carrying capacity over time. A comprehensive explanation of population growth would also require that we take account of other populations in the community with which it might compete or cooperate. For example, a growing number of bowling alleys might reduce the carrying capacity for movie theaters if both populations compete in the same niche of leisure entertainment. Or, the carrying capacity for hospitals might be increasing with increases in the number of insurance carriers and physicians' practices cooperating with the hospitals. However, for ease of explanation, we will defer inter-population relations until Chapter 11 and focus only on single populations in this chapter.

Density dependence

Before discussing extensions to the model of population development, we will articulate its key organizational implications in greater detail. *Density dependence* in the model refers to the relationship between population growth processes and the size of the population itself. Empirical generalizations concerning density dependence are now well-established, but their interpretation has been contested. As we discussed in the last chapter, Hannan and Freeman (1989) developed the density dependence model, arguing that the size of a population reflects two underlying processes: legitimation and competition. Increasing organizational density at the beginning of a new organizational form raises cognitive legitimacy, facilitating an increase in foundings. Later, at high levels of density, factors inhibiting foundings become dominant, such as heightened competition for resources. Considered jointly, these processes led Hannan and Freeman (1989) to predict a non-monotonic, inverse U-shaped association between organizational density and the rate of foundings.

Increasing density has a different effect on disbandings: rather than an inverted U-shaped pattern, density is predicted to have a U-shaped association with disbandings. At low levels of density, the level of competition with other organizations in the same population is modest, but disbandings are still high because legitimacy is low. As we noted in discussing the emergence of new populations, creditors, suppliers, employees, and customers will be wary of dealing with new organizations in an emerging population, thus lowering new organizations' life chances. Entrepreneurial learning will also be difficult in the early phase of population growth. Founders do not have successful models to imitate, and they will make numerous mistakes. As the new population becomes taken for granted, and founders learn to copy successful organizations, disbanding rates should drop. Eventually, however, additional organizations added to the population raise the level of competition to such an extent that survival becomes difficult and the disbanding rate rises again.

In early ecological studies, density was measured only by the number of organizations in a population, modeled by a linear and quadratic term for density. Hannan and Freeman (1989) specifically argued that the number of unions, rather than unions weighted by size, was critical in the historical development of the American labor movement. In later studies, ecologists broadened their view of density. Some speculated that the aggregate size of all organizations – *population mass* – and the size distribution of organizations within the population affected population dynamics (Barnett and Amburgey, 1990). A number of studies have measured population mass, including Barnett and Amburgey (1990), Baum and Mezias (1992), Barron (1999), and Ruef (2000). For example, Barnett and Amburgey (1990) studied telephone companies, and measured population mass by the total number of subscribers of all existing companies in a given year. Haveman (1994) extended the density-dependence model to encompass the process of strategic diversification by savings and loan firms. She showed that competitive pressures and legitimacy, and thus entry into new markets, depended on the mass of incumbents in a new market.

On the whole, however, studies of mass dependence within organizational populations have proven to be empirically inconclusive (Barron et al., 1994; Barron, 1999). Weaknesses in the mass dependence account led Barnett (1997) to propose two qualifications in his model of competitive intensity. He hypothesized that organizations typically generate a level of competition proportional to their age and size. Mature populations feature larger and older organizations and therefore display greater levels of aggregate competition than populations at earlier stages of evolution. Barnett's model also recognized that organizations that are *both* large and old may be relatively innocuous entities in terms of competitive intensity. These *weak survivors* often thrive because they conform to institutionalized norms and expectations (Scott, 2001), rather than because they are efficient or innovative. The presence of weak survivors can yield a pattern of resurgence in the density of some mature industries.

A parallel critique of simple density-dependence accounts argues that density might not have the same effects in all populations. If organizations in a population cannot differentiate themselves from one another, then the competitive strength of larger organizations may be felt throughout the population, resulting in dominance by a small number of organizations (Baum, 1996). By contrast, if organizations find ways to differentiate themselves from one another, then small or specialized organizations and strategic groups may coexist in the same population with much larger organizations (Caves and Porter, 1977). For example, Carroll's (1985) resource-partitioning model of niche segmentation – discussed later in this chapter – implies that competition within a population may be fragmented if some forms focus their fitness on specialized niches within their environments.

Facilitating effects of increasing density

We focus on the *consequences* of increasing density for founding and disbanding rates in this chapter, rather than on the legitimation process itself, which was a theme in the previous chapter. We have previously noted several studies that have reported a curvilinear effect of density. For example, Land et al. (1994) found a density effect in their study of U.S. minor-league baseball teams, with foundings initially increasing as density increased but then decreasing at higher densities. Similarly, Minkoff (1997) detected a curvilinear effect of density on foundings of feminist organizations in the United States between 1955 and 1985. Numerous other studies have produced additional support for the density dependence model (see Carroll and Hannan, 2000). Disconfirming results have appeared, but these often seem to be due to problems in research design, in particular *left-censored* observations that lead analysts to miss the early history of a population. Baum (1996) concluded that the basic empirical generalizations predicted by the model were sound, but he noted several criticisms of the density dependence argument.

Two alternative interpretations of the association between founding and disbanding rates and density have been proposed. First, legitimacy might only be an issue for new populations, not established ones. Density may also not be a sufficient condition for the legitimation of populations where many organizations lack a focused identity. Second, density might actually be a proxy for the effects of other forces, in addition to the process of legitimation. Processes associated with rising density include: the growth of organizational knowledge and opportunities for nascent entrepreneurs to learn effective routines and competencies; and the growth of extensive social networks. The latter two explanations can be read as supplementing or complementing, rather than challenging, Hannan and Freeman's model. We review each of the alternatives below.

Necessary and sufficient conditions for legitimation

Not all theorists accept the proposition that increasing density is a necessary condition for a population's legitimacy. In contrast to this argument, Delacroix et al. (1989) argued that most business organizations in modern capitalist societies do *not* face a legitimacy problem, as that issue was settled when private property rights were institutionalized. Zucker (1989) speculated that cognitive legitimacy for many new forms of organization should be thought of as 'yes or no' rather than 'more or less,' with the legitimacy issue dealt with early in a population's history. To some extent, subsequent refinements in ecological theory have confronted such criticisms. Carroll and Hannan (2000: 224) emphasized that the beneficial effects of density eventually reach a finite 'ceiling;' further additions to an organizational population beyond that point have little or no legitimating effect.

Other arguments question whether density, in and of itself, is a sufficient condition for a population's legitimacy. McKendrick and colleagues (2003) found that the beneficial effects of density held primarily for aggregates of organizations with 'focused identities.' In this formulation, independently founded firms (*de novo* entries) which are geographically clustered tend to contribute most to the cognitive legitimacy of a population. By contrast, ventures which are sponsored by existing firms (*de alio* entries) and are geographically dispersed contribute little to a population's legitimation.

Density as a proxy for other processes

Hannan and Carroll (1992: 69) argued that rising density controlled legitimation, rather than merely reflecting it. Zucker (1989), Miner (1993), Delacroix and Rao (1994), and Baum and Powell (1995), in contrast, claimed that changes in density were really a proxy for other processes, such as the evolution of a population's interdependencies with its environment. Baum and Oliver (1992), for example, identified increases in relational density as one explanation for density's effect, with *relational density* defined as direct ties between organizations and their institutional environment that give organizations the advantages of legitimacy, resources, and some buffering from environmental turbulence. Their argument was supported in a study of day care centers in Metropolitan Toronto. Hybels et al. (1994; see also Barley et al., 1992) obtained similar results when they examined patterns of vertical strategic alliances for American biotechnology firms between 1971 and 1989. More generally, processes that accompany growing density include increases in organizational knowledge and the growth of extensive social networks.

Growing density creates opportunities for learning effective entrepreneurial knowledge

Increases in density mean an increase in the number of work sites and thus an increase in the number of members with knowledge of a population. Potential entrepreneurs may hesitate to found an organization when they lack knowledge and proven recipes concerning its form. 'In such situations, existing organizations are the only training grounds for organization builders' (Hannan and Freeman, 1987: 918). Knowledge of competencies and routines gained on a job can arouse entrepreneurial confidence and also increase access to resources. Moreover, increasing density facilitates the formation of splits or spin-offs from already established organizations.

'Spin-off' can be used as a generic term that includes not only new businesses assisted by a parent firm with capital and other resources, but also any businesses started by one or more individuals who have previously worked in the industry (Garvin, 1983; Romanelli, 1989: 217). In some industries, many workers leave to start their own business. Hart and Denison (1987) called the firms spawning new firms *incubators*. Many small manufacturing firms in New York state were founded by entrepreneurs who developed their ideas while working for someone else, and who maintained many ties to their former employers (Young and Francis, 1991). In Winnipeg, Canada, about 20 percent of the firms in four industries studied by Dyck (1997) were founded by two or more persons who had previously worked together in a different organization. Phillips (2002) developed a *genealogical approach* to internal demography, seeking to understand how the flow of key personnel from an existing organization to a new one would contribute to transfers of skills and routines.

In firms with internal labor markets, ceilings on intra-organizational mobility due to the size of upper cohorts may induce employees with entrepreneurial intentions to leave, thus increasing the founding rate in a population, especially in the early stages of expansion (Brittain and Freeman, 1980). As businesses grow, they hire many workers in the early stages of their careers. Eventually the youngest cohorts of such workers bump up against the cohorts immediately above them, who are also fairly young. In their attempts to make sense of their organizational experiences and plan their careers, workers in small companies with youthful age structures realize that they have little chance of moving up rapidly. Employees in these organizational contexts thus are likely to quit to create their own firms (Dobrev and Barnett, 2005) or to join newly founded businesses. So, population growth fuels the organizational formation process whenever workers interpret slow intra-firm promotions in a fast-growing industry as a signal to look elsewhere for opportunities.

Silicon Valley provides an excellent illustration of the powerful effect of organizationally induced entrepreneurship on a region's economic evolution (Brittain and Freeman, 1980; Saxenian, 1994). One of the inventors of the transistor, William Shockley, left Bell Labs in 1954 and first tried to create a firm in Massachusetts, with the help of Raytheon. He gave up that attempt and moved to Palo Alto, where he had been a graduate student at Stanford University, to found the Shockley Transistor Corporation. 'Shockley hired a team of top-caliber engineers but proved to be an inept manager. Two years after the firm's founding, eight of its leading engineers, later known as the 'traitorous eight,' decided to leave and found a competing venture' (Saxenian, 1994: 25). Fairchild Semiconductor, the firm they founded, grew rapidly, spurred on by large military contracts.

None of the team who founded Fairchild Semiconductor stayed with it more than 10 years, and some left to found firms that became household names in the semiconductor industry, such as Intel. Of the 31 semiconductor firms founded in the 1960s in Silicon Valley, most owed their origins to persons associated with Fairchild Semiconductor. Some of the founders left to become venture capitalists, helping to fund startups in the Valley. Unlike persons who left big computer industry firms in the Route 128 region of Massachusetts, departing employees of Silicon Valley firms usually remained on good terms with their ex-employers. By maintaining weak ties to their former firms, they helped to create a network of information sharing that strengthened the entrepreneurial infrastructure of the region (Saxenian, 1994). A similar pattern of spin-offs from established firms was observed in the region of Italy around the city of Bologna, know as 'packaging Valley' because of the concentration of firms specializing in special-purpose packaging machines (Lorenzoni and Lipparini, 1999).

Another source of spin-offs arises from relations between employees and innovative users, who may alert employees to bottlenecks, gaps, or other problems with effective uses of their firm's products/services (Ruef, 2002a). Employees can either report these problems to the firm, or use the information to strike out on their own. For this reason, Garvin (1983) argued that spin-offs are more common in the early stages of an industry, when constraints on population size are low. Employers provide individuals 'with the ability to attract resources and knowledge about where to allocate those resources. [They also provide] models for organizing new firms (both positive examples to be emulated and negative examples to be avoided)' (Freeman, 1983: 33). In Japan, growth through spin-offs is a common tactic among large firms throughout an industry's life course. Large companies take equity positions in the new firms and often allow the firms' management considerable latitude in developing the business (Gerlach, 1992).

Growing density facilitates the growth of extensive social networks

Denser populations result in more frequent contacts between organizations using a new form and outsiders. As we discussed in Chapter 4, nascent entrepreneurs involved in diverse networks gain access to more opportunities than those involved in homogeneous networks. Rising population density may create more opportunities for nascent entrepreneurs to make new contacts and increase the diversity of their ties. In particular, workers in subunits heavily involved in boundary-crossing transactions with their environments have many chances to learn about potential opportunities.

Networks of relations built by larger organizations extend deeply into local communities. For example, employees in a government regulatory agency who have extensive field contacts with regulated organizations have more chances to learn of business opportunities than supervisors trapped behind desks in central offices. Baker and Aldrich (1994) observed such startup activity among Environmental Protection Agency (EPA) employees in the Research Triangle Area of North Carolina. Former EPA employees used their knowledge of government regulations concerning air and water pollution to start consulting firms that assisted others in complying with the regulations. If outsiders learn enough in such contacts to permit them to construct a viable imitation, then the number of organizations founded by persons *not* employed in the population ought to increase with increases in density.

Increasing ties between organizations may lead to successful *collective action* to stabilize and somewhat dampen competitive forces, through tactics such as price leadership and design standards. If business interest associations find ways to overcome the problem of mobilizing diverse firms, they can achieve economies of scale in political and legal action. In the last chapter, we noted that trade associations and other forms of collective action are critical in the process of gaining legitimacy for a new population. Trade associations, in turn, symbolize that a population is viable. For example, mass producers and their association, the Wine Institute, dominated the wine industry in California in the 1970s and 1980s. When the population of farm wineries in California grew large enough to challenge the mass producers, they created an independent trade association called the Premium Winemakers of America (Swaminathan, 1995: 657–658). To the extent that potential entrepreneurs read such conditions as raising their chances of successfully copying an effective form, they may be encouraged to enter the industry.

One of the first international observers to note that networks sometimes emerged on their own from interactions among specific firms was Lorenzoni (Lorenzoni and Lipparini, 1999; Lorenzoni and Ornati, 1988). Lorenzoni and his colleagues studied inter-firm interactions in the textile manufacturing area of Prato, Italy, where firms specialized in the production of apparel made from wool fabrics. He found that economic action had moved from individual firms dealing with one another to a pattern called a network or *constellation pattern*. This pattern emerged because a set of relationships arose over time between the firms in which pure economic exchange no longer governed transactions. Instead, short-term interests were downplayed in favor of longer-term relationships, and firms cooperated with one another in ways that reduced the fragmentation of the industry. Leading firms played the role of champions in initially organizing sets of firms. Later, they receded into the background as interactions between the firms moved from dyadic relationships with the leading firm to interrelationships with most of the other firms in the constellation. Alliances moved from a hub and spoke pattern, to a wheel, and finally to a fully connected network pattern.

Networks of organizations and associated collective action might not only generate more foundings but also cause a decline in disbandings. Members commonly share know-how within trade associations and industry councils. These organizations often publish journals and hold trade fairs at which valuable information is widely disseminated. In some cases, the sharing of helpful information may represent a form of *collective learning* that can be distinguished from direct learning from experience by individual organizations (Miner and Haunschild, 1995). Through organizational units formed by collective action, organizational members observe the impact of new routines and competencies on the fate of other organizations, go on to adopt new practices, and, possibly, lower their risk of disbanding. For example, when U.S. semiconductor firms imitated Japanese research consortia (Aldrich and Sasaki, 1995), their resulting activities influenced not only the semiconductor industry, but also other populations supplying the industry.

Inhibiting effects of increasing density

Eventually, increasing population size exacerbates competitive forces to such an extent that founding rates decline and disbanding rates increase. When a population approaches carrying capacity, several negative effects become apparent, including a reluctance by investors to fund new organizations, and a dwindling supply of potential organizers, customers, and suppliers. Nascent entrepreneurs may realize that the population they wished to enter has become overcrowded, and rethink their intentions. Resources become tied up in existing organizations, making the assembling of resources for new organizations much more difficult than in the past. Organizational boundaries may become acutely fragile, as intense competition makes it difficult for founders to retain valued employees and prime locations. Consequently, further increases in density lead to a decrease in foundings and an increase in disbandings.

Many studies have shown that increases in organizational density past a certain point *lower* founding rates and raise disbanding rates. Indeed, most of the studies of density dependence reviewed by Baum (1996) and Carroll and Hannan (2000) supported the model. For example, as the population of four-year women's colleges in Massachusetts, New York, and Pennsylvania grew between 1855 and 1968, the rate of foundings decreased, net of institutional changes (Studer-Ellis, 1995a). Few colleges disbanded, and so the population continued to grow, albeit at a reduced rate. Ranger-Moore et al. (1991) found that increases in density beyond a certain threshold reduced the founding rates of Manhattan banks over the period 1791 to 1980 and American life insurance companies over the period 1759 to 1937, although the effects were stronger at the city than at the national level.

To capture the growth-inhibiting implications of population density, organizational ecologists argue that competition increases as geometric function of density (Hannan and Carroll, 1992). This functional relationship can easily be derived by imagining the possible set of bilateral interactions among a group of competitors. Assuming that there only two competitors (**A** and **B**), there are also only two types of basic competitive interactions (as **A** initiates a competitive strategy against **B**, or, conversely, **B** initiates a strategy against **A**). By adding a third competitor, **C**, however, the possible interactions expand to six ($A \rightarrow B$, $B \rightarrow A$, $A \rightarrow C$, $B \rightarrow C$, $C \rightarrow A$, $C \rightarrow B$). More generally, given a population density of **N**, there are $N(N-1)$ possible competitive interactions. Consequently, organizational ecologists argue that diffuse competition in a population is most appropriately expressed as a function of N^2.

Lagged effects

Our discussion thus far has laid out the basic density-dependence model of population growth and considered some basic critiques. We now turn to extensions of the model, beginning with effects that may exhibit a temporal lag. The classic model of density-dependence assumes that the number of extant organizations in a population have a relatively immediate impact on founding and disbanding processes. In addition to this contemporaneous impact of density, a number of lagged effects have been proposed, including the impact of prior disbandings, the impact of prior foundings, and delayed effects arising from density itself.

Prior disbandings

Prior numbers of disbandings have been hypothesized to affect founding and disbanding rates by their effects on resource availability and on entrepreneurial knowledge and intentions. First, some resources are tied up within the boundaries of existing organizations, and entrepreneurs only have access to them when those organizations disband. Many foundings replace defunct organizations, as disbandings create openings in niches that then become available to new organizations (e.g. physical plant locations). Prior disbandings also free resources for use by existing organizations, thus lowering current organizations' likelihood of disbanding. For example, when high-technology firms fail in Silicon Valley, other firms seeking their expertise quickly re-hire their core staff of engineers (Saxenian, 1994). To the extent that such engineers bring valuable skills to their new firms, the disbanded firms have inadvertently improved the life chances of the remaining firms.

Second, potential founders' enthusiasm for business ownership may be dampened by high disbanding rates. High numbers of disbandings can be a signal to nascent entrepreneurs that a population has exceeded its carrying capacity, thus discouraging them from proceeding. The signaling power of disbandings depends in part on founders investing enough resources in scanning their environments to accurately assess true disbanding rates. However, even if nascent entrepreneurs themselves ignore the signals, potential employees, creditors, and suppliers may not.

Research on disbandings' effects on subsequent foundings and disbandings has produced equivocal results. With regard to *founding rates,* early research on the impact of prior disbandings was encouraging. However, since Delacroix and Carroll's (1983) pioneering study of newspaper foundings, investigators have found mixed results. Some studies have failed to find significant effects (Baum and Oliver, 1992; Land et al., 1994) and others have reported only a negative impact (Barnett and Amburgey, 1990). Subsequent research has shown that the effects of prior density are more important for foundings than prior disbandings. Studies of the effect of prior disbandings on subsequent *disbanding* rates have also generated mixed results (Baum, 1996).

Why has research on the effect of disbandings been so inconclusive? Confounding factors – cognitive heuristics used by nascent entrepreneurs, lack of relevant and salient information, and ambiguity in interpreting information – seem to moderate any direct effects of prior disbandings. Nascent entrepreneurs who carry through on their intentions appear to evaluate opportunities differently than others, manifesting overconfidence in their abilities to succeed even in difficult circumstances, and underestimating the risks posed (Busenitz and Barney, 1997; de Meza and Southey, 1996). Accordingly, high levels of disbandings probably discourage only a small fraction of nascent entrepreneurs from continuing with their intentions.

Entrepreneurs may also be unresponsive to disbanding levels simply because they cannot obtain decision-relevant information. Population-level information on disbandings is difficult to obtain and thus most nascent entrepreneurs have idiosyncratic knowledge about disbandings. They acquire fragments of incomplete information by reading newspapers or talking to people within their target industry. Xu and Ruef (2004) found, however, that entrepreneurs still had more accurate information on disbanding risks than the general population.

Prior foundings

Prior foundings have been hypothesized to affect subsequent events in ways similar to prior disbandings: perceptually, as a signal about the opportunity structure, and materially, as a drain on available resources, as resources are captured by established organizations. First, if nascent entrepreneurs learn from their environments by imitating others, they might read high levels of foundings as a signal that opportunities are growing in a population. Up to a point, foundings may be subject to bandwagon effects, as emphasized in the literature on boom-and-bust cycles (Kindleberger, 1996). Second, there are probably diminishing returns to the positive effects of prior foundings. At very high levels of foundings, resources and the pool of potential entrepreneurs are depleted.

Prior numbers of foundings are likely to increase subsequent disbandings to the extent that poorly prepared or overly optimistic founders were drawn into the population by the apparent boom in the population. Research on the cognitive heuristics and decision-making patterns of nascent entrepreneurs suggests that positive signals may magnify the normal overconfidence exhibited by potential founders, thus stimulating additional foundings (Busenitz and Barney, 1997). The precise consequences of niche-crowding produced by a rush of foundings may depend heavily on population density, as environments are much less forgiving at higher densities, when competition for resources is fierce, than at lower densities, when resources are abundant.

Are prior foundings a symbol to entrepreneurs and their resource providers of potential opportunities or are they an indication of already-committed resources? Untangling the two interpretations of prior foundings is not an easy task, and much prior research has not done so. In statistical models, prior foundings can only capture crowding due to foundings overshooting an environment's capacity *if* density is left out, or if old organizations do not crowd the environment as much as new ones. Emerging developments in cognitive psychology and decision making have given us a greater theoretical understanding of the ways in which nascent entrepreneurs view their environments. We need more research on the cognitive heuristics and biases of nascent entrepreneurs to uncover the extent to which potential entrepreneurs monitor prior foundings and disbandings and how they interpret the signals from such events.

Density delay

Carroll and Hannan (1989) coined the term *density delay* to explain an empirical regularity they observed across a number of populations: organizations founded during periods of higher density experience persistently higher disbanding rates than organizations founded during lower density periods. They offered three explanations for this finding

(Lomi and Larsen, 1998: 221–223). First, as we discussed in Chapter 8, a *liability of resource scarcity* confronts cohorts of founders in high-density periods. Resource scarcity limits their ability to construct coherent organizations with stable boundaries. Instead, many founders create organizations that are fragile and unprepared for harsh conditions. Second, founders also face a condition of *tight niche packing* that forces them to draw on the crumbs of resources left to them by already established organizations. Because they are forced to the margins of the environment, they must fight fiercely for any resources left by older and more central organizations. Third, a *trial by fire effect* may produce higher mortality in the short run but lower mortality in the long run for organizations founded in high-density environments. In the short run, the fragile organizations are selected out, leaving the stronger organizations to survive to old age.

Swaminathan (1996) examined the relative power of these explanations in his study of Argentinean newspapers and U.S. breweries. As predicted, he found that adverse founding conditions increased disbanding rates in both populations. In the long run, however, the trial by fire experience produced survivors with a lower disbanding rate in their later years. Before this finding may be generalized to other populations, it must be replicated in populations where the length of the initial adverse selection period differs and also in populations that vary in their distribution of 'frail' organizations (Lomi and Larsen, 1998: 223). The possibility of a density delay effect means that prior foundings, by themselves, are not a good predictor of subsequent disbandings. An analysis also needs to take into account the size of a population, relative to the resources in its environment.

Recent research has uncovered a second form of density delay, tied not to competitive conditions at founding but instead to the delays that entrepreneurs experience in reacting to changing environmental conditions (Lomi et al., 2005). As we noted in Chapter 4, considerable amounts of time often elapse during the gestation phase of a new venture, as nascent entrepreneurs struggle to acquire funding, develop a product or service, recruit employees or other members, and become legally established. This lag time during gestation has two effects. First, the population density observed by entrepreneurs as they initiate a new venture may misrepresent the level of competition and cognitive legitimation they experience once that venture becomes operational, several months or several years later (Ruef, 2006). Second, incumbents within a population are also likely to underestimate the level of competition, judging the attractiveness of a niche based on other incumbents and discounting pre-operational entrants. Ruef's (2006) study of American medical schools between 1765 and 1930 suggested that the separation of pre-operational and operational organizations in a population can yield predictions that are more consistent with the density-dependence model than predictions based on aggregate density alone.

Segregating processes

Another set of extensions to the density-dependence model involves the long-standing recognition that organizations within populations tend to be segregated by resource niche and geographic location, among other dimensions (Carroll and Hannan, 2000). Research on these segregating processes has produced theories bearing on resource partitioning and spatial agglomeration, respectively.

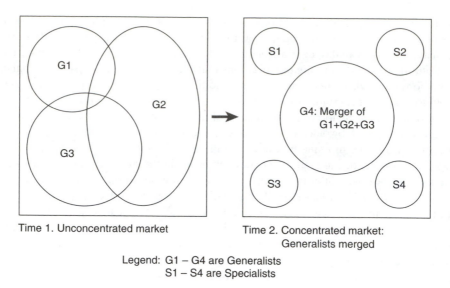

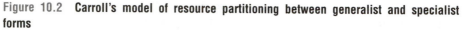

Time 1. Unconcentrated market

Time 2. Concentrated market:
Generalists merged

Legend: G1 – G4 are Generalists
S1 – S4 are Specialists

Figure 10.2 **Carroll's model of resource partitioning between generalist and specialist forms**

Resource partitioning

Intra-population segregation depends, in part, on whether individual organizations spread their activities over a wide or a narrow portion of the population's niche (Hannan and Freeman, 1977). *Specialists* concentrate their fitness in a narrow homogeneous band, and do exceptionally well when environmental conditions favor that band. *Generalists*, by contrast, spread their fitness over a wider, heterogeneous range, and do better than specialists when environments vary across diverse states with some degree of uncertainty. To the extent that widely differing states of the environment place very different demands on organizations, specialists will lose out to generalists. Generalists will triumph because they maintain the capacity to compete in several different environmental states, as opposed to the specialists' single state.

But, *is* a single niche strategy optimal for a given level of environmental variability or can organizations with different strategies coexist? Carroll (1985) argued that generalism and specialism not only coexist, but are also fundamentally interrelated. He noted that the generalists' broad appeal to multiple market segments potentially leaves many small, specialized niches open, depending on the market's level of concentration. In unconcentrated markets, generalists and specialists compete for the same resources, giving an edge to the generalists. However, as concentration increases, generalists engage in fierce competition for the center of the market, whereas specialists exploit peripheral niches and avoid direct competition with generalists. The niche has been partitioned into some segments held by specialists and others held by generalists, thus creating a condition of *resource partitioning*.

We give an example in Figure 10.2. Following Carroll (1985), let us assume that the organizational population in question involves metropolitan newspapers. At Time 1, three generalists aim for the center of the market, which is the location for maximum access to the greatest number of customers (readers). They are forced to differentiate themselves, as the market will not support all three newspapers occupying exactly the same niche. Thus, if they wish to survive, they must move toward the corners of the space, although they still overlap and thus compete for some of the same customers. The three generalists have done such a good job of soaking up the resource space that they have left little room, around the edges, for specialists.

Now let us assume that, over time, the market becomes more concentrated. A single generalist newspaper now dominates the market, occupying the center. It may hold the center because it has bought out the others, or they may have simply disbanded in the face of its superior competitive tactics. The dominance of the generalist has left space in the environment for specialists to operate, and four have occupied the available space. The proliferation of specialists may seem to be restricted to the case of an unevenly distributed resource space, with mass markets being desired locations for generalists. However, Péli and Nooteboom (1999) have shown that even homogeneous resource environments can give rise to specialists under some niche-packing assumptions. In particular, if the dimensions differentiating the resource space multiply over time – due to refinements in customer tastes or member perceptions, for instance – then the opportunities for specialists will increase as well.

Will this outcome be stable over time? Carroll pointed out that the mix of generalists and specialists depends upon several conditions: the degree of heterogeneity in the market, whether there are economies of scale in operations, and whether organizations can change strategies easily. The more heterogeneous the market, the more difficult it is for a generalist to produce one newspaper that appeals to all segments. Attempts to do so in one product – with specialized sections – will likely raise costs and could mean the loss of customers looking for more specialized information. A generalist could try producing multiple papers, but that becomes increasingly costly as differences grow between segments. Generalists benefit from economies of scale, and producing multiple products rather than a single product robs them of their advantage.

Paradoxically, even homogeneous markets can work against generalists in the long run. Evolutionary insights into the effects of market homogeneity can be seen in a study of newspaper readers across 11 Dutch provinces. Boone and colleagues (2002) analyzed the readership of daily papers along a number of demographic dimensions, including age, religious background, political preference, and education. They found that provinces with a relatively homogeneous set of readers were most likely to have a high concentration of generalist newspapers competing based on scale. This competitive condition, in turn, decreased the viability of generalist organizations and increased the viability of specialists. In a sense, the very success of generalists undermined their own position. Generalists also stabilize the market by their visibility and fairly predictable actions. For example, from this perspective, Microsoft Corporation's dominance of the personal computer operating system market has allowed producers of more specialized desktop applications to prosper.

Resource partitioning has been documented in industries as diverse as brewing, cooperative banking, auditing, microprocessor production, and automobile manufacturing (Carroll and Hannan, 2000). All of these industries are characterized by economies of scale in production, and all 'experienced a resurgence of specialist producers after these [scale] economies had been governing organizational evolution for some time' (Carroll and Swaminathan, 1992: 94). For example, as concentration increased in the American brewing industry between 1975 and 1990, the disbanding rate of microbreweries decreased, although the disbanding rate for large mass-production breweries was unchanged. In the American microprocessor industry, as concentration increased, new entrants in the industry were specialists, rather than generalists (Wade, 1995). They served specialized segments of the microprocessor market that placed a premium on high performance.

Another substantive example of resource partitioning can be found in the American wine industry. Between 1941 and 1990, Swaminathan (1995) found strong evidence that increasing concentration raised the founding rate of specialist farm wineries. Farm wineries created premium wine on a small scale and marketed their products as locally- rather than mass-produced. Their emergence as a sub-population reversed a long-term trend toward declining numbers of producers and increasing concentration of sales in the wine industry. 'At the end of 1990, 1,099 farm wineries were in operation, all except 30 having been founded over the period 1969–1990' (Swaminathan, 1995: 657). The major factor affecting the rate of farm winery foundings over time was rising density within their own sub-population, but Swaminathan also found that mass producers competed with farm wineries. In states with larger numbers of mass production wineries, farm winery foundings were lower, whereas numbers of non-state producers had no significant effect. Also, as resource partitioning theory would predict, industry concentration had a negative impact on the founding rate of generalist wine producers.

Considering research on organizational niches more generally, two departures from resource partitioning theory should be noted. First, several studies have begun to measure niche overlap among organizations directly, rather than relying on ideal-type distinctions between generalists and specialists. For instance, Baum and Singh (1994b, 1994c) analyzed day care centers in metropolitan Toronto between 1971 and 1989. They created two measures of the degree of niche overlap between the day care centers, focusing on degree of overlap in the age ranges of the children served. Overlap density was measured as the aggregate overlap of an organization's resource requirements with those of all others in the population. Non-overlap density was measured as the aggregate of all the resource non-overlaps with others. In accordance with their predictions, overlap density decreased founding rates and raised disbanding rates, whereas non-overlap density increased founding rates and lowered disbanding rates.

Why did density have these effects? Apparently, information about the distribution of day care centers, by age range of children served, was easily available to potential founders, allowing them to avoid tightly packed niches. Similarly, institutional support in the form of resources to start a day care center was more readily forthcoming when authorities perceived that a proposed center was not intended for an already overcrowded niche. Recent extensions to such niche overlap arguments have addressed the contextual influence of market concentration, as well. In their study of the American automobile industry, Dobrev and colleagues (2002) found that the effect of niche overlap on organizational mortality shifted from positive to negative with increases in market concentration. They argued that concentrated markets encourage organizations with similar niches, especially generalists, to engage in alliance formation and implicit collusion. However, they could not directly assess such interorganizational relationships.

A second departure from resource partitioning theory has occurred as some researchers speculate that the forces underlying partitioning and competition over dominant designs might be linked (Wade, 1995, 1996). As economies of scale become more important, organizations using the dominant design tend to cluster toward the center of the market. Those large organizations that might have sponsored techno-logical innovation remain tied to their existing user bases that have investments in the dominant design. Thus, they are likely to neglect the periphery of the market, leaving it to specialist organizations. Specialists benefit from the stabilizing influence of the generalists but also are free to innovate in serving peripheral niches. For example, spe-cialized farm wineries in the United States benefited from mass-production wineries' neglect of small upscale niches (Swaminathan, 1995: 658–660). Variations at the periphery might spark competence-destroying changes that produce the next great discontinuity in the population's technological trajectory.

Geographic scale and agglomeration

A second dimension often used to segregate populations is the physical location of organizations or establishments. One important issue in this regard concerns the geo-graphic scale at which population density should be measured. Evolutionary theory proposes that we focus on the level at which variation and selection forces are strongest. Some organizations compete at local levels, some at regional levels, and others at a national or international level. For instance, Ranger-Moore et al. (1991) found that increases in density had a stronger inhibiting effect on foundings of banks, which were studied at a city level, than on foundings of insurance companies, which were studied at a national level. Similarly, in his study of bank branches and head-quarters in Tokyo between 1894 and 1936, Greve (2002) found that founding rates depended on local neighborhood density. More generally, Hannan and colleagues (1995) argued that the geographic scale at which competition operated was often more local than that at which legitimation processes transpired. The cultural templates defining an organizational form tend to flow more freely across spatial boundaries than the material resources invoked in competitive interaction. Using a data set of auto-mobile manufacturers in five European countries between 1886 and 1981, Hannan et al. (1995) found some support for this multi-level density-dependent model, with competition typically occurring within country boundaries and legitimation occurring across the European context as a whole.

The forces affecting foundings may also operate on a different scale than dis-bandings. In research on the American brewing industry, Carroll and Wade (1991) found the strongest effects of density on foundings at local levels, with disbandings most affected by non-local density. They speculated that entrepreneurs might base their decisions on assessments of local competitive conditions, even though non-local conditions provide the most relevant information on the odds of survival. Local envi-ronments that appear benign are actually embedded in larger competitive environ-ments that might be quite harsh. This asymmetry bears further investigation with direct data on entrepreneurs' *perceptions* of environmental munificence.

In addition to the issue of geographic scale, analysts have questioned whether we should view spatial segregation in terms of discrete and discontinuous boundaries ver-sus continuous distances between different regions. A discrete boundaries approach seems most useful when political or cultural boundaries generate meaningful constraints or benefits for organizational populations. For instance, Saxenian (1994) argued that California's Silicon Valley and Boston's Route 128 have distinctive identities that can-not be reduced to the physical or human geography of these regions. In a similar study,

Molotch and colleagues (2000) compared Santa Barbara and Ventura, California. They found dramatically different populations of voluntary and business organizations, despite the fact that both cities have an almost identical climate, topography, and early history in cattle ranching and citrus agriculture. McKendrick and colleagues (2003: 69–70) extended this logic to stress that multiple identities may be attached to different locations: 'although places have a real physical environment and a spatial dimension, they are not defined by a precise geographic boundary[;] rather, they become known with regard to different spheres of social action and so may have multiple identities: political, cultural, social, and economic.'

In contrast to this discrete perspective on space, economic geographers often view spatial segregation in terms of continuous, physical distances (Appold, 1995; Ellison and Glaeser, 1997; Sorenson and Audia, 2000). Following classic location theory (Weber, 1928), geographers argue that physical distances impose real limitations on the ability of organizations to secure inputs from their logistical networks and to reach users or supporters. For instance, the spatial markets of acute-care hospitals are often represented as catchment areas, based on the distances that patients can feasibly travel to get to a hospital (Ruef, 1997). In health care, discrete political or cultural jurisdictions mean little because patients will travel across such boundaries to receive health care. However, in primary and secondary education, such jurisdictions mean a great deal because students do not typically travel more than five miles to school.

Assuming that the issues of scale and conceptualization of spatial difference have been resolved, organizational theorists can consider how geographic segregation affects the distribution of organizational populations. Given the liabilities associated with regional competition for members, users, and inputs, one might suppose that organizations will distance themselves from each other, evolving toward a relatively uniform distribution across geographic space. In reality, the opposite is true: most organizational populations exhibit *spatial agglomeration*, clustering more in some geographic regions than in others. We have identified four approaches to explaining this phenomenon.

First, some geographic locales may simply offer locational advantages that others lack, such as convenient access to inputs needed by an organizational form or strong local demand for a product or service. Strategy theorists, however, have criticized the economic benefits touted by this perspective, noting that they are unlikely to be sustainable in the long run. For example, agglomeration on a sufficient scale will tend to drive up the cost of local factor inputs. Using an implicit evolutionary argument, Porter and Wayland (1995) argued, instead, that sustained locational advantage tends to be fostered by geographic environments that may appear unattractive on the surface, but which promote the selection and retention of favorable organizational features. Thus, it may be more advantageous for an organization to locate in an area with sophisticated and demanding local users than in an area where users are passive and easily satisfied, provided that organizational members learn from the experience.

Second, economic geographers argue that scale economies tend to result from spatial agglomeration. Similar organizations may benefit from proximity to common suppliers or users, in terms of minimizing transportation and transaction costs (Weber, 1928; Appold, 1995). They may also tap into a more extensive and better-trained pool of labor than the workforce which develops around geographically-isolated organizations. Unfortunately, the empirical evidence for these hypothesized scale economies has been inconclusive. For example, in a study of footwear production in the United States,

Sorenson and Audia (2000) found that plants in regions with spatial agglomeration failed at a much higher rate than isolated plants. When we focus on disbanding events, it appears that local competition can often trump the benefits of regional scale economies.

Third, a social networks perspective on agglomeration emphasizes founding events. It assumes that nascent entrepreneurs want to network with other individuals involved in similar organizations, to acquire tacit knowledge, seek out financial and human capital, and build self-confidence (Sorenson and Audia, 2000). Because such networks are constrained by physical distance, entrepreneurial efforts become concentrated in specific geographic regions. Analysts studying spin-offs or the development of new entrants resulting from the disintegration of large firms offer a complementary explanation. They point out that many of the organizational 'apples' do not fall far from the proverbial 'tree,' leading to the formation of geographically-focused industrial districts (Scott, 1988).

Fourth, cultural perspectives propose an identity-based explanation for spatial agglomeration. If organizational forms (and, thus, populations) tend to be identified with specific geographic regions, then spatial agglomeration helps those forms develop a focused identity (McKendrick et al., 2003). For instance, cultural perceptions of musical theater in the United States are intimately tied to geographic locales such as Broadway and Branson, Missouri (Uzzi and Spiro, 2005). Spatial agglomeration of musical theaters encourages their promotion by local journalists, retailers, and politicians. Consequently, the cognitive and sociopolitical legitimacy of these organizations tends to be higher than if they were geographically dispersed.

Naturally, spatial agglomeration can interact with other segregating dimensions to produce more complex patterns of organizational clustering. Research on Manhattan hotels has found that new hotels tend to locate near hotels that differ in size but are similar in price, thus avoiding size-localized competition but benefiting from agglomeration with similarly priced hotels (Baum and Haveman, 1997). Localized competition may open up gaps in population distributions for a variety of features: size, geography, niche, or some combination of these dimensions. Selection pressures thus produce clusters of organizations at various points, rather than a continuous distribution.

Carrying capacity

A final extension of density-dependence models addresses variation in carrying capacity due to broader societal changes. In this section, we focus on factors that are sometimes exogenous to particular organizational populations, although mobilization by entrepreneurs and incumbent organizations may be critical in shaping these factors, producing considerable endogeneity in resource availability (Lomi et al., 2005). We have identified two aspects of societies that shape the environment for populations: cultural norms and values; and governmental and political activities and policies. Changing norms and values alter entrepreneurial intentions and the willingness of resource providers to support new ventures. Government actions and political events create new institutional structures for entrepreneurial action, encouraging some activities and thwarting others (Dobbin and Dowd, 1997; Schneiberg and Bartley, 2001).

Changing cultural norms and values

Cultural norms and values affect entrepreneurs' interpretations of social and economic opportunities (Stinchcombe, 1965). In the last chapter, we examined the social forces affecting the legitimacy of particular populations. In this section, we draw heavily on the institutional approach to address cultural shifts that may affect the carrying capacity of multiple populations. Institutional theorists give sociocultural norms and values a prominent role, on the grounds that 'the wider setting contains prescriptions regarding the types of organizational actors that are socially possible and how they can conceivably be structured' (Meyer et al., 1987: 15). In institutional accounts, the causes of changes in norms and values are sometimes obscure. By contrast, we focus on *collective action* by organizations whose interests are at stake.

Political leaders, entrepreneurs, and disenfranchised members may undertake crusades to change public perceptions and interpretations of organizational actions, as examples from Japan and Scotland demonstrate. In Japan, the nature of economic activity had to be re-defined between the 15th and 16th centuries before secular profit-oriented activity became legitimate in the eyes of the public. While entrepreneurship on the part of monasteries and temples was widely accepted as part of the medieval Buddhist economy (Collins, 1997), secular capitalism was largely unknown before the Muromachi period (1333–1460). Organized peasant uprisings, called *monto*, began to deprive the most traditional temples of their land rents in the 1470s and shifted public opinion in favor of market-oriented temples. Moves toward a secular economy were finalized during the wars of unification, when military leaders promoted norms against the accumulation of monastic property and in favor of autonomy for entrepreneurial merchants and artisans (Collins, 1997: 860).

In Scotland, an opinion survey in the early 1990s reported that people rated entrepreneurs 'below manual workers such as plumbers and bus drivers on their list of admired professions' (Buxton, 1994). Even though many people expressed an interest in creating a new business, the pervasively anti-entrepreneurial norms of the region discouraged potential founders. Similarly, Davidsson (1995) noted that cultural norms supporting entrepreneurship varied widely across regions in Sweden, depending on the industrial structure of an area. In Scotland, in the mid-1990s four banks reacted to the reported anti-entrepreneurial norms by creating an alliance called Scottish Enterprise. The small business loan scheme focused on encouraging more people to follow through on their interests. After the Labor Party's victory in national elections in 1997, a similar program was created for the rest of Great Britain, focused on moving people off welfare rolls and into self-employment.

Economic enterprise in 19th-century America, although not facing quite the same level of resistance as merchants in Japan or entrepreneurs in Scotland, also had to overcome perceptions that business activities conflicted with traditional societal values. For example, we noted in the last chapter that early life insurance companies' attempts in the United States to place a financial value on human life were rejected as profaning the sacredness of death (Zelizer, 1978). Life was defined as divine and religious leaders railed against the commercialization of a sacred event. However, a host of social and economic changes – especially the spread of notions of economic risk and speculation – fostered a growing awareness of the economic value of life and death. The life insurance industry redirected its marketing campaign to emphasize that a good family man was merely providing for his loved ones by purchasing insurance, and consumers gradually accepted the industry. The commercialization of death did not remove all the rituals associated with it, because the funeral home industry co-opted the sacred symbols associated with disposal of the dead and used them to secure its niche (Torres, 1988).

Just as business interest associations often campaign to change public perceptions of the industries they represent, voluntary and non-profit associations engage in similar practices. In the United States, 'Catholic women's colleges led the movement to train women for vocations, such as teaching and social work, thereby breaking the monopoly of the liberal arts emphasis in women's colleges' (Studer-Ellis, 1995a: 1054). As Catholic women's colleges were founded, they served as role models for other potential founders, consequently raising the founding rate for all women's colleges. The expanding population of women's colleges helped reshape norms regarding appropriate careers for educated women in American society. In Germany, the rise of the ecological movement and spiritualism in the 1980s generated an alternative sector that included health food shops and fortune tellers (Bögenhold, 1987). In mid-19th-century Denmark, the Danish Red Cross and other voluntary associations were founded partially as a response to the changing values placed on individual rights (Christensen and Molin, 1995).

As we noted in Chapter 4, the missing ingredient for most organizational entrepreneurs is not initial capital, but rather the knowledge of where to begin. Norms and values influence nascent entrepreneurs' understandings of current conditions and help shape the way in which entrepreneurial ambitions are expressed, e.g. toward traditional lines of action or toward actions that challenge the status quo. Will ambitious people become government officials or independent entrepreneurs? Will upward mobility be interpreted as a function of nepotism, good luck, or ability? Will revolutionaries advance their cause by turning to violent protests or the popular press? The examples we presented above, including changes in Denmark, Germany, Japan, Scotland, and the United States, suggest that cultural norms deserve greater attention from organizational scholars.

Governmental and political activities

Sovereign nation-states affect the creation of organizations by establishing necessary preconditions, such as political stability and calculable law, and by supporting institutional arrangements regarding the allocation of resources, such as state-supported corporations or banks. Scott (2003: 210) noted that 'the nation-state is the prime sovereign in the modern world; the major source of legitimate order; the agent defining, managing, and overseeing the legal framework of society.' The strength of the state affects political stability and ideological legitimacy, but even weak states may facilitate and protect new forms. Educational systems, improvements in transportation and communication networks, and national economic planning and other state investments affect the terms on which resources are made available to entrepreneurs and may raise founding rates and lower disbanding rates. In contrast, political repression can boost the cost of organizing and even block it altogether, thus lowering founding rates. As Aldrich noted in reviewing the role of the state, 'the state must surely be the *major* force affecting organizational formation in the twentieth century' (Aldrich, 1979: 164).

Table 10.2   Political processes and events affecting population reproduction

Political turbulence:	Political events that disrupt ties between organizations and their resource base, e.g. strikes and protest movements
Regulation:	Governmental activities that erect barriers to populations, or otherwise regulate organizational actions, e.g. airline and railroad deregulation
Direct government support:	Policies that enhance legitimacy, stimulate demand, or provide direct subsidies to a population
Macro-economic policy:	Policies that affect economic growth and decline

Political-institutional factors affect organizational events on a wider and more diffuse basis than other processes because they shape values, alter expectations, and change public policies (Lindblom, 1977). Nascent entrepreneurs construct organizations out of the resources they mobilize at *local* levels, and thus many of the processes affecting founding rates are specific to neighborhood or community environments. However, political forces occurring at regional or societal levels influence the availability of broad classes of resources and the legitimacy of certain kinds of organizing processes. We focus on *regional* and *national* forces in the rest of this chapter.

Foundings and disbandings are particularly sensitive to four kinds of political processes: (1) political turbulence because of heightened competition and conflict; (2) changes in government regulation; (3) direct government stimulation via enhanced legitimacy or subsidies; and (4) overall macro-economic policies. Table 10.2 provides definitions of these processes. Below, we present examples from Europe and Asia, as well as the United States.

Political turbulence

Political turbulence can disrupt established ties between organizations and resources, rearranging organizational boundaries and freeing resources for use by new organizations (Carroll et al., 1988; Stinchcombe, 1965). For example, progressive steps in the economic unification of the European Union since 1958 had major effects on organizations' life chances, removing many of the barriers to trans-European marketing of goods and services. Existing organizations were organized to operate within a single national space, or across national boundaries. However, they were not necessarily prepared to deal with larger, multi-national spaces. Consequently, new lobbying groups have proliferated as a reaction to increases in international trade and legislation (Fligstein and Sweet, 2002). The incorporation of the economies of the formerly socialist Eastern European countries into the European Union has produced even stronger effects, including the rise of many new populations. As Stark (2001) emphasized, this period of turbulence has not only been characterized by a transfer of property from public to private hands, but also by the emergence of new property forms that blur the distinction between public and private, eroding traditional organizational boundaries in the process.

Political turbulence in 19th-century Argentina and Ireland increased newspaper foundings, not only because more politically oriented newspapers were formed, but also because 'news' of all sorts increased and established social relations were fractured

(Delacroix and Carroll, 1983). In their study of San Francisco Bay Area newspaper foundings, Carroll and Huo (1986: 851–853) replicated this finding, as they found that political turmoil had a substantial effect on the foundings of all types of papers, not just political ones. Regional labor unrest, by contrast, decreased foundings, perhaps by raising barriers to entry for new employers. In their study of Finnish newspapers operating between 1771 and 1963, Amburgey et al. (1988: 172) found that some state regimes attempted to exert greater control over the society than other regimes, raising failure rates. They also noted that political newspapers were 'much more likely to be suppressed by the state than their counterparts, with the exception of right-wing newspapers.' They did not analyze founding rates.

In contrast to the above studies, Minkoff (1997) discovered that neither the number of feminist nor the number of black protest events had a significant impact on the foundings of feminist organizations in the United States between 1955 and 1985. The availability of foundation sponsorship for organizations and programs serving women and minorities grew substantially during this period. Despite the increase, the amount of funding available had no effect on foundings of feminist organizations, nor did the passage of laws by Congress advancing women's status. Instead of funding or visible protest activity, growing population size itself did the most to raise feminist organization foundings.

Government regulation

In Chapter 8, we noted that political and legal events often mark the beginning of a new historical period that significantly changes the environment for populations. Government laws and regulations can affect founding and disbanding rates in several ways by enacting protective legislation and changing the rules regulating a population.

First, governments often erect barriers to entry to protect favored industries or set strict entry criteria, thus suppressing foundings. For example, the National Credit Union Administration in the United States, beginning in 1936, created and enforced a policy that only chartered new credit unions that did not conflict with already existing ones (Amburgey and Dacin, 1994). In 1936, the Italian Banking Act created the same safe harbor for Rural Cooperative Banks in Italy (Lomi, 1995). In Japan, for decades the Large Scale Retail Store Law allowed 'small shop owners the power to block construction of any store over a certain size in their area.' The law was not revised until 1990 (Miyashita and Russell, 1994: 130).

Protectionist policies have often been explained by theories of *regulatory capture*, which posit that 'firms [within an industry] can manipulate public officials and harness the state for rent-seeking purposes via campaign contributions, job offers, withholding information, and bribery' (Schneiberg and Bartley, 2001: 105). The empirical evidence for capture theories is mixed, however. Examining the case of fire insurance regulation in the U.S. between 1906 and 1930, for instance, Schneiberg and Bartley (2001) found that rate regulation seemed more responsive to the interests of small manufacturers and farmers than insurance industry cartels.

Evidence of regulatory capture is equally mixed for other organizational populations. In the railroad industry in Massachusetts, between 1825 and 1897, legislatures enacted state-level pro-cartel policies as a way of stabilizing freight rates and protecting public capital. Pro-cartel policies dampened competition among incumbents and apparently guaranteed revenues to all firms. Dobbin and Dowd (1997) hypothesized that nascent entrepreneurs were encouraged to enter the industry because pro-cartel policies created a stable environment. However, they also cited research showing that railroad building in the western United States was most vigorous when cartels broke down, a result that would appear to be more consistent with theories of regulatory capture.

The radio broadcasting industry in the United States represents a case of *ideological capture*, rather than regulatory capture, according to Lippmann (forthcoming). In his analysis of that industry between 1920 and 1934, he examined the process through which commercial broadcasters influenced the National Radio Conferences and the Federal Radio Act (FRA), the first regulatory legislation to govern the broadcasting industry. He observed that private corporate actors effectively shaped the FRA, and the subsequent creation of the Federal Communications Commission, such that commercial interests were the main beneficiaries, shutting out broadcasters from the non-profit section. Lippmann outlined a set of conditions under which private influence on the state is likely to be realized, arguing that private interests are likely to succeed at ideological capture when they are highly mobilized and frame their intentions, purposes, and visions of themselves and their role in an industry in a manner similar to the prevailing ideologies of important state actors. As a result, state policy becomes anchored in ideological principles that favor a particular set of private interests.

Second, governments play a central role in regulating populations that affect public goods, such as health, education, and safety. Two organizational populations in the United States whose fate has been heavily affected by government regulation are the beer brewing and wine industries (Swaminathan, 1995; Wade et al., 1998). In research on the American wine industry, Swaminathan (1995) found that state winery laws had a more powerful effect on the foundings of specialist wineries than forces increasing wine consumption. Between 1844 and 1919, laws prohibiting the sale of alcohol were passed in 34 states, although some lasted only a few years. In 1913, the federal Webb-Kenyon Act prohibited the transport of alcohol through a state that had enacted a prohibition law, and foundings were substantially lower in the years that followed. Breweries in states adjacent to those passing prohibition laws actually benefited initially, as their founding rates increased to meet the demands from 'dry' states. However, as more states adjacent to the 'wet' state passed prohibition laws, foundings declined. Potential entrepreneurs were apparently worried about future legislation in their own state. Wade et al. (1998) noted that legislative success in one state apparently mobilized activists in other states to try their luck, and they often succeeded. They also noted that the growing number of breweries affected political contests over prohibition, with the passage of prohibition legislation being less likely as brewery density increased.

Government regulations can provoke the founding of new organizations because existing firms sometimes deliberately create new businesses to avoid regulations targeting them. In Germany, as well as in other European Union nations, firms above a certain number of workers are subject to governmental regulations regarding workers' participation, and so some firms avoid this by setting up new firms. Meyerhoefer (1982) discovered that almost one-third of the 263 large firms in his West German sample had started another firm between 1975 and 1980. In Italy, many governmental regulations apply to craft-based (artisan) manufacturing firms when they exceed 22 employees, causing some owners to restrict their growth, thus making room for new firms to enter the market (Lazerson, 1988). In the United States, size thresholds also affect the applicability of many federal regulations, such as the Age Discrimination in Employment Act, which applies to employers with 20 or more employees.

Direct government support

Government policies may encourage the founding of organizations and lower rates of disbanding through enhanced legitimacy via the symbolic consequences of governmental action and through direct subsidies. Minkoff (1994: 141) argued that federal government actions in the United States in the 1960s and 1970s served as a signal 'to activists that external actors were more or less supportive of their agenda, and organizers and external patrons reacted accordingly.' She cited the example of President Lyndon Johnson's Great Society Programs of the mid-1960s, which raised the salience of 'the plight of the poor' and encouraged social activism by persons and organizations outside of the public sector. A *professionalization of reform* occurred, as social workers, officials in local agencies, and non-profit organizations became involved in efforts aimed at ameliorating poverty (Moynihan, 1970). In Norway, governmental support for regional economic development reflects its symbolic commitment to boosting the living conditions of people at the periphery of society. Spilling and Bolkesjø (1998) found that public assistance was a significant motivating factor for entrepreneurs living in targeted rural regions of Norway.

Legislative initiatives have raised the founding rate of many different populations in the United States. For example, enactment of the National Industrial Recovery Act in the United States substantially raised the founding rate of business interest associations, although the effect was short-lived (Aldrich et al., 1990). Passage of the 19th Amendment to the United States constitution in 1920, acknowledging women's right to vote, substantially raised the founding rate of women's colleges over the next two decades (Studer-Ellis, 1995a). However, somewhat surprisingly, the founding rate for industrial unions did not change significantly as a result of the passage of the Wagner Act in 1935, which gave extensive legal protection to union organizing activities (Hannan and Freeman, 1987).

Government policies providing not only symbolic legitimacy but also financial support often target particular organizations serving particular kinds of constituencies. Three Canadian studies examined government provision of services to voluntary organizations, children, and members of consumer and worker cooperatives. Foundings of voluntary social service organizations between 1970 and 1982 in the Toronto area increased during the period when the provincial government provided additional funding to that sector (Tucker et al., 1990). Also in Toronto between 1971 and 1989, founding rates of day care centers increased after the government raised the budget of the Toronto Social Services Division (Baum and Oliver, 1992). Favorable tax policies by the Canadian government had a significant negative effect on disbandings among worker cooperatives in Atlantic Canada between 1920 and 1987 (Staber, 1993).

In the European Union, beginning in the 1990s, national governments substantially increased their support for policies fostering small- and medium-sized enterprises (SMEs). EU leaders have endorsed policy initiatives favoring SMEs and tried to create a favorable business climate for startups. For example, the European Charter for Small Enterprises, approved by EU leaders in June 2000, stressed the importance of small enterprises and entrepreneurship for national economic development (ENSR, 2004). Many have created special government ministries for SMEs, whereas others have created special departments within established ministries. For example, Belgium and Luxembourg set up Ministries of the Middle Class, representing crafts, trading companies, and the catering trades. Germany and the Netherlands created an SME department within their Ministries of Economic Affairs, and France established special SME departments within the Ministries of Industry and the Ministries of

Trade, Craft, and Services. In the United Kingdom, a Minister of State for small firms was established, as well as a Small Firms Division within the Department of Trade and Industry.

Western European governments have also promoted science-based industries. In Germany, government support for high-technology businesses has encouraged foundings, beginning in the 1980s (Bögenhold, 1987). Foundings of science and technology parks by public institutions, such as communities and governments, as well as private investors, increased in the 1980s. Loans were provided to high-technology companies at especially low interest rates, and research grants from the Ministry of Research and Technology facilitated startups. In the last quarter of the 20th century, government agencies and investors made similar efforts to create science and technology parks in France, Italy, England, and Japan. Studies in the United States and abroad have shown that most of the parks have been disappointments, not repaying the public resources invested in them (Luger and Goldstein, 1991; Massey et al., 1992).

Macro-economic policy

Governments' macro-economic policies indirectly affect business foundings to the extent that they affect unemployment rates and economic growth. A number of studies have reported a positive association between levels of unemployment and numbers of foundings. Johnson (1986) investigated the association between unemployment rates, economic growth, and foundings for England. Another study examined the effects of the unemployment rates and the GNP growth rates on the rates of business founding in ten OECD countries between the early 1950s and 1987 (Bögenhold and Staber, 1990). For most countries, they detected a significant positive relationship between unemployment rates and rates of business foundings. The effects of GNP growth rates were less consistent, but they generally indicated a lower rate of foundings as economic conditions improved. These results do *not* necessarily mean that unemployed persons were becoming entrepreneurs, and studies have shown that most founders were gainfully employed in the period immediately preceding their founding activities. Rising unemployment may be associated with rising self-employment because high unemployment rates make it more difficult for people to get jobs that match their abilities and aspirations.

Research on founding rates has uncovered only weak evidence that economic growth and decline are immediately consequential for organizational creation. For instance, Delacroix and Carroll (1983) discovered that economic variables had no significant effects on newspaper foundings, and Carroll and Huo (1986) also reported that economic conditions (recessions, number of business failures) were not related to newspaper foundings. In Atlantic Canada, economic recessions had no significant effect on disbandings of cooperatives (Staber, 1993). However, in the Baden-Württemberg district of Germany between 1946 and 1993, Staber (1998) found that the mortality rate for textile firms increased significantly during periods of economic decline. The Great Depression of the 1930s in the United States slightly depressed the founding rate for minor-league baseball teams, but its effect was not statistically significant in regression models (Land et al., 1994: 806).

Summary

Societal-level cultural and political forces probably have their greatest impact when a new population emerges, constraining and imprinting new organizations in distinctive ways (Stinchcombe, 1965). We argued in the last chapter that institutional processes give shape to organizational forms, transforming initial differences that may have emerged by chance into differences with significant social consequences. After a population is established, foundings and disbandings respond more to endogenous intra- and inter-population processes than to exogenous institutional forces. However, as populations grow and organizations within them engage in collective action, population processes and institutional forces become entangled. Thus, in addition to focusing on population dynamics, we need to focus on the co-evolving social forces that set the context for organizational foundings and disbandings. Our final research case study addresses how the demographic composition of organizational populations may affect the nature of their institutional context, considering Ingram and Rao's (2004) study of the passage of pro- and anti-chain store legislation in the United States.

Research Illustration 10.1   Population Processes and Legislative Outcomes

Ingram and Rao (2004) considered how competition among organizational forms manifests itself in legislative contention. Drawing from an archival data set on retailer regulation in the United States, they tracked all instances of pro- and anti-chain store legislation at the state level between 1923 (the attempted passage of the first anti-chain bill) and 1970. Over the same time period, they also collected data on the population of retailers in each state, distinguishing among independent stores, chain stores, and the retail segments in which all stores were competing. Their evolutionary account sought to explain variation in pro- and anti-chain laws as a consequence of the density and segregation among different kinds of retailers.

Early instances of anti-chain store legislation, passed in Maryland, North Carolina, and Georgia during the 1920s, rested on the claim that chains operating more than five stores in a circumscribed area ought to be disallowed (Ingram and Rao, 2004: 452). Following judicial setbacks to this early legislation, laws in Indiana and North Carolina introduced a novel variation, distinguishing only between single-unit and multi-unit organizations. After the Indiana law was upheld by the U.S. Supreme court, a wave of anti-chain legislation occurred, with more than half of all states enacting such regulation in the years before World War II. Meanwhile, the chain stores themselves mobilized against such restrictive efforts, led by the National Chain Store Association's (NCSA) efforts to repeal anti-chain bills.

Ingram and Rao suggested that the same density-dependent and segregating forces involved in intrapopulation processes also influenced the legal context of organizational populations. For instance, we have argued that density reflects the cognitive legitimacy and mobilizing capacity associated with an organizational form. Consequently, the density of independent retailers in various states should increase the propensity of those states to pass anti-chain legislation and, conversely, the density of chain retailers should increase the propensity to pass pro-chain legislation. Like density-dependence itself, however, this straightforward account must be qualified by attention to segregating processes and carrying capacity. In particular, Ingram and Rao predicted that the ability of independent stores to organize effectively may have been diminished by their level of heterogeneity, as reflected in their tendency to occupy distinct retail niches. Moreover, they argued that the viability of anti-chain legislation could have depended on pro-chain allies that independent entrepreneurs must mobilize against, including agricultural co-ops that had chain contracts and unions that had signed collective bargaining agreements with chain stores.

Analyzing the enactment of anti-chain legislation, Ingram and Rao found broad empirical evidence for their claims, with the density and concentration of independent stores increasing legislative propensity, and the density of chain stores decreasing propensity. These results held even after controlling for allies that may have mobilized for or against the legislation. However, Ingram and Rao failed to obtain corresponding results for the repeal of anti-chain legislation. What accounts for this asymmetry? From an evolutionary perspective, we suggest that variation and selection mechanisms affecting regulatory contexts are quite distinctive from retention mechanisms. While variation and selection may be subject to strong intrapopulation processes, the preservation of laws (and the organizational forms they support) may be played out in a broader societal context. Once institutionalized and embedded in a state's commercial culture, norms and values regarding 'fair competition' may be slow to change. Further studies of regulation across industries are required to explore this proposition more definitively.

Conclusions

From an evolutionary perspective, foundings allow the preservation and spread of organizational forms, replicating competencies and routines and possibly winning a larger space for a population. Without the activities of founders, constantly replenishing the stock of organizations, high rates of disbanding guarantee the disappearance of most populations. Moreover, resource constraints on growth, especially in a population's early years, may doom a new organizational form to insignificance if its participants do not take collective action to increase the carrying capacity for that form.

In this chapter, we have focused on founding and disbanding rates at the population level. We have examined conditions that affect the rate at which organizations are added to or removed from an existing population. Although mergers and acquisitions are dramatic and economically significant events for some populations, they are comparatively rare events. Studies show that foundings of new organizations, and disbandings of existing organizations, are highly dependent upon the events experienced by already existing organizations in a population.

Intra-population processes – prior foundings, disbandings, density, and other factors associated with a growing population – structure the environment into which foundings are born. Inter-population processes – the nature of relations between populations, whether competing or cooperating, and actions by dominant organizations – affect the distribution of resources in the environment and the terms on which they are available to entrepreneurs. We will focus more extensively on such forces when we discuss community evolution in the next chapter. Societal-level factors – cultural norms, government policies, and political events – shape the macro-context within which the other processes occur. Thus, we must always specify for what socio-historical period our explanations are valid, embedding them in their social context.

Study Questions

1. Organizational theorists and industrial economists often distinguish between 'first movers' that enter a population early in its life cycle and 'followers' that enter relatively late. What advantages and disadvantages accrue to these two entry strategies? What characteristics are likely to distinguish the organizations pursuing them?

2. Many accounts of decline in organizational populations rely on exogenous changes in carrying capacity (e.g. falling demand by users). What extensions of the density-dependence model help to explain such decline, even in the presence of *stable* carrying capacity? Thinking concretely about populations that have experienced decline; are some of these mechanisms more plausible than others?

Exercises

Continue your examination of the organizational population you selected for analysis in Chapter 9, answering the following questions:

1. Trace the density of organizations within the population at some selected time points. Aside from the pioneers, who were some of the early movers into the population? Did these tend to be *de novo* or *de alio* entrants? From a qualitative evaluation of the population's history, do you believe that it faced legitimacy problems early on? Has competition become a problem more recently?

2. What do you know about concentration (of revenues, sales, or members) within the organizational population? Who are the current industry leaders? Do any of them trace their roots to the pioneers of the population? Have any specialist niches appeared; if so, what organizations appear to be the top competitors in those?

3. Think about some of the environmental pressures on the population as a whole. What regulations have had a significant historical impact? Are there labor unions or professional/trade associations that have changed the way organizations in this population operate? Has the population reacted to more general cultural or economic trends?

11

Community Evolution

An organizational community is a spatially or functionally bounded set of populations, linked by ties of commensalism and symbiosis. *Commensalism* refers to competition and cooperation between similar units, whereas *symbiosis* refers to mutual interdependence between dissimilar units. Within a community, processes of competition and cooperation sort populations into differentiated niches, and dominant populations drive others into subordinate positions and ancillary roles, resulting in community-level differentiation and integration. We focus mainly on the temporal aspect of communities, examining the growth of new communities and population interdependence within them.

Why are organizational communities important? First, the emergence of organizational communities shapes the social environment and affects the course of societal evolution. For example, in 20th-century America, the communication network based on telephones grew from a dispersed and fragmented set of independent local phone companies into an interconnected national system. Its development involved struggles between populations offering competing technologies, feuding political jurisdictions, and ultimately federal regulation (Barnett and Carroll, 1993; Starr, 2004). Second, organizational communities set the context within which new populations emerge. In Chapter 9, we noted that new populations must find spaces for themselves within environments packed with competing populations, as well as populations ready to lend their support.

In this chapter, we begin with Hawley's (1950) conception of the community level of analysis, review other conceptions, and then offer our own. Relations between populations comprise the essential subject matter of community analysis, and so we offer a typology of eight forms of population interdependence. Interdependence results from processes of differentiation and integration that sort new organizations and populations into community niches. We examine two aspects of these processes: entrepreneurs' roles in building new populations by exploiting discontinuities in technology, norms and values, and laws and regulations; and collective action by interest groups and associations that builds community level legitimacy, especially when collective action targets the state. In presenting our arguments, we use several recent examples of organizational communities, focusing in particular on biotechnology.

Definitions: changing conceptions of community

Early human ecologists offered definitions of 'community' that emphasized its spatial aspect (Park et al., 1925), but Hawley (1950) argued that human ecology should focus on its *relational* aspect: patterns of symbiosis and commensalism in populations. Based on notions of community in general ecology, the parent field of human ecology, Hawley (1950: 67) proposed that 'the community ... is in the nature of a collective response to the habitat.' He explicitly excluded from human ecology the study of adaptations made by individual units to environments, arguing that other disciplines were better equipped to deal with problems concerning individuals. Hawley emphasized two aspects of communities that became the focus of subsequent debate: relations between populations within a community, and the boundary between a community and its environment.

In the 1970s, Hannan and Freeman (1977) posed an explicitly community-level question with their emphasis on similarities and differences between populations. However, in subsequent years, ecological theories focused mostly on how selection processes create uniformity and stability in existing populations, rather than on how new populations and communities develop. In reaction, Astley (1985) contended that research on organizational ecology should also focus on the dynamics of community ecology, particularly community evolution, to explain how new organizational forms arise. He argued that basic innovations, representing dramatic technological change, stimulate the creation of new organizational forms. New forms spawn new populations and, potentially, new organizational communities.

In the 1980s and 1990s, the concept of community evolution became somewhat diffuse, as authors disagreed in subtle ways over how to conceptualize 'community.' Different labels, including organizational field (DiMaggio and Powell, 1983), societal sector (Scott and Meyer, 1983), and organizational community (Astley, 1985), came into broad use. In one critique, DiMaggio (1994) observed that a consistent definition of community was lacking. Authors often equated an organizational community with a population, a sub-community, an interorganizational network, or an industry. Some theorists focused on particular *units* of analysis, whereas others focused on the types of *relations* between units. For example, Astley (1985: 224) defined an organizational community as a set of diverse, internally homogeneous populations that are fused together into functionally integrated systems based on interdependencies in their core technologies. By contrast, Barnett (1994) followed Hawley's emphasis on the relationships comprising a functioning community.

Contemporary perspectives on organizational communities tend to be relational, drawing on two kinds of empirical strategies for assessing coevolutionary processes. First, a number of studies have attempted to measure interpopulation flows of members, materials, or symbols directly. McPherson (1983; Popielarz and McPherson, 1995) pioneered an approach that characterized the niche overlap between populations of voluntary organizations in terms of the common socio-demographic characteristics of their membership. Sørensen (2004) recently extended this approach to describe competition among populations of business firms as a function of their tendency to recruit employees from similar labor markets. A parallel strategy has long existed for analyzing competition in product markets, placing organizational populations in structurally equivalent niches insofar as they require similar material inputs and produce substitutable outputs (Burt, 1992). Some investigators have extended this logic to less tangible, cultural processes of categorization. For example, Ruef (2000) considered how normative and regulatory discourse by professionals in the American health care community linked organizational forms and thus contributed to their symbolic similarity.

A second perspective on organizational communities infers co-evolutionary dynamics from processes of population growth and decline. Following classical treatments in organizational ecology (Hannan and Freeman, 1977), two populations are said to be interdependent insofar as the density of one affects the viability of the other (and, possibly, vice versa). This empirical approach to community interdependence has become important in addressing cross-population effects that mix material and symbolic elements. For instance, Simons and Ingram (2004) studied ideological competition in Israel, imputing competitive and cooperative relationships between kibbutzim, moshavim, corporations, and credit cooperatives. They found that the kibbutzim and moshavim, as similar forms of agricultural cooperatives, engaged in commensalistic competition. Meanwhile, the growth of credit cooperatives supported the development of both forms, whereas increases in the density of Israeli corporations suppressed them. Barnett and Woywode (2004) employed a similar approach in their study of interdependencies among different forms of Viennese newspapers between 1918 and 1938. Competition was greatest between forms that were ideologically adjacent (e.g. leftist and centrist papers), as opposed to those that were dissimilar (leftist and right-wing papers).

The two empirical approaches to conceptualizing organizational communities each carry advantages and disadvantages. Directly measuring niche overlap in the community entails a formidable exercise in data collection and requires that analysts identify niche dimensions that simultaneously support multiple and often diverse populations. Indirectly estimating population interdependencies from their ecological dynamics becomes impossible in any community containing more than a handful of organizational forms. In effect, the number of possible relationships to be estimated in the community matrix overwhelms the number of observations on population growth or decline, unless investigators make *ad hoc* assumptions concerning interdependencies (Sørensen, 2004). Investigators using this approach also cannot distinguish symbiotic relationships from certain forms of commensalism because they lack the independent data needed to judge the similarity of organizational forms.

Given the diversity of perspectives on organizational communities, we developed our own definition for purposes of this chapter, building on Hawley's original conceptualization. His arguments continue to influence theory and research in this area, and a definition should retain the essential elements he emphasized. Thus, it should include the idea of functional interdependence between units (commensalistic and symbiotic relations). A definition should also preserve evolutionary theory's emphasis on a future that is constructed rather than designed. Communities *emerge* from relationships between units that involve competition, cooperation, dominance, and symbiotic interdependence, rather than coming into being according to plan.

We restrict the definition to organizations and populations oriented toward a common technological, normative, or legal-regulatory core. The geographic scope of a community is an empirical question. A community may well encompass an entire regional, national, or global economic system, depending on the core chosen. The extent of interdependence between social actors is also ultimately an empirical question, and investigators must make informed choices in setting boundaries around a set of interdependent activities. We thus offer the following definition: an *organizational community* is *a set of co-evolving organizational populations joined by ties of commensalism and symbiosis through their orientation to a common technology, normative order, or legal-regulatory regime.* Investigators define it for a particular historical period.

Relations between populations

Relations between populations in an evolving community revolve simultaneously around two axes. The symbiotic axis refers to the inter-dependence of unlike forms, i.e. units of dissimilar functions, and the commensalistic axis refers to the interdependence of like forms, i.e. units of similar functions (Hawley, 1950). In an established community, cohesion and integration result from the concurrent actions of populations along both axes. Competition between similar populations and conflict between dissimilar populations may prevent emerging communities from developing further. Just as many emerging populations fail to achieve a place in a community, developing communities face the prospect of disintegration and dissolution. We first describe the types of relations in general terms and then give specific examples. Our definitions follow Hawley (1950), although we recognize that biological ecologists and some population ecologists have adopted somewhat different definitions (Roughgarden, 1983).

Symbiosis denotes a mutual dependence between dissimilar units, whereas *commensalism* means that units make similar demands on the environment. Commensalism, 'literally interpreted, means eating from the same table' (Hawley, 1950: 39). Although people often use the term 'commensalism' to mean cooperation or *mutualism*, it actually ranges from full dyadic mutualism to full dyadic competition. For example, Hawley noted that the most common expression of commensalism is *competition*, in which populations seek the same resources. The extent of competition between populations depends on the relative size of each and the degree of similarity or niche overlap between them. As we noted in Chapter 9, a population's *realized niche* may be substantially smaller than its *fundamental niche* because of competition from other populations.

Commensalism can also lead to mutualism, if populations making similar demands on the environment combine their efforts, intentionally or otherwise. In Chapter 9, we gave examples of cooperation within populations that resulted in collective action to improve an emerging population's position, such as by forming trade associations or industry councils. In a similar fashion, as we will show later, cross-population mutualism can improve the joint standing of those involved. For example, in 1998 the American Institute of Certified Public Accountants cooperated with associations of e-commerce firms to create a Web page symbol that not only signaled the legitimacy of Web sites, but also emphasized the commercial significance of accounting firms.

Based on the distinction between symbiotic and commensalistic relations, we can distinguish eight types of relations between populations, as shown in Table 11.1 (see Brittain and Wholey, 1988). In the table, symbols in parentheses precede each form of interaction, denoting the impact each population has on the other. Six constitute various forms of commensalism (competition and cooperation), and a seventh is symbiosis. We have included dominance as an eighth type of relation between populations.

Table 11.1   **Eight possible relations between organizational populations**

I. Commensalism

(–, –) Full competition: growth in each population detracts from growth in the other; e.g. competition between voluntary associations for members from the same socio-demographic groups (McPherson, 1983)

(–, 0) Partial competition: relations are asymmetric, with only one having a negative effect on the other; e.g. right-wing newspapers increased the failure rate of centrist papers in interwar Vienna (Barnett and Woywode, 2004)

(+, –) Predatory competition: one population expands at the expense of the other; e.g. sharecropping and share tenancy arrangements developed at the expense of plantations in the postbellum South (Ruef, 2004)

(0, 0) Neutrality: populations have no effect on each other; e.g. founding rates of commercial and savings banks in Manhattan had no effect on each other between 1792 and 1980 (Ranger-Moore et al., 1991)

(+, 0) Partial mutualism: relations are asymmetric, with only one population benefiting from the presence of the other; e.g. the growth of brew pubs between 1975 and 1990 stimulated foundings of microbreweries, but not vice versa (Carroll and Swaminathan, 1992)

(+, +) Full mutualism: two populations in overlapping niches benefit from the presence of the other; e.g. small and large railroads and telephone companies benefited from the other's presence (Barnett, 1995; Dobbin, 1994)

II. Symbiosis

(+, +) Symbiosis: two populations are in different niches and benefit from the presence of the other; e.g. venture capitalists make profits by investing in high-technology firms, thereby enabling both populations to grow (Brittain, 1994)

III. Dominance

A dominant population controls the flow of resources to other populations (Hawley, 1950); effects depend on the outcome of commensalistic and symbiotic relations

Legend: Signs in parentheses refer to the effect of one population, A, on a second population, B:
+ positive effect
0 no effect
– negative effect

Dominance emerges as a hierarchical relation between populations, based on the outcome of symbiotic and commensalistic interactions.

Because the term 'cooperation' carries a connotation of intentional behavior, and forms of positive population interdependence may be accidental and inadvertent, we use the term 'mutualism' instead of cooperation in Table 11.1. Traditionally, ecological studies tended to emphasize competitive behavior between organizations and populations of organizations, whereas institutional approaches tended to highlight symbiotic and mutualistic relations. However, over the past decade, many investigators have integrated the two. Institutional theorists have contributed to the emergent view of inter-population relations by arguing that coordinating mechanisms can manage a variety of competitive, symbiotic, and mutualistic interdependencies among populations (e.g. Scott et al., 2000: Chapter 8). As we noted in Chapter 3, resource dependence perspectives have likewise contributed to our understanding of relational interdependence, though they tend to rely on organizations, rather than populations, as their units of analysis.

Commensalism

We have identified six types of commensalistic relations. They range from full competition, through neutrality, to full mutualism.

Full competition
Growth in each population detracts from growth in the other because their fundamental niches overlap. In his study of *competitive niche overlap*, McPherson (1983) examined competition for members between voluntary associations in Omaha, Nebraska, by measuring the extent to which they competed for persons of similar characteristics. He examined the actual distribution of organizational members along the four dimensions of age, occupation, sex, and education, and defined K, or carrying capacity, as the number of potential members with such characteristics in the community. By making assumptions about the system being in equilibrium, McPherson estimated the extent to which voluntary associations were in competition with each other for the same types of members. McPherson and Ranger-Moore (1991) and McPherson and Rotolo (1996) continued this line of research by estimating the dynamics of competition between populations resulting from demographic changes. Ruef (2000) pursued a related argument in research on the health care field, noting a tendency toward full competition among organizational forms that were classified as occupying similar – but not identical – niches in the discourse of policy makers, administrators, physicians, and allied health professionals.

Partial competition
Inter-population relations are asymmetric, with only one having a negative effect on the other. In Vienna, when right-wing (e.g. national socialist) newspapers became numerous during the interwar period (1918–1938), they increased the failure rate of centrist papers (Barnett and Woywode, 2004). The right-wing papers drew on many readers that had traditionally been bourgeois or clerical in their orientation, and thus generated competition through ideological 'adjacency.' At the same time, the extremist orientation of right-wing readers meant that few could be swayed to bourgeois or clerical causes. Consequently, the prevalence of centrist newspapers had no adverse effect on right-wing publications.

Predatory competition
One population expands at the expense of another. Ruef (2004) studied the displacement of plantations by sharecropping and share tenancy forms in the postbellum South from 1865 to 1880. The proliferation of the sharecropping form stimulated landowners' desires to break wage plantations into smaller agricultural tenancies, thus representing a direct case of predatory competition over land resources. Interestingly, however, competition between mid-sized farms and plantations was limited during the years immediately following the Civil War, with these two populations even exhibiting some degree of mutualism. Accordingly, Ruef argued that some of the predatory competition exercised by sharecropping and share tenancy arrangements

should be seen in symbolic, rather than material, terms. In effect, the increasing density of the newer agricultural forms signaled that the legitimacy of large-scale agriculture based on gang labor was coming to an end.

Neutrality

Two populations in the same community have no influence on each other, although they do affect other populations in the community. In the financial services community, founding rates of commercial banks in Manhattan between 1792 and 1980 had no effects on savings bank foundings, and vice versa (Ranger-Moore et al., 1991). In the United States' health care community, independent physicians' practices fought against the certification of health maintenance organizations (HMOs), as we noted in Chapter 9. However, Wholey et al. (1993) showed that founding rates of group HMOs and independent practice associations (IPAs) were unrelated.

We offer one note of caution. 'Neutrality' is the most likely inter-population relation across the spectrum of all populations, but authors would exhaust themselves, and their readers, were they to catalog all the inter-population relations of little or no consequence. We expect to observe mostly loosely coupled social systems because evolutionary selection forces favor them (Aldrich, 1979: 80–86). Simon (1962), for example, asserted that loosely coupled hierarchies predominate in nature. Nevertheless, our methods for detecting and depicting community structure probably miss many neutral inter-population relations. Consequently, the communities depicted in most analyses appear much more tightly coupled than would be the case if investigators had tracked down and listed all their potential inter-population relations. Such selection biases inevitably result from the choices researchers must make in telling coherent tales about their subjects.

Partial mutualism

Inter-population relations are asymmetric, with only one population benefiting from the presence of the other. Prior to the 1930s, surges in foundings of industrial unions were associated with an increased founding rate for craft unions, but not vice versa (Hannan and Freeman, 1987). Craft union density had no effect on industrial union foundings. Another instance of partial population interdependence occurred in the United States between 1941 and 1984, when growth in wine imports apparently expanded the niche for domestic American wineries (Delacroix and Solt, 1988). Foreign imports, rather than crowding out American producers, actually made novel products acceptable to consumers, whetting their appetites for table wines rather than fortified wines. One result was an increase in foundings of domestic wineries. In a related life-style industry, Carroll and Swaminathan (1992) found evidence of partial mutualism between brew pubs and microbreweries in the United States between 1975 and 1990, with the growth of brew pubs stimulating the founding of microbreweries, but not vice versa.

Full mutualism

Two populations are in overlapping niches and benefit from the presence of the other. Dobbin (1994) pointed out that railroads, like telephone companies (Barnett, 1990), were often characterized at early points in their life cycles by mutualism between small and large firms. The large networks of major railroads and phone companies enhanced the survival chances of the smaller firms that connected to them, and the smaller firms benefited the larger firms by enlarging the market area they served.

When a major trunk rail line was constructed to connect several major cities, smaller spur lines could be built to minor cities. Similarly, single exchange and multiple exchange phone companies in Pennsylvania from 1879 to 1934 enjoyed fully mutualistic relations. Within the populations of firms that adopted the same transmission system of common battery power, smaller, single-exchange systems complemented larger, multi-exchange systems. They increased each other's growth rates while decreasing failure rates in 'smoothly functioning, viable networks capable of large-scale operation' (Barnett, 1995: 285).

Symbiosis

In a symbiotic relation, two populations exist in different niches and benefit from the presence of the other. Relationships between growing businesses needing capital and the firms supplying it are often contentious, but they are also an excellent example of symbiotic relations. In the United States, venture capital firms have played several important symbiotic roles in the emergence of new, technology-based communities (Gorman and Sahlman, 1989). First, they have provided funding for growing firms that are too young and unknown to obtain funding from more traditional sources, such as banks. Second, as early investors, venture capital firms have legitimated risky investments for other, more conservative investors. The early involvement of venture capital firms in a deal often reassures hesitant investors. Third, venture capital firms have served as facilitators and catalysts for the creation of alliances, acting as brokers in bringing complementary organizations together (Podolny, 2001).

Saxenian's (1994) richly detailed case study emphasized contrasting patterns of inter-population symbiotic relations in two regions: Silicon Valley and the Route 128 region around Boston. Beginning in the late 1930s, with the founding of Hewlett-Packard, Silicon Valley entrepreneurs, educators, venture capitalists, and other local residents developed a system that promoted 'collective learning and flexible adjustment among specialist producers of a complex of related technologies' (Saxenian, 1994: 2). Early on, dense social networks between firms were encouraged by an open labor market and a spirit of technical innovation that created a feeling of mutualism among the high-tech engineers and managers. Firms were clustered into a tightly constrained geographical area, promoting face-to-face interactions in seminars and workshops, as well as after working hours.

Law firms played a particularly important symbiotic role in Silicon Valley's emergence as an organizational community, as we noted in Chapter 8. As law firms gained more experience between 1976 and 1990 in writing financing agreements between venture capital firms and startups, such agreements became more standardized (Suchman et al., 2001). Standardization was least likely in contracts involving law firms and lead investors outside of Silicon Valley, such as those located in San Francisco. Moreover, the gap in standardization between Silicon Valley and other firms was greatest in the early 1980s, when the pace of growth in symbiotic and mutualistic relations between venture capital firms, law firms, and hi-tech firms was at its peak. Nelson and Winter (1982) noted that repeated interaction between customers, suppliers, and others often creates a local population language that is nearly opaque to outsiders.

Law firms thus played a major role in shaping the market for hi-tech startup financing through venture capitalists. They helped establish a governance framework for complex financial transactions by fostering market development and suppressing business disputes (Suchman and Cahill, 1996: 690–691). First, they absorbed some of the uncertainty in complex dealings by getting involved as a third-party buffer. Second, they helped create and diffuse community norms and standards, thus lowering the risks of opportunistic actions. Third, the local norms they helped create were transformed into national ones as law firms and regulators outside Silicon Valley followed their lead.

In contrast to pervasive symbiosis and mutualism found in Silicon Valley, firms in the Route 128 region around Boston perpetuated a competitive system in which large, independent firms looked to their own internal resources for much of what they needed, rather than developing links with other firms in the area. The region's culture encouraged stability and self-reliance, promoting competition based on secrecy and corporate loyalty (Saxenian, 1994: 3). The major universities in the Boston area, MIT and Harvard, kept their distance from smaller companies, preferring ties to large firms that could fund the universities' own research priorities. DEC and other large firms experienced financial difficulties in the 1980s, as the bottom fell out of the minicomputer market. Route 128's lack of a network-based collaborative community culture dealt it a severe blow from which it had trouble recovering, in contrast to Silicon Valley's recovery after its troubles in the 1980s. For a critical analysis of two other regions often compared to Silicon Valley – the 'Third Italy' and Baden-Württemberg industrial districts – see Harrison (1994) and Staber and Sharma (1994).

Dominance

As commensalistic and symbiotic relations develop within emerging communities, a hierarchy of influence and power emerges. Hawley (1950: 221) argued that inequality inevitably results from functional differentiation because 'certain functions are by their nature more influential than others; they are strategically placed in the division of labor and thus impinge directly upon a larger number of other functions.' From an evolutionary perspective, units occupying central locations are well positioned to play coordinating roles (Aldrich, 1979: 327–340). New organizational forms that enable organizations to communicate or connect with others more quickly occupy niches with an initially overwhelming advantage because of the strong demand for their services. Examples of forms playing such intermediary roles include money lending and credit institutions in the financial sector and wholesaling organizations in the retail sector. For instance, the largest CPA firms in the United States have molded the structure of the entire accounting industry because they attract the largest clients. Their practices were imitated by middle-sized accounting firms (Han, 1994).

Populations at the center of communities thus exercise dominance because they control the flow of resources to others. 'Such influence may be exercised directly or indirectly through control over the allocation of space to different activities, the determination of who shall be employed, the regulation of credit, the censoring of news and information regarding the community, and in many other ways' (Hawley, 1950: 221). Dominance results naturally as populations adapt to the structure of resource flows within a community, but organizations and populations may also act strategically to enhance their dominant positions. Hawley noted that organizations often band together in collective activities that affect the conditions of existence for others, such as in price-fixing cartels and collusion that creates restraints on trade.

Government has historically occupied the most dominant position, as it 'holds the police power through which it exercises many regulatory functions' (Hawley, 1950: 229). For example, when 34 states passed laws between 1904 and 1919, mandating interconnections among independent phone companies, the result was a significant increase in mutualism between small and large firms (Barnett and Carroll, 1993: 108–110). However, governments at every level of jurisdiction, from villages to the nation-state, are heavily circumscribed in their authority by political boundaries. Hawley wrote mainly about cities and regions in the United States, and he was well aware that governments play a predominantly reactive role in the flow of resources into such geographically delimited communities. Most state governments have created economic development offices that attempt to lure large firms into their territory by offering tax subsidies, cheap land, and funds for workforce retraining. As Grant (1995) noted, businesses can manipulate these incentives, particularly if employers use spatial relocation as a bargaining chip in negotiations with state governments. The power of large business units can therefore relegate other units, such as regional government, to subordinate status.

Theories of capitalist class integration, upper-class cohesion, and bank centrality in capitalist economies go beyond Hawley's ecological analysis (Mizruchi, 1996). In these theories, dominance results from strategic acts by self-aware or at least self-interested actors. In most of these accounts, powerful actors use director interlocks to shape the flow of resources between organizations and owners or top executives. They need not be aware of a larger collective interest for their actions to have systemic effects. Even if the individual firms act primarily out of self-interest, the aggregate affect of their actions can be substantial if a group of them behave similarly (Mizruchi, 1992: 42–47). However, as Mizruchi (1996: 273) noted, 'there are virtually no systematic data on firms' motives for interlocking.' Researchers have inferred motives by examining patterns of interlocking, observing that interlocks seem to follow from the flow of resource dependence.

Some theorists have argued that interlocks are an accidental by-product of top executives' attempts at career advancement rather than strategic inter-firm moves (Zajac, 1988). Mizruchi (1996: 278) argued that the theories are complementary, not substitutes, as a tie can reflect multiple structural conditions: 'a business transaction between the firms; a social tie between the firm leaders; and a limited availability of suitable candidates as a result of already established obligations involving other firms.' The resulting network arrangements tend to be highly robust, recovering quickly from the accidental dissolution of individual ties or external strategic threats. Their durability in spanning communities of diverse business organizations rests partially on their properties as *small-world* networks, as found in research on ownership links among German firms (Kogut and Walker, 2001) and on board interlocks in the United States (Davis et al., 2003). Small-world networks are characterized by a relatively small number of intermediate ties between organizations and a high degree of clustering, with clusters often forming around powerful brokers (Kogut and Walker, 2001). Although the description of interlocks as small-world networks is now fairly well established, we need more research on the origins of these structures and how they contribute to relations of dominance and influence in organizational communities.

Summary of relations between populations

A community-level analysis presumes that the fates of many populations are closely linked via their orientation to a common technology, normative order, or legal-regulatory regime. Relations between populations within communities take a wide variety of forms, indirect as well as direct, rippling through populations as communities develop. Research on inter-population relations has progressed slowly because of the difficulties involved in studying multiple populations and in obtaining direct measures of inter-dependence. Accordingly, most investigators have focused on one or two organizational populations, rather than on entire communities. As Baum (1996: 92) noted 'because few studies attempt to predict the form of specific interpopulation interactions, we know very little about when competition or mutualism will exist between organizations.' Until more studies move from the population to the community level, our understanding will necessarily remain incomplete. Our application of evolutionary theory to community evolution in this chapter thus focuses on a few specific examples.

How do organizational communities form?

Communities emerge not only from forces that generate new organizations and populations, but also from new commensalistic and symbiotic relations between populations. In previous chapters, we have explored the foundings of new organizations and the development of new populations. To those accounts we now add a new dimension: activities that cut across populations. We begin with discontinuities in existing populations and communities caused by technical, normative, and regulatory innovations that are exploited by entrepreneurs, provoking transformations in existing populations or the emergence of new ones. Processes of competition, mutualism, and symbiosis sort the affected populations into differentiated niches, characterized by hierarchy and dominance. Depending upon their strength, these processes may bind populations into a community sharing a common fate.

We draw our examples chiefly from one organizational community – biotechnology – but we also use examples from others, particularly radio broadcasting (Leblebici et al., 1991) and the commercial World Wide Web community (Hunt and Aldrich, 1998). In biotechnology, the organizational community consists of 'dedicated biotechnology firms, investors, government agencies, universities, suppliers, private research labs, and … large diversified corporations' (Barley et al., 1992: 315). Although based upon basic discoveries made about the structure of DNA in the 1950s by Watson and Crick, it only emerged in the 1970s, when its commercial potential was recognized and exploited. Table 11.2 shows the populations involved.

Our explanatory framework contains three components. First, we focus on three types of catalysts for new organizational communities: technological innovations, transformation of norms and values, and new regulatory regimes. Second, we examine the forces animating organizational emergence – entrepreneurs and funding sources – and the conditions under which successive cohorts of organizations enter. Finally, we argue that emerging communities depend on supra-organizational legitimating forces, such as consortia and other forms of collective action.

New and transformed populations

Innovations are the catalyst for new and transformed populations, as we argued in Chapters 8 and 9. Three kinds of discontinuities seem to play particularly important

Table 11.2   **The commercial community of biotechnology**

Governance structures	• Government agencies(FDA, NIH, Dept. of Agriculture) • Consortia and alliances(Biotechnology Industrial Association)
Commercial users and suppliers	• Commercial users(Monsanto) • Suppliers of goods and services(Beckman Instruments, Biotechnology Review Associates)
Usage promoters	• State biotechnology centers(North Carolina Biotechnology Center)
Infrastructural populations	• Universities(MIT, Stanford) • Public/private institutes(Whitehead) • Investors(Venture capital, banks, pension funds) • Hospitals(involved in clinical trials or R&D)
Core technology	• Dedicated biotechnology firms(Biogen, Genentech)

roles as catalysts for changes that generate entirely new communities: (1) shifts in societal norms and values, (2) changes in laws and regulations; and (3) technological innovations. The first two have been discussed in previous chapters, and so we will only briefly review them here. We focus mainly on technological innovation.

Norms and values

Shifts in societal norms and values may create conditions facilitating the development of new populations. If such populations develop mutualistic or symbiotic relations, they can become the nucleus of a new organizational community. The alternative-institutions movement in the United States gained normative legitimacy for a brief period in the late 1960s and early 1970s, as opponents of big business won a foothold in some regions (Rothschild, 1979). For example, in Santa Barbara, California, a symbiotically linked community of organizations developed that offered medical care, a legal service, a newspaper, and education. Mutualistic relations developed across the organizations, and members used the knowledge gained to found many other alternative organizations. The movement lost momentum when its advocates failed to win federal support for cooperative banks and forms of worker ownership other than traditional employee stock ownership plans. However, the movement's legacy lives on in some urban areas – as reflected, for instance, in Santa Barbara's rich network of health and human service organizations and a tradition of civic engagement (Molotch et al., 2000). In addition, the communal and normative goals of the movement survived, in modified form, in the 'quality of working life' initiatives in human resource management in the 1970s and 1980s (Kanter, 1972; Kanter and Stein, 1979).

Laws and regulations

Changes in laws and regulations may also lead to new organizational communities because of the resulting symbiotic networks of government agencies, non-profit organizations, law firms, consultants, research institutes, and academic programs (Galaskiewicz, 1979). In the United States, the Civil Rights Act of 1964, the Equal Employment Opportunity Act of 1972, and the Americans with Disabilities Act of 1990 created national legislation defining protected groups. The Acts created agencies to administer and enforce the rights of groups, defined in the law, to equal treatment by employers (Edelman, 1990, 1992; Dobbin and Sutton, 1998). The Environmental Protection Act, as well as many companion state laws, and the Occupational Safety and Health Act of 1970 placed restrictions on organizations' actions vis-à-vis the environment and their employees. These laws and subsequent regulations generated populations of law firms and consulting organizations specializing in compliance, as well as organizations intended to aid other organizations in operational compliance activities (Baker and Aldrich, 1994). Mutualism between organizations similarly affected by legislation led to lobbying groups and political action committees (Mizruchi, 1992).

Technology

Technological innovation constitutes a major catalyst for the creation of a new organizational community to the extent that it prompts the creation of new organizational forms. Rarely do single key events generate new organizational populations, based on a technological breakthrough. Instead, from an evolutionary view, technological innovation typically results from a cumulative series of interrelated acts of variation, selection, and retention, eventually culminating in commercial applications (Van de Ven and Garud, 1994). Long-term changes in scientific discovery in the 20th century have continually generated technological innovations with commercial potential (Dosi, 1988). Some of the innovations have been seized upon by entrepreneurs and pursued with such vigor that new populations were formed, such as the radio broadcasting industry in the 1920s (Lippmann, forthcoming; Starr, 2004: Chapter 10). Although many of the new populations failed, some of those that prospered became segments of existing communities. Others became the nucleus of new organizational communities.

Because a population's product or service often comprises part of a larger symbiotic system of components, its evolutionary path depends on changes in other populations. Many innovations are related to some aspect of a technological system, which can be thought of as composed of core and peripheral subsystems (Tushman and Murmann, 1998). For example, most micro-electronic devices are sold as components of more complex systems (Barley et al., 1992: 316), unlike biotechnology products, which are sold directly to end users. A period of incremental change may be relatively stable with respect to the core subsystem, but it may be quite dynamic with respect to innovations in peripheral subsystems. Individuals and organizations can cause temporary uncertainty by creating peripheral subsystems that complement the core technology. These new innovations become the basis for populations symbiotically linked to the population producing the core subsystem.

In biotechnology, two discoveries in the 1970s revolutionized molecular biology, and attracted the attention of researchers, entrepreneurs, and investors. In 1973, scientists at Stanford and the University of California at San Diego developed recombinant DNA, a technique for inserting DNA from one organism into the genes of another. Their discovery proved 'the feasibility of transforming everyday microorganisms into cheap and prolific facilities for manufacturing proteins characteristic of other species' (Barley et al., 1992: 314), allowing the production of growth hormones, interferon, and human insulin. In 1975, British scientists developed a technique for producing monoclonal antibodies, a vast improvement over earlier polyclonal techniques, making low cost production of large quantities of vaccines and immunoassays possible. These early efforts were widely disseminated and shared, mainly by scientists in research universities.

Technological innovation has been described as *either* competence-enhancing *or* competence-destroying, as we noted in earlier chapters (Tushman and Anderson, 1986). However, another possibility exists. Technological breakthroughs might go beyond current organizational knowledge but still allow established populations to participate in a new community. Rather than a dichotomy between competence-destroying and competence-enhancing innovations, Hunt and Aldrich (1998) proposed a third category of innovations: *competence-extending*. From this perspective, competence-extending innovations permit existing organizations to pursue new opportunities that allow them to stretch their existing competencies into complementary ventures. Unlike competence-enhancing opportunities, these new ventures are not a straightforward extension of their current routines and competencies and therefore cannot be pursued with minimal effort. At the same time, however, these opportunities are not direct threats to their existing business pursuits and competencies. Instead, they represent potential opportunities for expanding their domains by pursuing new markets through exploiting new competencies.

The biotechnology community offers an example of this process. Initially, established firms in the pharmaceutical, chemical, agricultural, and energy industries lacked many of the distinctive competencies required to participate in the biotechnology sector. By entering into strategic alliances and ownership relations with pioneering biotechnology ventures, however, these established firms gained knowledge and influence in the field (Stuart et al., 1999). Many have since created their own programs to pursue research on recombinant DNA and cell fusion technologies. These pursuits were not simply an enhancement of existing competencies, but rather involved leveraging resources and competencies in new ways to gain access to an emerging commercial niche.

Three forces driving organizational formation

Three interdependent forces drive the growth of organizations in new communities. First, entrepreneurs create new organizational forms or modify existing ones in response to technological, normative, or regulatory changes. Second, in commercial communities, funding sources selectively support many new firms that grow and also allow the transformation of existing firms. Populations of linked professions, such as law and accounting firms, may also play a symbiotic role that benefits new organizations. Third, as organizations enter at different stages of community growth, variation, selection, and retention mechanisms favor distinct organizational forms. This may contribute to a pattern of ecological 'nestedness' in organizational communities, whereby the presence of certain core and infrastructural populations tends to precede that of more peripheral organizational forms.

The role of entrepreneurs

Community evolution depends upon a steady stream of organizational foundings for the growth of new populations and the revitalization of established ones. In the early days of community creation, *de novo* entrants often produce the distinctive organizational forms that initiate new populations, as we discussed in Chapter 10. The populations making up the biotechnology community, for example, were opened up by pioneering entrepreneurial firms moving quickly and rather haphazardly, rather than established firms that were seeking to diversify. By the mid-1980s, 'over 500 freestanding dedicated biotechnology firms had been established worldwide to pursue some form of genetic engineering' (Barley et al., 1992: 315). The early biotechnology firms were mostly independent dedicated biotechnology firms, rather than divisions or spin-offs from existing companies (Hybels et al., 1994). Scientists striving to commercialize discoveries from their university laboratories founded many of these small, science-based companies. By the mid-1990s, independent startups appeared to have achieved more success than those initially sponsored by older and larger firms. Nonetheless, biotech firms benefited considerably when they established strategic alliances and equity relations with older, prominent partners. Because of the pervasive uncertainty involved in evaluating these unproven startups, interorganizational relations with established firms helped to signal legitimacy, improving such outcomes as time-to-IPO and market capitalization (Stuart et al., 1999).

Ryan et al. (1995: 339–342) offered two explanations for entrepreneurial success in biotechnology. First, founders of the specialized startups understood the technology and were committed to it. By contrast, top managers at established firms knew biotechnology only from a distance and failed to grasp the conditions necessary to promote pioneering research. Second, because biotechnology developed so rapidly and on so many fronts, large firms could not keep up with every development. Instead, they adopted a strategy of waiting to see which initiatives seemed to have potential. They then invested in them through alliances, joint ventures, and acquisitions.

Spatial agglomeration also played a role in the success of *de novo* biotechnology startups. From a community perspective, a crucial issue is whether entrepreneurs initiating new organizational forms locate in areas with appropriate supporting populations. In the case of biotechnology in the United States, startup efforts have been heavily clustered in a handful of regions, including the Bay Area, San Diego, Boston, Seattle, and North Carolina's Research Triangle (Powell, 2001). These regions also boast an impressive infrastructure of research universities, research hospitals, non-profit institutes, and investment firms.

As new populations achieve legitimacy and founders learn the required competencies, founding rates increase because of enhanced entrepreneurial understanding of new forms and a more generous flow of resources to startups. In some cases, technological progress towards greater reliability, breadth of application, efficiency of production, and ease of use may occur during this period as well (Miner and Haunschild, 1995). Across the entire evolving community, partial or full mutualism heightens legitimacy and organizational learning. Such developments mean that new populations generated at later stages in the community's growth will experience more favorable founding conditions than earlier populations. For example, in biotechnology, American firms founded in the 1980s became embedded in mutualistic *networks of learning* that gave them access to knowledge gained through research and development by previous firms (Powell et al., 1996). Uzzi's (1997) study of the apparel industry in New York showed that fine-grained information transfer across firms created population-level learning that raised the competencies of all the firms involved.

In Denmark, Kreiner and Schultz (1993) found similar informal collaborative networks between scientists in biotechnology firms and universities in the late 1980s. However, unlike the American networks, the Danish networks were constructed outside official channels, as individual researchers built them by appropriating organization resources and diverting them into unauthorized projects. Community-wide mutualistic norms of sharing triumphed over biotechnology firms' desire to protect proprietary secrets. As Abrahamson and Rosenkopf (1993) noted, even a small number of network links can have a substantial effect on the diffusion of innovations across populations. Because biotechnology was a set of techniques that were widely disseminated, rather than a product, no single product or firm emerged as dominant in the 1970s and 1980s.

Funding sources: the symbiotic role of venture capitalists

Venture capital firms and stock underwriting firms are not the major suppliers of capital to growing firms in the United States. Nonetheless, their actions have had a disproportionate effect in certain population segments of American industry. Venture capitalists provided funds for the expansion of entrepreneurial firms in several emerging communities over the past few decades (Richtel, 1998). In particular, the semiconductor and biotechnology communities have benefited from high levels of venture capital investment (Brittain, 1994; Eisenhardt and Schoonhoven, 1990).

Venture capital firms generally only disburse funds to entrepreneurs who have established a track record, and stock underwriters assist firms with initial public offerings of stock (IPOs) only when they show solid potential for growth. Unlike banks, however, venture capital firms do not insist on collateral in the form of physical assets and property. Instead, they are willing to consider the intellectual capital of a new venture. Venture capitalists generally invest in a portfolio of firms through which they can achieve a solid return on their investment through IPOs or acquisitions. However, despite the mobility of capital, geographic proximity appears to be a crucial factor influencing these investment decisions. Thus, Powell (2001: 48) found that 'over 40 percent of the venture capital funding for U.S. biotech companies in the late 1990s was between a venture firm and a biotech located within twenty-five miles of each other.' The local nature of these investment processes contributed to spatial agglomeration and the formation of regional communities of organizations. As of 2005, some venture capital firms were seeking to branch out into international investments, thus moving into potentially difficult territory in which they had no local networks or knowledge.

The first biotechnology firm in the United States went public in 1980, and of the hundreds of new firms founded through 1996, slightly over 200 eventually went public. For 106 firms on which Deeds et al. (2004) were able to obtain data, the average size of an IPO was $19 million. The amount raised was influenced not only by a firm's characteristics, but also by the industry's perceived legitimacy. Federal approval of new biotech-derived drugs substantially enhanced the chances for commercial success of the firms' products, and positive articles in the press about the biotech industry raised the industry's legitimacy and investor confidence in the offerings. The efficacy and safety of the products, as certified by the FDA, made the positive media coverage credible and thus increased the flow of funds to the industry. However, because venture capitalists were unwilling to fund all the needs of biotech firms, they increasingly turned to investment banks and alliances with large pharmaceutical companies in the late 1980s and early 1990s (Stuart et al., 1999).

Venture capital firms also make symbiotic contributions to community evolution by spreading knowledge of effective forms and linking firms in different populations. For the new firms in which they invest, venture capitalists often assemble teams of skilled managers by selecting from diverse but related industries. Silicon Valley law firms have also been involved in facilitating new venture formation. For example, law firms working with venture capital firms played an information-mediating role for startup companies, helping institutionalize routines in areas such as recruiting officers and structuring equity arrangements (Suchman et al., 2001; Suchman and Cahill, 1996).

Ecological nestedness

Our discussion of the emergence of dedicated biotechnology firms, supported by venture capital and specialized law firms, raises a more general analytical question. For any spatially-bounded organizational community, what factors determine the order in which organizational forms emerge during the community development process? In the case of biotechnology, for instance, to what extent are universities and other regional infrastructural populations a prerequisite to the founding of biotechnology startups? And, in turn, to what extent is the presence of dedicated biotech firms a prerequisite to the appearance of usage promoters and commercial users or suppliers in the community (see Table 11.2)?

Bio-ecologists gauge the extent to which communities are hospitable to biodiversity by studying the rank-order appearance of species in an area (Cody and Diamond, 1975; Atmar and Patterson, 1993). Recently, organizational theorists have extended this logic to human communities, noting that the *ecological nestedness* of communities can be analyzed by examining the order in which organizational populations appear across places (Hanneman, 2005). Consider the two matrices shown in Figure 11.1. For both matrices, a sample of hypothetical communities (labeled A through E) has been cross-tabulated with the organizational populations found in those communities (with gray cells indicating the presence of a population). Matrix A displays a pattern of strict hierarchical nesting across communities. All communities in the cross-tabulation have at least one gas station, and a subset also has fast food restaurants and convenience stores. Progressively smaller subsets feature supermarkets and museums. The communities on the right side of the matrix represent inhospitable environments for organizations. Only those organizational forms that can thrive on minimal resources – the proverbial 'roaches' of the organizational world – survive in these communities. By contrast, the communities on the left in the matrix support a wide variety of organizational forms.

In most real-world communities, we can expect deviations from a strict pattern of nesting, as Hanneman (2005) observed in his sample of 298 settlements in New Mexico. Matrix B in Figure 11.1 illustrates a pattern with such deviations. Community B, for instance, has managed to attract a supermarket, even though no convenience store has been established there. Community C features a museum, even though it lacks a rudimentary supermarket to provision its residents. To the extent that organizational forms and communities deviate significantly from a pattern of ecological nesting, we label them 'idiosyncratic' forms and places. For example, community C may be idiosyncratic because its organizational community caters primarily to out-of-town visitors rather than locals. We need further research to understand the variables that may produce such idiosyncratic cases, including factors such as community size, age, residential demography, transportation and communication networks, and the like (Hanneman, 2005).

Evolutionary theory calls attention to two other methodological questions in analyzing ecological nestedness. First, should analysts expect a pattern of nesting as a consequence of selection and retention mechanisms or as a consequence of intentional variation? If selective retention operates, we would generally expect to observe ecological nesting in cross-sectional data, because a community's resource mix affects which organizational populations survive. Applying this argument to the hypothetical examples in Figure 11.1, for instance, we can surmise that at some point entrepreneurs

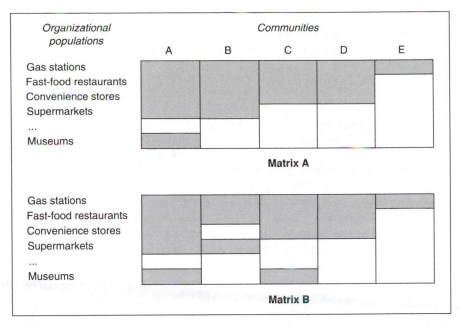

Figure 11.1   Two hypothetical patterns of ecological nestedness, displayed in cross-tabulations of organizational populations and communities

attempted to open a supermarket in community E but quickly failed. If, however, ecological nesting results primarily from intentional variation, then entrepreneurs in inhospitable communities would simply avoid such ill-advised founding efforts. Under such circumstances, organizational researchers need longitudinal data to uncover the typical sequence of nested population emergence.

Second, what is the geographic scope of the community being analyzed for ecological nestedness? Our hypothetical examples have conveniently focused on service sector organizations that rely on walk-in traffic, thus supporting an analysis that emphasizes local infrastructure and transportation networks. However, for many populations, such as those comprising the biotechnology community, the geographic scope is less clear. Can a comparison of biotech forms in different regions – San Diego, the Bay Area, and North Carolina's Research Triangle – inform an analysis of ecological nestedness? Or does the scope of interdependency in this community require analysis across national contexts? As we noted earlier in this chapter, the geographic scope of a community is an empirical question, depending on the nature and strength of interdependence among the organizational forms being analyzed.

Summary of three forces

Entrepreneurs in emerging communities work within a different context than those in established communities. As they create new organizational forms or modify existing ones, they must cope with incomplete networks of learning and immature mutualistic relations. However, populations linked symbiotically to the new or transformed populations can provide knowledge, capital, and other support to offset some of the liabilities of newness. For example, professional occupations, such as lawyers and accountants, may play an important symbiotic role. In other cases, the regional presence of predecessor forms may enhance the survival of a new population, especially when communities exhibit a pattern of ecological nestedness. Cognitive and sociopolitical legitimacy are as important for new communities as for new populations, and we turn next to that issue.

Legitimacy and collective action

A developing community's viability depends on the extent to which its core populations gain cognitive and sociopolitical legitimacy, as well as on the perceived value of the core populations' products or services (Miner and Haunschild, 1995). Government and regulatory bodies, for example, are faced with decisions regarding the extent to which they need to become involved in the burgeoning community, as overseers and as supporters. Innovating organizations must also consider how to modify or interpret the innovation to make it readily understandable to their customers or constituency. In making modifications, organizations and regulatory agencies engage in collective action to establish standards, both within and across populations. Established standards, by lowering barriers to entry and partially leveling the playing field between established organizations and startups, provide enhanced opportunities for new groups of entrepreneurs to join the community. Often, because of variations generated to work around existing barriers, entrepreneurs devise significant improvements to innovations that further enhance a population's legitimacy.

The greater the dependence of an emerging community on new organizational forms and populations, the more serious its legitimacy problems (Baum and Oliver, 1992; Dacin, 1997; Ruef, 2000). How does a developing organizational community achieve legitimacy? In most cases, no 'guiding hand' governs from the community center, directing strategic moves toward legitimacy. Instead, community legitimacy depends on three processes. First, new organizations and populations must struggle to achieve legitimacy in their own right, in accord with the processes described in Chapters 4 and 9. Legitimacy problems are most acute for the first populations in the community. Later, follower populations will have an easier time, especially if they enjoy spillovers in cognitive and sociopolitical legitimacy from their predecessors (Ruef, 2000). Second, populations achieve legitimacy more easily if they work together with other populations to establish standards and advance joint interests. Mutualism and symbiosis may emerge without regard to population members' intentions, as we noted in defining types of inter-population relations. Regardless of how it is achieved, mutualistic action by competing organizations is critical in industrial societies where government plays a dominant role. Third, across the entire community, institutional actors, such as government, educational organizations, and the media create the laws, regulations, and symbolic resources sustaining organizational communities. We describe these three processes in the following sections.

Organizational efforts

Organizations in newly created populations need to foster trust among the constituencies with which they interact, whether those constituencies consist of users, potential members, or other organizations within the nascent community, as we noted in Chapter 9. Given the paucity of information concerning new ventures, pioneering firms cannot base their initial trust-building strategies solely on impersonal evidence, such as technological efficiency or legal form. They must also concentrate on framing what they do in such a way that it becomes taken for granted. To enhance cognitive legitimacy, organizations may connect their innovations to existing knowledge through the use of symbolic language and behaviors. For example, in developing a novel system of electric lighting in the 1880s, Thomas Edison drew on numerous familiar elements of gas lighting technology, including reliance on central generation of power, underground mains, and gas meters and fixtures (Hargadon and Douglas, 2001). While many of these decisions proved to be technically inferior, they allowed Edison to imitate widely-recognized gas systems and thereby disguise some of the novelty of his design.

A century later in biotechnology, a similar problem arose because many founders were university scientists with no previous business experience. As a result, their firms appeared to lack management skills and had low credibility with the business community. Many dealt with those problems by hiring high-status executives from outside the firm to manage their operations, handle relations with outsiders, and enhance their firm's legitimacy. As in the case of Edison's strategy, the incorporation of such familiar business icons often had more symbolic than material implications. In their study of biotech IPO's, Deeds and colleagues (2004) found that firms with senior managers who graduated from top-ten business schools did *not* raise more capital than ventures lacking such management.

To enhance their cognitive and moral legitimacy, founders may also develop and communicate internally-consistent stories offering a compelling vision that they are behaving in a reasoned and trustworthy manner (Lounsbury and Glynn, 2001; Martin, 2002). For example, early founders of new commercial enterprises on the World Wide Web were effectively invisible to their potential customers, who saw only the firm's home page, not the organization itself. Because they could not rely on a recognizable 'bricks-and-mortar' presence to help convey their promise, they had to find some other way of communicating the credibility of their enterprises to the potential market. For many of them, the solution to this problem meant devoting a portion of their home pages to providing an overview of the company's history, as well as statements about their current business strategy.

Within- and cross-population actions and institutional support

Collective action can make population- and community-level learning much easier, as organizations share information and work on solutions to common problems affecting many populations (Miner and Haunschild, 1995). Although individual organizations might be able to achieve their own legitimacy, accomplishing population- and community-level legitimacy is problematic if these organizations engage in unbridled full competition to advance their own interests and fail to promote their mutual interests (Aldrich and Fiol, 1994; Wade, 1995). A lack of standard designs, for example, may block the diffusion of knowledge and understanding, thus constraining the new activities. Therefore, selection pressures compel founders of new organizations to find strategies for establishing stable sequences of mutualistic relations within their emerging population. They also benefit if they find ways to create symbiotic relations with organizations in other populations. Such actions include developing dominant designs and community-wide standards through the establishment of industry councils, cooperative alliances, trade associations, and other vehicles for collective action (Haunschild, 1993). Once established, these new collective units can concentrate on symbiotic relations with government, educational institutions, and the media. For example, the transportation network based on automobiles grew not only because of convergence on dominant designs and improvements in manufacturing efficiency, but also because of trade associations, special purpose magazines and journals, consumer lobbying groups, highway contractors, and strong state support (Carroll and Hannan, 1995; Rao, 1994).

Interest groups and associations

Following the logic of collective action, the combined activities of groups across populations has a more powerful influence on standards and regulations than the actions of isolated organizations or action sets (Aldrich and Whetten, 1981; Olson, 1965). For example, in the cochlear implant industry, the American Association of Otolaryngology 'initiated a committee of representatives from industry, clinics, audiology, psychoacoustics, and other disciplines to study and recommend technical standards' (Van de Ven and Garud, 1994: 436). In biotechnology, several practices promoted a relatively unified technological community: professors took sabbaticals at biotechnology firms, postdoctoral students circulated between universities and firms, and firms made laboratory conditions so attractive that they created a labor market for scientists that cut across universities and industry (Powell et al., 1996: 123).

The commercialization of the World Wide Web represents an interesting case precisely because collective action organizations – alliances, coalitions, and consortia – formed so quickly and managed to recruit the largest firms in the affected industries to join. As a community of symbiotically linked populations, many of the Web's interest groups were multi-industry, rather than limited to membership from only one population. For example, the World Wide Web Consortium, which set standards for the Web, included more than 100 members. All major software firms joined, as did the major hardware firms, such as IBM, Sun Microsystems, and Silicon Graphics (Lohr, 1995). Other groups that were formed to promote Internet standards included the Internet Engineering Task Force (IETF), the Internet Assigned Number Authority, the Federal Networking Council, and the Internet Society. Between 1993 and 1997, four International World Wide Web Conferences were held in Europe and the United States, where Web service providers and businesses discussed ways to resolve some of the common issues they faced. The American Institute of Certified Public Accountants developed a certification program, called the CPA Web Trust, which gave a seal of approval to vendors doing business on the Web who followed secure practices.

Because of a growing interest in conflicts over standards within evolving technological communities, rich case histories are now available for a number of industries in the United States, e.g. Rao (1994), Rosenkopf and Tushman (1994), and Garud et al. (2002). These studies document the importance of inter-organizational networks and alliances in socially constructing acceptable population-level standards. For example, arguments over how to pay for public radio broadcasting in the United States were fueled by the actions of 'an unsavory group at the periphery of the industry'

(Leblebici et al., 1991: 345). The Department of Commerce initiated annual Radio Conferences to promote the development of self-regulation (Lippmann, forthcoming).

Populations of semi-legitimate organizations on the fringe of communities may push central populations into consortia and alliances, thus raising the level of learning throughout all populations. They also keep alive models of organizing that preserve the heterogeneity of organizational forms in populations (Clemens, 1997). As with all collective action, interest groups and consortia in developing communities face the problem of free riders and defections by organizations pursing their own interests. Organizations may try to 'free ride' on the efforts of others because they know that they will benefit from collective success, regardless of their own contribution. As we noted in Chapter 9, collectivities that survive generally maintain organizational discipline by providing strong incentives for members to contribute and not defect. They also create a compliance structure for monitoring, detecting, and sanctioning defections. The World Wide Web's roots in the scientific community predated its commercialization, and thus associations promoting standards for the Web drew upon the strong communal norms of open standards and sharing that characterized the Internet. Defection from group standards was highly visible because the defector's products/services returned error messages to users. In biotechnology, in similar fashion, norms carried over from the university-based scientific community facilitated collective action, although not as strongly as for the Web. Biotechnology faced much greater legitimacy problems than the Web, and depended heavily on governmental actions affecting its fate.

In the late 1980s, the Industrial Biotechnology Association appealed to the President's Council on Competitiveness to pressure federal agencies to weaken regulations perceived as hindering the growth of the biotech industry. These efforts were rewarded in early 1992 with a sign that sociopolitical approval had been achieved at the highest levels of government. President George Bush issued a new government policy on biotechnology which said that genetically engineered products should not be assumed to be inherently dangerous and that biotechnology products should not receive greater scrutiny than products produced by conventional means (Hilts, 1992). In November, 1995, the Secretary of the Department of Health and Human Services, which oversees the Food and Drug Administration (FDA), announced that the FDA was eliminating special restrictions on drugs made by biotechnology companies and would now treat them the same as drugs made by traditional pharmaceutical firms.

While the example suggests that collective action leading to government intervention can be critical in the emergence of a community, this perspective must be tempered by attention to organizational inertia in regulatory activities. In a statistical study of FDA approval times for 450 drugs, Carpenter (2002) found that partisan activities and the ideology of congressional majorities and presidents had no significant impact on waiting times. Instead, media coverage and the density and resources of interest groups were two primary factors in reducing regulatory delay. Interestingly, the effect of interest group prevalence was non-linear: as the density of groups increased initially, collective action became more difficult, owing perhaps to lack of consensus or free riders. Collective action became easier as density increased further, however, because very large numbers of interest groups for some diseases (e.g. arthritis and diabetes) signaled the importance of expediency in drug approval (Carpenter, 2002: Figure 1). More generally, the study suggests that associations and interest groups can affect regulatory policy, even without the support of intermediaries, such as politicians or legislators.

The state: support and regulation

Governmental support and assistance can create a stable nucleus for an evolving organizational community and thus accelerate the speed with which new populations linked to the community achieve legitimacy. State-sponsored associations, alliances, and other activities can also create strong incentives for organizations and populations to engage in mutualistic activities, as well as a compliance structure for reducing the likelihood of competitive activities. Regardless of whether a community is generated by technological innovations, shifts in norms and values, or changes in laws and regulations, state actions play a key role in its evolution. Two domains are particularly significant: support for research, and enactment and enforcement of new laws and regulations.

Government support for research

In communities with deep roots in technological innovation, research and development sponsored by the government often built the essential infrastructure, as documented in several studies. In the cochlear implant industry, for example, the first commercial activity was preceded by 22 years of non-commercial research (Van de Ven and Garud, 1994). Research on electronically enhancing human hearing was conducted by academics and sponsored by grants from government, public research foundations, and philanthropists. The commercial radio community grew not only from entrepreneurial activity and collective action by commercial firms, but also from 'the emergence and active participation of military, legislative, and regulatory bodies' (Rosenkopf and Tushman, 1994: 413–414). The U.S. Navy was involved because it made heavy use of radio technology in its operations, and it lobbied for federal legislation giving priority to its needs.

In the case of the Web, government agencies were involved early on in the development efforts. The Defense Department created DARPAnet, the forerunner of the Internet, and the National Science Foundation (NSF) and other research agencies actively encouraged the Internet as a medium for communication between scientists (Hafner and Lyon, 1996). The communication backbone of the Internet and the Web was paid for by the NSF, which eventually privatized the network. Eventually, scientists wanted to be able to exchange graphics as well as text, and such exchanges were made possible after two scientists at CERN in Switzerland created the first Web browser. Graphics technology was further developed by the NCSA, a government-sponsored research institution at the University of Illinois at Urbana/Champaign. As companies began to realize the commercial potential in the technology, the NCSA began licensing the technology to commercial organizations for further exploitation and development.

Government support significantly affects the extent to which standards develop across organizational communities. Guler and colleagues (2002) studied the global adoption of ISO-9000 quality certificates, a set of management norms promoted by the International Organization for Standardization (ISO) based in Switzerland. Although certification is voluntary, government institutions wield a major influence on adoption, even in the absence of explicit regulation. Governments consume significant amounts of goods and services and thus can 'exert coercive pressures by asking suppliers and contractors to conform to certain procedures and standards' (Guler et al., 2002: 212). The early wave of ISO-9000 adoptions thus primarily affected organizational communities defined by their involvement with the state, including the energy, defense, and telecommunications sectors. The number of certificates subsequently issued in 85 countries between 1993 and 1998 correlated significantly with government expenditures, measured as a percentage of GDP (Guler et al., 2002).

Laws and regulations

In the United States' political system of divided executive and legislative branches, containing independent regulatory agencies, newly organized industries ultimately must co-opt, neutralize, form alliances with, and otherwise come to terms with government agencies. Trade associations and other collective action entities focus much of their efforts on direct access to agencies themselves. In political systems with unified executive and legislative branches, as in most European and Asian nations, support from political parties and career civil servants is essential. For example, in Japan, Ministry of Finance career officials wield substantial influence over the banking system, and many retire from the Ministry to take high-level positions in financial institutions. Regardless of a political system's structure, individual efforts to form organizations and create new populations will be severely hampered without governmental approval.

For example, the early biotechnology industry developed in an environment of great uncertainty, because firms did not have a clear idea of what products would be regulated and what safety tests would be required by the Environmental Protection Agency, the Food and Drug Administration, and the Department of Agriculture. Accordingly, the Industrial Biotechnology Association lobbied the FDA, the EPA and other agencies in an attempt to create a more certain regulatory environment. An FDA ruling in 1981, approving the first diagnostic kit based on a monoclonal antibody, significantly raised the founding rate of biotech firms in the years that followed (Shan et al., 1991). Nevertheless, the biotechnology community continued to fight a long-running battle with government regulators. As we have already noted, only in 1995 did the industry begin receiving the same treatment from the FDA as traditional pharmaceutical firms.

Educational institutions

Educational institutions also play a role in how rapidly emerging communities achieve legitimacy. Budding populations can establish symbiotic links with educational institutions by incorporating the skills and knowledge needed for success in the populations into school curricula. In the United States, biotechnology firms attempted to enhance their legitimacy by identifying themselves with elite research universities, such as Harvard, Stanford, and the University of California-San Francisco (Deeds et al., 2004). In many cases, faculty inventors of key technologies actually started new firms. The perceived value of the new firms arose from inventive technological advances, such as the use of restriction enzymes and recombinant DNA. In turn, the legitimacy of the firms and their technologies was heightened by links to the universities.

Mass and specialized media – television, magazines, journals, newsletters, and newspapers – also play a symbiotic role in communities, disseminating information within and between populations. Information diffusion increases the likelihood that potential entrepreneurs will recognize opportunities for combining old resources in new ways (Ruef, 2002a), or at least recognize opportunities in already existing populations. The media – especially journalists in print media – played a very key role in establishing the legitimacy of the World Wide Web. In 1993, for example, there were only 34 magazine articles and 13 articles in major newspapers that mentioned the Web. During 1994, however, those figures had jumped to 686 and 743 respectively; and during 1995 they reached totals of 6,365 and 10,054. In the early days, many of the articles were published in technical journals and focused on describing what the Web was and how browser technology worked. Eventually, articles appeared in mainstream outlets, focusing on how the Web could affect commercial activity. As the legitimacy of the Web became even more established, references to the Web (usually through provision of a home page address) became integrated into stories of all kinds, such as announcements of upcoming rock concerts and descriptions of new movie releases.

Summary: legitimacy and collective action

A developing organizational community's likelihood of achieving legitimacy depends on commensalistic, symbiotic, and dominance relations between populations. Indeed, the difference between an aggregation of interdependent populations and an organizational community turns on community-level legitimacy, as our examples from the field of biotechnology make clear. Populations must first develop sufficient legitimacy to win their own place in a community. Then, if members succeed in forming collective action organizations, such organizations have the potential for establishing standards and advancing the interests of community members. Examples from biotechnology show effective mutualistic action by organizations that normally compete. Many of their activities were directed at the state, which plays a dominant role in most communities.

Legitimacy contributes to the ongoing development of the community, influencing further differentiation and interdependence. Innovations and shared standards promote additional entrepreneurial entries into the community, and entrepreneurial initiatives eventually lead to changes by established firms. Web consultants and Web-page design firms, for example, drove established firms seeking a Web presence into creating sites that did much more than simply provide information to consumers (Schwartz, 1997). Some firms created sites allowing consumers to send feedback to the firm, sign up for emailed update bulletins, and click through to other firms offering complementary products or services. In addition, a new population of firms seeking to establish Web-based economic transaction standards (e.g. CyberCash, Clickshare, and PayPal) pushed traditional credit card companies into alliances with Web-oriented software firms, such as Netscape and Microsoft. As these alliances grew, at the organizational and population levels, they further enhanced the technology and legitimacy of the Web. Strong alliances also prompted the increased involvement of organizations and groups outside of the Web community, such as government and regulatory agencies, and academic and research institutions.

The speed with which the Web developed and established its legitimacy was unprecedented in organizational history, and may well foreshadow changes in the speed with which organizational communities develop in the 21st century (Hunt and Aldrich, 1998). Many processes and events facilitating the Web's legitimacy came together very early in its life cycle. Because the Web emerged from research on the Internet, which had been established for over 20 years, it began with a significant degree of institutional support. Its roots in the Internet also provided the Web with a certain degree of regulatory legitimacy from its earliest days. Because the technology was so accessible, both to developers and users, it not only quickly became available for use by many firms, but also gained cognitive and normative legitimacy. The concerted early effort to establish a set of technological standards not only enhanced technological compatibility, but also increased the technology's normative legitimacy. Because of the conjuncture of technological compatibility with enhanced legitimacy, entrepreneurs and established firms were encouraged to create new ventures that exploited the commercial possibilities inherent in the new technology.

Conclusions

The co-evolution of an organizational community depends on simultaneous processes of variation, selection, retention, and struggle at the population level, aggregated across the multiple populations constituting the community. Variation arises through processes such as foundings of new organizations, technological innovation, proactive legitimation strategies attempted by entrepreneurs and organizations, and collective action efforts by sets of organizations and populations. Selection forces arise from processes such as the struggle over a dominant design and the fit between legitimization strategies and prevailing social and cultural norms. Selection forces are also apparent in the response of external stakeholders to entrepreneurs' attempts to pursue collective action and to raise funds. Retention forces are reflected in processes such as the embedding of a dominant design in the architecture of new products and processes, and the institutionalization of a population's human resource needs in college curricula. They are also found in the tacit and informal rules used by external stakeholders to evaluate organizations, and the bureaucratization of the associations created by collective action. Thus, the same evolutionary model used to explain organizational foundings and the emergence of new populations can also be applied to community evolution.

Organizational evolution is intertwined with the dynamics of community legitimation. The development of technological, normative, or legal standards for a particular population has widespread consequences for the entire community to which it belongs. In some cases, innovations may represent a form of *collective learning* that can be distinguished from direct learning from experience by individual organizations (Miner and Haunschild, 1995). Through organizational units formed by collective action, populations of organizations may observe the impact of population-level routines on the fate of other populations, adopt new population-level practices, and thereby influence the fate of communities with which they are linked. For example, as we noted in the last chapter, when semiconductor firms in the United States created research and development consortia to develop and share population-level knowledge, they affected the entire community of firms involved in computers and electronics (Aldrich and Sasaki, 1995). Deliberate population-level learning thus influenced the spread of organizational knowledge and, consequently, the scope of community evolution.

Legitimacy is critical in determining whether a community will become fully developed. Organizations may act independently to promote their cognitive and normative legitimacy with individual stakeholders, but they also collaborate with other organizations in collective action (Aldrich and Whetten, 1981). Some of these collective efforts focus on establishing a set of standards for the community, whereas others are aimed at publicizing a community's needs to individuals and organizations, especially institutions, outside the community. In the past, information traveled slowly, was costly to obtain, and difficult to interpret. In the age of powerful information technologies, new populations and communities may no longer have to wait years for technological competencies to diffuse across populations. In the 21st century, global communication networks and high-technology information delivery systems have dramatically increased the diffusion rate of technological competencies and legitimating activities.

Study Questions

1. Pick a population you know well. What strategies can organizations or organizational populations use to reduce cross-population effects that have negative consequences for them?
2. Assume that we apply the term *robust communities* to describe patterns of interdependencies among organizational populations that are highly resistant to change over time. What characteristics would you expect to find in these communities?
3. Using the principles of entrepreneurial networking from Chapter 4, explain how the patterns of ecological nestedness in Figure 11.1 might occur. Consider what community characteristics affecting entrepreneurial networks might explain the differences between Matrices A and B.

Exercises

1. Consider the community context of the organizational population you have analyzed in Chapters 9 and 10. Describe the interdependencies of the population with other organizational forms. Do these relations entail commensalism, symbiosis, and/or dominance? How did those relations emerge historically? To what extent has collective action between the populations promoted the legitimacy of the community as a whole?
2. Conduct fieldwork in your local community to determine which organizational populations seem over- and under-represented. Use concepts and principles from this chapter to explain your findings.

APPENDIX: Research Design and Evolutionary Analysis

Overview of research Illustrations

We purposefully chose the case studies in this book to illustrate the diversity of research designs employed in organizational analysis. In Table A.1, we characterize this diversity along three dimensions: (1) *unit of analysis*; (2) *mode of data collection*; and (3) *observation plan*. Although the research designs are clearly not exhaustive – for instance, laboratory experiments are noticeably absent – they do include many of the most common approaches. We highlight the advantages and disadvantages of each.

As we argued in Chapter 2, scholars take different positions on the appropriate *unit of analysis* in evolutionary organizational studies. In many respects, organizations as a whole constitute a natural choice, insofar as they are boundary-maintaining entities with activities directed toward their own perpetuation. However, when scholarly interest centers on the emergence of new organizations or variation within existing ones, researchers must disaggregate the units further. Social groups in organizations (e.g. work groups, departments, divisions) and social routines represent two viable alternatives, as illustrated in the studies by Ruef and colleagues (2003) and Pentland (1992; Pentland and Rueter, 1994), respectively. Methodological individualists argue for further disaggregation, focusing on individual persons as carriers of routines, competencies, and status characteristics. This emphasis is especially useful when evolutionary processes affect the life histories of individuals, as noted in Li and Walder's (2001) study of institutional change in Maoist and post-Maoist China.

For other studies of organizational evolution, the timescale of variation, selection, and retention processes may transcend the lifespan of individuals and organizations. Studies at this scale benefit from a focus on organizational populations or even communities as units of analysis (e.g. Ingram and Rao, 2004). For this purpose, researchers commonly use the single population census, which emphasizes complete historical coverage of an organizational population, the observation of all major vital events (such as foundings and disbandings), and careful measurement of institutional and material context (Carroll and Hannan, 2000). Given growing

Table A.1   **Research designs employed in research illustrations**

Chapter	Research illustrations (source)	Unit of analysis	Mode of data collection	Observation plan
2	The Evolution of Bureaucracy (Langton, 1984)	Organization*	Archival	Retrospective
4	The Structure of Founding Teams (Ruef et al., 2003)	Social group	Interview	Prospective**
6	Routines as a Foundation for Organizational Forms (Pentland, 1992)	Social routine	Participant observation	Prospective
8	Elite Recruitment and Social Change in China (Li and Walder, 2001)	Individual	Mail survey and interview	Retrospective
10	Population Processes and Legislative Outcomes (Ingram and Rao, 2004)	Organizational population	Archival	Retrospective

* While focusing his case study primarily on Wedgwood's pottery factory, Langton (1984: 336) stresses that the process of bureaucratization must be studied as well at the level of the individual worker and the organizational population as a whole.

**Panel study includes retrospective components as well.

interest in the evolution of organizational communities, some scholars have also deployed a multi-population census, which tracks a number of interdependent populations simultaneously. Resource limitations may require limited temporal coverage and less precise measurement of vital events (Ruef, 2000).

The *mode of data collection* is largely orthogonal to the unit of analysis. In circumstances with limited direct access to the participants involved in an evolutionary process, analysts tend to rely on archival databases, such as those represented in directories, newspaper accounts, organizational records, diaries, and the like. For example, historical analyses of organizations usually rely on data archives. When direct access to participants can only be arranged for a limited period, researchers often employ interviews or mailed surveys. For units of analysis beyond the individual or small group, researchers may apply these instruments to multiple respondents within an organization or population, raising the question of inter-respondent reliability (Marsden, 2005). Finally, if researchers desire prolonged access to participants, they can use ethnographic methods to track evolutionary processes through field observation and varying levels of personal participation.

The type of *observation plan*, the third dimension of the research designs reviewed in Table A.1, addresses whether data are collected only at one time point (cross-sectionally) or at multiple time points (longitudinally). It also considers whether data will be collected after an evolutionary process has occurred (retrospectively) or while it is occurring (prospectively). As seen in the Table, we have omitted the first distinction since all research designs intended to address evolutionary processes entail some longitudinal component. Researchers tend to collect such data retrospectively when their interest centers on an extended period or process of historical interest. They are more apt to use prospective designs when their interest centers on activities that may be completed over a brief period.

Table A.2   **Strengths and weaknesses of design features**

Research design feature	Strengths	Weaknesses
Units of analysis		
Small (Individuals, Social Groups, Routines)	Fine-grained observation of routines, competencies, and status characteristics	Failure to observe emergent properties
Large (Organizations, Populations, Communities)	Holistic observation of structural and cultural characteristics	Risk of reification; loss of subjective dimension
Mode of data collection		
Archival	Access to informants not required	Measures limited by existing archives
Interview or survey	Requires only limited access to informants; measures can be tailored to interests of investigator	Investigator must identify useful informants and measures in advance
Direct observation	Unanticipated informants and measures may emerge during observation period	Extensive time spent with informants; observations may be difficult to structure
Observation plan		
Prospective	Absence of success bias or retrospective rationalization	Attrition among respondents; demands on time of investigator
Retrospective	Record of historical processes reconstructed through one-time data collection event	Success bias among sampled units; recall bias among informants

Strengths and weaknesses of non-experimental research designs

As we summarize in Table A.2, all research designs confront analysts with a mix of strengths and weaknesses. With respect to choosing a unit of analysis, for instance, studies of small units (examining individuals, social groups, or routines) afford investigators unique opportunities to observe organizational processes at a fine-grained level, often with some insight into the subjective dispositions of entrepreneurs or organizational members. This subjective dimension sometimes gets lost or reified in designs studying larger units, as investigators address structural and cultural characteristics in a more holistic fashion. Conversely, investigators who emphasize organizations, populations, and communities as their units of analysis are better positioned to observe emergent properties that may be missed in research designs for smaller units.

The strengths and weaknesses of different modes of data collection follow directly from the degree of access to informants they require. In archival research, investigators need not have any access to informants, but the measures collected will be limited to those present in existing archives. Typically, information in official archives has been collected for administrative purposes, making it very difficult to use for research purposes. Interviews or surveys allow investigators to tailor their measures to their specific evolutionary perspective. However, with the exception of respondent-driven instruments and open-ended questions, investigators must specify in advance both the sampling frame of informants and the operationalization of measures. Direct observation requires the most extensive access to participants in an evolutionary process, while allowing informants and measures to 'emerge' during the study period, along the lines advocated by proponents of grounded theory (Golden-Biddle and Locke, 1997; Strauss, 1978). Nevertheless, such observations must still be structured afterwards for the sake of interpretation.

The problem of success bias, noted in Chapter 2, is intimately tied to the choice of retrospective versus prospective research designs in evolutionary analysis. Retrospective designs suffer the greatest risk of success bias, because they often sample from units that have survived until analysts have collected data from them. Even in the absence of such obvious instances of success bias, the problem may appear in more subtle ways. The retrospective reliance on archival data in organizational ecology, for instance, is predicated on the assumption that such archives exist and, consequently, that organizational populations have attained some level of success that makes them amenable to analysis. Similarly, retrospective interviews with successful and unsuccessful managers are subject to different recall biases, as these informants try to make sense of past experiences (Weick, 1995). Prospective research designs not only mitigate these concerns, but also impose considerable demands on the time of investigators. Moreover, attrition – the loss of cases from prospective designs over time due to non-response or selection mechanisms – can whittle away even large samples, leaving investigators with limited ability to draw inferences.

References

Abbott, Andrew. 1992. 'From Causes to Events: Notes on Narrative Positivism.' *Sociological Methods & Research*, 20, 4 (May): 428–455.

Abernathy, William and Kim B. Clark. 1985. 'Innovation: Mapping the Winds of Creative Destruction.' *Research Policy*, 14: 3–22.

Abrahamson, Eric. 1991. 'Managerial Fads and Fashions: The Diffusion and Rejection of Innovations.' *Academy of Management Review*, 16, 3 (July): 586–612.

Abrahamson, Eric and Lori Rosenkopf. 1993. 'Institutional and Competitive Bandwagons: Using Mathematical Modeling as a Tool to Explore Innovation Diffusion.' *Academy of Management Review*, 18, 3 (July): 487–517.

Acker, Joan. 1990. 'Hierarchies, Jobs, Bodies: A Theory of Gendered Organizations.' *Gender and Society*, 4, 2 (June): 139–158.

Ahrne, Göran. 1994. *Social Organizations: Interaction Inside, Outside, and Between Organizations*. London: Sage.

Ahuja, Gautam. 2000. 'Collaboration Networks, Structural Holes, and Innovation: A Longitudinal Study.' *Administrative Science Quarterly*, 45, 3 (September): 425–455.

Akard, Patrick J. 1992. 'Corporate Mobilization and U.S. Economic Policy in the 1970s.' *American Sociological Review*, 57, 5 (October): 597–615.

Albach, Horst. 1983. *Zur Versorgung der Deutschen Wirtschaft mit Risikokapital*. IFM-Materialien Nr. 9. Bonn, Germany: Institut für Mittelstandsforschung.

Albert, Stuart and David A. Whetten. 1985. 'Organizational Identity.' pp. 263–295 in L. Cummings and B. Staw (eds.), *Research in Organizational Behavior*. Greenwich, CT: JAI Press.

Alchian, Armen A. and Harold Demsetz. 1972. 'Production, Information Costs, and Economic Organization.' *American Economic Review*, 62, 5 (December): 777–795.

Alchian, Armen A. and S. Woodward. 1988. 'The Firm is Dead: Long Live the Firm: A Review of Oliver E. Williamson's *The Economic Institutions of Capitalism*.' *Journal of Economic Literature*, 26, 4 (December): 65–79.

Aldrich, Howard E. 1971. 'Organizational Boundaries and Interorganizational Conflicts.' *Human Relations*, 24 (August): 279–287.

Aldrich, Howard E. 1972. 'Sociability in Mensa: Characteristics of Interaction Among Strangers.' *Urban Life and Culture*, 1 (July): 167–186.

Aldrich, Howard E. 1975. 'Tight Versus Loose Coupling: Some Arguments and a Model.' Paper presented at a Conference on Design of Inter-organizational Relations in the Public Sector, International Institute of Management, West Berlin, June.

Aldrich, Howard E. 1976a. 'Resource Dependence and Interorganizational Relations Between Local Employment Service Offices and Social Services Sector Organizations.' *Administration and Society*, 7, 1 (February): 419–454.

Aldrich, Howard E. 1976b. 'An Interorganizational Dependency Perspective on Relations Between the Employment Service and Its Organization Set,' pp. 233–266 in R. Killman et al. (eds), *The Management of Organization Design*. Amsterdam: Elsevier.

Aldrich, Howard E. 1979. *Organizations and Environments*. Englewood Cliffs, NJ: Prentice-Hall.

Aldrich, Howard E. 1988. 'Paradigm Wars: Donaldson Versus the Critics of Organization Theory.' *Organization Studies*, 9, 1 (January): 19–25.

Aldrich, Howard E. and Ellen R. Auster. 1986. 'Even Dwarfs Started Small.' pp. 165–198 in Barry M. Staw and Larry L. Cummings (eds), *Research in Organizational Behavior*, Vol. 8. Greenwich, CT: JAI Press.

Aldrich, Howard E., John Cater, Trevor Jones, and Dave McEvoy. 1983. 'From Periphery to Peripheral: The South Asian Petite Bourgeoisie in England.' pp. 1–32 in Ida Harper Simpson and Richard Simpson (eds), *Research in the Sociology of Work*, Vol. 2. Greenwich, CT: JAI Press.

Aldrich, Howard E., Amanda Elam, and Pat Ray Reese. 1996. 'Strong Ties, Weak Ties, and Strangers: Do Women Business Owners Differ from Men in Their Use of Networking to Obtain Assistance?' pp. 1–25 in Sue Birley and Ian MacMillan (eds), *Entrepreneurship in a Global Context*. London: Routledge.

Aldrich, Howard E. and Marlene C. Fiol. 1994. 'Fools Rush In? The Institutional Context of Industry Creation.' *Academy of Management Review*, 19, 4 (October): 645–670.

Aldrich, Howard E., Arne L. Kalleberg, Peter V. Marsden, and James Cassell. 1989. 'In Pursuit of Evidence: Strategies for Locating New Businesses.' *Journal of Business Venturing*, 4, 6 (November): 367–386.

Aldrich, Howard E. and Amy Kenworthy. 1999. 'The Accidental Entrepreneur: Campbellian Antinomies and Organizational Foundings.' pp. 19–33 in Joel A. C. Baum and Bill McKelvey (eds), *Variations in Organization Science: In Honor of Donald T. Campbell*. Newbury Park, CA: Sage.

Aldrich, Howard E. and Nancy Langton. 1998. 'Human Resource Management Practices and Organizational Life Cycles.' pp. 349–357 in Paul Reynolds et al. (eds), *Frontiers of Entrepreneurship Research 1997*. Babson Park, MA: Babson College, Center for Entrepreneurial Studies.

Aldrich, Howard E. and Jeffrey Pfeffer. 1976. 'Environments of Organizations.' pp. 79–105 in *Annual Review of Sociology, 2*. Palo Alto, CA: Annual Reviews.

Aldrich, Howard E., Pat Ray Reese, and Paola Dubini. 1989. 'Women on the Verge of a Breakthrough?: Networking Among Entrepreneurs in the United States and Italy.' *Journal of Entrepreneurship and Regional Development*, 1, 4: 339–356.

Aldrich, Howard E. and Albert J. Reiss, Jr. 1976. 'Continuities in the Study of Ecological Succession: Changes in the Race Composition of Neighborhoods and Their Businesses.' *American Journal of Sociology*, 81, 4 (January): 846–866.

Aldrich, Howard E., Linda Renzulli, and Nancy Langton. 1998. 'Passing on Privilege: Resources Provided by Self-employed Parents to their Self-employed Children.' pp. 291–317 in Kevin Leicht (ed.), *Research in Social Stratification and Mobility*. Greenwich, CT: JAI Press.

Aldrich, Howard E. and Tomoaki Sakano. 1998. 'Unbroken Ties: How the Personal Networks of Japanese Business Owners Compare to Those in Other Nations.' pp. 32–52 in Mark Fruin (ed.), *Networks and Markets: Pacific Rim Investigations*. New York: Oxford University Press.

Aldrich Howard E., and Toshihiro Sasaki. 1995. 'R & D Consortia in the United States and Japan.' *Research Policy*, 24, 2 (March): 301–316.

Aldrich, Howard E. and Udo H. Staber. 1988. 'Organizing Business Interests: Patterns of Trade Association Foundings, Transformations, and Deaths.' pp. 111–126 in Glenn R. Carroll (ed.), *Ecological Models of Organization*. Cambridge, MA: Ballinger.

Aldrich, Howard E. and Roger Waldinger. 1990. 'Ethnicity and Entrepreneurship.' pp. 111–135 in *Annual Review of Sociology* 16. Palo Alto, CA: Annual Reviews.

Aldrich, Howard E. and David Whetten. 1981. 'Making the Most of Simplicity: Organization Sets, Action Sets, and Networks.' pp. 385–408 in P. Nystrom and William H. Starbuck (eds), *Handbook of Organizational Design*. New York: Oxford University Press.

Aldrich, Howard E. and Gabriele Wiedenmayer. 1993. 'From Traits to Rates: An Ecological Perspective on Organizational Foundings.' pp. 145–195 in Jerome Katz and Robert H. Brockhaus (eds), *Advances in Entrepreneurship, Firm Emergence, and Growth*, Vol. 1. Greenwich, CT: JAI Press.

Aldrich, Howard E., Catherine Zimmer, Udo H. Staber, and John J. Beggs. 1990. 'Trade Association Foundings in the 20th Century.' Paper presented at the annual meeting of the American Sociological Association, Washington, DC.

Aldrich, Howard E., Catherine R. Zimmer, Udo H. Staber, and John J. Beggs. 1994. 'Minimalism, Mutualism, and Maturity: The Evolution of the American Trade Association Population in the 20th Century.' pp. 223–239 in Joel A.C. Baum and Jitendra V. Singh (eds), *Evolutionary Dynamics of Organizations*. New York: Oxford University Press.

Amburgey, Terry L. and Tina Dacin. 1994. 'As the Left Foot Follows the Right? The Dynamics of Strategic and Structural Change.' *Academy of Management Journal*, 37, 6 (December): 1427–1452.

Amburgey, Terry L., Dawn Kelly, and William Barnett. 1993. 'Resetting the Clock: The Dynamics of Organizational Change and Failure.' *Administrative Science Quarterly*, 38, 1 (March): 51–73.

Amburgey, Terry L., Marjo-Riitta Lehtisalo, and Dawn Kelly. 1988. 'Suppression and Failure in the Political Press: Government Control, Party Affiliation, and Organizational Life Chances.' pp. 153–174 in Glenn R. Carroll (ed.), *Ecological Models of Organization*. Cambridge, MA: Ballinger.

Amburgey, Terry L. and Anne S. Miner. 1992. 'Strategic Momentum: The Effects of Repetitive, Positional, and Contextual Momentum on Merger Activity.' *Strategic Management Journal*, 13, 5 (June): 335–348.

Amburgey, Terry L. and Hayagreeva Rao. 1996. 'Organizational Ecology: Past, Present, and Future Directions.' *Academy of Management Journal*, 39, 5 (October): 1265–1286.

Aminzade, Ronald. 1992. 'Historical Sociology and Time.' *Sociological Methods & Research*, 20, 4 (May): 456–480.

Anderson, Phillip and Michael Tushman. 1990. 'Technological Discontinuities and Dominant Designs: A Cyclical Model of Technological Change.' *Administrative Science Quarterly*, 35, 4 (December): 604–633.

Andrews, Edmund L. 1992. 'House Votes to Put Stricter Rules on "900" Pay – Call Phone Services.' *New York Times*, February 25, A1.

Appelbaum, Eileen, Thomas Bailey, Peter Berg, and Arne L. Kalleberg. 2000. *Manufacturing Advantage: Why High-Performance Work Systems Pay Off*. Ithaca, NY: Cornell University Press.

Appold, Stephen J. 1995. 'Agglomeration, Interorganizational Networks, and Competitive Performance in the U.S. Metalworking Sector.' *Economic Geography*, 71, 1 (January): 27–54.

Argote, Linda. 1993. 'Group and Individual Learning Curves: Individual, System, and Environmental Components.' *British Journal of Social Psychology*, 32, 1 (March): 31–51.

Argote, Linda, Sara L. Beckman, and Dennis Epple. 1990. 'The Persistence and Transfer of Learning in Industrial Settings.' *Management Science*, 36, 2 (February): 140–154.

Argote, Linda and Dennis Epple. 1990. 'Learning Curves in Manufacturing.' *Science*, 247 (February): 920–924.

Argyris, Chris and Donald Schön. 1978. *Organizational Learning*. Reading, MA: Addison-Wesley.

Arrow, Kenneth J. 1962. 'The Economic Implications of Learning by Doing.' *Review of Economic Studies*, 29: 155–173.

Arrow, Kenneth J. 1987. 'Oral History I: An Interview.' pp. 191–242 in G.R. Feiwel (ed.), *Arrow and the Ascent of Modern Economic Theory*. Basingstoke: Macmillan.

Arthur, W. Brian. 1989. 'Competing Technologies, Increasing Returns, and Lock-in by Historical Events: The Dynamics of Allocation Under Increasing Returns.' *The Economic Journal*, 99 (March): 116–131.

Astley, W. Graham. 1985. 'The Two Ecologies: Population and Community Perspectives on Organizational Evolution.' *Administrative Science Quarterly*, 30, 2 (June): 224–241.

Astley, W. Graham and Edward J. Zajac. 1990. 'Beyond Dyadic Exchange: Functional Interdependence and Sub-unit Power.' *Organization Studies*, 11, 4: 481–501.

Atmar, Wirt and Bruce D. Patterson. 1993. 'The Measure of Order and Disorder in the Distribution of Species in Fragmented Habitat.' *Oecologia*. 96, 3 (December): 373–382.

Axelrod, Robert, Will Mitchell, Robert E. Thomas, D. Scott Bennett, and Erhard Bruderer. 1995. 'Coalition Formation in Standard-setting Alliances.' *Management Science*, 41, 9 (September): 1493–1508.

Baker, Ted. 1995. *Stodgy Too Fast: Human Resource Practices and the Development of Inertia in Start Up Firms*. Unpublished MA thesis, Department of Sociology, University of North Carolina at Chapel Hill.

Baker, Ted. 1999. *Doing Well by Doing Good: The Bottom Line on Workplace Practices*. Washington, DC: The Economic Policy Institute.

Baker, Ted and Howard E. Aldrich. 1994. 'Human Resource Management and New Ventures.' Paper presented to the Babson College Conference on Entrepreneurship, Wellesley, MA, June.

Baker, Ted, Anne S. Miner, and Dale T. Easley. 2003. 'Improvising Firms: Bricolage, Account Giving, and Improvisational Competencies in the Founding Process.' *Research Policy*, 32: 255–276.

Baker, Wayne E. and Robert F. Faulkner. 1993. 'The Social Organization of Conspiracy in the Heavy Electrical Equipment Industry.' *American Sociological Review*, 58, 6 (December): 837–860.

Baldwin, John, Lin Bian, Richard Dupuy, and Guy Gellatly. 2000. *Failure Rates for New Canadian Firms: New Perspectives on Entry and Exit*. Ottawa, Ontario: Statistics Canada.

Barley, Stephen R. 1990. 'The Alignment of Technology and Structure through Roles and Networks.' *Administrative Science Quarterly*, 35, 1 (March): 61–103.

Barley, Stephen R., John Henry Freeman, and Ralph C. Hybels. 1992. 'Strategic Alliances in Commercial Biotechnology.' pp. 311–347 in Nitin Nohria and Robert G. Eccles (eds), *Networks and Organizations: Structure, Form, and Action*. Boston, MA: Harvard University Business School.

Barley, Stephen R. and Gideon Kunda. 2004. *Gurus, Hired Guns, and Warm Bodies: Itinerant Experts in a Knowledge Economy*. Princeton, NJ: Princeton University Press.

Barnard, Chester I. 1938. *The Functions of the Executive*. Cambridge, MA: Harvard University Press.

Barnett, William P. 1990. 'The Organizational Ecology of a Technological System.' *Administrative Science Quarterly*, 35, 1 (March): 31–50.

Barnett, William P. 1994. 'The Liability of Collective Action: Growth and Change Among Early American Telephone Companies.' pp. 337–354 in Joel A.C. Baum and Jitendra

V. Singh (eds), *Evolutionary Dynamics of Organizations*. New York: Oxford University Press.

Barnett, William P. 1995. 'Telephone Companies.' pp. 277–289 in Glenn R. Carroll and Michael T. Hannan (eds), *Organizations in Industry: Strategy, Structure, and Selection*. New York: Oxford University Press.

Barnett, William P. 1997. 'The Dynamics of Competitive Intensity.' *Administrative Science Quarterly*, 42, 1 (March): 128–160.

Barnett, William P. and Terry L. Amburgey. 1990. 'Do Larger Organizations Generate Stronger Competition?' pp. 78–102 in Jitendra V. Singh (ed.), *Organizational Evolution: New Directions*. Beverly Hills, CA: Sage.

Barnett, William P. and Glenn R. Carroll. 1987. 'Competition and Mutualism Among Early Telephone Companies.' *Administrative Science Quarterly*, 32, 3 (September): 400–421.

Barnett, William P. and Glenn R. Carroll. 1993. 'How Institutional Constraints Affected the Organization of Early U.S. Telephony.' *Journal of Law, Economics, and Organization*, 9, 1: 98–126.

Barnett, William P. and Glenn R. Carroll. 1995. 'Modeling Internal Organizational Change.' pp. 217–236 in *Annual Review of Sociology, 21*. Palo Alto, CA: Annual Reviews.

Barnett, William P., Henrich R. Greve, and Douglas Y. Park. 1994. 'An Evolutionary Model of Organizational Performance.' *Strategic Management Journal*, 15, S (Winter): 11–28.

Barnett, William P. and Michael Woywode. 2004. 'From Red Vienna to the Anschluss. Ideological Competition among Viennese Newspapers during the Rise of National Socialism.' *American Journal of Sociology*, 109, 6 (May): 1452–1499.

Barney, Jay B. 1986. 'Types of Competition and the Theory of Strategy: Toward an Integrative Framework.' *Academy of Management Review*, 11, 4 (October): 791–800.

Baron, James N., Frank R. Dobbin, and P. Devereaux Jennings. 1986. 'War and Peace: The Evolution of Modern Personnel Administration in U.S. Industry.' *American Journal of Sociology*, 92, 2 (September): 350–383.

Baron, James, Michael T. Hannan and M. Diane Burton. 1999. 'Building the Iron Cage: Determinants of Managerial Intensity in the Early Years of Organizations.' *American Sociological Review*, 64, 4 (August): 527–547.

Baron, James, Michael T. Hannan and M. Diane Burton. 2001. 'Labor Pains: Change in Organizational Models and Employee Turnover in Young, High-Tech Firms.' *American Journal of Sociology*, 106, 4 (January): 960–1012.

Baron, James N., P. Devereaux Jennings and Frank R. Dobbin. 1988. 'Mission Control? The Development of Personnel Systems in U.S. Industry.' *American Sociological Review*, 53, 4 (August): 497–514.

Baron, Robert A. and Gideon D. Markman. 2003. 'Beyond Social Capital: The Role of Entrepreneurs' Social Competence in their Financial Success.' *Journal of Business Venturing*, 18, 1 (January): 41–60.

Barron, David N. 1995. 'Credit Unions.' pp. 137–162 in Glenn R. Carroll and Michael T. Hannan (eds), *Organizations in Industry: Strategy, Structure, and Selection*. New York: Oxford University Press.

Barron, David N. 1999. 'The Structuring of Organizational Populations.' *American Sociological Review*, 64, 3 (June): 421–445.

Barron, David. N. 2001. 'Simulating the Dynamics of Organizational Populations: A Comparison of Three Models of Organizational Entry, Exit and Growth.' pp. 209–242 in Alessandro Lomi and Erik R. Larsen (eds), *Dynamics of Organizations: Computational Modeling and Organization Theories*. Menlo Park, CA: MIT Press.

Barron, David N., Elizabeth West, and Michael T. Hannan. 1994. 'A Time to Grow and a Time to Die: Growth and Mortality of Credit Unions in New York City, 1914–1990.' *American Journal of Sociology*, 100, 2 (September): 381–421.

Bartunek, Jean M. and B.L. Betters-Reed. 1987. 'The Stages of Organizational Creation.' *American Journal of Community Psychology*, 15, 3 (June): 287–303.

Bates, Timothy. 1997. 'Financing Small Business Creation: The Case of Chinese and Korean Immigrant Entrepreneurs.' *Journal of Business Venturing*, 12, 2 (March): 109–124.

Baudrillard, Jean. 1983. *Simulations*. New York: Semiotext(e).

Baum, Joel A.C. 1996. 'Organizational Ecology.' pp. 77–114 in Stewart R. Clegg, Cynthia Hardy, and Walter Nord (eds), *Handbook of Organization Studies*. London: Sage.

Baum, Joel A.C. and Terry L. Amburgey. 2002. 'Organizational Ecology.' pp. 304–326 in Joel A.C. Baum, (ed.), *Companion to Organizations*. Oxford, UK: Blackwell Publishers, Ltd.

Baum, Joel A.C. and Paul Ingram. 1998. 'Survival-enhancing Learning in the Manhattan Hotel Industry, 1898–1980.' *Management Science*, 44: 996–1016.

Baum, Joel A.C. and Heather A. Haveman. 1997. 'Love Thy Neighbor? Differentiation and Agglomeration in the Manhattan Hotel Industry, 1898–1990.' *Administrative Science Quarterly*, 42, 2 (June): 304–338.

Baum, Joel A.C., Helaine J. Korn, and Suresh B. Kotha. 1995. 'Dominant Designs and Population Dynamics in Telecommunications Services: Founding and Failure of Facsimile Transmission Service Organizations, 1965–1992.' *Social Science Research*, 24, 2 (June): 97–135.

Baum, Joel A.C. and Bill McKelvey (eds), 1999. *Variations in Organization Science: In Honor of Donald T. Campbell*. Newbury Park, CA: Sage.

Baum, Joel A.C. and Stephen J. Mezias. 1992. 'Localized Competition and Organizational Failure in the Manhattan Hotel Industry, 1989–1990.' *Administrative Science Quarterly*, 37, 4 (December): 580–604.

Baum, Joel A.C. and Christine Oliver. 1992. 'Institutional Embeddedness and the Dynamics of Organizational Populations.' *American Sociological Review*, 57, 4 (August): 540–559.

Baum, Joel A.C. and Walter W. Powell. 1995. 'Cultivating an Insititutional Ecology of Organizations: Comment on Hannan, Carroll, Dundon, and Torres.' *American Sociological Review*, 60, 4 (August): 529–538.

Baum, Joel A.C. and Jitendra V. Singh (eds). 1994a. *Evolutionary Dynamics of Organizations*. New York: Oxford University Press.

Baum, Joel A.C. and Jitendra V. Singh. 1994b. 'Organizational Niche Overlap and the Dynamics of Organizational Founding.' *Organization Science*, 5, 4 (November): 483–501

Baum, Joel A.C. and Jitendra V. Singh. 1994c. 'Organizational Niche Overlap and the Dynamics of Organizational Mortality.' *American Journal of Sociology*, 100, 2 (September): 346–380.

Bechky, Beth. 2003. 'Object Lessons: Workplace Artifacts as Representations of Occupational Jurisdiction.' *American Journal of Sociology*, 109, 3 (November): 720–752.

Becker, Gary S. 1975. *Human Capital* (2nd edition). New York: Columbia University Press.

Becker, Howard, Blanche Geer, Everett C. Hughes, and Anselm L. Strauss. 1961. *Boys in White: Student Culture in Medical School*. London: Transaction Publishers.

Becker, Markus C. 2004. 'Organizational Routines: A Review of the Literature.' *Industrial and Corporate Change*, 13, 4 (August): 643–677.

Bellah, Robert N., Richard Madsen, William M. Sullivan, Ann Swidler, and Steven Tipton. 1996. 'Individualism and the Crisis of Civic Membership.' *The Christian Century*, 113, 16 (May 8): 510–516.

Berger, Peter and Thomas Luckmann. 1966. *The Social Construction of Reality*. New York: Doubleday.

Berk, Richard A. 1983. 'An Introduction to Sample Selection Bias in Sociological Data. ' *American Sociological Review*, 48, 3 (June): 386–398.

Berry, David C. and Donald E. Broadbent, 1984. 'On The Relationship between Task Performance and Associated Verbalizable Knowledge.' *The Quarterly Journal of Experimental Psychology*, 36A, 2 (May): 209–231.

Bielby, William T. and Denise Delgado Bielby. 1999. 'Organizational Mediation of Project-Based Labor Markets.' *American Sociological Review*, 64, 1 (February): 64–85.

Biggart, Nicole W. 1988. *Charismatic Capitalism*. Chicago, IL: University of Chicago Press.

Biggart, Nicole W. and Richard Castanias, II. 1992. 'Taiwan Capital Markets: An Economic and Sociological Perspective.' Unpublished paper, Graduate School of Administration, University of California, Davis.

Blau, Judith R. 1993. *Social Contracts and Economic Markets*. New York: Plenum.

Blau, Judith R. 1995. 'Art Museums.' pp. 87–114 in Glenn R. Carroll and Michael T. Hannan (eds), *Organizations in Industry: Strategy, Structure, and Selection*. New York: Oxford University Press.

Blau, Peter M. 1955. *The Dynamics of Bureaucracy*. Chicago, IL: University of Chicago Press.

Blau, Peter M. 1964. *Exchange and Power in Social Life*. New York: John Wiley.

Blau, Peter M. 1970. 'A Formal Theory of Differentiation in Organizations.' *American Sociological Review*, 35, 2 (April): 201–218.

Boden, Deidre. 1994. *The Business of Talk: Organizations in Action*. London: Polity Press.

Bodfish, Morton. 1931. *History of Building and Loans in the United States*. Chicago, IL: United States Building and Loan League.

Boeker, Warren. 1988. 'Organizational Origins: Entrepreneurial and Environmental Imprinting at the Time of Founding.' pp. 33–51 in Glenn. R. Carroll (ed.), *Ecological Models of Organization*. Cambridge, MA: Ballinger.

Boettger, Richard D. and Charles R. Greer. 1994. 'On the Wisdom of Rewarding A While Hoping for B.' *Organization Science*, 5, 4 (November): 569–582.

Bögenhold, Dieter. 1987. *Der Gründerboom: Realität und Mythos der Neuen Selbständigkeit*. Frankfurt: Campus.

Bögenhold, Dieter and Udo H. Staber. 1990. 'Selbständigkeit als ein Reflex auf Arbeitslosigkeit? – Makrosoziologische Befunde Einer International Vergleichenden Studie.' *Kölner Zeitschrift für Soziologie und Sozialpsychologie*, 42: 265–279.

Boisot, Max and John Child. 1988. 'The Iron Law of Fiefs: Bureaucratic Failure and the Problem of Governance in the Chinese Economic Reforms.' *Administrative Science Quarterly*, 33, 4 (December): 507–527.

Bolton, Michelle K. 1993. 'Organizational Innovation and Substandard Performance: When is Necessity the Mother of Innovation?' *Organization Science*, 4, 1 (February): 57–75.

Boone, Christophe, Glenn R. Carroll, and Arjen van Witteloostuijn. 2002. 'Resource Distributions and Market Partitioning: Dutch Daily Newspapers, 1968 to 1994.' *American Sociological Review*, 67, 3 (June): 408–431.

Boone, Christophe, Woody van Olffen, Arjen van Witteloostuijn, and Bert De Brabander. 2004. 'The Genesis of Top Management Team Diversity: Selective Turnover among Top Management Teams in Dutch Newspaper Publishing: 1970–94,' *Academy of Management Journal*, 47, 5 (October): 633–656.

Botti, Hope Finney. 1995. 'Misunderstandings: A Japanese Transplant in Italy Strives for Lean Production.' *Organization*, 2, 1 (February): 55–86.

Botti, Hope Finney and Guiseppe Bonazzi. 1994. 'Asymmetric Expectations: Cross-National Coalitions in a Japanese Transplant in Italy.' Unpublished paper presented at the annual meeting of the Association for Japanese Business Studies, Vancouver, Canada, January 8th.

Boyd, Robert and Peter J. Richerson. 1985. *Culture and the Evolutionary Process*. Chicago, IL: University of Chicago Press.

Bradach, Jeffrey L. 1998. *Franchise Organizations*. Boston, MA: Harvard Business School Press.

Bradach, Jeffry L. and Robert G. Eccles. 1989. 'Price, Authority, and Trust: From Ideal Types of Plural Forms.' pp. 97–117 in *Annual Review of Sociology, 15*. Palo Alto, CA: Annual Reviews.

Breines, Wini. 1980. 'Community and Organization: The New Left and Michels' Iron Law.' *Social Problems*, 27, 4 (April): 419–429.

Brittain, Jack. 1994. 'Density-Independent Selection and Community Evolution.' pp. 355–378 in Joel A.C. Baum and Jitendra V. Singh (eds), *Evolutionary Dynamics of Organizations*. New York: Oxford University Press.

Brittain, Jack and John Henry Freeman. 1980. 'Organizational Proliferation and Density Dependent Selection.' pp. 291–338 in John R. Kimberly, Robert H. Miles, and Associates (eds), *The Organizational Life Cycle*. San Francisco, CA: Jossey-Bass.

Brittain, Jack and Douglas R. Wholey. 1988. 'Competition and Coexistence in Organizational Communities: Population Dynamics in Electronic Components Manufacturing.' pp. 195–222 in Glenn R. Carroll (ed.), *Ecological Models of Organization*. Cambridge, MA: Ballinger.

Brown, Shona L. and Kathleen M. Eisenhardt. 1997. 'The Art of Continuous Change: Linking Complexity Theory and Time-Paced Evolution in Relentlessly Shifting Organizations.' *Administrative Science Quarterly*, 42, 1 (March): 1–34.

Bruderer, Erhard and Jitendra Singh. 1996. 'Organizational Evolution, Learning and Selection: A Genetic-Algorithm-Based Model.' *Academy of Management Journal*, 39, 5 (October): 1322–1349.

Brunsson, Nils. 1985. *The Irrational Organization*. New York: John Wiley.

Brush, Candida G. 1992. 'Research on Women Business Owners: Past Trends, a New Perspective, and Future Directions.' *Entrepreneurship: Theory and Practice*, 16, 4 (Summer): 5–30.

Budros, Art. 1997. 'The New Capitalism and Organizational Rationality: The Adoption of Downsizing Programs, 1979–1994.' *Social Forces*, 76, 1 (September): 229–249.

Burgelman, Robert A. 1983. 'Corporate Entrepreneurship and Strategic Management: Insights from a Process Study.' *Management Science*, 29, 12 (December): 1349–1364.

Burgelman, Robert A. 1984. 'Designs for Corporate Entrepreneurship in Established Firms.' *California Management Review*, 26, 3 (Spring): 154–166.

Burgelman, Robert A. and Brian S. Mittman. 1994. 'An Intraorganizational Ecological Perspective on Managerial Risk Behavior, Performance, and Survival: Individual, Organizational, and Environmental Effects.' pp. 53–75 in Joel A.C. Baum and Jitendra V. Singh (eds), *Evolutionary Dynamics of Organizations*. New York: Oxford University Press.

Burkhardt, Marlene E. and Daniel J. Brass. 1990. 'Changing Patterns or Patterns of Change: The Effects of a Change in Technology on Social Network Structure and Power.' *Administrative Science Quarterly*, 35, 1 (March): 104–127.

Burns, Lawton R. and Doug R. Wholey. 1993. 'Adoption and Abandonment of Matrix Management: Effects of Organizational Characteristics and Interorganizational Networks.' *Academy of Management Journal*, 36, 1 (February): 106–138.

Burns, Tom R. and Thomas Dietz. 1992. 'Cultural Evolution: Social Role Systems, Selection, and Human Agency.' *International Sociology*, 7, 3 (September): 259–284.

Burrell, Gibson. 1988. 'Modernism, Post Modernism and Organizational Analysis 2: The Contribution of Michel Foucault.' *Organization Studies*, 9, 2 (March-April): 221–235.

Burris, Val. 1987. 'The Political Partisanship of American Business: A Study of Corporate Political Action Committees.' *American Sociological Review*, 52, 6 (December): 732–744.

Burt, Ronald S. 1982. *Toward a Structural Theory of Action*. New York: Academic Press.

Burt, Ronald S. 1983. *Corporate Profits and Cooptation: Networks of Market Constraints and Directorate Ties in the American Economy*. New York: Academic Press.

Burt, Ronald S. 1992. *Structural Holes: The Social Structure of Competition*. Cambridge, MA: Harvard University Press.

Burton, M. Diane. 1995. *The Emergence and Evolution of Employment Systems in High Technology Firms*. Unpublished Ph.D. dissertation, Stanford University.

Burton, M. Diane, Jesper B. Sorensen, and Christine Beckman. 2002. 'Coming from Good Stock: Career Histories and New Venture Formation.' *Research in the Sociology of Organizations*, 19: 229–262.

Busenitz, Lowell W. and Jay B. Barney. 1997. 'Differences Between Entrepreneurs and Managers in Large Organizations: Biases and Heuristics in Strategic Decision-Making.' *Journal of Business Venturing*, 12, 1 (January): 9–30.

Butler, John Sibley. 1991. *Entrepreneurship and Self-Help Among Black Americans*. New York: SUNY Press.

Buxton, James. 1994. 'Raising the Birthrate.' *Financial Times*, November 22.

Buzzanell, Patrice M. 1995. 'Reframing the Glass Ceiling as a Socially Constructed Process: Implications for Understanding and Change.' *Communication Monographs*, 62, 4 (December): 327–354.

Calás, Marta. 1993. 'Deconstructing 'Charismatic Leadership': Re-Reading Weber from the Darker Side.' *Leadership Quarterly*, 4, 3/4: 305–328.

Campbell, Donald T. 1969. 'Variation and Selective Retention in Socio-Cultural Evolution.' *General Systems*, 14: 69–85.

Campbell, Donald T. 1982. 'The "Blind-Variation-and-Selective-Retention" Theme.' In J.M. Broughton and D.J. Freeman-Moir (eds), *The Cognitive-Developmental Psychology of James Mark Baldwin: Current Theory and Research in Genetic Epistemology*. Norwood, NJ: Ablex Publishing.

Campbell, Donald T. 1994. 'How Individual and Face-to-Face-Group Selection Undermine Firm Selection in Organizational Evolution.' pp. 23–38 in Joel A. C. Baum and Jitendra V. Singh (eds), *Evolutionary Dynamics of Organizations*. New York: Oxford University Press.

Campbell, Karen E. 1988. 'Gender Differences in Job-Related Networks.' *Work and Occupations*, 15, 2 (May): 179–200.

Campion, Michael A., Gina J. Medsker, and A. Catherine Higgs. 1993. 'Relations Between Work Group Characteristics and Effectiveness: Implications for Designing Effective Work Groups.' *Personnel Psychology*, 46, 4 (Winter): 823–850.

Cannella, Albert A., Jr. and Michael Lubatkin. 1993. 'Succession as a Sociopolitical Process: Internal Impediments to Outsider Selection.' *Academy of Management Journal*, 36, 4 (August): 763–793.

Cannella, Albert and Wei Shen. 2001. 'So Close and Yet So Far: Promotion versus Exit for CEO Heirs Apparent.' *Academy of Management Journal*, 44, 2 (April): 252–270.

Cappelli, Peter, Laurie Bassi, Harry Katz, David Knoke, Paul Osterman, and Michael Useem. 1997. *Change at Work*. New York: Oxford University Press.

Carland, James W., Frank Hoy, W.R. Boulton, and Jo Ann C. Carland. 1984. 'Differentiating Entrepreneurs from Small Business Owners: A Conceptualization.' *Academy of Management Review*, 9, 2 (April): 354–359.

Carley, Kathleen. 1991. 'A Theory of Group Stability.' *American Sociological Review*, 56, 3 (June): 331–354.

Caronna, Carol and W. Richard Scott. 1999. 'Field and Organizational Governance Structures: The Case of Kaiser Permanente and the U.S. Healthcare Field.' pp. 68–86 in D. Brock, M. Powell, and C.R. Hinings (eds.), *Restructuring the Professional Organization: Accounting, Health and Law*. London: Routledge Press.

Carpenter, Daniel P. 2002. 'Groups, the Media, Agency Waiting Costs, and FDA Drug Approval.' *American Journal of Political Science*, 46, 3 (July): 490–505.

Carroll, Glenn R. 1985. 'Concentration and Specialization: Dynamics of Niche Width in Populations of Organizations.' *American Journal of Sociology*, 90, 6 (May): 1262–1283.

Carroll, Glenn R. 1993. 'Sociological View on Why Firms Differ.' *Strategic Management Journal*, 14, 4 (May): 237–249.

Carroll, Glenn R., Jacques Delacroix, and Jerry Goodstein. 1988. 'The Political Environment of Organizations: An Ecological View.' pp. 359–392 in Barry M. Staw and Larry L. Cummings (eds), *Research in Organizational Behavior, Vol. 10*. Greenwich, CT: JAI Press.

Carroll, Glenn R. and Michael T. Hannan. 1989. 'Density Delay and the Evolution of Organizational Populations: A Model and Five Empirical Tests.' *Administrative Science Quarterly*, 34, 3 (September): 411–430.

Carroll, Glenn R. and Michael T. Hannan. 1995. 'Automobile Manufacturers.' pp. 195–214 in Glenn R. Carroll and Michael T. Hannan (eds), *Organizations in Industry: Strategy, Structure, and Selection*. New York: Oxford University Press.

Carroll, Glenn R. and Michael T. Hannan. 2000. *The Demography of Corporations and Industries*. Princeton, NJ: Princeton University Press.

Carroll, Glenn R. and J. Richard Harrison. 1994. 'On the Historical Efficiency of Competition between Organizational Populations.' *American Journal of Sociology*, 100, 3 (November): 720–749.

Carroll, Glenn R., Heather A. Haveman, and Anand Swaminathan. 1992. 'Careers in Organizations: An Ecological Perspective.' pp. 112–144 in David Featherman, Richard Lerner, and Marion Perlmutter (eds), *Life-Span Development and Behavior, 11*. Hillsdale, NJ: Lawrence Erlbaum Associates.

Carroll, Glenn R. and Yangchung Paul Huo. 1986. 'Organizational Task and Institutional Environments in Ecological Perspective: Findings from the Local Newspaper Industry.' *American Journal of Sociology*, 91, 4 (January): 838–873.

Carroll, Glenn R. and Karl Ulrich Mayer. 1986. 'Job-Shift Patterns in the Federal Republic of Germany: The Effects of Social Class, Industrial Sector, and Organizational Size.' *American Sociological Review*, 51, 3 (June): 323–341.

Carroll, Glenn R. and Elaine Mosakowski. 1987. 'The Career Dynamics of Self-Employment.' *Administrative Science Quarterly*, 32, 4 (December): 570–589.

Carroll, Glenn R. and Anand Swaminathan. 1992. 'The Organizational Ecology of Strategic Groups in the American Brewing Industry from 1975 to 1990.' *Industrial and Corporate Changes*, 1, 1: 65–97.

Carroll, Glenn R. and James B. Wade 1991. 'Density Dependence in the Organizational Evolution of the American Brewing Industry Across Different Levels of Analysis.' *Social Science Research*, 20, 3: 271–302.

Carter, Nancy M. 1994. 'Reducing Barriers Between Genders: Differences in New Firm Start-Ups.' Center for the Study of Entrepreneurship, Marquette University. Milwaukee, WI. Unpublished paper presented at the meeting of the Academy of Management, Dallas, TX.

Carter, Nancy M., William B. Gartner, and Paul D. Reynolds. 1996. 'Exploring Startup Sequences.' *Journal of Business Venturing*, 11, 3, (May): 151–166.

Carter, Nancy M., William B. Gartner, and Paul D. Reynolds. 2004. 'Firm Founding.' pp. 311–323 in William Gartner, Kelly Shaver, Nancy Carter, and Paul Reynolds (eds), *Handbook of Entrepreneurial Dynamics: The Process of Business Creation*. Thousand Oaks, CA: Sage.

Cartwright, Dorwin and Frank Harary. 1956. 'Structural Balance: A Generalization of Heider's Theory.' *Psychological Review*, 63: 277–93.

Casciaro, Tiziana and Mikolaj J. Piskorski. 2005. 'Power Imbalance, Mutual Dependence, and Constraint Absorption: Resource Dependence Theory Revisited.' *Administrative Science Quarterly*, forthcoming.

Caves, Richard E. and Michael E. Porter. 1977. 'From Entry Barriers to Mobility Barriers.' *Quarterly Journal of Economics*, 91, 2 (May): 241–261.

Chandler, Alfred D., Jr. 1962. *Strategy and Structure*. Cambridge, MA: MIT Press.

Chandler, Alfred D., Jr. 1977. *The Visible Hand*. Cambridge, MA: Harvard University Press.

Charles, Maria and David B. Grusky. 2004. *Occupational Ghettos: The Worldwide Segregation of Women and Men*. Stanford, CA: Stanford University Press.

Cheng, Man Tsun. 1991. 'The Japanese Permanent Employment System.' *Work and Occupations*, 18, 2 (May): 148–171.

Chi, Michelene T.H., Robert Glaser, and Marshall J. Farr. 1988. *The Nature of Expertise*. Hillsdale, NJ: Erlbaum.

Child, John. 1972. 'Organization Structure, Environment, and Performance – The Role of Strategic Choice.' *Sociology*, 6, 1 (January): 1–22.

Child, John. 1973. 'Predicting and Understanding Organization Structure.' *Administrative Science Quarterly*, 18, 2 (June): 168–185.

Christensen, Soren and Jan Molin. 1995. 'Origin and Transformation of Organizations: Institutional Analysis of the Danish Red Cross.' pp. 67–90 in W. Richard Scott and Soren Christensen (eds), *The Institutional Construction of Organizations: International and Longitudinal Studies*. Newbury Park, CA: Sage.

Chura, Hillary. 1995. 'Computer Software Visionary Makes Millions.' *Raleigh News & Observer*, September 17, 4F.

Clark, Burton. 1956. 'Organizational Adaptation and Precarious Values.' *American Sociological Review*, 21, 3 (June): 327–336.

Clark, Burton. 1970. *The Distinctive College: Antioch, Reed, and Swarthmore*. Chicago: Aldine.

Clark, Burton. 1972. 'The Organizational Saga in Higher Education.' *Administrative Science Quarterly*, 17, 2 (June): 178–184.

Clark, Peter B. and James Q. Wilson. 1961. 'Incentive Systems: A Theory of Organizations.' *Administrative Science Quarterly*, 6, 3 (September): 129–166.

Clegg, Stewart. 1989. 'Radical Revisions: Power, Discipline and Organizations.' *Organization Studies*, 10, 1: 97–115.

Clegg, Stewart R. and Cynthia Hardy. 1996. 'Organizations, Organization and Organizing.' pp. 1–28 in Stewart R. Clegg, Cynthia Hardy, and Walter Nord (eds), *Handbook of Organization Studies*. London: Sage.

Clemens, Elisabeth S. 1993. 'Organizational Repertoires and Institutional Change: Women's Groups and the Transformation of U.S. Politics, 1890–1920.' *American Journal of Sociology*, 98, 4 (July): 755–798.

Clemens, Elisabeth S. 1997. *The People's Lobby: Organizational Innovation and the Rise of Interest Group Politics in the United States, 1890–1925*. Chicago: University of Chicago Press.

Cody, Martin L., and Jared M. Diamond. 1975. *Ecology and the Evolution of Communities*. Cambridge, MA: Harvard University Press.

Cohen, Michael D. and Paul Bacdayan. 1994. 'Organizational Routines are Stored as Procedural Memory: Evidence from a Laboratory Study.' *Organization Science*, 5, 4 (November): 554–568.

Cohen, Michael D. and Lee S. Sproull. 1991. 'Editors' Introduction: Special Issue on Organizational Learning.' *Organization Science*, 2, 1 (February): i–ii.

Cohen, Wesley M. and Daniel A. Levinthal. 1990. 'Absorptive Capacity: A New Perspective on Learning and Innovation.' *Administrative Science Quarterly*, 35, 1 (March): 128–152.

Cole, Robert E. 1985. 'The Macropolitics of Organizational Change: A Comparative Analysis of the Spread of Small-Group Activities.' *Administrative Science Quarterly*, 30, 4 (December): 560–585.

Coleman, Donald C. 1987. 'The Uses and Abuses of Business History.' *Business History*, 39 (April): 141–156.

Coleman, James S. 1957. *Community Conflict*. Glencoe, IL: Free Press.

Coleman, James S. 1974. *Power and the Structure of Society*. New York: W.W. Norton.

Collins, Randall. 1979. *The Credential Society*. New York: Academic Press.

Collins, Randall. 1997. 'An Asian Route to Capitalism: Religious Economy and the Origins of Self-Transforming Growth in Japan,' *American Sociological Review*, 62, 6 (December): 843–865.

Contacts Target Marketing Group. 1994. *Market Planner*. Vancouver, Canada: Contacts Target Marketing Group.

Cooper, Arnold C. and Dan Schendel. 1976. 'Strategic Responses to Technological Threats.' *Business Horizons*, 19, 1 (February): 61–69.

Corning, Peter A. 1974. 'Politics and the Evolutionary Process.' *Evolutionary Biology*, 7: 253–294.

Cortada, James W. 1993. *Before the Computer: IBM, NCR, Burroughs, and Remington Rand and the Industry They Created, 1865–1956*. Princeton, NJ: Princeton University Press.

Coser, Lewis. 1974. *Greedy Institutions: Patterns of Undivided Commitment*. New York: Free Press.

Crozier, Michel. 1964. *The Bureaucratic Phenomenon*. Chicago: University of Chicago.

Cullen, John B., Kenneth S. Anderson, and Douglas B. Baker. 1986. 'Blau's Theory of Structural Differentiation Revisited: A Theory of Structural Change or Scale?' *Academy of Management Journal*, 29, 2 (June): 203–229.

Curtis, James E., Edward G. Grabb, and Douglas E. Baer. 1992. 'Voluntary Association Membership in Fifteen Countries: A Comparative Analysis.' *American Sociological Review*, 57, 2 (April): 139–152.

Cyert, Richard M. and James G. March. 1963. *The Behavioral Theory of the Firm*. Englewood Cliffs, NJ: Prentice-Hall.

Czarniawska, Barbara. 1997. *Narrating the Organization: Dramas of Institutional Identity*. Chicago: University of Chicago Press.

Dacin, M. Tina. 1997. 'Isomorphism in Context: The Power and Prescription of Institutional Norms.' *Academy of Management Journal*, 40, 1 (February): 46–81.

Damanpour, Fariborz. 1988. 'Innovation Type, Radicalness, and the Adoption Process.' *Communication Research*, 15, 5 (October): 545–567.

Darr, Eric L, Linda Argote, and Dennis Epple. 1995. 'The Acquisition, Transfer, and Depreciation of Knowledge in Service Organizations: Productivity in Franchises.' *Management Science*, 41, 11 (November): 1750–1762.

David, Paul A. 1985. 'Clio and the Economics of QWERTY.' *American Economic Review*, 75, 2 (May): 332–337.

David, Paul A. and Shane Greenstein. 1990. 'The Economics of Compatibility Standards: An Introduction to Recent Research.' *Economics of Innovation and New Technology*, 1: 3–42.

David, Robert J. and Shin-Kap, Han 2004. 'A Systematic Assessment of the Empirical Support for Transaction Cost Economics.' *Strategic Management Journal*, 25, 1 (January): 39–58.

Davidsson, Per. 1995. 'Culture, Structure, and Regional Levels of Entrepreneurship,' *Entrepreneurship & Regional Development*, 7, 1: 41–62.

Davis, Amy E. and Howard E. Aldrich. 2004. 'Work Participation History.' pp 115–128 in William Gartner, Kelly Shaver, Nancy Carter, and Paul Reynolds (eds), *Handbook of Entrepreneurial Dynamics: The Process of Business Creation.* Thousand Oaks, CA: Sage.

Davis, Amy E., Linda Renzulli, and Howard E. Aldrich. Forthcoming. 'Mixing or Matching? The Influence of Voluntary Associations on the Occupational Diversity and Density of Business Owners' Networks,' *Work and Occupations.*

Davis, Gerald F. 1991. 'Agents Without Principles? The Spread of the Poison Pill Through the Intercorporate Network.' *Administrative Science Quarterly,* 36, 4 (December): 583–613.

Davis, Gerald F. 1994. 'The Interlock Network as a Self-Reproducing Social Structure.' Unpublished paper, Kellogg Graduate School of Management, Northwestern University, Evanston, Illinois.

Davis, Gerald F., Kristina A. Diekmann, and Catherine H. Tinsley. 1994. 'The Deinstitutionalization of Conglomerate Firms in the 1980s.' *American Sociological Review,* 59, 4 (August): 547–570.

Davis, Gerald F., Mina Yoo, and Wayne E. Baker. 2003. 'The Small World of the American Corporate Elite, 1982–2001.' *Strategic Organization,* 1, 3 (August): 301–326.

Davis, James A. 1963. 'Structural Balance, Mechanical Solidarity, and Interpersonal Relations.' *American Journal of Sociology,* 68, 4 (January): 444–62.

Dawkins, Richard. 1986. *The Blind Watchmaker.* New York: Norton.

Deeds, David L., Paul Y. Mang, and Michael L. Frandsen. 2004. 'The Influence of Firms' and Industries' Legitimacy on the Flow of Capital into High-Technology Ventures.' *Strategic Organization,* 2, 1 (February): 9–34.

Dees, J. Gregory and Jennifer A. Starr. 1992. 'Entrepreneurship Through an Ethical Lens: Dilemmas and Issues for Research and Practice.' pp. 89–116 in Donald L. Sexton and John D. Kasarda (eds), *The State of the Art of Entrepreneurship.* Boston: PWS-Kent.

Delacroix, Jacques and Glenn R. Carroll. 1983. 'Organizational Foundings: An Ecological Study of the Newspaper Industries of Argentina and Ireland.' *Administrative Science Quarterly,* 28, 2 (June): 274–291.

Delacroix, Jacques and M.V. Hayagreeva Rao. 1994. 'Externalities and Ecological Theory: Unbundling Density Dependence.' pp. 255–268 in Jitendra V. Singh and Joel A. C. Baum (eds), *Evolutionary Dynamics of Organizations.* Oxford: Oxford University Press.

Delacroix, Jacques and Michael Solt. 1988. 'Niche Formation and Foundings in the California Wine Industry, 1941–1984.' pp. 53–68 in Glenn R. Carroll (ed.), *Ecological Models of Organization.* Cambridge, MA: Ballinger.

Delacroix, Jacques and Anand Swaminathan. 1991. 'Cosmetic, Speculative, and Adaptive Organizational Change in the Wine Industry: a Longitudinal Study.' *Administrative Science Quarterly,* 36, 4 (December): 631–661.

Delacroix, Jacques, Anand Swaminathan, and Michael E. Solt. 1989. 'Density Dependence Versus Population Dynamics: An Ecological Study of Failings in the California Wine Industry.' *American Sociological Review,* 54, 2 (April): 245–262.

Delaney, Kevin J. 1992. *Strategic Bankruptcy: How Corporations and Creditors use Chapter 11 to their Advantage.* Berkeley, CA: University of California Press.

De Meza, David and Clive Southey. 1996. 'The Borrower's Curse: Optimism, Finance, and Entrepreneurship.' *The Economic Journal,* 106 (March): 375–386.

DeNardo, James. 1985. *Power in Numbers: The Political Strategy of Protest and Rebellion.* Princeton, NJ: Princeton University Press.

Dennett, Daniel C. 1995. *Darwin's Dangerous Idea: Evolution and the Meanings of Life.* London: Penguin Books.

Denrell, Jerker C. 2003. 'Vicarious Learning, Undersampling of Failure, and the Myths of Management.' *Organization Science,* 14, 3 (May/June): 277–243.

Denrell, Jerker C. and James G. March. 2001. 'Adaptation as Information Restriction: The Hot Stove Effect.' *Organization Science*, 12, 5 (September): 523–538.

DiMaggio, Paul J. 1986. 'Structural Analysis of Organizational Fields: A Blockmodel Approach.' pp. 335–370 in B. Staw and L. Cummings (eds), *Research in Organizational Behavior*. Greenwich, CN: JAI Press.

DiMaggio, Paul J. 1988. 'Interest and Agency in Institutional Theory.' pp. 3–21 in Lynne G. Zucker (ed.), *Institutional Patterns and Organizations*. Cambridge, MA: Ballinger.

DiMaggio, Paul J. 1991. 'Constructing an Organizational Field as a Professional Project: U.S. Art Museums, 1920–1940.' pp. 267–292 in Walter W. Powell and Paul J. DiMaggio (eds), *The New Institutionalism in Organizational Analysis*. Chicago, IL: University of Chicago Press.

DiMaggio, Paul J. 1994. 'The Challenge of Community Evolution.' pp. 444–450 in Joel A.C. Baum and Jitendra V. Singh (eds), *Evolutionary Dynamics of Organizations*. New York: Oxford University Press.

DiMaggio, Paul J. 1997. 'Culture and Cognition.' pp. 263–287 in *Annual Review of Sociology* 23. Palo Alto, CA: Annual Reviews.

DiMaggio, Paul (ed). 2001. *The Twenty-First Century Firm: Changing Economic Organization in International Perspective*. Princeton, NJ: Princeton University Press.

DiMaggio, Paul J. and Walter W. Powell. 1983. 'The Iron Cage Revisited: Institutional Isomorphism and Collective Rationality in Organizational Fields.' *American Sociological Review*, 48, 2 (April): 147–160.

DiMaggio, Paul J. and Walter W. Powell. 1991. 'Introduction.' pp. 1–40 in Walter W. Powell and Paul J. DiMaggio (eds), *The New Institutionalism in Organizational Analysis*. Chicago: University of Chicago Press.

Dobbin, Frank. 1994. *Forging Industrial Policy: The United States, Britain, and France in the Railway Age*. New York: Cambridge University Press.

Dobbin, Frank and Timothy J. Dowd. 1997. 'How Policy Shapes Competition: Early Railroad Foundings in Massachusetts.' *Administrative Science Quarterly*, 42, 3 (September): 501–529.

Dobbin, Frank and John R. Sutton. 1998. 'The Strength of a Weak State: The Rights Revolution and the Rise of Human Resources Management Divisions.' *American Journal of Sociology*, 104, 2 (September): 441–476.

Dobbin, Frank, John Sutton, John Meyer, and W. Richard Scott. 1993. 'Equal Opportunity Law and the Construction of Internal Labor Markets.' *American Journal of Sociology*, 99: 396–427.

Dobrev, Stanislav D. and William P. Barnett. 2005. 'Organizational Roles and Transition to Entrepreneurship.' *Academy of Management Journal*, 48, 3 (June): 433–449.

Dobrev, Stanislav D., Tai-Young Kim, and Glenn R. Carroll. 2002. 'The Evolution of Organizational Niches: U.S. Automobile Manufacturers, 1885–1981.' *Administrative Science Quarterly*, 47, 2 (June): 233–264.

Dodge, H. Robert, Sam Fullerton, and John E. Robbins. 1994. 'Stage of the Organizational Life Cycle and Competition as Mediators of Problem Perception for Small Businesses.' *Strategic Management Journal*, 15, 2 (February): 121–134.

Donaldson, Lex. 1995. *American Anti-Management Theories of Organization: A Critique of Paradigm Proliferation*. Cambridge: Cambridge University Press.

Dosi, Giovanni. 1988. 'Sources, Procedures, and Microeconomic Effects of Innovation.' *Journal of Economic Literature*, 26, 4 (December): 1120–1171.

Dow, Gregory K. 1988. 'Configurational and Coactivational Views of Organizational Structure.' *Academy of Management Review*, 13, 1 (January): 53–64.

Drake, St. Clair, and Horace R. Cayton. 1945. *Black Metropolis: A Study of Negro Life in a Northern City*. New York: Harper & Row.

Draper, Elaine A. 1991. *Risky Business: Genetic Testing and Exclusionary Practices in the Hazardous Workplace*. Cambridge: Cambridge University Press.

Duncan, Joseph W. and Douglas P. Handler. 1994. 'The Misunderstood Role of Small Business.' *Business Economics*, 29, 3 (July): 1–6.

Duneier, Mitchell. 1999. *Sidewalk*. New York: Farrar, Straus and Giroux.

Dunne, Timothy, Mark J. Roberts, and Larry Samuelson. 1988. 'Patterns of Firm Entry and Exit in U.S. Manufacturing Industries.' *Rand Journal of Economics*, 19, 4 (Winter): 495–515.

Dyck, Bruno. 1997. 'Exploring Organizational Family Trees: A Multigenerational Approach for Studying Organizational Births.' *Journal of Management Inquiry*, 6, 3 (September): 222–233.

Edelman, Lauren B. 1990. 'Legal Environments and Organizational Governance: The Expansion of Due Process in the American Workplace.' *American Journal of Sociology*, 95, 6 (May): 1401–1440.

Edelman, Lauren B. 1992. 'Legal Ambiguity and Symbolic Structures: Organizational Mediation of Civil Rights Law.' *American Journal of Sociology*, 97, 6 (May): 1531–1576.

Edelman, Lauren B. and Mark C. Suchman. 1997. 'The Legal Environment of Organizations.' pp. 479–515 in *Annual Review of Sociology, 23*. Palo Alto, CA: Annual Reviews.

Edwards, Bob and Sam Marullo. 1995. 'Organizational Mortality in a Declining Social Movement: The Demise of Peace Movement Organizations in the End of the Cold War.' *American Sociological Review*, 60, 6 (December): 908–927.

Edwards, Clive T. and Rod Samimi. 1997. 'Japanese Interfirm Networks: Exploring the Seminal Sources of Their Success.' *Journal of Management Studies*, 34, 4 (July): 489–510.

Edwards, Richards. 1979. *Contested Terrain*. New York: Basic Books.

Eisenhardt, Kathleen M. 1989a. 'Agency Theory: An Assessment and Review.' *Academy of Management Review*, 14, 1 (January): 57–74.

Eisenhardt, Kathleen M. 1989b. 'Making Fast Strategic Decisions in High-Velocity Environments.' *Academy of Management Journal*, 32, 3 (September): 543–576.

Eisenhardt, Kathleen M. and Claudia Bird Schoonhoven. 1990. 'Organizational Growth: Linking Founding Team, Strategy, Environment, and Growth Among U.S. Semiconductor Ventures, 1978–1988.' *Administrative Science Quarterly*, 35, 3 (September): 504–529.

Ekeh, Peter. 1974. *Social Exchange Theory: The Two Traditions*. Cambridge, MA: Harvard University Press.

Elder, Glen H., Jr. 1969. 'Appearance and Education in Marriage Mobility.' *American Sociological Review*, 34, 4 (August): 519–533.

Elder, Glen H., Jr. 1999. *Children of the Great Depression: Social Change in Life Experiences*. Boulder, CO: Westview Press (originally published in 1974).

Elder, Glen H. and Angela M. O'Rand. 1995. 'Adult Lives in a Changing Society.' pp. 452–475 in Karen S. Cook, Gary Alan Fine, and James S. House (eds), *Sociological Perspectives on Social Psychology*. Boston: Allyn and Bacon.

Ellison, Glenn and Edward Glaeser. 1997. 'Geographic Concentration in U.S. Manufacturing Industries: A Dartboard Approach.' *Journal of Political Economy*, 105, 5 (October): 889–927.

Emerson, Richard M. 1962. 'Power-Dependence Relations.' *American Sociological Review*, 27, 1 (February): 31–40.

Emerson, Richard M. 1972. 'Exchange Theory, Part I: A Psychological Basis for Social Exchange,' and 'Exchange Theory, Part II: Exchange Relations, Exchange Networks, and Groups as Exchange Systems.' In Joseph Berger et al. (eds), *Sociological Theories in Progress, Vol. II*. Boston: Houghton Mifflin.

Emery, Fred E. and Eric L. Trist. 1965. 'The Casual Texture of Organizational Environments.' *Human Relations*, 18: 21–32.

Emirbayer, Mustafa and Ann Mische. 1998. 'What is Agency?' *American Journal of Sociology*, 103, 4 (January): 962–1023.

Ensel, Walter M. 1979. *Sex, Social Ties, and Status Attainment*. Unpublished Ph.D. dissertation, Department of Sociology, State University of New York at Albany.

ENSR. 2004. *The European Observatory for SMEs: Highlights from the 2003 Observatory*. Luxembourg: Office for Official Publications of the European Communities.

Espeland, Wendy Nelson and Paul M. Hirsch. 1990. 'Ownership Changes Accounting Practice and the Redefinition of the Corporation.' *Accounting, Organizations, and Society*, 15, 1: 77–96.

Feagin, Joe R. and Nikitah Imani. 1994. 'Racial Barriers to African American Entrepreneurship: An Exploratory Study.' *Social Problems*, 41, 4 (November): 562–584.

Feldman, Martha S. and Brian T. Pentland. 2003. 'Reconceptualizing Organizational Routines as a Source of Flexibility and Change.' *Administrative Science Quarterly*, 48, 1 (December): 94–118.

Fernandez, Roberto M. 1997. 'Spatial Mismatch: Housing, Transportation and Employment in Regional Perspective.' In B. Weisbrod and J. Worthy (eds.), *The Urban Crisis: Linking Research to Action*. Evanston, IL: Northwestern University Press.

Fernandez, Roberto M. and Nancy Weinberg. 1997. 'Sifting and Sorting: Personal Contacts and Hiring in a Retail Bank.' *American Sociological Review*, 62, 6 (December): 883–902.

Fichman, Mark and Daniel A. Levinthal. 1991. 'Honeymoons and the Liability of Adolescence: A New Perspective on Duration Dependence in Social and Organizational Relationships.' *Academy of Management Review*, 16, 2 (April): 442–468.

Fiet, James O. 2002. *The Systematic Search for Entrepreneurial Discoveries*. Westport, CT: Quorum Books.

Fine, Gary. 1984. 'Negotiated Order and Organizational Cultures.' pp. 239–262 in *Annual Review of Sociology, 10*. Palo Alto, CA: Annual Reviews.

Fiol, C. Marlene. 1991. 'Managing Culture as a Competitive Resource: An Identity-Based View of Sustainable Competitive Advantage.' *Journal of Management*, 17, 1 (March): 191–211.

Fiol, C. Marlene, Drew Harris, and Robert House. 1999. 'Charismatic Leadership: Strategies for Effecting Social Change.' *Leadership Quarterly*, 10, 3 (Autumn): 449–482.

Fischer, Claude S. 1982. *To Dwell Among Friends*. Chicago, IL: University of Chicago Press.

Fischer, Harald and Timothy Pollock. 2004. 'Effects of Social Capital and Power on Surviving Transformational Change: The Case of Initial Public Offerings.' *Academy of Management Journal*, 47: 463–481.

Fisher, Walter R. 1985. 'The Narrative Paradigm: An Elaboration.' *Communication Monographs*, 52: 347–367.

Fiske, Susan T. and Shelley E. Taylor. 1991. *Social Cognition* (2nd edition). New York: McGraw-Hill.

Fligstein, Neil. 1985. 'The Spread of the Multi-division Form Among Large Firms, 1919–1979.' *American Sociological Review*, 50, 3 (June): 377–391.

Fligstein, Neil. 1990. *The Transformation of Corporate Control*. Cambridge, MA: Harvard.

Fligstein, Neil. 1996. 'Markets as Politics: A Political-Cultural Approach to Market Institutions.' *American Journal of Sociology*, 102, 1 (July): 1–33.

Fligstein, Neil, and Peter Brantley. 1992. 'Bank Control, Owner Control, or Organizational Dynamics: Who Controls the Large Modern Corporation?' *American Journal of Sociology*, 98, 2 (September): 280–307.

Fligstein, Neil and Robert Freeland. 1995. 'Theoretical and Comparative Perspectives on Corporate Organizations.' pp. 21–43 in *Annual Review of Sociology*, 21. Palo Alto, CA: Annual Reviews.

Fligstein, Neil and Alec S. Sweet. 2002. 'Constructing Polities and Markets: An Institutionalist Account of European Integration.' *American Journal of Sociology*, 107, 5 (March): 1206–1243.

Florida, Richard and Martin Kenney. 1991. 'The Transfer of Japanese Industrial Organization to the U.S.' *American Sociological Review*, 56, 3 (June): 381–398.

Freear, J., J.E. Sohl, and William E. Wetzel. 1995. 'Who Bankrolls Software Entrepreneurs?' *Babson College Entrepreneurship Research Conference*, London, UK: April 9–13.

Freeborn, Donald and Clyde Pope. 1994. *Promise and Performance in Managed Care.* Baltimore, MD: Johns Hopkins Press.

Freeland, Robert F. 2001. *The Struggle for Control of the Modern Corporation: Organizational Change at General Motors, 1924–1970.* Cambridge: Cambridge University Press.

Freeman, John H. 1983. 'Entrepreneurs as Organizational Products: Semiconductor Firms and Venture Capital Firms.' pp. 33–52 in Gary D. Libecap (ed.), *Advances in the Study of Entrepreneurship, Innovation, and Economic Growth, Vol. 1.* Greenwich, CT: JAI Press.

Friedkin, Noah. 1999. 'Choice Shift and Group Polarization.' *American Sociological Review*, 64, 6 (December): 856–875.

Frost, Peter J., Larry F. Moore, Meryl Reis Louis, Craig C. Lundberg, and Joanne Martin. 1985. *Organizational Culture.* Beverly Hills, CA: Sage.

Frost, Peter J., Larry F. Moore, Meryl Reis Louis, Craig C. Lundberg, and Joanne Martin. 1991. *Reframing Organizational Culture.* Newbury Park, CA: Sage.

Galaskiewicz, Joseph. 1979. 'The Structure of Community Organizational Networks.' *Social Forces*, 57, 4 (June): 1346–1364.

Galaskiewicz, Joseph. 1985. 'Interorganizational Relations.' pp. 281–304 in *Annual Review of Sociology, 11.* Palo Alto, CA: Annual Reviews.

Galvin, Tiffany L. 2002. 'Examining Institutional Change: Evidence from the Founding Dynamics of U.S. Health Care Interest Associations,' *Academy of Management Journal*, 45, 4 (August): 673–696.

Ganguly, Pom. 1982. 'Births and Deaths of Firms in the UK in 1980.' *British Business* (January 29–February 5): 3–4.

Garfinkel, Harold. 1967. *Studies in Ethnomethodology.* Englewood Cliffs, NJ: Prentice-Hall.

Gartner, William B. 1988. '"Who Is an Entrepreneur?" Is the Wrong Question.' *American Journal of Small Business*, 12, 4 (Spring): 11–32.

Gartner, William B. 2001. 'Is There an Elephant in Entrepreneurship? Blind Assumptions in Theory Development.' *Entrepreneurship Theory & Practice*, 25, 4 (June): 27–39.

Gartner, William B., Kelly G. Shaver, Nancy M. Carter, and Paul D. Reynolds (eds). 2004. *Handbook of Entrepreneurial Dynamics: The Process of Business Creation.* Thousand Oaks, CA: Sage.

Garud, Raghu, Sanjay Jain, and Arun Kumaraswamy. 2002. 'Institutional Entrepreneurship in the Sponsorship of Common Technological Standards: The Case of Sun Microsystems and Java.' *Academy of Management Journal*, 45, 1 (February): 196–214.

Garvin, David A. 1983. 'Spin-Offs and the New Firm Formation Process.' *California Management Review*, 25, 1 (Fall): 3–20.

Geddes, Barbara. 1990. 'How the Cases You Choose Affect the Answers You Get: Selection Bias in Comparative Politics.' *Political Analysis*, 2: 131–150.

Georgiou, Petro. 1973. 'The Goal Paradigm and Notes Towards a Counter Paradigm.' *Administrative Science Quarterly*, 18, 3 (September): 291–310.

Gerlach, Michael L. 1992. *Alliance Capitalism: The Social Organization of Japanese Business*. Berkeley, CA: University of California Press.

Gersick, Connie J.G. 1991. 'Revolutionary Change Theories: A Multilevel Exploration of the Punctuated Equilibrium Paradigm.' *Academy of Management Review*, 16, 1 (January): 10–36.

Gersick, Connie J.G. 1994. 'Pacing Strategic Change: The Case of a New Venture.' *Academy of Management Journal*, 37, 1 (January): 9–45.

Gersick, Connie J.G. and J. Richard Hackman. 1990. 'Habitual Routines in Task-Performing Groups.' *Organizational Behavior and Human Decision Processes*, 47, 1 (October): 65–97.

Gherardi, Slyvia. 1994. 'The Gender We Think, The Gender We Do In Our Everyday Organizational Lives.' *Human Relations*, 47, 6 (June): 591–610.

Giddens, Anthony. 1985. *The Constitution of Society*. London: Macmillan.

Gifford, Sharon. 1997. 'Limited Attention and the Role of the Venture Capitalist.' *Journal of Business Venturing*, 12, 6, (November): 459–482.

Gimeno, Javier, Timothy B. Folta, Arnold C. Cooper, and Carolyn Y. Woo. 1997. 'Survival of the Fittest? Entrepreneurial Human Capital and the Persistence of Underperforming Firms.' *Administrative Science Quarterly*, 42, 4 (December): 750–783.

Ginsberg, Ari and Joel A.C. Baum. 1994. 'Evolutionary Processes and Patterns of Core Business Change.' pp. 127–151 in Joel A.C. Baum and Jitendra V. Singh (eds), *Evolutionary Dynamics of Organizations*. New York: Oxford University Press.

Glynn, Mary Ann, Theresa K. Lant, and Frances J. Milliken. 1994. 'Mapping Learning Processes in Organizations: A Multi-Level Framework Linking Learning and Organizing.' pp. 43–83 in *Advances in Managerial Cognition and Organizational Information Processing*, Vol. 5. Greenwich, CT: JAI Press.

Goffman, Erving. 1961. *Asylums*. Garden City, NY: Doubleday, Anchor Books.

Goffman, Erwing. 1967. *Interaction Ritual*. New York: Pantheon.

Golden-Biddle, Karen and Karen D. Locke. 1997. *Composing Qualitative Research*. Thousand Oaks, CA: Sage.

Gorman, Michael and William A. Sahlman. 1989. 'What Do Venture Capitalists Do?' *Journal of Business Venturing*, 4, 4 (July): 231–248.

Gottfried, Heidi and Laurie Graham. 1993. "Constructing Difference: The Making of Gendered Subcultures in a Japanese Automobile Assembly Plant.' *Sociology*, 27, 4 (November): 611–628.

Granovetter, Mark. 1973. 'The Strength of Weak Ties.' *American Journal of Sociology*, 78, 6 (May): 1360–1380.

Granovetter, Mark. 1985. 'Economic Action and Social Structure: The Problem of Embeddedness.' *American Journal of Sociology*, 91, 3 (November): 481–510.

Granovetter, Mark. 1993. 'The Nature of Economic Relationships.' pp. 3–41 in Richard Swedberg (ed.), *Explorations in Economic Sociology*. New York: Russell Sage Foundation.

Granovetter, Mark. 1995. *Getting a Job: A Study of Contacts and Careers* (2nd Edition). Chicago: University of Chicago Press.

Granovetter, Mark and Patrick McGuire. 1998. 'The Making of an Industry: Electricity in the United States.' pp. 147–173 in Michel Callon (ed.), *The Law of Markets*. Oxford: Blackwell.

Grant, Don Sherman. 1995. 'The Political Economy of Business Failures across the American States, 1970–1985: The Impact of Reagan's New Federalism.' *American Sociological Review*, 60, 6 (December): 851–873.

Gray, Virginia and David Lowery. 1996. *The Population Ecology of Interest Representation: Lobbying Communities in the American States*. Ann Arbor, MI: University of Michigan Press.

Greiner, Larry E. 1972. 'Evolution and Revolution as Organizations Grow.' *Harvard Business Review*, 76, 3 (May): 37–46.

Greve, Henrich. 2002. 'An Ecological Theory of Spatial Evolution: Local Density Dependence in Tokyo Banking, 1894–1936.' *Social Forces*, 80, 3 (March): 847–880.

Greve, Henrich. 2003. *Organizational Learning from Performance Feedback: A Behavioral Perspective on Innovation and Change*. Cambridge, UK: Cambridge University Press.

Griffin, Larry J. 1992. 'Temporality, Events, and Explanation in Historical Sociology.' *Sociological Methods and Research*, 20, 4 (May): 403–427.

Gulati, Ranjay and Martin Gargiulo. 1999. 'Where Do Interorganizational Networks Come From?' *American Journal of Sociology*, 104, 5 (March): 1439–1493.

Guler, Isin, Mauro F. Guillén, and John Muir Macpherson. 2002. 'Global Competition, Institutions, and the Diffusion of Global Practices: The International Spread of ISO 9000 Quality Certificates.' *Administrative Science Quarterly*, 47, 2 (June): 207–232.

Gusfield, Joseph R. 1963. *Symbolic Crusade: Status Politics and the American Temperance Movement*. Urbana, IL: University of Illinois Press.

Guthrie, Doug and Louise M. Roth. 1999. 'The State, Courts, and Maternity Policies in U.S. Organizations: Specifying Institutional Mechanisms.' *American Sociological Review*, 64, 1 (February): 41–63.

Hackman, J. Richard. 1987. 'The Design of Work Teams.' pp. 314–342 in Jay W. Lorsch (ed.), *Handbook of Organizational Behavior*. Englewood Cliffs, NJ: Prentice-Hall.

Hafner, Katie and Matthew Lyon. 1996. *Where Wizards Stay Up Late: The Origins of the Internet*. New York: Simon & Schuster.

Halaby, Charles N. 1986. 'Worker Attachment and Workplace Authority.' *American Sociological Review*, 51, 5 (October): 634–649.

Halaby, Charles N. 1988. 'Action and Information in the Job Mobility Process: The Search Decision.' *American Sociological Review*, 53, 1 (February): 9–25.

Halliday, Terrence, Michael J. Powell, and Mark W. Granfors. 1987. 'Minimalist Organizations: Vital Events in State Bar Associations, 1870–1930.' *American Sociological Review*, 52, 4 (August): 456–471.

Hamilton, Barton H. 2000. 'Does Entrepreneurship Pay? An Empirical Analysis of the Returns to Self-Employment.' *Journal of Political Economy*, 108, 3 (June): 604–631.

Han, Shin-Kap. 1994. 'Mimetic Isomorphism and Its Effect on the Audit Services Market.' *Social Forces*, 73, 2 (December): 637–663.

Hannan, Michael T. 1998. 'Rethinking Age Dependence in Organizational Mortality: Logical Formalizations.' *American Journal of Sociology*, 104, 1 (July): 126–164.

Hannan, Michael T. and Glenn R. Carroll. 1992. *Dynamics of Organizational Populations: Density, Legitimation, and Competition*. New York: Oxford University Press.

Hannan, Michael T. and Glenn R. Carroll. 1995. 'An Introduction to Organizational Ecology.' pp. 17–31 in Glenn R. Carroll and Michael T. Hannan (eds), *Organizations in Industry: Strategy, Structure, and Selection*. New York: Oxford University Press.

Hannan, Michael T., Glenn R. Carroll, Elizabeth A. Dundon, and John C. Torres. 1995. 'Organizational Evolution in a Multinational Context: Entries of Automobile Manufacturers in Belgium, Britain, France, Germany, and Italy.' *American Sociological Review*, 60, 4 (August): 509–528.

Hannan, Michael T. and John Henry Freeman. 1977. 'The Population Ecology of Organizations.' *American Journal of Sociology*, 82, 5 (March): 929–964.

Hannan, Michael T. and John Henry Freeman. 1984. 'Structural Inertia and Organizational Change.' *American Sociological Review*, 49, 2 (April): 149–164.

Hannan, Michael T. and John Henry Freeman. 1986. 'Where Do Organizational Forms Come from?' *Sociological Forum*, 1, 1 (March): 50–72.

Hannan, Michael T. and John Henry Freeman. 1987. 'The Ecology of Organizational Founding: American Labor Unions, 1836–1975.' *American Journal of Sociology*, 92, 4 (January): 910–943.

Hannan, Michael T. and John Henry Freeman. 1989. *Organizational Ecology*. Cambridge, MA: Harvard University Press.

Hannan, Michael T., Laszlo Pólos, and Glenn R. Carroll. 2003. 'Cascading Organizational Change.' *Organization Science*, 14, 5 (September): 463–482.

Hanneman, Robert. 2005. 'Nestedness in Community Organizational Ecology.' Working Paper, Department of Sociology, University of California-Riverside.

Hardin, Russell. 1976. 'Stability of Statist Regimes: Industrialization and Institutionalization.' pp. 147–168 in T. Burns and W. Buckley (eds), *Power and Control*. London: Sage Publications.

Hargadon, Andrew B. and Yellowlees Douglas. 2001. 'When Innovations Meet Institutions: Edison and the Design of the Electric Light.' *Administrative Science Quarterly*, 46, 3 (September): 476–501.

Harris, Stanley G. 1994. 'Organizational Culture and Individual Sensemaking: A Schema-Based Perspective.' *Organization Science*, 5, 3 (August): 309–321.

Harrison, Bennett. 1994. 'The Italian Industrial Districts and the Crisis of the Cooperative Form: Part I.' *European Planning Studies*, 2, 1: 3–22.

Hart, Stuart and Daniel R. Denison. 1987. 'Creating New Technology-Based Organizations: A System Dynamics Model.' *Policy Studies Review*, 6, 3 (February): 512–528.

Hashimoto, Masanori and John Raisian. 1985. 'Employment Tenure and Earnings Profiles in Japan and the United States.' *American Economic Review*, 75, 4 (September): 721–735.

Hatcher, Larry and Timothy L. Ross. 1991. 'From Individual Incentives to an Organization-Wide Gainsharing Plan: Effects of Teamwork on Product Quality.' *Journal of Organizational Behavior*, 12, 3 (May): 169–183.

Haunschild, Pamela R. 1993. 'Interorganizational Imitation: The Impact of Interlocks on Corporate Acquisition Activity.' *Administrative Science Quarterly*, 38, 4 (December): 564–592.

Haveman, Heather A. 1992. 'Between a Rock and a Hard Place: Organizational Change and Performance Under Conditions of Fundamental Environmental Transformation.' *Administrative Science Quarterly*, 37, 1 (March): 48–75.

Haveman, Heather A. 1993a. 'Organizational Size and Change: Diversification in the Savings and Loan Industry after Deregulation.' *Administrative Science Quarterly*, 38, 1 (March): 20–50.

Haveman, Heather A. 1993b. 'Ghosts of Managers Past: Managerial Succession and Organizational Mortality.' *Academy of Management Journal*, 36, 4 (August): 864–881.

Haveman, Heather A. 1993c. 'Follow the Leader: Mimetic Isomorphism and Entry into New Markets.' *Administrative Science Quarterly*, 38, 4 (December): 593–627.

Haveman, Heather A. 1994. 'The Ecological Dynamics of Organizational Change: Density and Mass Dependence in Rates of Entry into New Markets.' pp. 152–166 in Joel A.C. Baum and Jitendra V. Singh (eds), *Evolutionary Dynamics of Organizations*. New York: Oxford University Press.

Haveman, Heather A. and Lisa E. Cohen. 1994. 'The Ecological Dynamics of Careers: The Impact of Organizational Founding, Dissolution, and Merger on Job Mobility.' *American Journal of Sociology*, 100, 1 (July): 104–152.

Haveman, Heather A. and Hayagreeva Rao. 1997. 'Structuring a Theory of Moral Sentiments: Institutional and Organizational Coevolution in the Early Thrift Industry.' *American Journal of Sociology*, 102, 6 (May): 1606–1651.

Hawley, Amos. 1950. *Human Ecology*. New York: Ronald.

Hawthorn, Geoffrey. 1988. 'Three Ironies in Trust.' pp. 111–126 in Diego Gambetta (ed.), *Trust: Making and Breaking Cooperative Relations*. New York: Basil Blackwell.

Hegtvedt, Karen A. and Barry Markovsky. 1994. 'Justice and Injustice.' pp. 257–280 in Karen Cook, Gary Alan Fine, and James S. House (eds), *Sociological Perspectives on Social Psychology*. Boston: Allyn and Bacon.

Henderson, Rebecca. 1993. 'Underinvestment and Incompetence as Responses to Radical Innovation: Evidence from the Photolithographic Alignment Equipment Industry,' *RAND Journal of Economics*, 24, 2 (Summer): 248–270.

Henderson, Rebecca M. and Kim B. Clark. 1990. 'Architectural Innovation: The Reconfiguration of Existing Product Technologies and the Failure of Established Firms.' *Administrative Science Quarterly*, 35, 1 (March): 9–30.

Hermalin, Benjamin E. and Michael S. Weisbach. 1998. 'Endogenously Chosen Boards of Directors and Their Monitoring of the CEO.' *American Economic Review*, 88, 1 (March): 96–118.

Hesterly, William S., Julia Liebeskind, and Todd R. Zenger. 1990. 'Organizational Economics: An Impending Revolution in Organization Theory?' *Academy of Management Review*, 15, 3 (July): 402–420.

Heydebrand, Wolf V. 1989. 'New Organizational Forms.' *Work and Occupations*, 16, 3 (August): 323–357.

Hilts, Philip J. 1992. 'Bush to Ease Rules on Products Made by Altering Genes.' *New York Times* (February 25): A1, B7.

Hinings, C.R. and Royston Greenwood. 2002. 'Disconnects and Consequences in Organization Theory.' *Administrative Science Quarterly*, 47, 3 (September): 411–421.

Hirsch, Paul M., Ray Friedman, and Mitchell P. Koza. 1990. 'Collaboration or Paradigm Shift? Caveat Emptor and the Risk of Romance with Economic Models for Strategy and Policy Research.' *Organization Science*, 1, 1: 87–97.

Hirsch, Paul M. and Michael Lounsbury. 1997. 'Ending the Family Quarrel: Toward a Reconciliation of 'Old' and 'New' Institutionalism.' *American Behavioral Scientist*, 40, 4 (February): 406–418.

Hirschman, Albert O. 1972. *Exit, Voice, and Loyalty*. Cambridge, MA: Harvard University Press.

Hochschild, Arlie. 1983. *The Managed Heart: Commercialization of Human Feeling*. Berkeley, CA: University of California Press.

Hodgson, Geoffrey M. 1993. *Economics and Evolution: Bringing Life Back into Economics*. Cambridge, MA: Polity Press.

Hodgson, Geoffrey M. 2002. 'The Legal Nature of the Firm and the Myth of the Firm-Market Hybrid.' *International Journal of the Economics of Business*, 9, 1 (February): 37–60.

Hodgson, Geoffrey M. 2004a. 'Reclaiming Habit for Institutional Economics.' *Journal of Economic Psychology*, 25, 5 (October): 651–660.

Hodgson, Geoffrey M. 2004b. 'Opportunism is Not the Only Reason Why Firms Exist: Why an Explanatory Emphasis on Opportunism may Mislead Management Strategy.' *Industrial and Corporate Change*, 13, 2 (April): 401–418.

Hodgson, Geoffrey and Thorbjørn Knudsen. 2004. 'The Firm as an Interactor: Firms as Vehicles for Habits and Routines,' *Journal of Evolutionary Economics*, 14, 3 (July): 281–307.

Hoffman, Andrew J. 2000. *Competitive Environmental Strategy: A Guide to the Changing Business Landscape.* Washington, DC: Island Press.

Horowitz, Helen Lekfowitz. 1987. *Campus Life: Undergraduate Cultures from the End of the Eighteenth Century to the Present.* New York: A.A. Knopf.

Howard, Judith. 1994. 'Social Cognition.' pp. 90–117 in Karen Cook, Gary Alan Fine, and James S. House (eds), *Sociological Perspectives on Social Psychology.* Boston, MA: Allyn and Bacon.

Howell, Jane M. and Christopher A. Higgins. 1990. 'Champions of Technological Innovation.' *Administrative Science Quarterly*, 35, 2 (June): 317–341.

Hsu, Greta and Joel M. Podolny. 2005. 'Critiquing the Critics: An Approach for the Comparative Evaluation of Critical Schemas.' *Social Science Research*, 34, 1 (March): 189–214.

Huber, George P. 1991. 'Organizational Learning: The Contributing Processes and the Literature.' *Organization Science*, 2: 88–115.

Hughes, Thomas P. 1983. *Networks of Power: Electrification in Western Society, 1880–1930.* Baltimore, MD: Johns-Hopkins Press.

Hull, David. 2001. *Science and Selection: Essays on Biological Evolution and the Philosophy of Science.* Cambridge: Cambridge University Press.

Hunt, Courtney Shelton and Howard E. Aldrich. 1998. 'The Second Ecology: The Creation and Evolution of Organizational Communities as Exemplified by the Commercialization of the World Wide Web.' pp. 267–302 in Barry Staw and Larry L. Cummings (eds), *Research in Organizational Behavior*, Vol. 20. Greenwich, CT: JAI Press.

Hutchins, Edwin. 1991. 'Organizing Work by Adaptation.' *Organization Science*, 2, 1 (February): 14–39.

Hybels, Ralph C., Alan R. Ryan, and Stephen R. Barley. 1994. 'Alliances, Legitimation, and Founding Rates in the U.S. Biotechnology Field, 1971–1989.' Unpublished paper presented at the Academy of Management meetings, Dallas, Texas.

Hylmo, Annika and Patrice Buzzanell. 2002. 'Telecommuting as Viewed Through Cultural Lenses: An Empirical Investigation of the Discourses of Utopia, Identity, and Mystery.' *Communication Monographs*, 69, 4 (December): 329–356.

Iansiti, Marco and Tarun Khanna. 1995. 'Technological Evolution, System Architecture and the Obsolescence of Firm Capabilities.' *Industrial and Corporate Change*, 4, 2: 333–362.

Ingersoll, Virginia H. and Guy B. Adams. 1992. 'The Child Is 'Father' to the Manager: Images of Organizations in U.S. Children's Literature.' *Organization Studies*, 13, 4: 497–520.

Ingram, Paul and Joel A.C. Baum. 1997. 'Opportunity and Constraint: Organizations' Learning from the Operating and Competitive Experience of Industries.' *Strategic Management Journal*, 18 (Summer Special Issue): 75–98.

Ingram, Paul and Hayagreeva Rao. 2004. 'Store Wars: The Enactment and Repeal of Anti-Chain-Store Legislation in America.' *American Journal of Sociology*, 110, 2 (September): 446–487.

Internal Revenue Service. 2003. *Corporation Income Tax Returns. A Collection of Tables, Plus the Introduction, Changes in Law and Regulations, Description of the Sample and Limitations of the Data, and the Explanation of Terms.* Sections, Table 2. SOI-2000, Corporation Income Tax Returns, September 2003. URL: http://www.irs.gov/taxstats/article/0,id=112834,00.html. Accessed September 23, 2004.

Isaac, Larry W. and Larry J. Griffin. 1989. 'Ahistoricism in Time-Series Analyses of Historical Process: Critique, Redirection, and Illustrations from U.S. Labor History.' *American Sociological Review*, 54, 6 (December): 873–890.

Jacobs, Jerry A. 2005. 'ASR's Greatest Hits.' *American Sociological Review*, 70, 1 (February): 1–3.

Jacobs, Jerry A. and Kathleen Gerson. 2004. *The Time Divide: Work, Family, and Gender Inequality*. Cambridge, MA: Harvard University Press.

Jacoby, Sanford M. 2005. *The Embedded Corporation: Corporate Governance and Employment Relations in Japan and the United States*. Princeton, NJ: Princeton University Press.

James, Erika Hayes. 2000. 'Race-Related Differences in Promotions and Support: Underlying Effects of Human and Social Capital.' *Organization Science*, 11, 5: 493–508.

Jansen, Karen J. 2004. 'From Persistence to Pursuit: A Longitudinal Examination of Momentum during the Early Stages of Strategic Change.' *Organization Science*, 15, 3 (May–June): 276–294.

Japan Small Business Research Institute. 1995. *Japan's Small Businesses: The Challenge*. Tokyo: Ministry of International Trade and Industry.

Japan Statistics Bureau. 2001. *Establishment and Enterprise Census*. Ministry of Public Management, Home Affairs, Posts and Telecommunications. URL: http://www.stat.go.jp/english/data/jigyou/kakuhou/04.htm . Accessed September 7, 2004.

Jarley, Paul, Jack Fiorito, and John T. Delaney. 1997. 'A Structural Contingency Approach to Bureaucracy and Democracy in U.S. National Unions.' *Academy of Management Journal*, 40, 4 (August): 831–861.

Johnson, Anna G. and William Foote Whyte. 1977. 'The Mondragon System of Worker Production Cooperatives.' *Industrial and Labor Relations Review*, 31, 1 (October): 18–30.

Johnson, Peter S. 1986. *New Firms: An Economic Perspective*. London: Allen and Unwin.

Jones, Candace, William S. Herterly, and Stephen P. Borgatti. 1997. 'A General Theory of Network Governance: Exchange Conditions and Social Mechanisms.' *Academy of Management Review*, 22, 4 (October): 911–945.

Jovanovic, Boyan. 1982. 'Selection and the Evolution of Industry.' *Econometrica*, 50, 3 (May): 649–670.

Jovanovic, Boyan. 1984. 'Matching, Turnover, and Unemployment.' *Journal of Political Economy*, 92, 1 (February): 108–122.

Jurik, N.C. 1998. 'Getting Away and Getting By: The Experiences of Self-Employed Homeworkers.' *Work and Occupations*, 25, 1 (February): 7–35.

Kahneman, Daniel, Paul Slovic, and Amos Tversky. 1982. *Judgment Under Uncertainty: Heuristics and Biases*. New York: Cambridge University Press.

Kalleberg, Arne L. and Larry J. Griffin. 1978. 'Positional Sources of Inequality in Job Satisfaction.' *Work and Occupations*, 5, 4 (November): 371–401.

Kalleberg, Arne L., Peter V. Marsden, Howard E. Aldrich, and James W. Cassell. 1990. 'Comparing Organizational Sampling Frames.' *Administrative Science Quarterly*, 35, 4 (December): 658–688.

Kalleberg, Arne L., Barbara F. Reskin, and Kenneth Hudson. 2000. 'Bad Jobs in America: Standard and Nonstandard Employment Relations and Job Quality in the United States.' *American Sociological Review*, 65: 256–278.

Kamm, Judith B. and Aaron J. Nurick. 1993. 'The Stages of Team Venture Formation: A Decision Making Model.' *Entrepreneurship Theory and Practice*, 17, 2 (Winter): 17–27.

Kanter, Rosabeth Moss. 1972. *Commitment and Community; Communes and Utopias in Sociological Perspective*. Cambridge: Harvard University Press.

Kanter, Rosabeth Moss. 1977. *Men and Women of the Corporation*. New York: Basic Books.

Kanter, Rosabeth Moss. 1989. *When Giants Learn to Dance: Mastering the Challenge of Strategy, Management, and Careers in the 1990s*. New York: Simon and Schuster.

Kanter, Rosabeth Moss and Barry A. Stein (eds), 1979. *Life in Organizations: Workplaces as People Experience Them.* New York : Basic Books.

Kaplan, Jerry. 1994. *Startup: A Silicon Valley Adventure.* Boston, MA: Houghton Mifflin.

Karabel, Jerome. 2005. *The Chosen: The Hidden History of Admission at Harvard, Yale and Princeton.* Boston, MA: Houghton Mifflin.

Katz, Jerome and William B. Gartner. 1988. 'Properties of Emerging Organizations.' *Academy of Management Review*, 13 (July): 429–441.

Kaufman, Herbert. 1985. *Time, Chance, and Organizations.* Chatham, NJ: Chatham House Publishers.

Kelly, Dawn. and Terry L. Amburgey. 1991. 'Organizational Inertia and Momentum: A Dynamic Model of Strategic Change.' *Academy of Management Journal*, 34, 3 (September): 591–612.

Kelly, Erin L. 2003. 'The Strange History of Employer-Sponsored Child Care: Interested Actors, Uncertainty, and the Transformation of Law in Organizational Fields.' *American Journal of Sociology*, 109, 3 (November): 606–649.

Khandekar, Rajendra and John Young. 1985. 'Selecting a Legal Structure: A Strategic Decision.' *Journal of Small Business Management*, 23: 47–55.

Kim, Phillip H., Howard E. Aldrich, and Lisa A. Keister. 2004. 'Access (Not) Denied: The Impact of Financial, Human Capital, and Cultural Capital on Becoming a Nascent Entrepreneur.' Working Paper, University of North Carolina at Chapel Hill.

Kimberly, John R. 1980. 'Initiation, Innovation, and Institutionalization in the Creation Process.' pp. 18–43 in John R. Kimberly and Robert H. Miles (eds), *The Organizational Life Cycle.* San Francisco, CA: Jossey-Bass.

Kindleberger, Charles. 1996. *Manias, Panics and Crashes: A History of Financial Crises* (3rd edition). New York: John Wiley.

Kirzner, Israel M. 1997. 'Entrepreneurial Discovery and the Competitive Market Process: An Austrian Approach.' *Journal of Economic Literature*, 35, 1 (March): 60–85.

Klein, Jim and Martha Olson. 1996. *Taken for a Ride* (Videorecording). Hohokus, NJ: New Day Films.

Kleinman, Sherryl. 1996. *Opposing Ambitions.* Chicago, MA: University of Chicago Press.

Kleinman, Sherryl and Martha Copp. 1992. *Emotions and Field Work.* Newbury Park, CA: Sage.

Klepper, Steven and Elizabeth Graddy. 1990. 'The Evolution of New Industries and the Determinants of Market Structure.' *Rand Journal of Economics*, 21, 1 (Spring): 27–44.

Knoke, David. 1990. *Organizing for Collective Action: The Political Economics of Voluntary Associations.* Hawthorne, NY: A. De Gruyter.

Kochan, Thomas A. and Paul Osterman. 1994. *The Mutual Gains Enterprise: Forging a Winning Partnership Among Labor, Management, and Government.* Boston, MA: Harvard Business School Press.

Kogut, Bruce and Gordon Walker. 2001. 'The Small World of Germany and the Durability of National Networks.' *American Sociological Review*, 66, 3 (June): 317–335.

Kono, Clifford, Donald Palmer, Roger Friedland, and Matthew Zafonte. 1998. 'Lost in Space: The Geography of Corporate Interlocking Directorates.' *American Journal of Sociology*, 103, 4 (January): 863–911.

Krackhardt, David and Robert Stern. 1988. 'Informal Networks and Organizational Crises: An Experimental Simulation.' *Social Psychology Quarterly*, 51: 123–140.

Kramer, Roderick M. and Karen Cook (eds). 2004. *Trust and Distrust in Organizations: Dilemmas and Approaches.* New York: Russell Sage Foundation.

Krecker, Margaret L. 1994. 'Work Careers and Organizational Careers: the Effects of Age and Tenure on Worker Attachment to the Employment Relation.' *Work and Occupations*, 21, 3 (August): 251–283.

Kreiner, Glen E. and Blake E. Ashforth. 2004. 'Evidence Toward an Expanded Model of Organizational Identification.' *Journal of Organizational Behavior*, 25, 1 (February): 1–27.

Kreiner, Kristian and Majken Schultz. 1993. 'Informal Collaboration in R & D. The Formation of Networks Across Organizations.' *Organization Studies*, 14, 2 (February): 189–210.

Kunda, Gideon. 1992. *Engineering Culture: Control and Commitment in a High Tech Corporation*. Philadelphia, PA: Temple University.

Land, Kenneth C., Walter R. Davis, and Judith R. Blau. 1994. 'Organizing of the Boys of Summer: The Evolution of U.S. Minor-League Baseball, 1883–1990.' *American Journal of Sociology*, 100, 3 (November): 781–813.

Langlois, Richard N. and Paul L. Robertson. 1989. 'Explaining Vertical Integration: Lessons from the American Automobile Industry.' *Journal of Economic History*, 49, 2 (June): 361–376.

Langton, John. 1979. 'Darwinism and the Behavioral Theory of Sociocultural Evolution: An Analysis.' *American Journal of Sociology*, 85, 2 (September): 288–309.

Langton, John. 1984. 'The Ecological Theory of Bureaucracy: The Case of Josiah Wedgwood and the British Pottery Industry.' *Administrative Science Quarterly*, 29, 3 (September): 330–354.

Lant, Theresa K. and Stephen J. Mezias. 1990. 'Managing Discontinuous Change: A Simulation Study of Organizational Learning and Entrepreneurship.' *Strategic Management Journal*, 11: 147–179.

Larson, Andrea. 1992. 'Network Dyads in Entrepreneurial Settings: A Study of the Governance of Exchange Processes.' *Administrative Science Quarterly*, 37, 1 (March): 76–104.

Latour, Bruno. 1993. 'Can the Sociology of Science Contribute Anything to Organizational Sociology?' Keynote address at the meeting of European Group on Organization Studies, Paris, France, July 8th.

Laumann, Edward and David Knoke. 1987. *The Organizational State: Social Change in National Policy Domains*. Madison, WI: University of Wisconsin Press.

Lave, Jean and Etienne, Wenger 1991. *Situated Learning: Legitimate Peripheral Performance*. Cambridge, MA: Cambridge University Press.

Lawless, Michael W. And Philip C. Anderson. 1996. 'Generational Technological Change: Effects of Innovation and Local Rivalry on Performance.' *Academy of Management Journal*, 39, 5 (October): 1185–1217.

Lawless, Robert M. and Elizabeth Warren. 2005. 'The Myth of the Disappearing Business Bankruptcy.' *California Law Review*, forthcoming.

Lawrence, Barbara S. 1997. 'The Black Box of Organizational Demography.' *Organization Science*, 8, 1 (January/February): 1–22.

Lawrence, Paul R. and Davis Dyer. 1983. *Renewing American Industry*. New York: Free Press.

Lawrence, Paul R. and Jay Lorsch. 1967. *Organization and Environment*. Boston, MA: Graduate School of Business Administration, Harvard University.

Lazerson, Mark H. 1988. 'Organizational Growth of Small Firms: An Outcome of Markets and Hierarchies?' *American Sociological Review*, 53, 3 (June): 330–342.

Leblebici, Hussein, Gerald Salancik, Anne Copay, and Tom King. 1991. 'Institutional Change and the Transformation of Interorganizational Fields: An Organizational History of the U.S. Radio Broadcasting Industry.' *Administrative Science Quarterly*, 36, 3 (September): 333–363.

Lerner, Miri, Candida Brush, and Robert Hisrich. 1997. 'Israeli Women Entrepreneurs: An Examination of Factors Affecting Performance.' *Journal of Business Venturing*, 12, 4 (July): 315–339.

Levie, Jonathan and Michael Hay. 1998. 'Progress or Just Proliferation? A Historical Review of Stages Models of Early Corporate Growth.' Unpublished paper, London Business School, London, England.

Levine, Adeline Gordon. 1982. *Love Canal: Science, Politics, and People*. Lexington, MA: Lexington Books.

Levine, Sol and Paul E. White. 1961. 'Exchange as a Conceptual Framework for the Study of Interorganizational Relationships.' *Administrative Science Quarterly*, 5, 1 (March): 583–610.

Levinthal, Daniel. 1991. 'Organizational Adaptation and Environmental Selection – Interrelated Processes of Change.' *Organization Science*, 2, 1 (February): 140–145.

Levitt, Barbara and James G. March. 1988. 'Organizational Learning.' pp. 319–340 in *Annual Review of Sociology, 14*. Palo Alto, CA: Annual Reviews.

Li, Bobai and Andrew Walder. 2001. 'Career Advancement as Party Patronage: Sponsored Mobility into the Chinese Administrative Elite, 1949–1996.' *American Journal of Sociology*, 106, 5 (March): 1371–1408.

Lichtenstein, Sara and Baruch Fischhoff. 1977. 'Do Those Who Know More Also Know More About How Much They Know?' *Organizational Behavior and Human Performance*, 20, 2: 159–183.

Light, Ivan. 2005. 'The Ethnic Economy.' pp. 650–677 in Neil Smelser and Richard Swedberg (eds). *The Handbook of Economic Sociology* (2nd Edition). New York: Princeton University Press and Russell Sage Foundation.

Light, Ivan and Steven Gold. 2000. *Ethnic Economies*. San Diego, CA: Academic Press.

Lin, Nan, Walter M. Ensel, and John C. Vaughn. 1981. 'Social Resources and Strength of Ties: Structural Factors in Occupational Status Attainment.' *American Sociological Review*, 46, 4 (August): 393–405.

Lincoln, James R. and Arne L. Kalleberg. 1990. *Culture, Control, and Commitment: A Study of Work Organizations and Work Attitudes in the United States and Japan*. New York: Cambridge University Press.

Lindblom, Charles Edward. 1977. *Politics and Markets: The World's Political Economic Systems*. New York: Basic Books.

Link, Albert N. and Laura L. Bauer. 1989. *Cooperative Research in U.S. Manufacturing: Assessing Policy Initiatives and Corporate Strategies*. Lexington, MA: Lexington Books.

Lippmann, Stephen. Forthcoming. 'Public Airwaves, Private Interests: Competing Visions and Ideological Capture in the Regulation of U.S. Broadcasting, 1920–1934.' In Harland Prechel (ed.), *Research in Political Sociology: Politics and the Corporation, Vol. 14*. Greenwich, CT: JAI Press.

Lipset, Seymour M., Martin A. Trow, and James S. Coleman. 1956. *Union Democracy*. Glencoe, IL: Free Press.

Litwak, Eugene and Lydia Hylton. 1962. 'Interorganizational Analysis: A Hypothesis on Coordination.' *Administrative Science Quarterly*, 6, 1 (March): 395–420.

Loasby, Brian J. 1995. 'Running a Business: An Appraisal of *Economics, Organization, and Management* by Paul Milgrom and John Roberts.' *Industrial and Corporate Change*, 4, 2: 471–489.

Lodahl, Thomas M. and Stephen M. Mitchell. 1980. 'Drift in the Development of Innovative Organizations.' pp. 184–207 in John R. Kimberly, Robert H. Miles, and Associates (eds), *The Organizational Life Cycle*. San Francisco, CA: Jossey-Bass.

Lohr, S. 1995. 'Telecommunications Giants' Joint Internet Security Quest.' *New York Times*, December 18th: C2.

Lomi, Alessandro. 1995. 'The Population and Community Ecology of Organizational Founding: Italian Co-operative Banks, 1936–1989.' *European Sociological Review*, 11, 1 (May): 75–98.

Lomi, Alessandro and Erik R. Larsen. 1998. 'Density Delay and Organizational Survival: Computational Models and Empirical Comparisons.' *Computational & Mathematical Organization Theory*, 3, 4: 219–247.

Lomi, Alessandro, Erik R. Larsen, and John H. Freeman. 2005. 'Things Change: Dynamic Resource Constraints and System-Dependent Selection in the Evolution of Organizational Populations.' *Management Science*, 51, 6 (June): 882–903.

Lorenzoni, Gianni and Andrea Lipparini. 1999. 'The Leveraging of Interfirm Relationships as a Distinctive Organizational Capability: A Longitudinal Study.' *Strategic Management Journal*, 20, 4 (April): 317–338.

Lorenzoni, Gianni and Oscar A. Ornati. 1988. 'Constellations of Firms and New Ventures.' *Journal of Business Venturing*, 3, 1 (Winter): 41–58.

Lounsbury, Michael. 2001. 'Institutional Sources of Practice Variation: Staffing College and University Recycling Programs.' *Administrative Science Quarterly*, 46, 1 (March): 29–56.

Lounsbury, Michael and Mary Ann Glynn. 2001. 'Cultural Entrepreneurship: Stories, Legitimacy, and the Acquisition of Resources.' *Strategic Management Journal*, 22, 6/7 (June/July): 545–564.

Lowstedt, Jan. 1993. 'Organizing Frameworks in Emerging Organizations: A Cognitive Approach to the Analysis of Change.' *Human Relations*, 46, 4 (April): 501–526.

Luger, Michael and Harvey Goldstein. 1991. *Technology in the Garden: Research Parks and Regional Economic Development*. Chapel Hill, NC: University of North Carolina Press.

Lynn, Leonard H. and Timothy J. McKeown. 1988. *Organizing Business: Trade Associations in America and Japan*. Washington, DC: American Enterprise Institute for Public Policy Research.

March, James G. 1981. 'Footnotes to Organizational Change.' *Administrative Science Quarterly*, 26, 2 (June): 563–577.

March, James G. 1991. 'Exploration and Exploitation in Organizational Learning.' *Organization Science*, 2, 1 (February): 71–87.

March, James G. 1994. 'The Evolution of Evolution.' pp. 39–52 in Joel A.C. Baum and Jitendra V. Singh (eds), *Evolutionary Dynamics of Organizations*. New York: Oxford University Press.

March, James G. and Johan P. Olsen. 1976. *Ambiguity and Choice in Organizations*. Bergen, Norway: Universitetsforlaget.

March, James G., Martin Schulz, and Xueguang Zhou. 2000. *The Dynamics of Rules: Change in Written Organizational Codes*. Stanford, CA: Stanford University Press.

March, James G. and Zur Shapira. 1987. 'Managerial Perspectives on Risk and Risk Taking.' *Management Science*, 33: 1404–1418.

March, James G. and H. Simon. 1958. *Organizations*. New York: Wiley.

Mare, Robert D. 1991. 'Five Decades of Educational Assortative Mating.' *American Sociological Review*, 56, 1 (February): 15–32.

Marks, Stephen R. 1977. 'Multiple Roles and Role Strain: Some Notes on Human Energy, Time and Commitment.' *American Sociological Review*, 42, 6 (December): 921–936.

Marsden, Peter V. 1987. 'Core Discussion Networks of Americans.' *American Sociological Review*, 52, 1 (February): 122–131.

Marsden, Peter V. 2005. 'Informants in Establishment Surveys,' Working Paper, Department of Sociology, Harvard University.

Marsden, Peter V. and Karen Campbell. 1984. 'Measuring Tie Strength.' *Social Forces*, 63, 2 (December): 482–501.

Martin, Joanne. 1982. 'Stories and Scripts in Organizational Settings.' pp. 225–305 in H. Hastorf and A. Isen (eds), *Cognitive Social Psychology*. New York: Elsevier–North-Holland.

Martin, Joanne. 2002. *Organizational Culture: Mapping the Terrain*. Thousand Oaks, CA: Sage.

Martin, Joanne, Martha S. Feldman, Mary Jo Hatch, and Sim B. Sitkin. 1983. 'The Uniqueness Paradox in Organizational Stories.' *Administrative Science Quarterly*, 28, 3 (September): 438–453.

Martin, Joanne and Debra Meyerson. 1988. 'Organizational Culture and the Denial, Channeling, and Acknowledgment of Ambiguity.' pp. 93–125 in Louis R. Pondy, Richard Boland, Jr., and Howard Thomas (eds), *Managing Ambiguity and Change*. London: John Wiley.

Martin, Joanne, Sim B. Sitkin, and Michael Boehm. 1985. 'Founders and the Elusiveness of a Cultural Legacy.' pp. 99–124 in Peter J. Frost, Larry F. Moore, Meryl Reis Louis, Craig C. Lundberg, and Joanne Martin (eds), *Organizational Culture*. Newbury Park, CA: Sage.

Marx, Thomas. 1976. 'Technological Change and the Theory of the Firm: The American Locomotive Industry, 1920–1955.' *Business History Review*, 50, 1: 1–24.

Massey, Doreen, Paul Quintas, and David Wield. 1992. *High Tech Fantasies: Science Parks in Society, Science and Space*. London: Routledge.

McCaffrey, David P., Sue R. Faerman, and David W. Hart. 1995. 'The Appeal and Difficulties of Participative Systems.' *Organization Science*, 6, 6 (November–December): 603–627.

McDonald, Peggy. 1991. 'The Los Angeles Olympic Organizing Committee: Developing Organizational Culture in the Short Run.' pp. 26–38 in P.J. Frost, L.F. Moore, M.R. Louis, C.C. Lundberg, and Joanne Martin (eds), *Reframing Organizational Culture*. Newbury Park, CA: Sage.

McKelvey, Bill. 1982. *Organizational Systematics*. Berkeley, CA: University of California Press.

McKelvey, Bill and Howard E. Aldrich. 1983. 'Populations, Natural Selection, and Applied Organizational Science.' *Administrative Science Quarterly*, 28, 1 (March): 101–128.

McKendrick, David G. and Glenn R. Carroll. 2001. 'On the Genesis of Organizational Forms: Evidence from the Market for Disk Arrays.' *Organization Science*, 12, 6 (November/December): 661–682.

McKendrick, David G., Jonathon Jaffee, Glenn R. Carroll, and Olga M. Khessina. 2003. 'In the Bud? Analysis of Disk Array Producers as a (possibly) Emergent Organizational Form.' *Administrative Science Quarterly*, 48, 1 (March): 60–93.

McKendrick, Neil. 1961. 'Josiah Wedgwood and Factory Discipline.' *The Historical Journal*, 4, 1: 30–55.

McPherson, J. Miller. 1983. 'The Ecology of Affiliation.' *American Sociological Review*, 48, 4 (August): 519–532.

McPherson, J. Miller. 1990. 'Evolution in Communities of Voluntary Organizations.' pp. 224–245 in Jitendra V. Singh (ed.), *Organizational Evolution: New Directions*. Newbury Park, CA: Sage.

McPherson, J. Miller, Pamela A. Popielarz, and Sonja Drobnic. 1992. 'Social Networks and Organizational Dynamics.' *American Sociological Review*, 57, 2 (April): 153–170.

McPherson, J. Miller and James R. Ranger-Moore. 1991. 'Evolution on a Dancing Landscape: Organizations and Networks in Dynamic Blau Space.' *Social Forces*, 70, 1 (September): 19–42.

McPherson, J. Miller and Thomas Rotolo. 1996. 'Testing a Dynamic Model of Social Composition: Diversity and Change in Voluntary Groups.' *American Sociological Review*, 61, 2 (April): 179–202.

McPherson, J. Miller and Lynn Smith-Lovin. 1987. 'Homophily in Voluntary Organizations: Status Distance and the Composition of Face to Face Groups.' *American Sociological Review*, 52, 3 (June): 370–379.

McPherson, J. Miller, Lynn Smith-Lovin, and James Cook. 2001. 'Birds of a Feather: Homophily in Social Networks.' pp. 415–444 in *Annual Review of Sociology, 27*. Palo Alto, CA: Annual Reviews.

Meadows, Paul. 1967. 'The Metaphors of Order: Toward a Taxonomy of Organization Theory.' pp. 77–103 in Llewellyn Gross (ed.), *Sociological Theory: Inquiries and Paradigms*. New York: Harper & Row.

Melbin, Murray. 1987. *Night as Frontier: Colonizing the World After Dark*. New York: Free Press.

Merton, Robert K. 1957. *Social Theory and Social Structure*. London: The Free Press of Glencoe.

Meyer, Alan. 1982. 'Adapting to Environmental Jolts.' *Administrative Science Quarterly*, 27, 4 (December): 515–537.

Meyer, John W. 1994. 'Rationalized Environments.' pp. 28–54 in W. Richard Scott and John W. Meyer (eds), *Institutional Environments and Organizations: Structural Complexity and Individualism*. Thousand Oaks, CA: Sage.

Meyer, John W., John Boli, and George M. Thomas. 1987. 'Ontology and Rationalization in the Western Cultural Account.' pp. 12–37 in G.M. Thomas, John W. Meyer, Franciso O. Ramirez, and J. Boli (eds), *Institutional Structure: Constituting State, Society, and the Individual*. Newbury Park, CA: Sage.

Meyer, John W. and Brian Rowan. 1977. 'Institutionalized Organizations: Formal Structure as Myth and Ceremony.' *American Journal of Sociology*, 83, 2 (September): 340–363.

Meyer, John W. and W. Richard Scott. (eds) 1983. *Organizational Environments: Ritual and Rationality*. Beverly Hills, CA: Sage.

Meyer, Marshall W. and Lynne G. Zucker. 1989. *Permanently Failing Organizations*. Newbury Park, CA: Sage.

Meyerhoefer, W. 1982. 'Hemmnisse und Hilfen für Existenz- und Unternehmens-gründungen aus der Sicht Privater und Gewerblicher Gründer.' *IFO Studien zu Handels und Dienstleistungsfragen*, 21. München: IFO-Institut für Wirtschaftsforschung e. V. München.

Meyerson, Debra E. 1990. 'Uncovering Socially Undesirable Emotions: Experiences of Ambiguity in Organizations.' *American Behavioral Scientist*, 33, 3 (January): 296–307.

Meyerson, Debra E. 1991a. '"Normal" Ambiguity? A Glimpse of an Occupational Culture.' pp. 131–144 in Peter J. Frost, Larry F. Moore, Meryl Reis Louis, Craig C. Lundberg, and Joanne Martin (eds), *Reframing Organizational Culture*. Newbury Park, CA: Sage.

Meyerson, Debra E. 1991b. 'Acknowledging and Uncovering Ambiguities in Cultures.' pp. 254–270 in P.J. Frost, L.F. Moore, M.R. Louis, C.C. Lundberg, and Joanne Martin (eds), *Reframing Organizational Culture*. Newbury Park, CA: Sage.

Meyerson, Debra E. and Joanne Martin. 1987. 'Cultural Change: An Integration of Three Different Views.' *Journal of Management Studies*, 24, 6 (November): 623–647.

Meyerson, Debra E. and Maureen A. Scully. 1995. 'Tempered Radicalism and the Politics of Ambivalence and Change.' *Organization Science*, 6, 5 (September): 585–600.

Mezias, Stephen J. and Mary Ann Glynn. 1993. 'The Three Faces of Renewal: Institution, Revolution, and Evolution.' *Strategic Management Journal*, 14, 2 (February): 77–101.

Michels, Robert. 1962. *Political Parties*. Glencoe, IL: Free Press.

Miller, C. Chet and Laura B. Cardinal. 1994. 'Strategic Planning and Firm Performance: A Synthesis of More than Two Decades of Research.' *Academy of Management Journal*, 37, 6 (December): 1649–1665.

Milliken, Frances J. and Theresa K. Lant. 1991. 'The Effect of an Organization's Recent Performance History on Strategic Persistence and Change: The Role of Managerial Interpretations.' pp. 125–152 in Paul Shrivastava, Ann Huff, and Jane Dutton (eds), *Advances in Strategic Management, Vol. 7*. Greenwich, CT: JAI Press.

Mindlin, Sergio and Howard E. Aldrich. 1975. 'Interorganizational Dependence: A Review of the Concept and a Re-examination of the Findings of the Aston Group.' *Administrative Science Quarterly*, 20, 3 (September): 382–392.

Miner, Anne S. 1987. 'Idiosyncratic Jobs in Formalized Organizations.' *Administrative Science Quarterly*, 32, 3 (September): 327–351.

Miner, Anne S. 1991. 'The Social Ecology of Jobs.' *American Sociological Review*, 56, 6 (December): 772–785.

Miner, Anne S. 1992. 'Structural Evolution Through Idiosyncratic Jobs: The Potential for Unplanned Learning.' *Organization Science*, 1, 2: 195–210.

Miner, Anne S. 1993. 'Review of *Dynamics of Organizational Populations: Density, Competition, and Legitimation.*' *Academy of Management Review*, 18, 2 (April): 355–367.

Miner, Anne S. 1994. 'Seeking Adaptive Advantage: Evolutionary Theory and Managerial Action.' pp. 76–89 in Joel A.C. Baum and Jitendra V. Singh (eds), *Evolutionary Dynamics of Organizations*. New York: Oxford University Press.

Miner, Anne S., Terry L. Amburgey, and Timothy M. Stearns. 1990. 'Interorganizational Linkages and Population Dynamics: Buffering and Transformational Shields.' *Administrative Science Quarterly*, 35, 4 (December): 689–713.

Miner, Anne S. and Suzanne E. Estler. 1985. 'Accrual Mobility: Job Mobility in Higher Education Through Responsibility Accrual.' *Journal of Higher Education*, 56, 2 (March/April): 121–143.

Miner, Anne S. and Pamela R. Haunschild. 1995. 'Population Level Learning.' pp. 115–166 in Barry Staw and Larry L. Cummings (eds), *Research in Organizational Behavior*. Greenwich, CT: JAI Press.

Miner, Anne S. and Stephen J. Mezias. 1996. 'Ugly Duckling No More: Pasts and Futures of Organizational Learning Research.' *Organization Science*, 7, 1 (January-February): 88–99.

Miner, Anne S., Sri V. Raghavan, and Pamela S. Haunschild. 1999. 'Models of Imitation and the Convergence of Routines in a Population.' In Joel A.C. Baum and Bill McKelvey (eds), *Variations in Organization Science: In Honor of Donald T. Campbell*. Newbury Park, CA: Sage.

Minkoff, Debra C. 1994. 'The Institutional Structuring of Organized Social Action, 1955–1985.' pp. 135–171 in *Research in Social Movements, Conflict, and Change*, Vol. 17. Greenwich, CT: JAI Press.

Minkoff, Debra C. 1997. 'The Sequencing of Social Movements.' *American Sociological Review*, 62, 5 (October): 779–799.

Mintzberg, Henry. 1974. *The Nature of Managerial Work*. New York: Harper & Row.

Mitchell, Will. 1992. 'Are More Good Things Better: Or Will Technical and Market Capabilities Conflict When a Firm Expands?' *Industrial and Corporate Change*, 1, 2: 327–346.

Miyashita, Kenichi and David W. Russell. 1994. *Keiretsu: Inside the Hidden Japanese Conglomerates*. New York: McGraw-Hill.

Mizruchi, Mark S. 1982. *The American Corporate Network, 1904–1974*. Beverly Hills, CA : Sage Publications.

Mizruchi, Mark S. 1992. *The Structure of Corporate Political Action: Interfirm Relations and Their Consequences*. Cambridge, MA: Harvard University Press.

Mizruchi, Mark S. 1996. 'What Do Interlocks Do? An Analysis, Critique, and Assessment of Research on Interlocking Directorates.' pp. 271–298 in *Annual Review of Sociology, 22*. Palo Alto, CA: Annual Reviews.

Mizruchi, Mark S. and Lisa C. Fein. 1999. 'The Social Construction of Organizational Knowledge: A Study of the Uses of Coercive, Mimetic, and Normative Isomorphism.' *Administrative Science Quarterly*, 44, 4 (December): 653–683.

Mizruchi, Mark S. and Joseph Galaskiewicz. 1993. 'Networks of Interorganizational Relations.' *Sociological Methods & Research*, 22, 1 (August): 46–70.

Moe, Terry N. 1980. *The Organization of Interests*. Chicago, IL: University of Chicago Press.

Moffat, Michael. 1989. *Coming of Age in New Jersey: College in American Culture*. New Brunswick, NJ: Rutgers University Press.

Mokyr, Joel. 1992. 'Technological Inertia in Economic History.' *The Journal of Economic History*, 52, 2 (June): 325–338.

Molotch, Harvey, William Freudenberg, and Krista E. Paulsen. 2000. 'History Repeats Itself, but How? City Character, Urban Tradition, and the Accomplishment of Place.' *American Sociological Review*, 65, 6 (December): 791–823.

Montgomery, Cynthia A. 1995. 'Of Diamonds and Rust: A New Look at Resources.' pp. 251–268 in Cynthia A. Montgomery (ed.), *Resource-Based and Evolutionary Theories of the Firm: Towards a Synthesis*. Boston, MA: Kluwer Academic Publishers.

Moore, Dorothy P. and E. Holly Buttner. 1997. *Women Entrepreneurs: Moving Beyond the Glass Ceiling*. Thousand Oaks, CA: Sage.

Moorman, Christine and Anne S. Miner. 1998. 'Organizational Improvisation and Organizational Memory.' *Academy of Management Review*, 23, 4 (October): 698–723.

Morgenson, Gretchen. 1998. 'Stock Options are not a Free Lunch.' *Forbes*, May 18th.

Morrison, Elizabeth Wolfe. 1994. 'Role Definitions and Organizational Citizenship Behavior: The Importance of the Employee's Perspective.' *Academy of Management Journal*, 37, 6 (December): 1543–1567.

Moskowitz, Tobias J., and Annette Vissing-Jorgensen 2002. 'The Returns to Entrepreneurial Investment: A Private Equity Premium Puzzle?' *American Economic Review*, 92, 4 (September): 745–778.

Mouw, Ted. 2002. 'Are Black Workers Missing the Connection? The Effect of Spatial Distance and Employee Referrals on Interfirm Racial Segregation.' *Demography*, 39, 3 (August): 507–528.

Mouw, Ted. 2003. 'Social Capital and Finding a Job: Do Contacts Matter?' *American Sociological Review*, 68, 6 (December): 868–898.

Moynihan, Daniel Patrick. (ed.) 1970. *Toward a National Urban Policy*. New York: Basic Books.

Müller, Walter and Richard Arum. 2004. 'Self-Employment Dynamics in Advanced Economies.' pp. 1–35 in *The Reemergence of Self-Employment: A Comparative Study of the Self-Employment Dynamics and Social Inequality*, edited by R. Arum, and W. Müller. Princeton, NJ: Princeton University Press.

Mumby, Dennis K. and Linda L. Putnam. 1992. 'The Politics of Emotion: A Feminist Reading of Bounded Rationality.' *Academy of Management Review*, 17, 3 (July): 465–486.

Murmann, Johann P. 2003. *Knowledge and Competitive Advantage: The Coevolution of Firms, Technology, and National Institutions*. Cambridge: Cambridge University Press.

Nash, Nathaniel C. 1994. 'Germany Shuns Biotechnology.' *New York Times* (December 21): C1, C5.

Nelson, Reed E. 1993. 'Authority, Organization, and Societal Context in Multinational Churches,' *Administrative Science Quarterly*, 38, 4 (December): 653–682.

Nelson, Richard R. 1994. 'Evolutionary Theorizing About Economic Change.' pp. 108–136 in Neil Smelser and Richard Swedberg (eds), *The Handbook of Economic Sociology*. Princeton, NJ: Princeton University Press.

Nelson, Richard R. and Sidney Winter. 1982. *An Evolutionary Theory of Economic Change*. Cambridge, MA: Belknap.

Nemeth, Charlan Jeanne. 1995. 'Dissent As Driving Cognition, Attitudes, and Judgment.' *Journal of Social Cognition*, 13: 273–291.

Nemeth, Charlan Jeanne. 1997. 'Managing Innovation: When Less Is More.' *California Management Review*, 40, 1 (Fall): 59–74.

Nickerson, Jack A. and Brian S. Silverman. 2003. 'Why Firms Want to Organize Efficiently and What Keeps Them from Doing So: Inappropriate Governance, Performance, and Adaptation in a Deregulated Industry.' *Administrative Science Quarterly*, 48, 3 (September): 433–466.

Nilakant, V. and Hayagreeva Rao. 1994. 'Agency Theory and Uncertainty in Organizations: An Evaluation.' *Organization Studies*, 15, 5: 649–672.

Nonaka, Ikujiro and Hirotaka Takeuchi. 1995. *The Knowledge-Creating Company: How Japanese Companies Create the Dynamics of Innovation*. New York: Oxford University Press.

O'Reilly, Charles A. III and John Anderson. 1982. 'Personnel/Human Resource Management in the US: Some Evidence of Change.' *Journal of Irish Business and Administrative Research*, 4, 2 (October): 3–12.

O'Reilly, Charles A. III, David F. Caldwell, and William P. Barnett. 1989. 'Work Group Demography, Social Integration, and Turnover.' *Administrative Science Quarterly*, 34, 1 (March): 21–37.

Oliver, Christine. 1991. 'Strategic Responses to Institutional Processes. ' *Academy of Management Review*, 16, 1 (January): 145–179.

Oliver, Christine. 1992. 'The Antecedents of Deinstitutionalization.' *Organization Studies*, 13, 4: 563–588.

Olson, Mancur, Jr. 1965. *The Logic of Collective Action*. Cambridge, MA: Harvard University Press.

Orlikowski, Wanda J. and JoAnne Yates. 1994. 'Genre Repertoire: The Structuring of Communicative Practices in Organizations.' *Administrative Science Quarterly*, 39, 4 (December): 541–574.

Orloff, Ann Shola and Theda Skocpol. 1984. 'Why Not Equal Protection? Explaining the Politics of Public Social Spending in Britain, 1900–1911, and the United States, 1880s–1920.' *American Sociological Review*, 49, 6 (December): 726–750.

Osterman, Paul. 1994. 'How Common is Workplace Transformation and How Can We Explain Who Does It?' *Industrial and Labor Relations Review*, 47, 2 (January): 173–188.

Ouchi, William. 1981. *Theory Z*. Reading, MA: Addison-Wesley.

Palmer, Donald A., P. Devereaux Jennings, and Xueguang Zhou. 1993. 'Late Adoption of the Multidivisional Form by Large U.S. Corporations: Institutional, Political, and Economic Accounts.' *Administrative Science Quarterly*, 38, 1 (March): 100–131.

Pananond, Pavida. 1995. 'Comparison of Conglomeration Development: The American and the Thai Experiences.' Unpublished paper, Kenan-Flagler School of Business. University of North Carolina, Chapel Hill.

Park, Robert E., Ernest W. Burgess, and Roderick D. McKenzie, (eds). 1925. *The City*. Chicago, IL: University of Chicago Press.

Parsons, Talcott. 1956. 'Suggestions for a Sociological Approach to the Theory of Organization, I and II.' *Administrative Science Quarterly*, 1, (1/2): 63–85, 225–239.

Péli, Gábor and Bart Nootebaum. 1999. 'Market Partitioning and the Geometry of the Resource Space.' *American Journal of Sociology*, 104, 4 (January): 1132–1153.

Peng, Yusheng. 2004. 'Kinship Networks and Entrepreneurs in China's Transitional Economy.' *American Journal of Sociology*, 109, 5 (March): 1045–1074.

Pennings, Johannes M., Harry Barkema, and Sytse Douma. 1994. 'Organizational Learning and Diversification.' *Academy of Management Journal*, 37, 3 (June): 608–640.

Pentland, Brian T. 1992. 'Organizing Moves in Software Support Hot Lines.' *Administrative Science Quarterly*, 37, 4 (December): 527–548.

Pentland, Brian T. and Henry H. Rueter. 1994. 'Organizational Routines as Grammars of Action.' *Administrative Science Quarterly*, 39, 3 (September): 484–510.

Perrow, Charles. 1985. 'Comment on Langton.' *Administrative Science Quarterly*, 30, 2 (June): 278–283.

Perrow, Charles. 1986. *Complex Organizations* (3rd edition). New York: Scott Foresman.

Perrow, Charles. 1991. 'A Society of Organizations.' *Theory and Society*, 20, 6 (December): 725–762.

Perrow, Charles. 1999. *Normal Accidents: Living With High-Risk Technologies* (2nd edition). Princeton, NJ: Princeton University Press.

Pettigrew, Andrew. 1979. 'On Studying Organizational Culture.' *Administrative Science Quarterly*, 24, 4 (December): 570–581.

Pfeffer, Jeffrey. 1972. 'Merger as a Response to Organizational Interdependence.' *Administrative Science Quarterly*, 17, 2 (June): 218–228.

Pfeffer, Jeffrey. 1983. 'Organizational Demography.' pp. 299–357 in Barry M. Staw and Larry L. Cummings (eds), *Research in Organizational Behavior, Vol. 5*. Greenwich, CT: JAI Press.

Pfeffer, Jeffrey. 1993. 'Barriers to the Advance of Organizational Science: Paradigm Development as a Dependent Variable.' *Academy of Management Review*, 18, 4 (October): 599–620.

Pfeffer, Jeffrey. 2003. 'Introduction to the Classic Edition.' *The External Control of Organizations: A Resource Dependence Perspective* (2nd Edition). Stanford, CA: Stanford University Press.

Pfeffer, Jeffrey and James N. Baron. 1988. 'Recent Trends in the Structuring of Employment.' pp. 257–303 in Barry M. Staw and Larry L. Cummings (eds), *Research in Organizational Behavior, Vol. 10*. Greenwich, CT: JAI Press.

Pfeffer, Jeffrey and Gerald Salancik. 1978. *The External Control of Organizations*. New York : Harper & Row.

Phillips, Almarin. 1960. 'A Theory of Interfirm Organization.' *Quarterly Journal of Economics*, 74, 4 (November): 602–613.

Phillips, Damon J. 2002. 'A Geneological Approach to Organizational Life Chances: The Parent–Progeny Transfer among Silicon Valley Law Firms, 1946–1996.' *Administrative Science Quarterly*, 47, 3 (September): 474–506.

Picot, A., U.D. Laub, and D. Schneider. 1989. *Innovative Unternehmensgründungen: Eine Ökonomisch-Empirische Analyse*. Berlin, Heidelberg, New York: Springer.

Pierce, Jennifer L. 1995. *Gender Trials: Emotional Lives in Contemporary Law Firms*. Berkeley, CA: University of California.

Podolny, Joel M. 1994. 'Market Uncertainty and the Social Character of Economic Exchange.' *Administrative Science Quarterly*, 39, 3 (September): 458–483.

Podolny, Joel M. 2001. 'Networks as the Pipes and Prisms of the Market.' *American Journal of Sociology*, 107, 1 (July): 33–60.

Podolny, Joel M., Toby E. Stuart, and Michael T. Hannan. 1996. 'Networks, Knowledge, and Niches: Competition in the Worldwide Semiconductor Industry, 1984–1991.' *American Journal of Sociology*, 102, 3 (November): 659–689.

Polanyi, Karl. 1944. *The Great Transformation*. New York: Farrar and Rinehart.

Polanyi, Michael. 1966. *The Tacit Dimension*. London: Routledge & Kegan Paul.

Pólos, László, Michael T. Hannan, and Glenn R. Carroll. 2002. 'Foundations of a Theory of Social Forms.' *Industrial and Corporate Change*, 11, 1 (February): 85–115.

Popielarz, Pamela A. and J. Miller McPherson. 1995. 'On the Edge or In Between: Niche Position, Niche Overlap, and the Duration of Voluntary Association Memberships.' *American Journal of Sociology*, 101, 3 (November): 698–720.

Porac, Joseph F., Howard Thomas, and C. Baden-Fuller. 1989. 'Competitive Groups as Cognitive Communities: The Case of Scottish Knitwear Manufacturers.' *Journal of Management Studies*, 1989, 26, 4 (July): 397–416.

Porter, Michael and Rebecca E. Wayland. 1995. 'Global Competition and the Localization of Competitive Advantage.' pp. 63–105 in *Advances in Strategic Management, Vol. 11.* Greenwich, CT: JAI Press.

Portes, Alejandro and Julia Sensenbrenner. 1993. 'Embeddedness and Immigration: Notes on the Social Determinants of Economic Action.' *American Journal of Sociology*, 98, 6 (May): 1320–50.

Portes, Alejandro, William Haller, and Luis E. Guarnizo. 2002. 'Transnational Entrepreneurs: An Alternative Form of Immigrant Economic Adaptation.' *American Sociological Review*, 67, 2 (April): 278–298.

Powell, Walter W. 1990. 'Neither Market nor Hierarchy: Network Forms of Organization.' pp. 295–336 in Barry M. Staw and Larry L. Cummings (eds), *Research in Organizational Behavior, Vol. 12.* Greenwich, CT: JAI Press.

Powell, Walter W. 2001. 'The Capitalist Firm in the Twenty-First Century: Emerging Patterns in Western Enterprise.' pp. 33–68 in Paul DiMaggio (ed.) *The Twenty-First Century Firm: Changing Economic Organization in International Perspective.* Princeton: Princeton University Press.

Powell, Walter W., Kenneth W. Koput, and Larel Smith-Doerr. 1996. 'Interorganizational Collaboration and the Locus of Innovation: Networks of Learning in Biotechnology.' *Administrative Science Quarterly*, 41, 1 (March): 116–145.

PriceWaterhouseCoopers, Thomson Venture Economics and the National Venture Capital Association. 2004. *MoneyTree™ Survey.* http://www.nvca.org/ffax. html accessed September 7, 2004.

Pugh, Derek S., David J. Hickson, C. Robert Hinings, and C. Turner. 1968. 'Dimensions of Organizational Structure.' *Administrative Science Quarterly*, 13, 1 (June): 65–105.

Rafaeli, Anat and Robert I. Sutton. 1990. 'Busy Stores and Demanding Customers: How Do They Affect the Display of Positive Emotion?' *Academy of Management Journal*, 33, 3 (September): 623–637.

Rafaeli, Anat, and Robert I. Sutton. 1991. 'Emotional Contrast Strategies as Means of Social Influence: Lessons from Criminal Interrogators and Bill Collectors.' *Academy of Management Journal*, 34, 4 (December): 749–775.

Ranger-Moore, James R. 1997. 'Bigger May Be Better, But Is Older Wiser?: Organizational Age and Size in the New York Life Insurance Industry.' *American Sociological Review*, 62, 6 (December): 903–920.

Ranger-Moore, James, Jane Banaszak-Holl, and Michael T. Hannan. 1991. 'Density-Dependent Dynamics in Regulated Industries: Founding Rates of Banks and Life Insurance Companies.' *Administrative Science Quarterly*, 36, 1 (March): 36–65.

Rao, Hayagreeva. 1989. *The Social Organization of Trust: The Growth and Decline of Organizational Forms in the Savings and Loan Industry; 1960–1987.* Unpublished Ph.D. dissertation, Weatherhead School of Management, Case Western Reserve University, Cleveland, OH.

Rao, Hayagreeva. 1994. 'The Social Construction of Reputation: Certification Contests, Legitimation, and the Survival of Organizations in the American Automobile Industry: 1895–1912.' *Strategic Management Journal*, 15 (Winter): 29–44.

Rao, Hayagreeva. 1998. 'Caveat Emptor: The Construction of Nonprofit Consumer Watchdog Organizations.' *American Journal of Sociology*, 103, 4 (January): 912–961.

Rao, Hayagreeva and Robert Drazin. 2002. 'Overcoming Resource Constraints on Product Innovation by Recruiting Talent from Rivals: A Study of the Mutual Fund Industry; 1986–1994.' *Academy of Management Journal*, 45, 3 (June): 491–508.

Rao, Hayagreeva, Philippe Monin, and Rodolphe Durand. 2003. 'Institutional Change in Toque Ville: Nouvelle Cuisine as an Identity Movement in French Gastronomy.' *American Journal of Sociology*, 108, 4 (January): 795–843.

Rao, Hayagreeva and Kumar Sivakumar. 1999. 'Institutional Sources of Boundary-Spanning Structures: The Establishment of Investor Relations Departments in the *Fortune 500* Industrials.' *Organization Science*, 10, 1 (January–February): 27–42.

Reed, Michael I. 1988. 'The Problem of Human Agency in Organizational Analysis.' *Organization Studies*, 9, 1: 33–46.

Reed, Michael I. 1996. 'Organizational Theorizing: a Historically Contested Terrain.' pp. 31–56 in Stewart R. Clegg, Cynthia Hardy, and Walter R. Nord (eds), *Handbook of Organization Studies*. London: Sage.

Reed, Richard and Robert J. DeFillippi. 1990. 'Causal Ambiguity, Barriers to Imitation, and Sustainable Competitive Advantage.' *Academy of Management Review*, 15, 1 (January): 88–102.

Reiss, Albert J., Jr. 1992. 'The Trained Incapacities of Sociologists.' pp. 297–315 in Terrence Halliday and Morris Janowitz (eds), *Sociology and Its Publics*. Chicago, MA: University of Chicago Press.

Renzulli, Linda. 1998. *Small Business Owners, Their Networks, and the Process of Resource Acquisition*. Unpublished MA thesis, Department of Sociology, University of North Carolina at Chapel Hill.

Renzulli, Linda A. 2005. 'Organizational Environments and the Emergence of Charter Schools in the U.S.' *Sociology of Education* 78 (1): 1–26.

Renzulli, Linda, Howard E. Aldrich, and James Moody. 2000. 'Family Matters: Gender, Networks, and Entrepreneurial Outcomes.' *Social Forces*, 79, 2 (December): 523–546.

Renzulli, Linda A. and Vincent Roscigno. Forthcoming. 'Charter School Policy, Implementation, and Diffusion in the United States' *Sociology of Education*.

Reynolds, Paul D. 2000. 'National Study of U.S. Business Start-Ups: Background and Methodology.' pp. 153–228 in Jerome Katz (ed), *Advances in Entrepreneurship, Firm Emergence and Growth, Vol. 4*. Stamford, CT: JAI.

Reynolds, Paul D. 2005. *Entrepreneurship in the U.S.* Miami, FL: Eugenio Pino and Family Global Entrepreneurship Center, College of Business Administration, Florida International University.

Reynolds, Paul D. and Sammis B. White. 1997. *The Entrepreneurial Process: Economic Growth, Men, Women, and Minorities*. Westport, CN: Quorum Books.

Richtel, Matt. 1998. 'Venture Capital Is Alive, and Plentiful.' *New York Times*, April 6, C3.

Ridgeway, Cecilia, Elizabeth Boyle, Kathy Kuipers, and Dawn Robinson. 1998. 'How Do Status Beliefs Develop? The Role of Resources and Interaction.' *American Sociological Review*, 63: 331–350.

Ritzer, George. 2006. 'Metatheory.' In G. Ritzer (ed.), *Blackwell Encyclopedia of Sociology*. London: Blackwell (forthcoming).

Robins, James A. 1987. 'Organizational Economics: Notes on the Use of Transaction-Cost Theory in the Study of Organizations.' *Administrative Science Quarterly*, 32, 1 (March): 68–86.

Rogers, Everett M. 1995. *Diffusion of Innovations*. New York: The Free Press.

Romanelli, Elaine. 1989. 'Organization Birth and Population Variety: A Community Perspective on Origins.' pp. 211–246 in Barry M. Staw and Larry L. Cummings (eds), *Research in Organizational Behavior, Vol. 11*. Greenwich, CT: JAI Press.

Romanelli, Elaine. 1999. 'Blind (But Not Unconditioned) Variation: Problems of Copying in Socio-cultural Evolution.' pp. 79–91 in Joel A.C. Baum and Bill McKelvey (eds), *Variations in Organization Science: In Honor of Donald T. Campbell*. Newbury Park, CA: Sage.

Roscigno, Vincent J. and William F. Danaher. 2004. *The Voice of Southern Labor: Radio, Music, and Textile Strikes, 1929–1934*. Minneapolis, MN: University of Minnesota Press.

Rosenfeld, Rachel A. 1992. 'Job Mobility and Career Processes.' pp. 39–61 in *Annual Review of Sociology, 18*. Palo Alto, CA: Annual Reviews.

Rosenkopf, Lori and Michael L. Tushman. 1994. 'The Coevolution of Technology and Organization.' pp. 403–424 in Joel A.C. Baum and Jitendra V. Singh (eds), *Evolutionary Dynamics of Organizations*. New York: Oxford University Press.

Rosenwein, Robert E. and Donald T. Campbell. 1992. 'Mobilization to Achieve Collective Action and Democratic Majority/Plurality Amplification.' *Journal of Social Issues*, 48, 2: 125–138.

Rothschild, Joyce. 1979. 'The Collectivist Organization: An Alternative to Rational-Bureaucratic Models.' *American Sociological Review*, 44, 4 (August): 509–527.

Rothschild, Joyce and Raymond Russell. 1986. 'Alternatives to Bureaucracy: Democratic Participation in the Economy.' pp. 307–328 in *Annual Review of Sociology, 12*. Palo Alto, CA: Annual Reviews.

Rothschild, Joyce and J. Allen Whitt. 1986. 'Worker-owners as an Emergent Class: Effects of Cooperative Work on Job Satisfaction, Alienation and Stress.' *Economic and Industrial Democracy*, 7, 3 (August): 297–317.

Roughgarden, Jonathan. 1983. 'The Theory of Coevolution.' pp. 33–64 in D.J. Futuyama and M. Slatkin (eds), *Coevolution*. Sunderland, MA: Sinauer.

Roy, Donald. 1953. 'Work Satisfaction and Social Reward in Quota Achievement.' *American Sociological Review*, 18, 5 (October): 507–514.

Roy, William G. 1981. 'The Process of Bureaucratization in the U.S. State Department and the Vesting of Economic Interests, 1886–1905.' *Administrative Science Quarterly*, 26, 3 (September): 419–433.

Roy, William G. 1997. *Socializing Capital: The Rise of the Large Industrial Corporation in America*. Princeton, NJ: Princeton University Press.

Ruef, Martin. 1997. 'Assessing Organizational Fitness on a Dynamic Landscape: An Empirical Test of the Relative Inertia Hypothesis.' *Strategic Management Journal*, 18, 11 (December): 837–853.

Ruef, Martin. 2000. 'The Emergence of Organizational Forms: A Community Ecology Approach.' *American Journal of Sociology*, 106, 3 (November): 658–714.

Ruef, Martin. 2002a. 'Strong Ties, Weak Ties and Islands: Structural and Cultural Predictors of Organizational Innovation.' *Industrial and Corporate Change*, 11, 3 (June): 427–449.

Ruef, Martin. 2002b. 'Unpacking the Liability of Aging: Toward a Socially-Embedded Account of Organizational Disbanding.' *Research in the Sociology of Organizations*, 19: 195–229.

Ruef, Martin. 2004. 'The Demise of an Organizational Form: Emancipation and Plantation Agriculture in the American South, 1860–1880.' *American Journal of Sociology*, 109, 6 (May): 1365–1410.

Ruef, Martin. 2005. 'Origins of Organizations: The Entrepreneurial Process.' pp. 63–101 in Lisa Keister (ed), *Research in the Sociology of Work, Vol 15*. Greenwich, CT: JAI Press.

Ruef, Martin. 2006. 'Boom and Bust: The Effect of Entrepreneurial Inertia on Organizational Populations.' In Joel Baum, Stanislav Dobrev, and Arjen van Witteloostuijn (eds), *Advances in Strategic Management, Vol. 23*. forthcoming.

Ruef, Martin, Howard E. Aldrich, and Nancy M. Carter. 2003. 'The Structure of Founding Teams: Homophily, Strong Ties, and Isolation among U.S. Entrepreneurs.' *American Sociological Review*, 68, 2 (April): 195–222.

Ruef, Martin and W. Richard Scott. 1998. 'A Multidimensional Model of Organizational Legitimacy: Hospital Survival in Changing Institutional Environments.' *Administrative Science Quarterly*, 43, 4 (December): 877–904.

Russell, Raymond. 1985. *Sharing Ownership in the Workplace*. Albany, NY: State University of New York Press.

Ryan, Allan, John H. Freeman, and Ralph C. Hybels. 1995. 'Biotechnology Firms.' pp. 332–357 in Glenn R. Carroll and Michael T. Hannan (eds), *Organizations in Industry: Strategy, Structure, and Selection*. New York: Oxford University Press.

Rynes, Sara L. and Alison E. Barber. 1990. 'Applicant Attraction Strategies: An Organizational Perspective.' *Academy of Management Review*, 15, 2 (April): 286–310.

Rytina, Steve and David Morgan. 1982. 'The Arithmetic of Social Relations: The Interplay of Category and Network.' *American Journal of Sociology*, 88, 1 (July): 88–113.

Saloner, Garth, Andrea Shepard and Joel Podolny. 2001. *Strategic Management*. New York: John Wiley.

Sanders, Jimy and Victor Nee. 1996. 'Immigrant Self-Employment: The Family as Social Capital and the Value of Human Capital.' *American Sociological Review*, 61, 2 (April): 231–249.

Saxenian, Annalee. 1994. *Regional Advantage: Culture and Competition in Silicon Valley and Route 128*. Cambridge, MA: Harvard.

Schein, Edgar. 1990. 'Organizational Culture.' *American Psychologist*, 45, 2 (February): 109–119.

Schlozman, Kay Lehman and John T. Tierney. 1986. *Organized Interests and American Democracy*. New York: Harper & Row.

Schmitz, Christopher J. 1993. *The Growth of Big Business in the United States and Western Europe, 1850–1939*. London: Macmillan.

Schmookler, Jacob. 1962. 'Economic Sources of Inventive Activity.' *Journal of Economic History*, 22, 1 (March): 1–20.

Schneiberg, Marc and Tim Bartley. 2001. 'Regulating American Industries: Markets, Politics, and the Institutional Determinants of Fire Insurance Regulation.' *American Journal of Sociology*, 107, 1 (July): 101–146.

Schofer, Evan, and Marion Fourcade-Gourinchas. 2001. 'The Structural Contexts of Civic Engagement: Voluntary Association Membership in Comparative Perspective.' *American Sociological Review* 66, 6 (December): 806–828.

Schön, Donald. 1983. *The Reflective Practitioner: How Professionals Think in Action*. New York: Basic Books.

Schumpeter, Joseph. 1934. *The Theory of Economic Development* (originally published in 1911). Cambridge, MA: Harvard University Press.

Schwartz, Evan I. 1997. *Webonomics: Nine Essential Principles for Growing your Business on the World Wide Web*. New York: Broadway Books.

Scott, Allen J. 1988. *From the Division of Labor to Urban Form*. Berkeley, CA: University of California Press.

Scott, John Finley. 1965. 'The American College Sorority: Its Role in Class and Ethnic Endogamy.' *American Sociological Review*, 30, 4 (August): 514–527.

Scott, W. Richard. 1987. 'The Adolescence of Institutional Theory.' *Administrative Science Quarterly*, 32, 4 (December): 493–511.

Scott, W. Richard. 2001. *Institutions and Organizations* (2nd edition). Thousand Oaks, CA: Sage.

Scott, W. Richard. 2003. *Organizations: Rational, Natural, and Open Systems* (5th edition). Englewood Cliffs, NJ: Prentice-Hall.

Scott, W. Richard and Bruce L. Black. 1986. *The Organization of Mental Health Services: Societal and Community Systems*. Beverly Hill, CA: Sage.

Scott, W. Richard and John W. Meyer. 1983. 'The Organization of Societal Sectors.' pp. 129–154 in John W. Meyer and W. Richard Scott (eds), *Organizational Environments: Ritual and Rationality*. Beverly Hills, CA: Sage.

Scott, W. Richard, Martin Ruef, Peter Mendel, and Carol Caronna, 2000. *Institutional Change and Healthcare Organizations: From Professional Dominance to Managed Care*. Chicago, MA: University of Chicago Press.

Seabrook, John. 1994. 'Rocking in Shangri-La.' *The New Yorker* (October10): 64–78.

Selznick, Philip. 1949. *TVA and the Grass Roots*. Berkeley, CA: University of California.

Selznick, Philip. 1957. *Leadership in Administration*. New York: Harper & Row.

Selznick, Philip. 1969. *Law, Society, and Industrial Justice*. New York: Russell Sage Foundation.

Shaiken, Harley. 1986. *Work Transformed: Automation and Labor in the Computer Age*. Lexington, MA: Lexington Books.

Shan, Weijian, Jitendra V. Singh, and Terry L. Amburgey. 1991. 'Modeling the Creation of New Biotechnology Firms, 1973–1987.' pp. 78–82 in Jerry L. Wall and Lawrence R. Jauch (eds), *Academy of Management Best Papers Proceedings 1991*. Miami Beach, FL: Academy of Management.

Shane, Scott and S. Venkataraman. 2000. 'The Promise of Entrepreneurship as a Field of Research.' *Academy of Management Review*, 25, 1 (January): 217–226.

Shelanski, Howard A. and Peter G. Klein. 1995. 'Empirical Research in Transaction Costs Economics: A Review and Assessment.' *Journal of Law, Economics, and Organization*, 11, 2 (October): 335–361.

Shirai, Taishiro. 1983. *Contemporary Industrial Relations in Japan*. Madison, WI: University of Wisconsin Press.

Silverman, Brian S., Jack A. Nickerson, and John Freeman. 1997. 'Profitability, Transactional Alignment, and Organizational Mortality in the U.S. Trucking Industry.' *Strategic Management Journal*, 18, Special Issue (Summer): S31–52.

Simon, Herbert A. 1955. 'A Behavioral Model of Rational Choice.' *Quarterly Journal of Economics*, 69, 1 (February): 99–118.

Simon, Herbert A. 1962. 'The Architecture of Complexity.' *Proceedings of the American Philosophical Society*, 106, 6 (December): 467–482.

Simon, Herbert A. 1997. *Administrative Behavior* (4th edition). New York: Free Press.

Simon, Herbert A. 1985. 'Human Nature in Politics: The Dialogue of Psychology with Political Science.' *American Political Science Review*, 79, 2 (June): 293–304.

Simon, Herbert A. and Charles P. Bonini. 1958. 'On the Size Distribution of Business Firms.' *American Economic Review*, 48, 4 (September): 607–617.

Simons, Tal and Paul Ingram. 2004. 'An Ecology of Ideology: Theory and Evidence from Four Populations.' *Industrial and Corporate Change*, 13, 1 (February): 33–59.

Sine, Wesley D., Heather A. Haveman, and Pamela S. Tolbert. 2005. 'Risky Business? Entrepreneurship in the New Independent-Power Sector.' *Administrative Science Quarterly*, 50, 2 (June): 200–232.

Sitkin, Sim B. 1992. 'Learning Through Failure: The Strategy of Small Losses.' pp. 231–266 in Barry Staw and Larry L. Cummings (eds), *Research in Organizational Behavior, Vol. 14*. Greenwich, CT: JAI Press.

Sitkin, Sim B., Kathleen M. Sutcliffe, and Roger G. Schroeder. 1994. 'Distinguishing Control from Learning in Total Quality Management: A Contingency Perspective.' *Academy of Management Review*, 19, 3 (June): 537–564.

Skocpol, Theda. 1979. *States and Social Revolutions*. Cambridge: Cambridge University Press.

Small Business Administration. 1982. *The State of Small Business: A Report of the President*. Washington, DC: U.S. Government Printing Office.

Small Business Administration, Office of Advocacy. 1997. *Characteristics of Small Business Employees and Owners, 1997*. http://www.sba.gov/advo/stats/ ch_em97.pdf.

Small Business Administration. 1998. *Mergers and Acquisitions in the United States, 1990–1994*. Office of Advocacy, Small Business Administration, Washington, DC: U.S. Government Printing Office.

Small Business Administration, Office of Advocacy. 2002. *The Small Business Economy: A Report to the President*. Washington DC: United States Government Printing Office.

Small Business Administration, Office of Advocacy. 2003. *Small Business Economic Indicators for 2003*. Washington, DC: United States Government Printing Office.

Small Business Administration, Office of Advocacy. 2004. *The Small Business Economy: A Report to the President*. Washington, DC: United States Government Printing Office.

Small Business Administration Website FAQ. 2004. http://app1.sba.gov/faqs/faqIndexAll.cfm?areaid=24 Accessed September 8, 2004.

Smelser, Neil J. 1998. 'The Rational and the Ambivalent in the Social Sciences.' *American Sociological Review*, 63, 1 (February): 1–15.

Smigel, Erwin O. 1964. *The Wall Street Lawyer: Professional Organization Man?* New York: Free Press.

Smircich, Linda. 1983. 'Concepts of Culture and Organizational Analysis.' *Administrative Science Quarterly*, 28, 3 (September): 339–358.

Smith, Eric L. 1996. 'The Great Black Hope.' *Black Enterprise*, 26, 7 (February): 150.

Snow, David A., E. Burke Rochford, Jr, Steven K. Worden, and Robert D. Benford. 1986. 'Frame Alignment Processes, Micromobilization, and Movement Participation.' *American Sociological Review*, 51, 4 (August): 464–481.

Sober, Elliot. 1984. *The Nature of Selection: Evolutionary Theory in Philosophical Focus*. Cambridge, MA: MIT Press.

Sørensen, Jesper. 2004. 'Recruitment-Based Competition Between Industries: A Community Ecology.' *Industrial and Corporate Change*, 13, 1 (February): 149–170.

Sorenson, Olav and Pino G. Audia. 2000. 'The Social Structure of Entrepreneurial Activity: Geographic Concentration of Footwear Production in the United States, 1940–1989.' *American Journal of Sociology*, 106, 2 (September): 424–462.

Spencer, Herbert. 1898. *The Principles of Sociology*. New York: D. Appleton.

Spilling, Olav R. 1996. *SMB-typologi: Om klassifisering av små og mellomstore bedrifter.* [SME typologies: on classifying small and medium-sized firms]. Oslo, Norway: Norwegian School of Management, Discussion Paper 6/1996.

Spilling, Olav R. and Torjus Bolkesjø. 1998. 'Motivation for Entrepreneurship in Different Contexts: Some Reflections on Entrepreneurial Typologies.' Paper presented at the 10th Nordic Conference on Small Business Research, Växjö, Sweden.

Staber, Udo H. 1993 'Worker Cooperatives and the Business Cycle: Are Cooperatives the Answer to Unemployment?' *American Journal of Economics and Sociology*, 52: 129–143.

Staber, Udo H. 1998. 'Inter-Firm Cooperation and Competition in Industrial Districts,' *Organization Studies*, 19, 4: 701–724.

Staber, Udo H. and Howard E. Aldrich. 1983. 'Trade Association Stability and Public Policy.' pp. 163–178 in Richard Hall and Robert Quinn (eds), *Organization Theory and Public Policy*. Beverly Hills, CA: Sage.

Staber, Udo H. and Basu Sharma. 1994. 'The Employment Regimes of Industrial Districts: Promises, Myths, and Realities.' *Industrielle Beziehungen: Zeitschrift für Arbeit, Organisation und Management*, 1, 4: 321–346.

Staggenborg, Suzanne. 1989. 'Stability and Innovation in the Women's Movement: A Comparison of Two Movement Organizations.' *Social Problems*, 36, 1 (February): 75–92.

Starbuck, William H. 1965. 'Organizational Growth and Development.' pp. 451–533 in James G. March (ed.), *Handbook of Organizations*. Chicago, IL: Rand McNally.

Stark, David. 2001. 'Ambiguous Assets for Uncertain Environments: Heterarchy in Postsocialist Firms.' pp. 69–104 in Paul DiMaggio (ed.), *The Twenty-First Century Firm: Changing Economic Organization in International Perspective*. Princeton, NJ: Princeton University Press.

Starr, Paul. 2004. *The Creation of the Media: Political Origins of Modern Communications*. New York: Basic Books.

Stasser, Garold. L.A. Taylor, and C. Hanna. 1989. 'Information Sampling in Structured and Unstructured Discussion of Three- and Six-person Groups.' *Journal of Personality and Social Psychology*, 57, 1 (January): 67–78.

Staw, Barry M., Lance E. Sandelands, and Jane E. Dutton. 1981. 'Threat-rigidity Effects in Organizational Behavior: A Multilevel Analysis.' *Administrative Science Quarterly*, 26, 4 (December): 501–524.

Stearns, Linda Brewster and Kenneth D. Allan. 1996. 'Economic Behavior in Institutional Environments: The Corporate Merger Wave of the 1980s.' *American Sociological Review*, 61, 4 (August): 699–718.

Stephens, Evelyne Huber and John D. Stephens. 1982. 'The Labor Movement, Political Power, and Workers' Participation in Western Europe.' pp. 215–249 in *Political Power and Social Theory, Vol. 3*. Greenwich, CT: JAI Press.

Stevenson, Howard H. and David E. Gumpert. 1985. 'The Heart of Entrepreneurship.' *Harvard Business Review*, 63, 2 (March-April): 85–94.

Stevenson, William B. and Jean M. Bartunek. 1996. 'Power, Interaction, Position, and the Generation of Cultural Agreement in Organizations.' *Human Relations*, 49, 1 (January): 75–105.

Stewart, Alex. 1989. *Team Entrepreneurship*. Newbury Park, CA: Sage.

Stewart, Alex. 1998. *The Ethnographer's Method*. Thousand Oaks, CA: Sage.

Stewman, Shelby. 1988. 'Organizational Demography.' pp. 173–202 in *Annual Review of Sociology, 14*. Palo Alto, CA: Annual Reviews.

Stinchcombe, Arthur L. 1964. *Rebellion in a High School*. Chicago, MA: Quadrangle.

Stinchcombe, Arthur L. 1965. 'Social Structure and Organizations.' pp. 142–193 in James G. March (ed.), *Handbook of Organizations*. Chicago, MA: Rand McNally.

Stoeberl, Philipp A., Gerald E. Parker, and Seong-Jong Joo. 1998. 'Relationship between Organizational Change and Failure in the Wine Industry: An Event History Analysis.' *Journal of Management Studies*, 35, 4 (July): 537–555.

Storey, David J. 1994. *Understanding the Small Business Sector*. London: Routledge.

Story, Ronald. 1980. *The Forging of an Aristocracy: Harvard and the Boston Upper Class, 1800–1870*. Middletown, CT: Wesleyan University Press.

Strang, David and Michael W. Macy. 2001. 'In Search of Excellence: Fads, Success Stories, and Adaptive Emulation.' *American Journal of Sociology*, 107, 1 (July): 147–182.

Strang, David and Sara Soule. 1998. 'Diffusion in Organizations and Social Movements: From Hybrid Corn to Poison Pills.' pp. 265–290 in *Annual Review of Sociology, 24*. Palo Alto, CA: Annual Reviews.

Stratton, Kay. 1989. 'Union Democracy in the International Typographers Union: Thiry Years Later.' *Journal of Labor Research*, 10, 1 (Winter): 119–135.

Strauss, Anselm L. 1978. *Negotiations*. San Francisco, CA: Jossey-Bass.

Stuart, Toby E., Ha Hoang, and Ralph C. Hybels. 1999. 'Interorganizational Endorsements and the Performance of Entrepreneurial Ventures.' *Administrative Science Quarterly*, 44, 2 (June): 315–349.

Studer-Ellis, Erich. 1995a. 'Springboards to Mortarboards: Massachusetts, New York, and Pennsylvania Women's College Foundings.' *Social Forces*, 73, 3 (March): 1051–1070.

Studer-Ellis, Erich. 1995b. 'Women's College Evolution, 1960 to 1990: Coed or Not Coed?' Paper presented at the Annual Meeting of American Sociological Association, Washington, DC, August 1995.

Suchman, Mark C. 1995. 'Managing Legitimacy: Strategic and Institutional Approaches.' *Academy of Management Review*, 20, 3 (July): 571–610.

Suchman, Mark C. and Mia L. Cahill. 1996. 'The Hired-Gun as Facilitator: The Case of Lawyers in Silicon Valley.' *Law and Social Inquiry*, 21, 3: 679–712.

Suchman, Mark C. and Lauren B. Edelman. 1996. 'Legal Rational Myths: The New Institutionalism and the Law and Society tradition.' *Law and Social Inquiry*, 21, 4 (Fall): 903–941.

Suchman, Mark C., Daniel J. Steward, and Clifford A. Westfall. 2001. 'The Legal Environment of Entrepreneurship: Observations on the Legitimation of Venture Finance in Silicon Valley.' pp. 349–382 in Claudia B. Schoonhoven and Elaine Romanelli (eds), *The Entrepreneurship Dynamic: Origins of Entrepreneurship and the Evolution of Industries*. Stanford, CA: Stanford University Press.

Suehiro, Akira. 1992. 'Capitalist Development in Postwar Thailand: Commercial Bankers, Industrial Elites, and Agribusiness Groups.' pp. 35–63 in Ruth McVey (ed.), *Southeast Asian Capitalists*. Ithaca, NY: Cornell University Press.

Sutton, John. 1997. 'Gibrat's Legacy.' *Journal of Economic Literature*, 35, 1 (March): 40–59.

Sutton, Robert I. and Anita L. Callahan. 1987. 'The Stigma of Bankruptcy: Spoiled Organizational Image and Its Management.' *Academy of Management Journal*, 30, 3 (September): 405–436.

Swaminathan, Anand. 1995. 'The Proliferation of Specialist Organizations in the American Wine Industry: 1941–1990.' *Administrative Science Quarterly*, 40, 4 (December): 653–680.

Swaminathan, Anand. 1996. 'Environmental Conditions at Founding and Organizational Mortality: A Trial-by-Fire Model.' *Academy of Management Journal*, 39, 5 (October): 1350–1377.

Swanson, Guy E. 1971. 'An Organizational Analysis of Collectivities.' *American Sociological Review*, 36, 4 (August): 607–623.

Swidler, Ann. 1986. 'Culture in Action: Symbols and Strategies.' *American Sociological Review*, 51, 2 (April): 273–286.

Teece, David J. 1986. 'Profiting from Technological Innovation: Implications for Integration, Collaboration, Licensing, and Public Policy,' *Research Policy*, 15, 6 (December): 285–305.

Teece, David J. 1987. 'Profiting from Technological Innovation: Implications for Integration, Collaboration, Licensing, and Public Policy.' pp. 185–219 in David Teece (ed.), *The Competitive Challenge*. Cambridge, MA: Ballinger.

Thaler, Richard H. 1994. *The Winner's Curse: Paradoxes and Anomalies of Economic Life*. Princeton, NJ: Princeton University Press.

Thomas, Joe and Ricky Griffin. 1983. 'The Social Information Processing Model of Task Design: A Review of the Literature.' *Academy of Management Review*, 8, 4 (October): 672–682.

Thomas, Robert. 1994. *What Machines Can't Do*. Cambridge, MA: MIT Press.

Thompson, James D. 1967. *Organizations in Action*. New York: McGraw-Hill.

Thornton, Patricia H. 2004. *Markets from Culture: Institutional Logics and Organizational Decisions in Higher Education Publishing*. Stanford, CA: Stanford University Press.

Tiedens, Larissa Z. 2001. 'Anger and Advancement versus Sadness and Subjugation: The Effect of Negative Emotion Expressions on Social Status Conferral.' *Journal of Personality and Social Psychology*, 80, 1 (January): 86–94.

Tilly, Charles. 1998. *Durable Inequality*. Berkeley, CA: University of California Press.

Tolbert, Pamela and Lynne Zucker. 1996. 'The Institutionalization of Institutional Theory.' pp. 175–190 in Stewart R. Clegg, Cynthia Hardy, and Walter Nord (eds), *Handbook of Organization Studies*. Thousand Oaks, CA: Sage.

Torres, David L. 1988. 'Professionalism, Variation, and Organizational Survival.' *American Sociological Review*, 53, 3 (June): 380–394.

Tracy, Sarah J. 2004. 'Dialectic, Contradiction, or Double Bind? Analyzing and Theorizing Employee Reactions to Organizational Tension.' *Journal of Applied Communication Research*, 32, 2 (May): 119–146.

Trethewey, Angela. 1999. 'Isn't It Ironic: Using Irony to Explore the Contradictions of Organizational Life.' *Western Journal of Communication*, 63, 2 (Spring) : 140–167.

Trevino, Linda Klebe, and Bart Victor. 1992. 'Peer Reporting of Unethical Behavior.' *Academy of Management Journal*, 35, 1 (March): 38–64.

Trice, Harrison M. and Janice M. Beyer. 1991. 'Cultural Leadership in Organizations.' *Organization Science*, 2, 2 (May): 149–169.

Tripsas, Mary. 1997. 'Unraveling the Process of Creative Destruction: Complementary Assets and Incumbent Survival in the Typesetter Industry,' *Strategic Management Journal*, 18 (Special Summer Issue): 119–142.

Tucker, David J., Jitendra V. Singh, and Agnes Meinhard. 1990. 'Organizational Form, Population Dynamics, and Institutional Change: The Founding Pattern of Voluntary Organizations.' *Academy of Management Journal*, 33, 1 (March): 151–178.

Tushman, Michael L. and Philip Anderson. 1986. 'Technological Discontinuities and Organizational Environments.' *Administrative Science Quarterly*, 31, 3 (September): 439–465.

Tushman, Michael L. and Johann P. Murmann. 1998. 'Dominant Designs, Innovations Types, and Organizational Outcomes.' pp. 231–266 in B.M. Staw and Larry L. Cummings (eds), *Research in Organizational Behavior, Vol 20*. Greenwich, CT: JAI Press.

Tversky, Amos and Daniel Kahneman. 1981. 'The Framing of Decisions and the Psychology of Choice.' *Science*, 211, 4481 (January): 453–458.

Tyre, Marcie J. and Wanda J. Orlikowski. 1994. 'Windows of Opportunity: Temporal Patterns of Technological Adaptation in Organizations.' *Organization Science*, 5 (February): 98–118.

UCLA. 2003. 'College Student Survey.' Higher Education Research Institute, Graduate School of Education and Information Studies, University of California, Los Angeles.

U.S. Department of Commerce. 1992. Bureau of the Census. *Characteristics of Business Owners*. CB092–1. U.S. Government Printing Office.

U.S. Department of Commerce. 2001. *1997 Economic Census: Survey of Women-Owned Business*. U.S. Government Printing Office.

U.S. Department of Commerce. 2003. *Statistical Abstract of the United States: The National Data Book*. U.S. Government Printing Office.

U.S. Department of Labor, Bureau of Labor Statistics. 2003. *Work Experience of the Population in 2002*. USDL 03–911.

U.S. Department of Labor. 2004a. 'Employee Tenure Summary.' Washington, DC: United States Department of Labor Report # 04–1829, September 29th.

U.S. Department of Labor. 2004b. 'Number of Jobs Held, Labor Market Activity, and Earnings Growth Among Younger Baby Boomers.' Washington, DC: United States Department of Labor Report # 04–1678, August 25th.

U.S. Department of Labor. 2004c. 'National Compensation Survey: Employee Benefits in Private Industry in the United States, March 2003.' Washington, DC: United States Department of Labor Report # 04–02, April.

Uzzi, Brian. 1997. 'Social Structure and Competition in Interfirm Networks: The Paradox Of Embeddedness.' *Administrative Science Quarterly*, 42, 1 (March): 35–67.

Uzzi, Brian. and Jarrett Spiro. 2005. 'Collaboration and Creativity: Big Differences from Small World Networks.' *American Journal of Sociology*, 111, 2 (September).

Vallas, Steven P. 2003. 'Why Teamwork Fails: Obstacles to Workplace Change in Four Manufacturing Plants.' *American Sociological Review*, 68, 2 (April): 223–250.

Van de Ven, Andrew H. and Raghu Garud. 1994. 'The Coevolution of Technical and Institutional Events in the Development of an Innovation.' pp. 425–443 in Joel A.C. Baum and Jitendra V. Singh (eds), *Evolutionary Dynamics of Organizations*. New York: Oxford University Press.

Van de Ven, Andrew H. and Marshall Scott Poole. 1995. 'Explaining Development and Change in Organizations.' *Academy of Management Review*, 20, 3 (July): 510–540.

Van Maanen, John and Stephen Barley. 1984. 'Occupational Communities: Culture and Control in Organizations.' pp. 287–365 in Barry M. Staw and Larry L. Cummings (eds), *Research in Organizational Behavior, Vol 6*. Greenwich, CT: JAI Press.

Van Maanen, John and Gideon Kunda. 1989. 'Real Feelings: Emotional Expression and Organizational Culture.' pp. 43–103 in Barry M. Staw and Larry L. Cummings (eds), *Research in Organizational Behavior, Vol. 11*. Greenwich, CT: JAI Press.

Van Osnabrugge, Mark. 1998. *Comparison of Business Angels and Venture Capitalists: Financiers of Entrepreneurial Firms*. London: British Venture Capital Association.

Vanderpool, Tim. 2001. 'Lawsuits Tee Off Against Male Golf Clubs.' *Christian Science Monitor*, 93, 225 (October 16th): 3.

Vaughan, Diane. 1983. *Controlling Unlawful Organizational Behavior: Social Structure and Corporate Misconduct*. Chicago, MA: University of Chicago Press.

Vaughan, Diane. 1996. *The Challenger Launch Decision: Risky Technology, Culture, and Deviance at NASA*. Chicago, MA: University of Chicago Press.

Vaughan, Diane. 1999. 'The Dark Side of Organizations: Mistake, Misconduct, and Disaster.' pp. 271–305 in *Annual Review of Sociology, 25*. Palo Alto, CA: Annual Reviews.

Vogel, David. 1973. 'The Power of Business in America: A Reappraisal.' *British Journal of Political Science*, 13, 1 (January): 19–43.

Voss, Kim and Rachel Sherman. 2000. 'Breaking the Iron Law of Oligarchy: Union Revitalization in the American Labor Movement.' *American Journal of Sociology*, 106, 2 (September): 303–349.

Wade, James B. 1995. 'Dynamics of Organizational Communities and Technological Bandwagons: An Empirical Investigation of Community Evolution in the Microprocessor Market.' *Strategic Management Journal*, 16, (Summer Special Issue): 111–133.

Wade, James B. 1996. 'A Community Level Analysis of Sources and Rates of Technological Variation in the Microprocessor Market.' *Academy of Management Journal*, 39, 5 (October): 1218–1244.

Wade, James B., Anand Swaminathan, and Michael Scott Saxon. 1998. 'Normative and Resource Flow Consequences of Local Regulations in the American Brewing Industry, 1845–1918.' *Administrative Science Quarterly*, 43, (4): 905–935.

Wageman, Ruth. 1995. 'Interdependence and Group Effectiveness.' *Administrative Science Quarterly*, 40, 1 (March): 145–180.

Wagner, John A. III. 1995. 'Studies of Individualism–Collectivism: Effects on Cooperation in Groups.' *Academy of Management Journal*, 38, 1 (February): 152–172.

Waldinger, Roger and Michael I. Lichter. 2003. *How the Other Half Works*. Berkeley, CA: University of California Press.

Wallerstein, Immanuel. 1974. *The Modern World-System: Capitalist Agriculture and the Origins of the European World-Economy in the Sixteenth Century*. New York: Academic Press.

Walsh, James P. 1988. 'Top Management Turnover Following Mergers and Acquisitions.' *Strategic Management Journal*, 9, 2 (March/April): 173–183.

Walsh, James P. 1995. 'Managerial and Organizational Cognition: Notes from a Trip Down Memory Lane.' *Organization Science*, 6, 3 (May/June): 280–321.

Walsh, James P. and Gerardo Rivera Ungson. 1991. 'Organizational Memory.' *Academy of Management Review*, 16, 1 (January): 57–91.

Warren, Roland Leslie, Stephen M. Rose, and Ann F. Bergunder. 1974. *The Structure of Urban Reform: Community Decision Organizations in Stability and Change*. Lexington, MA: Lexington Books.

Washington, Marvin. 2004. 'Field Approaches to Institutional Change: The Evolution of the National Collegiate Athletic Association, 1906–1995.' *Organization Studies*, 25, 3 (March): 393–414.

Weber, Alfred. 1928. *Theory of the Location of Industries*. Chicago, MA: University of Chicago Press.

Weber, Caroline L. 1994. *The Effects of Personnel and Human Resource Management Practices on Firm Performance: A Review of the Literature*. Report submitted to Queen's University – University of Ottawa Economic Projects.

Weber, Max. 1947. *The Theory of Social and Economic Organization* (translated and edited by A.M. Henderson and Talcott Parsons). New York: Oxford University Press.

Weber, Max. 1963. *Gesammelte Aufsätze zur Religionssoziologie*. Tübingen, Germany: J.C.B. Mohr.

Weber, Max. 1978. *Economy and Society: An Outline of Interpretive Sociology* (edited by Guenther Roth and Claus Wittich). Berkeley, CA: University of California Press.

Wegner, T.G. and Daniel M. Wegner. 1995. 'Transactive Memory.' pp. 654–656 in S.R. Manstead and M. Hewstone (eds), *The Blackwell Encyclopedia of Social Psychology*. Oxford: Blackwell.

Weick, Karl E. 1976. 'Educational Organizations as Loosely Coupled Systems.' *Administrative Science Quarterly*, 21, 1, (March): 1–19.

Weick, Karl E. 1979. *The Social Psychology of Organizing*. Reading, MA: Addison-Wesley.

Weick, Karl E. 1991. 'The Vulnerable System: An Analysis of the Tenerife Air Disaster.' pp. 117–130 in Peter J. Frost, Larry F. Moore, Meryl Reis Louis, Craig C. Lundberg, and Joanne Martin (eds), *Reframing Organizational Culture*. Newbury Park, CA: Sage.

Weick, Karl E. 1995. *Sensemaking in Organizations*. Thousand Oaks, CA: Sage.

Weick, Karl E. and Karlene Roberts. 1993. 'Collective Mind in Organizations: Heedful Interrelating on Flight Decks.' *Administrative Science Quarterly*, 38, 3 (September): 357–381.

Weick, Karl E. and Frances Westley. 1996. 'Organizational Learning: Affirming an Oxymoron.' pp. 440–458 in Stewart R. Clegg, Cynthia Hardy, and Walter Nord (eds), *Handbook of Organization Studies*. London: Sage.

Welbourne, Theresa M. 1997. 'Pay For What Performance? Using the Role-Based Performance Scale.' *Journal of Strategic Performance Measurement*, 1 (5): 13–20.

Welbourne, Theresa M. and Alice O. Andrews. 1996. 'Predicting the Performance of Initial Public Offerings: Should Human Resource Management be in the Equation?' *Academy of Management Journal*, 39, 4 (August): 891–919.

Welbourne, Theresa M. and Linda A. Cyr. 1999. 'The Human Resource Executive Effect in Initial Public Offering Firms.' *Academy of Management Journal*, 42: 616–629.

Welbourne, Theresa M. and Luis R. Gomez-Mejia. 1995. 'Team Incentives in the Workplace.' pp. 236–247 in M.L. Rock and L.A. Berger (eds), *The Compensation Handbook: A State-of-the Art Guide to Compensation Strategy and Design*. New York: McGraw-Hill.

Welsh, M. Ann and E. Allen Slusher. 1986. 'Organizational Design as a Context for Political Activity.' *Administrative Science Quarterly*, 31, 3 (September): 389–402.

Westney, D. Eleanor. 1987. *Imitation and Innovation: The Transfer of Western Organizational Patterns to Meiji Japan*. Cambridge, MA: Harvard University Press.

Weston, J. Fred, Kwang S. Chung, and Susan E. Hoag. 1990. *Mergers, Restructuring, and Corporate Control*. Englewood Cliffs, NJ: Prentice-Hall.

Westphal, James, Ranjay Gulati, and Stephen M. Shortell. 1997. 'Customization or Conformity: An Institutional and Network Perspective on the Content and Consequences of TQM Adoption.' *Administrative Science Quarterly*, 42, 2 (June): 366–394.

Wholey, Douglas R., Jon B. Christianson, and Susan M. Sanchez. 1993. 'Professional Reorganization: The Effect of Physician and Corporate Interests on the Formation of Health Maintenance Organizations.' *American Journal of Sociology*, 99, 1 (July): 164–200.

Williamson, Oliver E. 1981. 'The Economics of Organization: The Transaction Cost Approach.' *American Journal of Sociology*, 87, 3 (November): 548–577.

Williamson, Oliver E. 1985. *The Economic Institutions of Capitalism: Firms, Markets, Relational Contracting*. New York: Free Press.

Williamson, Oliver E. 1994. 'Transaction Cost Economics and Organization Theory.' pp. 77–107 in Neil Smelser and Richard Swedberg (eds), *The Handbook of Economic Sociology*, Princeton, NJ: Princeton University Press.

Willis, Paul E. 1977. *Learning to Labour: How Working Class Kids Get Working Class Jobs*. Farnborough: Saxon House.

Wilson, Kenneth and Alejandro Portes. 1980. 'Immigrant Enclaves: An Analysis of the Labor Market Experiences of Cubans in Miami.' *American Journal of Sociology*, 86, 2 (September): 295–315.

Winborg, Joakim and Hans Landstrom. 2000. 'Financial Bootstrapping in Small Businesses: Examining Managers' Resource Acquisition Behaviors.' *Journal of Business Venturing* 16, 3 (May): 235–254.

Winter, Sidney G. 1984. 'Schumpeterian Competition in Alternative Technological Regimes.' *Journal of Economic Behavior and Organization*, 5, 3–4 (Sept/Dec): 287–320.

Wood, Wendy and Jeffrey Quinn. 2005. 'The Power of Repetition in Daily Life: Habits and Intentions Guide Actions.' Unpublished paper, Department of Psychology, Duke University, Durham, North Carolina.

Wood, Wendy, Jeffrey M. Quinn, and Deborah Kashy. 2002. 'Habits in Everyday Life: Thoughts, Emotions, and Action.' *Journal of Personality and Social Psychology*, 83, 6 (December): 1281–1297.

Wuthnow, Robert. 1987. *Meaning and Moral Order: Explorations in Cultural Analysis*. Berkeley, CA: University of California Press.

Xu, Hongwei and Martin Ruef. 2004. 'The Myth of the Risk-Tolerant Entrepreneur.' *Strategic Organization*, 2, 4 (November): 331–355.

Xu, Hongwei and Martin Ruef. Forthcoming. 'Boundary Formation in Emergent Organizations.' In Martin Ruef and Michael Lounsbury (eds), *Research in the Sociology of Organizations, Vol. 24*.

Young, Ed. 1989. 'On the Naming of the Rose: Interests and Multiple Meanings as Elements of Organizational Culture.' *Organization Studies*, 10, 2: 187–206.

Young, Ruth and Joe D. Francis. 1991. 'Entrepreneurship and Innovation in Small Manufacturing Firms.' *Social Science Quarterly*, 72, 1 (March): 149–162.

Yuchtman, Ephraim and Stanley Seashore. 1967. 'A System Resource Approach to Organizational Effectiveness.' *American Sociological Review*, 32, 6 (December): 891–903.

Zajac, Edward J. 1988. 'Interlocking Directorates as an Interorganizational Strategy: A Test of Critical Assumptions.' *Academy of Management Journal*, 31, 2 (June): 428–438.

Zajac, Edward J. and Matthew S. Kraatz. 1993. 'A Diametric Forces Model of Strategic Change: Assessing the Antecedents and Consequences of Restructuring in the Higher Education Industry.' *Strategic Management Journal*, 14, Special Issue (Summer): 83–102.

Zajac, Edward J. and James D. Westphal. 1996. 'Director Reputation, CEO-Board Power, and the Dynamics of Board Interlocks.' *Administrative Science Quarterly*, 41, 3 (September): 507–529.

Zald, Mayer N. 1970. *Organizational Change: The Political Economy of the YMCA*. Chicago, MA: University of Chicago Press.

Zald, Mayer and Michael Berger. 1978. 'Social Movements in Organizations: Coup d'État, Insurgency, and Mass Movements.' *American Journal of Sociology*, 83, 4 (January): 823–861.

Zald, Mayer N. and Patricia Denton. 1963. 'From Evangelism to General Service: The Transformation of the YMCA.' *Administrative Science Quarterly*, 8, 3 (September): 214–234.

Zelizer, Vivian A. 1978. 'Human Values and the Market: The Case of Life Insurance and Death in 19th-Century America.' *American Journal of Sociology*, 84, 3 (November): 591–610.

Zeune, G.D. 1993. 'Ducks in a Row: Orchestrating the Flawless Stock Offering.' *Corporate Cashflow*, 14, 2: 18–21.

Zimmer, Catherine and Howard E. Aldrich. 1987. 'Resource Mobilization Through Ethnic Networks: Kinship and Friendship Ties of Shopkeepers in England.' *Sociological Perspectives*, 30, 4 (October): 422–455.

Zorn, Dirk. 2004. 'Here a Chief, There a Chief: The Rise of the CFO.' *American Sociological Review*, 69, 3 (June): 345–364.

Zuboff, Shoshana. 1988. *In the Age of the Smart Machine*. New York: Basic Books.

Zucker, Lynne G. 1986. 'Production of Trust: Institutional Sources of Economic Structure, 1840–1920.' pp. 53–112 in Barry M. Staw and Larry L. Cummings (eds), *Research in Organizational Behavior, Vol. 8*. Greenwich, CT: JAI Press.

Zucker, Lynne G. 1987. 'Institutional Theories of Organization.' pp. 443–464 in *Annual Review of Sociology, 13*. Palo Alto, CA: Annual Reviews.

Zucker, Lynne G. 1988. 'Where Do Institutional Patterns Come from? Organizations as Actors in Social Systems.' pp. 23–49 in Lynne G. Zucker (ed.), *Institutional Patterns and Organizations*. Cambridge, MA: Ballinger.

Zucker, Lynne G. 1989. 'Combining Institutional Theory and Population Ecology: No Legitimacy, No History.' *American Sociological Review*, 54, 4 (August): 542–545.

Zuckerman, Ezra. 1999. 'The Categorical Imperative: Securities Analysts and the Illegitimacy Discount.' *American Journal of Sociology*, 104, 5 (March): 1398–1438.

Zuckerman, Ezra. 2004. 'Structural Incoherence and Stock Market Activity.' *American Sociological Review*, 69, 3 (June): 405–432.

Author Index

Abbott, A., 163, 164
Abrahamson, E., 25, 255
Adams, G., 44
Ahrne, G., 1, 93
Ahuja, G., 31
Akard, P., 203
Albach, H., 85
Alchian, A., 56, 109
Aldrich, H., 2, 4, 22, 23, 29, 30, 34, 37,
    38, 51, 52, 53, 61, 65, 69–81, 86, 87,
    95–100, 103, 112, 126, 130, 133, 139,
    140, 168, 174, 184, 186, 192, 200,
    203, 206, 213, 219, 220, 231, 235,
    246, 248, 250–2, 259, 260, 264–8
Allan, K., 10, 146
Amburgey, T., 11, 26, 37, 62, 136,
    138, 142, 155, 170, 176, 196,
    215, 221, 233, 263
Aminzade, R., 168
Anderson, P., 20, 47, 67, 68, 96, 173,
    175, 187, 188, 252
Andrews, A., 89, 96, 109, 111, 201
Appelbaum, E., 153
Appold, S., 228
Argote, L., 47, 120
Argyris, C., 47
Arrow, K., 94, 190
Arthur, W., 178, 189, 190
Arum, R., 62, 65
Ashforth, B., 95, 115
Astley, W., 37, 52, 241
Atmar, W., 255
Audia, P., 189, 228, 229
Auster, E., 62, 140
Axelrod, R., 194

Bacdayan, P., 48, 76
Baden-Fuller, C., 189
Baker, T., 68, 77, 79, 100, 103, 109,
    112, 153, 219, 252
Baker, W., 2
Baldwin, J., 84
Banaszak-Holl, J., 220, 227, 244, 245, 246
Barber, A., 96

Barkema, H., 58
Barley, S., 2, 44, 46, 78, 95, 134,
    136, 143, 150, 217
Barnard, C., 25
Barnett, W., 11, 37, 38, 66, 126, 132, 138,
    155, 167, 170, 215, 217, 221,
    240, 241, 242, 244–9
Barney, J., 81, 189, 221, 222
Baron, J., 21, 96, 97, 102, 106, 107,
    111, 112, 124, 134, 135, 156
Baron, R., 188
Barron, D., 38, 167, 199, 215
Bartley, T., 229, 233
Bartunek, J., 124, 162
Bates, T., 70
Baudrillard, J., 3
Baum, J., 14, 30, 38, 62, 83, 133, 138,
    141, 156, 166, 167, 173, 190, 206,
    215–17, 220, 221, 226, 229,
    235, 250, 258
Bechky, B., 6
Becker, G., 78
Becker, H., 44
Becker, M., 29
Beckman, C., 78
Beckman, S., 120
Bellah, R., 56
Bennett, S., 194
Berger, M., 152
Berger, P., 29, 39, 41
Bergunder, A., 165
Berk, R., 32
Berry, D., 116
Betters-Reed, B.L., 162
Beyer, J., 124
Bielby, D., 2
Bielby, W., 2
Biggart, N., 44, 88, 107
Black, B., 2
Blau, J., 120, 127, 216, 221, 236
Blau, P., 6, 7, 51 94, 96
Boden, D., 120, 126
Bodfish, M., 199
Boehm, M., 124, 125

Denison, D., 89, 217
Dennett, D., 16, 18, 32, 35, 49, 58
Denrell, J., 47, 79, 81
Denton, P., 135, 143
Diamond, J., 256
Diekmann, K., 134, 146, 172
Dietz, T., 19
DiMaggio, P., 39–43, 47, 50, 114–16,
    151, 168, 172, 176, 199, 241
Dobbin, F., 21, 43, 97, 108, 156, 170,
    202, 229, 233, 244, 246, 251
Dobrev, S., 37, 66, 126, 174, 217, 226
Dodge, H., 161
Donaldson, L., 53
Dosi, G., 190, 252
Douglas, Y., 68, 259
Dow, G., 45, 94
Dowd, T., 229, 233
Drake, S., 73
Draper, E., 19, 204
Drazin, R., 78
Duncan, J., 62, 83, 136
Duneier, M., 44
Dunne, T., 208
Dyck, B., 217
Dyer, D., 1, 20

Easley, D., 68, 77, 79
Eccles, R., 55
Edelman, L., 43, 152, 170, 201, 251
Edwards, B., 175
Edwards, C., 171
Edwards, R., 106
Eisenhardt, K., 19, 88, 152, 255
Elam, A., 79
Elder, G., 128, 132, 168
Ellison, G., 228
Emerson, R., 51, 52, 149
Emery, F., 7
Emirbayer, M., 18
Ensel, W., 100
Epple, D., 120
Espeland, W., 152, 172
Estler, S., 104

Farr, M., 105
Faulkner, R., 2
Feagin, J., 73
Fein, L., 42
Feldman, D., 6, 29, 117
Fernandez, R., 100, 101, 146
Fichman, M., 83, 167
Fiet, J., 64
Fine, G., 43, 123, 127, 129
Fiol, C., 30, 37, 61, 82, 100, 122, 184, 186, 259
Fischer, C., 70
Fischer, H., 142
Fischhoff, B., 116
Fisher, W., 82
Fiske, S., 76
Fligstein, N., 40, 53, 54, 134, 135, 140,
    172, 176, 232

Florida, R., 171
Folta, T., 21, 22
Fourcade-Gourinchas, M., 8
Francis, J., 217
Freear, J., 87
Freeland, R., 40, 53, 54, 176
Freeman, J., 35–7, 43, 115, 136–7, 140,
    155, 166, 183, 186, 213, 214–18,
    224, 235, 241–2, 246
Friedkin, N., 22, 121
Friedman, R., 57
Frost, P., 122
Fullerton, S., 161

Galaskiewicz, J., 51, 54, 251
Galvin, T., 193
Ganguly, P., 14
Garfinkel, H., 45
Gargiulo, M., 48, 140
Gartner, W., 62–7
Garud, R., 192, 197, 202,
    252, 260, 262
Garvin, D., 139, 217, 218
Geddes, B., 7
Geer, B., 44
Georgiou, P., 25, 45, 92, 94
Gerlach, M., 171, 218
Gersick, C., 121, 160
Gerson, K., 93
Gherardi, S., 128
Giddens, A., 17
Gifford, S., 89
Gimeno, J., 21, 22
Ginsberg, A., 138
Glaeser, E., 228
Glaser, R., 105
Glynn, M., 47, 49, 50, 81, 82,
    139, 188, 259
Goffman, E., 95, 116, 122
Gold, S., 73
Golden-Biddle, K., 46, 270
Goldstein, H., 236
Gomez-Mejia, L., 110
Gorman, M., 89, 247
Gottfried, H., 129
Graddy, E., 182, 206
Graham, L., 72, 129
Granfors, M., 192
Granovetter, M., 8, 57, 69, 70, 99,
    100, 130, 142, 190, 207
Grant, D., 249
Gray, V., 200
Greenstein, S., 191
Greenwood, R., 163
Greer, C., 111
Greiner, L., 160
Greve, H., 38, 47, 138, 227
Griffin, L., 95, 120, 142, 159, 164, 167
Grusky, D., 129
Gulati, R., 48, 140
Guler, I., 262
Gumpert, D., 63

Index compiled by Judith Isabel Rodriguez, Christy Thomas, and the authors

Subject Index